HOW NATIVES THINK

Lucien Lévy-Bruhl

• • •

HOW NATIVES THINK

Authorized Translation by

LILIAN A. CLARE

•

With a new Introduction,
"Lucien Lévy-Bruhl and the
Concept of Cognitive Relativity," by

C. SCOTT LITTLETON

PRINCETON UNIVERSITY PRESS

Published by Princeton University Press, 41 William Street,
Princeton, New Jersey 08540

In the United Kingdom: Princeton University Press, Guildford, Surrey

Introduction copyright © 1985 by Princeton University Press

Library of Congress Cataloging in Publication Data will be found
on the last printed page of this book

Allen & Unwin / Knopf edition, 1926
Washington Square Press edition, 1966
Princeton edition, 1985

LCC 85-42622
ISBN 0-691-07298-1
ISBN 0-691-02034-5 (pbk.)

Reprinted by arrangement with George Allen & Unwin Ltd.

Clothbound editions of Princeton University Press books are printed
on acid-free paper, and binding materials are chosen for strength
and durability. Paperbacks, while satisfactory for personal collections,
are not usually suitable for library rebinding.

Printed in the United States of America by Princeton University
Press, Princeton, New Jersey

INTRODUCTION (1985)

Lucien Lévy-Bruhl and the Concept of Cognitive Relativity

BY C. SCOTT LITTLETON

I

WHEN Princeton University Press first broached the possibility that I might write an introduction to a new edition of Lucien Lévy-Bruhl's *How Natives Think*—originally published in 1910 as *Les fonctions mentales dans les sociétés inférieures*—I must admit that I had more than a few qualms. Like most anthropologists of my generation, I had been conditioned by my teachers to regard Lévy-Bruhl as something of an intellectual curiosity, a brilliant scholar who somehow managed to get it all wrong, a failed forerunner whose ideas pale into insignificance alongside those of such eminent contemporaries as Émile Durkheim and Max Weber. Indeed, almost every well-known British and American anthropologist writing in the late twenties and thirties had had at least something negative to say about him, and this critical assessment seemed to have stood the test of time.

Yet the project intrigued me. At the very least, this much maligned French philosopher-cum-sociologist deserved a retrospective assessment, and, although I fully expected to find myself concurring with Paul Radin, Robert Lowie, Bronislaw Malinowski, and other early critics, I decided to accept the assignment.

What follows does not, for the most part, conform to that expectation. After re-reading *How Natives Think* and several of his other early works, I have reached the conclusion that Lévy-Bruhl is well worth reprinting, and that he thoroughly deserves to be recalled from the intellectual limbo to which he has generally been consigned. Moreover, it is possible to suggest that in *How Natives Think* and elsewhere he managed to adumbrate a great many ideas which have only recently been put forward, in most cases by people who do not consider themselves to be in his intellectual debt. Most of these ideas involve what may be called, for lack of a better term, *cognitive relativity*, that is, the notion that the logic we bring to bear in our descriptions of the world is *not* universal, but rather a function of our immediate techno-environmental circumstances and our particular linguistic and ideological heritage, and that no one logic is necessarily superior to any other logic.

There is, as we shall see, an irony here, as Lévy-Bruhl has long been criticized for being ethnocentric, for apparently insisting that the Western thought-mode, or logic, is inherently better than the one he identified as common to folk and primitive societies. In retrospect, this criticism, as well as many of the other criticisms that have been levied against him, is unfounded. Indeed, the perspective employed by a great many contemporary anthropologists—few of whom could be labeled ethnocentric—is remarkably similar to that which pervades Lévy-Bruhl's work, including *How Natives Think*. This is especially true when it comes to the study of the range and diversity of human cognition; it was only after I had come to recognize this similarity that I began to change my mind about Lévy-Bruhl's position in the history of anthropological theory. It will therefore be necessary to review the growth and development of the three most "Lévy-Bruhlian" anthropological sub-fields, cognitive anthropology, structural anthropology (including "the new comparative mythology"), and symbolic anthropology, and to underscore the extent to which the conceptual frameworks currently brought to bear by them were in fair measure anticipated by the author of the book that follows.

I should add that my new-found respect for Lévy-Bruhl was also enhanced by reviewing some of the more positive assessments of his work that have appeared over the years, and especially the retrospective ones by E. E. Evans-Pritchard, Rodney Needham, Jan de Vries, Robin Horton, and several other contemporary scholars. These, too, need to be considered in some depth, for they belie the widespread assumption that the French philosopher has universally been consigned to the intellectual dustbin.

However, before examining these most important aspects of the matter, we must set the stage, as it were, and consider Lévy-

Bruhl in the context of his time, as well as the milieu in which his ideas took shape, the ideas themselves, and the intensely negative critical reactions they initially engendered.

II

It is, I think, fair to say that we are still coming to terms with the ideas and theories first annunciated between 1900 and 1914. Indeed, it is possible to suggest that the foundation of what we generally consider contemporary thought was laid down during that all too brief decade and a half between the death of Queen Victoria and the outbreak of World War I, and that nothing really fundamental has occurred since, at least in the realm of ideas.

Consider the record. In mathematics and philosophy, Einstein, Whitehead, Russell, Cassirer, Husserl, and Heisenberg had all formulated the theories that would later make them famous by the time the "guns of August" roared. And in the arts Picasso and his fellow *fauves*, as well as Stravinsky and Kafka, had revolutionized their respective métiers and had firmly established the basis for what may be termed the twentieth century sensibility. In the social and behavioral sciences the record is especially impressive. Freud, Frazer, Weber, Durkheim, Mauss, van Gennep, Pareto, Simmel, Boas, and de Saussure all did their most important work in those fifteen years; it was a time of intense intellectual creativity and ferment, perhaps the most intense this country has yet witnessed, and the author of *How Natives Think* was very much a part of it.

Born in 1857 to a middle-class Parisian family, Lévy-Bruhl graduated from the Lycée Charlemagne and, like many others of his class and economic circumstances, went on to attend the prestigious École Normale Supérieur, where he majored in philosophy. Unlike Durkheim, his Jewishness does not seem to have caused him any major problems at the École, and after his graduation in 1879 he had no trouble finding positions as a philosophy instructor at lycées in Poitiers and Amiens. In 1884 he returned to Paris to complete his doctorate, and after holding several posts at lycées in the capital, in 1896 was appointed to the faculty of the Sorbonne, where he eventually became Titular Professor of Modern Philosophy.

Although he maintained an interest in academic philosophy throughout his career and indeed lectured regularly on Descartes, Hume, and Shopenhauer, among others, shortly after his appointment to the Sorbonne Lévy-Bruhl's focus began to shift in the direction of the new science of sociology, then being shaped in France by Émile Durkheim and his colleagues. Like Durkheim, he had been imbued with neo-Kantianism while a student at the École Normale, and, as Lévy-Bruhl's biographer Jean Cazeneuve (1972:x–xi) points out, there was a natural affinity between the two scholars, especially at the outset of his career.

It was an exciting time to be in Paris, especially if one was becoming interested in sociology. The year Lévy-Bruhl joined the faculty of the University of Paris Durkheim published his famous *The Rules of the Sociology Method* (1896), which for the first time laid out a systematic methodology for the study of "social facts." In addition to his philosophical training, Durkheim had been profoundly influenced by Auguste Comte and Herbert Spencer, as well as the brilliant social historian N.-D. Fustel de Coulanges and the iconoclastic Scottish Semiticist William Robertson Smith, all of whom had stressed the social basis of religious thought, and Lévy-Bruhl seems also to have absorbed the ideas of these scholars as he found himself drawn ever more closely into the circle of scholars that regularly published in *L'année sociologique*, the influential journal that Durkheim and his disciples had recently launched.

The first fruit of this new interest was a comparative study of ethics, *La morale et la science des moeurs* (1903). In it he attempted to apply the empirical models Durkheim and others had developed to a cross-cultural analysis of primitive as well as contemporary ethical behavior. His goal was to establish a "science of morals," that is, to discover the rules underlying moral and ethical codes everywhere. But it soon became apparent that these codes varied widely according to the level of cultural complexity, and thus Lévy-Bruhl took his first plunge into anthropology. The result was an appreciation of cultural relativity that would loom large indeed—his critics to the contrary notwithstanding—in the balance of his work.

But it was a relativity tempered by the evolutionary process. Like most of his European and American contemporaries at the turn of the century, Lévy-Bruhl had come to accept, albeit cautiously, the fundamental assumptions of unilineal evolutionism. Formulated a generation earlier by Spencer, Bachofen, Tylor, Morgan, and others, these assumptions include (1) the idea of progress, (2) an unquestioned faith in the efficacy of the comparative method, and (3) the notion of psychic unity—that is, the idea that fundamental thought processes are the same everywhere and that if left alone *all* human communities would independently pass through the *same* intellectual stages (see, for example, Harris 1968:142f.). It was the third assumption that gave Lévy-Bruhl the most trouble, especially as he began to probe more deeply into the patterns of logic manifested in the moral codes characteristic of simple societies. And here we need to make explicit precisely what Lévy-Bruhl means by the word "logic."

He does not mean formal logic in the mathematical sense, that is, the logic that is brought to bear in the proof of a geometric theorem; nor does he imply that there is necessarily any fundamental difference in the way human beings reason when it comes to mundane matters of survival. Indeed, as he puts it in *How Natives Think*, to infer such a thing would be "going too far" (p. 68). Rather, by "logic" Lévy-Bruhl seems to mean the formal *rules* of rational thought deemed by Western logicians to be universal. And of these rules, as we shall see, by far the most important is the so-called "rule of non-contradiction": the rule that states that two objects cannot occupy the same space at the same time. Primitive "collective representations" seemed to violate this rule with impunity; indeed, the thought patterns characteristic of what he later came to call "primitive mentality" appeared to lack logic (i.e., the rule of non-contradiction) altogether. They conform rather to what can be described as a "prelogical" pattern in which the rules which we have taken for granted since Aristotle's time simply do not apply. At bottom, what bothered him was an apparent difference in *mentality*, a difference that seemed to violate the psychic unity dimension of unilineal evolutionism.

To be sure, the particular version of unilineal evolutionism espoused by Durkheim and his circle, which emphasized the notion that "elementary forms" should be isolated primarily so as to facilitate a better understanding of "higher" (i.e., later) developments, provided a framework in which this problem might be approached. For example, was the "prelogical" pat-

HOW NATIVES THINK

tern—or "mentality"—that Lévy-Bruhl had recognized in fact a key to understanding the evolution of formal logic and its attendant rules, in the same way that his fellow neo-Kantian (and friend) Ernst Cassirer (1953) had demonstrated that complex symbolic forms were generally prefigured in the simpler conceptions shared by our remote ancestors? But the more he pondered the matter, the more convinced he became that the difference between the two thought-modes was indeed inherent, and that the primitive mode, although clearly antecedent to logic as we generally define it, had to be understood on its own terms. "Prelogical" thought was thus more than simply an "elementary form" of a "higher" logic, that is, one which is clearly predicated on the rule of non-contradiction. On the contrary, it appeared to be predicated on a wholly different set of rules and principles, and he set for himself the task of explicating these rules and principles, as well as the particular kinds of "social facts" that gave rise to them.

At the same time, in concert with Marcel Mauss, Durkheim's nephew and most brilliant disciple, Lévy-Bruhl was becoming interested in myth and the myth-making process. And it is here that he first began to depart from the path followed by Durkheim and the majority of the circle. Like Sir James Frazer, Jane Harrison, Andrew Lang, and others who had come to reject the text-centered naturism advocated by the so-called "philological school" of comparative mythology (Max Müller, Adalbert Kuhn et al.), which had dominated mythological scholarship in the previous half-century (Feldman and Richardson 1972:480-3), Durkheim sought to place the primary emphasis on *ritual*, that is, on the behavioral aspects of religion, primitive and otherwise. But to Lévy-Bruhl, the rules—or better, perhaps, the mentality—and/or thought processes underlying myths were keys to understanding the nature of the human condition in its simplest manifestations. As Ivan Strensky (n.d.) points out, Mauss shared this concern with myth, despite his close ties with Durkheim, and provided a great deal of encouragement. Moreover, unlike Durkheim, Lévy-Bruhl had a strong background in psychology, having taken several courses in the subject at the clinic of Sainte Anne while he was at the École. Thus, both his neo-Kantian training and clinical experience predisposed him to place a strong emphasis on *mind* rather than on behavior per se.[1] It was myth, more than anything else, that provided insights into how the mind, especially the "primitive mind," worked, a mind free from the constraints of anything approaching formal, rule-based logic.

The initial results of this inquiry into the nature of primitive thought processes, a subject that would occupy most of his attention for the balance of his career, were published in the work that follows. It was, as Mauss (1939:252) notes, the book that established his reputation. Indeed, the ideas contained in *Les fonctions mentales dans le sociétés inférieures*, which was translated into English in 1926 by Lilian A. Clare,[2] were to have a profound, albeit negative, impact on a generation of anthropologists committed to a wholly different conception of how people (natives and otherwise) think, and none of his subsequent books were read (or criticized) with quite the same intensity.

In any event, the outbreak of World War I in 1914 caused Lévy-Bruhl, as a patriotic Frenchman, to put aside his studies for the duration of the conflict. Too old for active military service, he took an unpaid position in the Ministry of Munitions, where he served with distinction. In 1919 he was attached to the Section of Documentation of the Ministry of Foreign Affairs, and found himself actively involved in the preparations for the Versailles Peace Conference. During this period, despite his commitment to the war effort and the subsequent effort to establish a lasting peace, he managed to find time to write impassioned articles for the socialist journal *L'humanité*, which had been founded by his old friend Jean Jaures.[3]

It was not until the early twenties that he was able to return to his research into the nature of primitive thought. In 1922 he published *La mentalité primitive* (translated in 1923 as *Primitive Mentality*), and went on to publish four more books on various aspects of "prelogical" thought: *L'âme primitive* (1927; translated as *The "Soul" of the Primitive* in 1928), *Le surnaturel et la nature dans le mentalité primitive* (1931), *La mythologie primitive* (1935), and *L'expérience mystique et les symboles chez les primitives* (1938). His *Carnets*, or notebooks, in which he capitulated to his critics and all but abandoned the theory of "prelogical mentality," were published posthumously in 1949.

In the latter part of his career, Lévy-Bruhl's professional interests became more and more anthropological, and in 1925, together with Paul Rivet and his old friend Mauss, he founded the Institute of Ethnology in the University of Paris. However, two years later he resigned from the Institute, as he could no longer accept the Durkheimian "party-line" espoused by his colleagues. Shortly thereafter he also retired from his chair at the Sorbonne so as to concentrate on writing and research—and upon responding to the mounting critical assault that had been launched by Radin and others (see pp. xvi, xxi).

He also found time to travel widely. His trips, many of which were sponsored by the Alliance française, took him not only to the Continent, but also to the Far East, Central America, North America, and the Middle East, and thus he had an opportunity to at least visit (if not to do field work in) many parts of that "primitive world" he had so often written about.

Lévy-Bruhl died in March of 1939, discouraged, as Cazeneuve (1972:xvi) puts it, "by the clear awareness which he had of the imminent world disaster." But he had certainly made an impact on anthropology, albeit for the most part a negative one, and we must now consider in more detail the book most responsible for that impact.

III

In a great many respects, *How Natives Think* is Lévy-Bruhl's most Durkheimian book, the culmination of over a decade of close association with Durkheim, Mauss, and the rest of the *L'année sociologique* group. Drawing extensively on the well-known concept of "collective representations," that is, the shared representations of natural and social reality found in all human communities (see, for example, Durkheim and Mauss 1903, Durkheim 1912), Lévy-Bruhl states his case quite succinctly in the first chapter:

> The collective representations of primitives . . . differ very profoundly from our ideas or concepts, nor are they equivalent either. On the one hand, as we shall presently discover, they have not their logical character. On the other hand, not being genuine representations, in the strict sense of the term, they express, or rather imply, not only that the primitive actually has an image of the object in his mind, and thinks it real, but also that he has some hope or fear connected

with it, that some definite influence emanates from it. (pp 37–38)

Thus at the outset of this seminal book, the author makes it clear that the way "undeveloped peoples" look at the world is different in kind from the way we do, and that this primitive "way" involves the notion that all things, beings, or whatever are in some fashion linked together, that there is no distinction (not simply no clear distinction, but *no* distinction at all) between self and other, or between subject and object, past and present, animate and inanimate, etc. Interpretation—or better, perhaps, functional integration in the modern mathematical sense—is the key descriptive concept here (though he does not explicitly use it), and the notions of time and space as we conventionally understand them have no meaning.

Such a thought process, of course, does not merely violate the traditional rules of Western logic, such as the rule of non-contradiction; it has no connection whatsoever with these rules, and is predicated on what Lévy-Bruhl calls the "law of participation." Moreover, this so-called "law," which is expressed in an intricate set of interpenetrations among all the parts (human and otherwise) that go to make up a collective representation, is inherently *mystical*: "If I were to express in one word the general peculiarity of the collective representations which play so important a part in the mental activity of undeveloped peoples, I should say that this mental activity was a *mystic* one" (p. 38).

Primitive thought processes, then, are predicated on what he calls "mystical participation." And this, at bottom, is a manifestation of the "prelogical mentality" mentioned earlier. Characteristically, Lévy-Bruhl takes great pains to define exactly what he means by this controversial concept:

By *prelogical* we do not mean to assert that such a mentality constitutes a kind of antecedent stage, in point of time, to the birth of logical thought. Have there ever existed groups of human or pre-human beings whose collective representations have not been subject to the laws of logic? We do not know, and in any case, it seems to be very improbable. At any rate, the mentality of these undeveloped people which, for want of a better term, I call *prelogical*, does not partake of that nature. It is not *antilogical*; it is not *alogical* either. By designating it "prelogical" I merely wish to state that it does not bind itself down, as our thought does, to avoiding contradiction. It obeys the law of participation first and foremost. Thus oriented, it does not expressly delight in what is contradictory (which would make it merely absurd in our eyes), but neither does it take pains to avoid it. It is often wholly indifferent to it, and that makes it so hard to follow. (p. 78)

The foregoing extract expresses in a nutshell the central thesis of *How Natives Think*: primitives do not simply violate the laws of our vaunted logic, they are "wholly indifferent" to them. Moreover, "prelogical" thought is *not* absurd, but must be understood *on its own terms* as a wholly separate reality-construct predicated on the "law of participation."

To be sure, Lévy-Bruhl points out that in ordinary life there is in fact a great deal of conformity to what can be interpreted (by us) as the rules of logic—or at least the rule of non-contradiction. For example, hunters do make distinctions between living and dead animals, or between themselves and their prey, and the rule of non-contradiction generally holds when describing an immediate set of circumstances, such as the birth of a child or the exact location of a water-hole. But primitive thought is not *governed* by these rules, and "mystical participation" is apt to color the *interpretation* of any significant event, especially when it appears to involve other events. Thus, among Australian aboriginals, the birth of a child may be interpreted as the immediate result of a union between a man and a woman (earlier theories about their lack of any knowledge of the "facts of life" to the contrary notwithstanding),[4] and, at the same time, as the reincarnation of one or more totemic spirits, who also exist in a variety of other temporal and spatial contexts. A given event, such as a totemic initiation, may be interpreted both as a here-and-now situation, unique in its immediate circumstances and personnel, and as having happened in the "dream time," which links past, present, and future (to stretch our linguistic resources to their limits) and thereby forms a single sacred event-stream (cf. Stanner 1965). Thus, logic and prelogic manage to coexist in most societies without the tension experienced by civilized theologians like Tertullian, who ultimately concluded that he believed "because it is absurd."

The balance of the book is largely devoted to citing examples of "prelogical" thought in a wide variety of cultures and cultural contexts, including language. Indeed, Lévy-Bruhl's linguistic analyses, especially his discussion of the lexical and syntactical manifestations of "mystical participation," are interesting in light of post-Whorfian anthropological linguistics, and we shall consider them shortly.

He concludes by attempting to explain the evolution of "conceptual" thought, that is, thought based on the rule of non-contradiction. As might be expected, Lévy-Bruhl implicitly follows Durkheim's (1893) evolutionary scheme wherein "mechanical solidarity" necessarily gives way to "organic solidarity," and suggests that as the latter begins to take shape, thanks to the increasing sophistication of the division of labor and the corresponding decline in importance of kin-based, all-encompassing social groups, the growth of individualism, private property, and the like reduces the number of contexts in which "mystical participation" can function effectively as a mode of defining reality. In many respects, this is the weakest part of the book. For example, the author's assertion that among peoples such as the Australian aborigines, where social participation is direct and immediate, and where "prelogicality" necessarily reigns supreme, ". . . myths are meagre in number and of poor quality" (p. 368) is patently incorrect. All one need do is read any modern account of the cultures concerned (e.g., Stanner 1965); he will find them as myth-ridden as any ancient civilization. The same holds for the majority of African and Native American peoples.

However, in the end, Lévy-Bruhl recognizes that "prelogical" thought is by no means wholly absent from even the most advanced societies, and that despite several millennia of explicit attempts to codify the rules of formal logic, all of us, at least on occasion, find ourselves operating in this atavistic fashion; no traditional religious or philosophical system is wholly free from it. Again, the "prelogical" and the "conceptual" exist side by side, albeit uneasily, and the former is not simply a misapplied version of the latter. Again, Lévy-Bruhl sums it up with characteristic clarity and succinctness in his closing remarks: "[in modern society] the prelogical and the mystic are co-existent with the logical. . . . And if it be true that our mentality is both logical and prelogical, the history of religious dogmas and systems of philosophy may henceforth be explained in a new light" (p. 386).

IV

Almost from the moment it appeared, *How Natives Think* raised the hackles of a great many anthropologists, primarily because it appeared to violate the then emerging doctrine of "cultural relativity," that is, the assumption that all cultures must be assessed on their *own* terms, without reference to any absolute standards of measurement—such as whether or not a particular culture has evolved the rule of non-contradiction. At the same time, the idea of a "prelogical" mentality seemed to violate the intellectualist tradition, fostered by Tylor and Frazer, which held that man's mental processes were ultimately the same everywhere, and that the "irrational" behavior of primitives was predicated on misapplications of the universal rules of logic and/or reason rather than on a wholly different set of fundamental assumptions about the way the world works.

Among the earliest of his English-speaking critics was Bronislaw Malinowski, a firm adherent of the intellectualist approach, who, in his well-known essay, "Magic, Science and Religion," initially published in 1925, asks whether ". . . the savage has any rational outlook, any rational mastery of his surroundings, or is he, as M. Lévy-Bruhl and his school maintain, entirely 'mystical'?" (Malinowski 1948:26). The answer to this rhetorical question was, of course, no; on the basis of his intensive field work in the Trobriand Islands, the eminent Anglo-Polish anthropologist concluded that: ". . . every primitive community is in possession of a considerable store of knowledge, based on experience and reason." This, as we have just seen, is a sentiment that Lévy-Bruhl would have heartily endorsed, and indicates that Malinowski, like so many others who have attacked Lévy-Bruhl, failed to read the book carefully!

However, the most intransigent of Lévy-Bruhl's early anthropological critics were to be found in the United States. Indeed, almost every student and disciple of Franz Boaz, the German-born American anthropologist who, more than any single individual, laid the foundation for the modern concept of cultural relativity, had something negative to say about Lévy-Bruhl. And among the most persistent and hostile of these critics was the late Paul Radin, whose most famous book, *Primitive Man as Philosopher* (1927), was in fair measure inspired—in a negative way—by *How Natives Think*.

A devoted follower of Boas, Radin was thoroughly committed to the cause of cultural realtivity and the concomitant notion that there are no fundamental racial or ethnic differences when it comes to the way the mind works. That is, human beings everywhere are capable of rational thought; we may question the *premises* upon which primitives and other pre-modern peoples base their conclusions, but the logical processes are essentially the same the world over. Thus, to Radin, the notion of a "prelogical mentality" based on a wholly different "law" (i.e., the "law of participation") was totally unacceptable. Moreover, he challenges Lévy-Bruhl's presumed contention that primitive peoples are always "prelogical" and therefore are totally incapable of rational analysis, that is, analysis based on the implicit application of the rule of non-contradiction. As Radin puts it:

> . . . M. Lévy-Bruhl contends that no primitive man can properly distinguish between subject and object, that the relation between them predicated by him does not constitute what we would call a logical relation, but rather one which can best be described by a term he has introduced into the anthropological literature, *participation mystique* [i.e., "mystical participation"]. Primitive man, according to Lévy-Bruhl, never reaches the logical stage at all. (Radin 1927:230)

But as we have seen, Lévy-Bruhl does *not* contend that *all* primitive thought is predicated on the "law of participation." As in the case of Malinowski, one cannot help but assume that Radin failed to read him carefully, especially the last chapter. Nevertheless, he goes on to criticize both the "law" itself and its presumed universal applicability among primitives: "Primitive man in no sense merges himself with the object. He distinguishes subject and object quite definitely. . . . What he says is simply this: not all the reality of an object resides in our external perception of it. There is an internal side and there are also effects, constraints from subject to object and from object to subject" (Radin 1927:246).

In refutation of Lévy-Bruhl, Radin suggests that in all societies, primitive and otherwise, there are essentially two sorts of people: "men of action" and "thinkers." The former, everywhere in the majority, are prone to accept their perceptions uncritically and to relate to the phenomenal world without attempting to seek out and explain the logical interconnections among ideas and sensations. In behaving in such a fashion, such persons may appear to be "prelogical" when in the last analysis they are simply acting out of pragmatic necessity. In contrast, the "thinkers" are the paradigm builders, as it were, the ones who do apply the universal rules of logic in defining the world. Their premises may be absurd by Western standards, but they are as subject to the rule of non-contradiction in applying them as the most so-phisticated modern philosopher or logician. Thus, Radin (1927:246) concludes, Lévy-Bruhl's notion of a wholly different thought-base among primitive peoples is necessarily "off the mark."

Other American critics, such as Alexander Goldenweiser (1933) and Robert Lowie (1937), were neither as harsh—nor as inaccurate—as Radin, who continued to attack Lévy-Bruhl in later books (e.g., Radin 1937:231). But the basic complaint was the same: Lévy-Bruhl fails to appreciate the fundamental simi-larities in the way men think, whatever their overall level of cultural complexity. Goldenweiser, for example, after compli-menting the French philosopher on his erudition and his intel-lectual brilliance, goes on to call into question his interpretation of certain facts. Citing an essay by W.H.R. Rivers on the con-ception of death in Melanesia, he points out that Lévy-Bruhl's contention (see p. 269f.) that a person can be both alive and dead simultaneously is contrary to ethnographic observation. When a man or woman nears the end of life, he or she is socially defined as "dead," regardless of what we would call "vital signs," and therefore funeral rites begin. Thus: "No contradiction is in-volved, [Rivers] claims, for the individual is not really both dead and alive at the same time: for the natives he *is* dead, *mate*. The contradiction appears only if we combine our own attitude with that of the natives" (Goldenweiser 1933:182). By the same token, when a person who is by our standards objectively "dead" is believed to be in transit to another supernatural realm, that person is socially defined as "alive"; again, there is no inherent contradiction once the native's premises are taken into account.

Goldenweiser (1933:185) concludes by observing that Lévy-Bruhl's stress on the principle of "participation" deserves great credit, but that it is by no means confined to the "primitive mind": "Had Lévy-Bruhl compared the manifestation of logic in modern man and in his early precursor, as well as the manifestation of collective mentality in the same two settings, his conclusions would have been different."

Lowie, in his well-known *History of Ethnological Theory* (1937), says essentially the same thing: "The 'savage' thinks rationally as we do in comparable situations, that is, he uses the rule of thumb logic that suffices for everyday use. What Lévy-Bruhl describes as the 'law of participation' is the common foible of all humanity, not the peculiarity of primitive minds" (Lowie 1937:220-1). He goes on to criticize several aspects of Lévy-Bruhl's theory and method. For example, he takes him to task for ranging over the entire primitive world and presenting a composite picture of the so-called "primitive mind," one "that is made to embrace even the highly sophisticated natives of China and India" (Lowie 1937:220). By implication here, Lowie is criticizing Lévy-Bruhl's reliance on the comparative method à la Tylor, Frazer et al., something that the Boasians had come to reject along with "progress" and the rest of the assumptions shared by the classical evolutionists. The fact that Lévy-Bruhl saw fit to cite a plethora of examples from around the globe rather than attempt an in-depth analysis of a single culture made his work seem "old fashioned and therefore suspect," at least in the eyes of a particularist like Lowie (cf. Harris 1968:342f.).

Lowie also takes Lévy-Bruhl to task for ignoring individual variability and for failing to recognize that ". . . primitive man, irrational though he often appears in his abstract formulations and in the religious phases of his culture, is often as keen an observer as civilized man, and as logical a reasoner from his observations" (Lowie 1937:220).

In all fairness, many of these criticisms, especially those that point out possible errors in specific ethnographic interpretations (e.g., the Melanesian conception of death), are well taken. But what Radin, Goldenweiser, Lowie, and the rest *really* seem to have disliked most about Lévy-Bruhl was his apparent insistence that primitive peoples everywhere are somehow inherently different from—and, by extension, inferior to—more complex peoples like ourselves. As we have already seen, this was (or appeared to be) very much at odds with the notion of cultural relativity. The concept of "prelogical mentality" was redolent of ethno-centrism and had to be combatted. What his critics failed to realize, of course, was that Lévy-Bruhl was as much, if not more of a relativist than they were, and that the logical rules they implicitly assumed to be universal were in fact themselves cultural artifacts. But it would be a while before this could be appreci-ated—not until the seeds planted by Benjamin Lee Whorf (see pp. xx-xxi) and other pioneer anthropological linguists had begun to blossom in the late fifties and early sixties.

As I have indicated, Lévy-Bruhl was extremely sensitive to these criticisms (Radin to the contrary not withstanding), and, as we shall see, they precipitated some major modifications in his latter formulations of the theory. However, despite his vigorous attempts to demonstrate that "prelogical" thought is *not* restricted to the simpler human communities, and that primitives *do* behave rationally in most circumstances, the criticisms, at least from the Boasians, continued unabated.

Part of the problem was Lévy-Bruhl's terminology, which remained for the most part the same at it had been in *How Natives Think*. Expressions such as "prelogicality" (which he eventually abandoned), "undeveloped peoples," "primitive mentality," and even "the natives," no matter how carefully defined, were bound to infuriate a generation of anthropologists that had struggled to free their discipline from the shackles of ethnocentrism, and who, like Boas, were firmly committed to the proposition that all human beings everywhere are endowed with the same potential for cul-tural attainment. Indeed, this remains a problem for the modern reader, as the author of this introduction, who is firmly committed to what Geertz (1984) has recently called "anti anti-relativism," can readily attest.

Another widespread and persisting criticism relates to Lévy-Bruhl's lack of field experience; how could an armchair theorist, who had not undergone that peculiar *rite de passage* that endows one with full membership in the anthropological fraternity, have anything to say about "how natives think"? Even Evans-Pritchard (1934), who, as we shall see, was one of the few early critics to appreciate the importance of Lévy-Bruhl's work, saw fit to take him to task for not having had first-hand experience with the natives he wrote about so eloquently. This complaint has been echoed by more recent critics; indeed, it has become almost canonical among historians of the discipline. For example, in his widely read and otherwise highly original book *From Ape to Angel*, H. R. Hays (1958:303-4), asserts that "It is probable that Lévy-Bruhl would not have exaggerated his picture of native confusion to such an extent if he had engaged in field work."

Lévy-Bruhl himself seems to have been keenly aware of his deficiency here. In her introduction to an earlier edition of *How Natives Think*, Ruth Bunzel (1966:v), herself an old-line Boasian who shared many of the qualms just noted, recalls that in the course of her one meeting with Lévy-Bruhl, circa 1927, he pressed her for details about the Zuñi: ". . . here was someone who had actually lived among the Zuñi about whom he had written, and whose culture fascinated him, and he wanted to learn." He was thus fully cognizant of the importance of systematic, first-hand knowledge of the cultures he wrote about, and, in retrospect, more than made up for his own lack of field experience, by his judicious use of others' data. This is a point that Maurice Leenhardt (1949), a French missionary-cum-ethnologist, saw fit to underscore in his preface to Lévy-Bruhl's posthumously published *Carnets*.

Nevertheless, the Boasians' objections—to say nothing of those raised by Malinowski and other "rationalists"--took their toll, and by the late thirties Lévy-Bruhl found himself no longer able to defend the central concept of this book. As he puts it in the *Carnets* (quoted by Cazeneuve 1972:87): ". . . let us expressly rectify what I believed in 1910: there is not a primitive mentality distinguishable from the other by two characteristics which are peculiar to it (mystical and prelogical). There is a mystical mentality which is more marked and more easily observable among primitive peoples than in our societies, but it is present in every human mind." In short, as Malefijt (1974:191) observes, Lévy-Bruhl was ultimately his own best critic.

V

The foregoing, however, is only part of the story. As we have just seen, Leenhardt had kind things to say about Lévy-Bruhl's central thesis in his preface to the *Carnets*, and even his most adamant critics were compelled to acknowledge his vast erudition. Moreover, from the outset, a handful of scholars in anthropology and related disciplines not only took Lévy-Bruhl seriously, but also recognized the significance of his discoveries about the nature of "primitive mentality." For example, Joseph Needham (1925:28-29), a field worker of some renown, makes reference to "the daring and brilliant speculations of Professor Lévy-Bruhl," and indeed criticizes Goldenweiser for overestimating the rational basis of primitive thought. Although Needham goes on to criticize what he believes to be Lévy-Bruhl's underestimation of "savage" rationality, he nevertheless concludes that the latter's thesis is generally supported by the Melanesian data he had collected. The Dutch historian of religion G. Van der Leeuw (1928) saw fit to use Lévy-Bruhl's conception of "prelogical mentality" as his point of departure in an attempt to develop a case for the presence everywhere of what he calls an "asyntactical" thought-mode, one that manifests itself in dreams as well as in the beliefs and practices of primitive peoples. And the eminent American anthropologist Frederica de Laguna (1940:566), in an essay written shortly after Lévy-Bruhl's death, was critical of the latter's methodology, but nevertheless concluded that ". . . because he has attacked some of our unconscious assumptions he has enabled us to become more objectively critical of others. His pioneer formulation of the problem was a necessary preliminary to more adequate formulations, and his mistakes can be as illuminating as his durable contributions."

Another early admirer was the late E. E. Evans-Pritchard, who in 1934 published a lengthy defense of Lévy-Bruhl that stands in sharp contrast to the negative position taken by Radin, Goldenweiser, Malinowski, and the rest of his Boasian and "intellectualist" critics. To be sure, like Needham, he takes the French philosopher to task for underplaying the abundant evidence that primitives often think as rationally as we do when it comes to matters of immediate survival—Evans-Pritchard's own field work in Africa had clearly established this—and, as we have seen, he questions whether anyone who has not had first-hand contact with a tribal society can really come to grips with the way members of such a society think. But, on balance, Evans-Pritchard's assessment is extremely positive. Indeed, he goes so far as to assert that Lévy-Bruhl was easily the most brilliant of the Durkheimians and that his thesis thoroughly deserves to be taken seriously—a far cry from the way the Boasians perceived it

Thirty years later, in *Theories of Primitive Religion* (1965), Evans-Pritchard amplified his earlier assessment in light of subsequent developments in the field, and reached essentially the same conclusions (see also Evans-Pritchard 1981). In retrospect, he observes, the author of *How Natives Think*

> . . . was one of the first, if not the first, to emphasize that primitive ideas, which seem so strange to us, and indeed sometimes idiotic, when considered as isolated facts, are meaningful when seen as parts of patterns of ideas and behaviours, each part having an intelligible relationship to the others. He recognized that values form systems as coherent as the logical constructions of the intellect, that there is a logic of sentiments as well as of reason, though based on a different principle. His analysis is not like the just-so stories we have earlier considered [that is, the theories of Tylor, Frazer, Marett et al.], for he does not try to explain primitive magic and religion by a theory that purports to show how they might have come about, what is their cause or origin. He takes them as given, and seeks only to show their structure and the way they are evidence of a distinctive mentality common to all societies of a certain type. (Evans-Pritchard 1965:86)

I quote Evans-Pritchard here *in extenso* so as to lay to rest the misconception mentioned at the outset that contemporary anthropologists (or nearly contemporary, in Evans-Pritchard's case) have universally dismissed Lévy-Bruhl as unworthy of serious consideration.[5] Indeed, since the late forties, an increasing number of scholars have followed Evans-Pritchard's (and Leenhardt's) lead, bucking the Boasian-intellectualist "consensus" by taking the French philosopher's ideas to heart. For example, Adolf Jensen (1963:17) observes that "Lévy-Bruhl still remains the pre-eminent ethnopsychologist" when it comes to an understanding of the ways primitive peoples conceive of religious ideas, and goes on to assert that his posthumous repudiation of the concept of "primitive mentality" "did not nullify his earlier works and especially not their effect on other branches of society." In this vein, Mircea Eliade (1969:16), perhaps the most distinguished contemporary historian of religion, has observed that, "Though based on an erroneous hypothesis, Lévy-Bruhl's early works are not without merit; they helped to arouse interest in the spiritual creations of archaic societies." And Jan de Vries (1977:168), another eminent historian of religion, concludes his rather extensive discussion of Lévy-Bruhl's "law of participation" by asking, "Who would deny that in the perspective of the cosmos things show a mutual participation?" In such cases, de Vries observes, "all men are prelogical in circumstances where logic is insufficient." Finally, Annemarie de Waal Malefijt (1974:191) has seen fit to observe that

> . . . [Lévy-Bruhl's] critics often misunderstood his aims. Lévy-Bruhl felt that cultures can be legitimately studied by analyzing how patterned modes of thinking give rise to patterned social behavior. In this respect he has much in common with the culture-and-personality school of modern anthropology [i.e., cognitive anthropology] and he may be called one of the pioneers of this important movement.

To be sure, none of the scholars just cited has accepted Lévy-Bruhl's ideas—and especially the ideas expressed in *How Natives Think*—uncritically. All of them express an uneasiness about the assumption that prelogicality is uniquely primitive in its provenance. The point is that, unlike Radin et al., they took his concepts seriously and sought to apply them in their own conceptions of how the human mind works.

In addition to those just mentioned, three especially perceptive reassessments of Lévy-Bruhl by Needham (1972), Horton (1973), and O'Keefe (1983) need to be taken into account, as each underscores the inherent validity of the concept of cognitive relativity expressed in *How Natives Think*.

VI

In *Belief, Language, and Experience* (1972), a disquisition on the experiential dimension of religious beliefs, which is, in fact, dedicated to the memory of Lévy-Bruhl (together with that of Ludwig Wittgenstein), the eminent British anthropologist Rodney Needham concludes that the author of *How Natives Think* did indeed have something important to say, and that it was he, ". . . more than any other scholar, who turned inquiry out of the confined circuit laid down by Comte and his British successors, and who took up a quite new line of advance" (R. Needham 1972:181). As Needham sees it, Lévy-Bruhl did *not* begin with the assumption that the "European" thought-mode was inherently superior to any other mode, but rather was ". . . concerned to understand . . . certain features of ideation in primitive societies that could not be accounted for by the traditional notions of our own psychology and our own logic," adding that "This is a point of capital importance." He goes on to note that perhaps the most lasting legacy left by Lévy-Bruhl was the realization that there is no universal logic or thought-mode, and that it is incumbent upon students of the human condition to adopt a truly *relativist* perspective. In short, thanks to Lévy-Bruhl's seminal efforts:

> The premise of an absolute conception of human experience, against which cultural styles of thought and action can be objectively assessed, disintegrates; and its place is taken by an apprehension of conceptual relationships in which variant collective representatives of man and his powers confusedly contend. The task of social anthropology thus becomes to determine comparatively what means of resolution can be contrived, and whether there are any constant correspondences that can be made into points of reference for a universal and more reliable cartography of human nature. (R. Needham 1972:185)

Needham suggests that such "points of reference" may in fact exist, but that the rationalist assumptions shared by most of Lévy-Bruhl's critics (including the Boasians) are incapable of providing a viable framework for such an investigation.

In a similar vein, Robin Horton (1973), in an essay comparing Lévy-Bruhl and Durkheim and their respective impacts on the rise of "scientific" social science in the early years of this century, points out that although both scholars stressed the increased importance of individualism as a prime factor in the evolution of civilization and the concomitant emergence of rational thought (that is, the breakdown of Durkheim's "conscience collective"; for a recent discussion of this matter, see Wallwork 1984), there is a fundamental difference between how the two scholars per-

ceived the relationship between prerational and rational modes
of perception. To Durkheim, as Horton points out, the relationship was clearly evolutionary. The primitive way of looking
at the world was inherently simple and unsophisticated. However, to Lévy-Bruhl, the two modes remained antithetical, the
implications being that the one is no less sophisticated than the
other. Thus, there is no necessary reason to conclude that "prelogical" thought gradually evolved to "conceptual" thought;
rather, the newly emerged individualism was simply more compatible with non-contradiction than it was with participation.

In short, both Needham and Horton accord Lévy-Bruhl a
prominent place indeed in the galaxy of early twentieth century
contributors to social thought, and especially that branch thereof
that attempts to explain the ways the human mind organizes and
makes sense out of the world, or, in other words, the cognitive
patterns that have emerged in the course of man's evolutionary
experience. Thus, when it comes to cognition, there is as yet no
clear evidence to suggest that any one cognitive model or "map"
is necessarily more accurate than any other; rather, as Needham
so succinctly puts it, there are but "variant collective representations," each of which must be assessed on its *own* terms.

More recently, in a brilliant and remarkably comprehensive
study of the origin and social functions of magic, Daniel Lawrence O'Keefe (1982:88) has remarked that in his final formulation, Lévy-Bruhl is very close to the position espoused by the
philosopher Ludwig Wittgenstein, that is, both assert that the
principle of non-contradiction ". . . became a Western institution
which progressively hardened our concepts of all the physical
entities so as to build contradiction right into them." O'Keefe
goes on to suggest that the "sharp edges" that define objects (or
persons, places, times, etc.) in the Western consciousness are
"conceptual," and that magic is necessarily predicated on an alternate conception of temporal and spatial relationships. He concludes his brief but insightful discussion of Lévy-Bruhl by observing that in the final analysis the latter's original argument,
as stated in *How Natives Think*, was never really abandoned, but
rather was reformulated: "Primitive thought lacks the principle
of contradiction not in the sense that it does not obey the simple
contradiction [that is, in immediate circumstances] but because
its basic concept lacks the sharp edges that the principle of con-

tradiction as a social institution builds into them over the long course of [Western] civilization" (O'Keefe 1982:88). Clearly, O'Keefe has read his Lévy-Bruhl with care—something that cannot be said of a great many of his erstwhile detractors!

Having examined the other side of the critical coin, it remains for us to review the Lévy-Bruhlian dimension in contemporary anthropological theory per se. To be sure, this for the most part unconscious dimension has hitherto been obscured by the vast difference in the terminology employed by modern students of human cognition. Moreover, the Boasian-intellectualist critique of Lévy-Bruhl is still embedded in the history of anthropological theory (e.g., Hays 1958, Honigmann 1976), and the three most relevant sub-fields, cognitive anthropology, structural anthropology (Dumézilian as well as Lévi-Straussian), and symbolic anthropology, are, with one major exception, more closely linked to the phenomenology of Edmund Husserl and the linguistic tradition that began with Ferdinand de Saussure than they are to the theories propounded by Émile Durkheim. Nevertheless, as we shall see, the parallels are there, and they deserve to be noted.

VII

As I have just indicated, the three anthropological sub-fields in question are closely linked to two fundamental (and related) developments in twentieth-century scholarship: descriptive linguistics and the philosophical school of thought known as phenomenology. The former discipline took shape shortly after the turn of the century, thanks in no small measure to de Saussure's (1916) celebrated dichotomy between *la langue* and *la parole*, that is, between the infinitely varied speech patterns one actually encounters in discourse and the finite set of rules that give rise to these patterns, be they phonological or syntactic. As a result of this breakthrough, the study of languages escalated from what had been largely an historical discipline to a true descriptive science.

It would be impossible here to do justice to the complex history of descriptive (or structural) linguistics. But for my purposes the most important historical development is the notion, shared by virtually every post-Saussurian linguist, that at the base of any language is a set of assumptions or axioms, a "logic," if you will, that governs the formation of any and all utterances in that language. This "logic" is necessarily implicit, and the native speaker takes it for granted. But its presence is reflected whenever linguistic communication takes place. At the phonological level it is manifest in the finite number and, more importantly, arrangement of the *phonemes*, or minimal signalling units; at the level of vocabulary (or morphology) it is reflected in the *morphemes*, or minimal set of phonemes that carry meanings, and at the level of syntax and grammar it is reflected in the finite number of patterns that govern how morphemes are combined and re-combined into phrases and sentences, as well as more inclusive units of discourse.

By the late twenties several schools of descriptive linguistics had emerged. In Europe generally, and especially among members of what came to be known as the Linguistic Circle of Prague (N. S. Trubetzkoy, Roman Jakobson et al.) the emphasis was on the contrasts among phonemes, morphemes, syntactical systems, etc.; in the United States, thanks to the influence of Boas and his followers, the emphasis was more traditionally descriptive, and the linguistic features themselves were generally considered more important than the "spaces between them." However, in the late thirties, as political events in Europe forced the breakup of the Prague School and the subsequent migration of Jakobson and other European linguists to the United States, the differences between the "European" and "American" approaches to linguistics began to blur. In the late fifties Noam Chomsky and his transformationalist disciples percipitated yet another "revolution" in the scientific study of language, one that has still not run its course.

The second major development, phenomenology, is even more complex, both in its roots, which lie deep in the subsoil of nineteenth century German idealism, and its subsequent history. Nevertheless, the impact of this approach to the philosophy of mind has been profound, not only on the social sciences, but on twentieth century thought per se. The first modern phenomenologist was the eminent German philosopher Edmund Husserl. In *Logische Untersuchungen* (1900-01), *Ideen zu einen reinen Phänomenologie* (1913), and other works, Husserl attempted to demonstrate that there is no inherent or "objective" reality, but rather that we create the world "out there" by conceiving of it. To the extent that we share conceptions in common with others, we can be said to have reached an *agreement* as to the nature of the phenomenal world. Thus, reality is necessarily relativistic, a function of our respective cognitive orientations.

Directly or indirectly, Husserl's ideas influenced a host of twentieth century philosophers and social scientists, including Ludwig Wittgenstein, Martin Heidigger, Alfred Schutz, Maurice Merleau-Ponty, and the American sociologists Peter Berger and Harold Garfinkel—to say nothing of the controversial anthropologist Carlos Castaneda, who makes no bones whatsoever about his indebtedness to this school of philosophy in his ongoing attempts to interpret the "teachings" of his famous Yaqui Indian *guru*, don Juan Matus (see Littleton 1976:149). Moreover, although there is no evidence that Lévy-Bruhl was aware of Husserl's work at the time he wrote *How Natives Think*, it is highly probable that he became familiar with the phenomenological approach shortly thereafter; he was too competent a philosopher to have ignored it—even though he does not specifically cite Husserl in his later works—and it can be argued that the German philosopher eventually came to have an indirect, albeit significant impact on Lévy-Bruhl's ideas.[6] Indeed, it is not impossible to suggest that phenomenology—broadly defined—is one of the chief links between the theories shortly to be discussed and the ideas expressed in *How Natives Think*.

In any event, no discipline was more profoundly—albeit for the most part implicitly—influenced by Husserl's epistemology than the fledgling science of descriptive linguistics. If, as Husserl and his disciples maintained, reality is at bottom the artifact of an agreement, the only way such an agreement could be achieved is through discourse. Thus, language, or, more properly, the logic embedded in language, is by definition a prime factor in achieving an agreement as to the nature of the world. And as languages and their attendant logics differ substantially in time and space, it is impossible to understand the nature of a given "agreement" without reference to the structure of the language spoken by those who share it.

The first twentieth century linguist to make this point—to be sure, he did not do so in strictly phenomenological terms—was Edward Sapir. In a celebrated essay originally published in 1928, Sapir (quoted by Whorf 1956:134) observed that "Human beings do not live in the objective world alone, nor alone in the world of social activity as ordinarily understood, but are very much at the mercy of the particular language which has become the medium of expression of their society. . . . The fact of the matter is that the 'real world' is to a large extent unconsciously built up in the language habits of the group." Thus was phenomenology married to the science of language.

Sapir himself did not follow up this brilliant observation; that task fell to his most gifted student, the Hartford-based insurance underwriter-turned-linguist Benjamin Lee Whorf. In a remarkable series of essays published initially in the late thirties and early forties, Whorf (1956) systematically compared the Hopi Indian language to what he termed "Standard Average European," or SAE, an amalgam of the basic structural features shared by English, French, German, Spanish, and the rest of the modern Indo-European languages of central and western Europe. The result was a major breakthrough, for it soon became apparent that the Hopi "logic," as it were, was fundamentally different from that evolved by the SAE languages. For example, the Hopi conception of time is almost impossible to express in ordinary English; there is no tense as we know it, but rather a vast array of "validity-forms" and other features that specify aspects of an event. Indeed, this emphasis on *events* is itself profoundly different from the SAE emphasis on *things*, and the spaces occupied by them (Whorf 1956:147). Thus, it is not fortuitous that Western logicians saw fit to formalize a rule of non-contradiction, i.e., that two things cannot occupy the same space at the same time. To the Hopi, such a rule would be irrelevant, as "things" are, in the last analysis, but aspects of what can best be described as an event-stream. What is more, Whorf pointed out that this and other features of the Hopi language are reflected throughout Hopi culture, and that the Hopi image of the "real world" is indeed "unconsciously built up in the language habits of the group."

It should be emphasized that neither Sapir nor Whorf seem to have been consciously influenced by Lévy-Bruhl, any more than they were by Husserl. Nevertheless, the parallels between the ideas expressed in *How Natives Think* and the so-called "Sapir-Whorf" hypothesis are remarkable, to say the least. Lévy-Bruhl, as we have seen, devotes an important section of the book to the linguistic parameters of prelogicality, and, although he does not pursue the matter as deeply or as systematically as Whorf did in his Hopi-SAE comparisons, the implication that there is in fact a "linguistic microcosm" of one sort or another underlying the "law of participation" seems clear. Indeed, the following passage (p. 139) could easily have been written by Whorf:

> The essential characteristic of the mentality of a given social group should, it seems to me, be reflected to some extent in the language its members speak. In the long run the mental habits of the group cannot fail to leave some trace upon their modes of expression, since these are also social phenomena, upon which the individual has little, if any, influence. With differing types of mentality, therefore, there should be languages which differ in their construction.

To be sure, Lévy-Bruhl also cautiously suggests that the languages spoken by "undeveloped races" generally share some common characteristics, such as an excess of "mystical" words and a paucity of generalized categories that would permit the systematic delineation of "objective reality" (pp. 175-6). Few contemporary linguists would agree with this observation. Yet it should be noted that several of Whorf's disciples, among them the late Harry Hoijer (1964), subsequently discovered "linguistic microcosms" in other non-Western languages, such as Navajo, that are broadly analogous to the one he discovered in Hopi.[7] Thus, the suggestion that peoples whose techno-environmental adaptations are significantly less sophisticated than our own may share certain linguistic—and, by extension, conceptual—features in common, regardless of their immediate linguistic heritage, should not be dismissed out of hand.

In any event, it is clear that Lévy-Bruhl anticipated by almost three decades Whorf's (1956:152) conclusion that Western reality-constructs are *not* necessarily universal, but rather for the most part as much a function of the syntax in which they are couched as any other set of such constructs, civilized or primitive.

VIII

In the decades immediately following Whorf's death in 1941 the notion of cognitive relativity, as I have termed it, was developed in several directions as a new generation of cultural anthropologists, in fair measure inspired by Whorf's work, began to incorporate linguistic/phenomenological models into their conceptual frameworks. In a seminal monograph entitled *Language in Relation to a Unified Theory of the Structure of Human Behavior* (1954), Kenneth L. Pike, citing the well-known linguistic distinction between phonetics and phonemics (respectively, the objective study of speech sounds per se and the subjective analysis of the phonemes, or primary signalling units, of a given language), suggested that a similar distinction can be made when it comes to the description of human behavior generally. Heretofore, he pointed out, anthropologists had for the most part viewed culture (and/or cultures) from an *etic* standpoint. That is, the emphasis had been on universal categories, upon empirical generalizations that are external to any one culture—just as the speech sound we label "unvoiced apicodental stop" (English *t*) occurs in French, German, Swahili, and perhaps the majority of the world's languages. Indeed, most of the traditional categories and labels anthropologists have brought to bear—"clan," "lineage," "cross-cousin," "shaman," etc.—are etic categories, and are clearly analogous to phonetic phenomena such as "unvoiced apicodental stop." However, when the ethnographer's focus shifts to the finite set of categories unique to a given culture at a given time, the resulting account is an *emic* one, and is analogous to a description of the phonemes of a specific language (hence the label "emic").

To put it another way, an emic account necessarily involves a hierarchy of actor-relevant categories rather than simply the theoretical and/or logical framework subscribed to by the observer, just as the English *t* phoneme is, *qua* phoneme, something other than merely another manifestation of an unvoiced apicodental stop. In short, Pike's dichotomy between emics and etics, although still controversial in some quarters (e.g., Harris 1968:568f.), was a fundamental development in the evolution of cognitive anthropology. In retrospect, it proved to be a watershed.

The next important step was taken in 1957, three years after Pike's monograph appeared. In the context of a Georgetown University symposium on the relationship between anthropology and linguistics, Ward Goodenough, a cultural anthropologist, presented a paper that was to have far reaching effects. He begins by redefining the concept of culture in linguistic—and, implicitly, phenomenological—terms:

> A society's culture consists of whatever it is one has to know or believe in order to operate in a manner acceptable to its members, and do so in any role that they accept for any one of themselves. . . . By this definition, we should note that culture is not a material phenomenon; it does not consist of things, people, behavior, or emotions. It is rather an organization of these things. It is the forms of things that people have in mind, their models for perceiving, relating, and otherwise integrating them (Goodenough 1957:167).

After elaborating this new, anti-materialist definition and relating it explicitly to the study of language, Goodenough (1957:173) concludes his brief but ground-breaking paper with a challenge to the discipline that is still regarded in a great many circles as a confession of faith: "The great problem for a science of man is how to get from the objective world of materiality, with its infinite variability, to the subjective world of form as it exists in what, for lack of a better term, we must call the minds of our fellow men."

It did not take long for the profession, or at least a substantial portion thereof, to rise to Goodenough's challenge. As it turned out, he was not the only scholar thinking along these lines at the time, and by the end of the decade a new methodology had surfaced, one that was to become a major force in contemporary anthropology. Initially referred to as "ethnoscience," "componential analysis," "formal semantic analysis," or simply, in Sturtevant's (1964:99) apt phrase, "the new enthography," it was enthusiastically adopted by an otherwise diverse group of younger anthropologists who had become disenchanted with the prevailing materialist approach to culture (e.g., Steward 1955, Sahlins and Service 1960). In addition to Goodenough and Sturtevant, the pioneer contributors include Harold Conklin (1964), Charles Frake (1962, 1964a, 1964b, 1977), A. Kimball Romney and Roy D'Andrade (1964), John Gumperz (1964), Anthony F. C. Wallace (1962), Paul Kay (1970), and the late James Spradley

(1970, 1972, 1979). Most had been trained in (or at least exposed to) structural linguistics and were eager to get as far inside the minds of their fellow men as possible.

By the mid-sixties, the new methodology had become, in effect, a movement, and almost every cultural anthropologist in the United States was forced to come to terms with it in one way or another. Thus began the famous "emic-etic" controversy (e.g., Harris 1968:568f.), which has still not totally run its course (e.g., Honigmann 1976:330-4).

It would neither be possible nor germane to my purpose to follow all the twists and turns taken by what is now generally referred to as "cognitive anthropology" since the mid-sixties. Like most such movements, especially those which have an air of revealed truth about them, cognitive anthropology has produced its share of sects and sub-sects. What is germane, however, is the extent to which this contemporary approach to the study of human cognition resembles the one advocated by Lévy-Bruhl in 1910.

In the first place, the cognitive models elicited by Goodenough, Frake, Conklin, Spradley, and the rest, are all thoroughly emic. Like Lévy-Bruhl (and Whorf), their goal is to understand the "logic" of a particular culture *on its own terms*, without reference (in theory, at least) to any preconceived ideas about the way the human mind works. Thus, every culture will necessarily be characterized by a unique set of "cognitive maps" (cf. Spradley 1972) which define experience and which serve to orient the behavior of the participants in that culture. Moreover, like the basic constituents of language, the significant features of those maps will necessarily be finite rather than infinite: they form, as it were, a code which, when deciphered, will allow the investigator to make his or her way through what on the surface might appear to be an infinitely complex maze of specific behaviors, categories, symbols, and labels.

Lévy-Bruhl attempted to discover essentially the same sort of cognitive map for primitive culture as a whole: once the "law of participation" has been elicited, one can navigate the apparently illogical seas of "prelogical mentality" with relative ease. To be sure, he lumped a great many otherwise radically distinct cultures into a single undifferentiated mass, and this, of course, is a major difference between his brand of cognitive anthropology (or cognitive relativism) and that advocated by the "new ethnographers." But the point here is that both the author of *How Natives Think* and contemporary cognitive anthropology begin with the *same* basic assumption: there is no single congitive map that can guide one though the entire range of the human condition.

Secondly, both Lévy-Bruhl and the cognitive anthropologists share a concern with folk taxonomies and conceptual hierarchies. It is no accident that the emic approach has been most frequently applied in the analysis of cultural domains in which paradigms are most abundant: kinship terminology (e.g., Goodenough 1969, Romney and D'Andrade 1964), color terms (e.g., Berlin and Kay 1969), ethnobotany (e.g., Berlin, Breedlove, and Raven 1966), and other analogous sorts of labeling systems. Indeed, a widespread criticism of the method is that until it is able to progress beyond such taxonomies, it cannot really tell us all that much about how the "natives" actually think (cf. Keesing 1972:307-8). Nevertheless, Lévy-Bruhl, too, found himself constrained by paradigmatic evidence and the extent to which it serves as a primary mode of expression in primitive society. For example, in the chapter on numeration (Chapter 5) he devotes a great deal of space to the discussion of the compass, number systems, etc., and how the "law of participation" links them together into "prelogical" wholes (see especially pp. 185-7).

As has just been indicated, one of the principal differences between Lévy-Bruhl and the new ethnographers is that the former was concerned with what amounts to the "emics" of primitive culture as a whole. Thus, unlike Goodenough, and the rest, he was a thoroughgoing comparativist, and the cognitive model he managed to elicit from the ethnographic data available to him was not unique to any one primitive culture. In this respect he more closely resembles his fellow countryman Claude Lévi-Strauss.

IX

Lévi-Strauss, founding father, as it were, of the structuralist movement that has dominated French anthropological thought for more than a generation, is also deeply indebted to linguistic theory, especially that brand of it developed by the previously mentioned Prague School. Inspired by Roman Jakobson's contention that phonemic systems are everywhere predicated on the mediation of contrasts, he has attempted to demonstrate that the human mind itself operates according to a binary logic, and that a fundamental feature of *all* cognitive models, civilized as well as primitive, is a schema in terms of which seemingly inherent (and irreconcilable) oppositions are resolved. The arena in which he has most effectively demonstrated this thesis is that of myth (e.g., Lévi-Strauss 1958, 1964, 1966a, 1967; see also Littleton 1969, Leach 1970). His evidence comes from a broad spectrum of New World ethnography, from the Amazon Basin to British Columbia, with occasional excursions to others hemispheres and eras. Thus, like Lévy-Bruhl, Lévi-Strauss is a comparativist whose goal is to explicate how people think, and his seminal book, *La pensée sauvage* (1962; i.e., *The Savage Mind* [1966b]), was in many respects inspired by *How Natives Think* (cf. Lévi-Strauss 1966b:268).

But the theories expressed in these two similarly titled books (at least in their respective English versions) are in fact poles apart. To Lévi-Strauss, the "savage mind" is at bottom but a manifestation of the human mind per se (cf. Strutynski 1977), whereas to Lévy-Bruhl, as we have seen, "primitive mentality," although present to some degree in all human societies, is different *in kind* from the cognitive processes generally characteristic of Western culture. In short, unlike Lévy-Bruhl, Lévi-Strauss is a "cognitive absolutist"; that is, he is fundamentally committed to a *single*, all-pervasive model of how the human mind works, while the author of *How Natives Think*, like most contemporary cognitive anthropologists, is committed to the proposition that there are multiple (or at least two) modes when it comes to the ways our minds work.

X

In some respects, Lévy-Bruhl has much more in common with another contemporary French scholar, the eminent Indo-Euro-peanist Georges Dumézil, who is also sometimes considered a pioneer structuralist (cf. Lévi-Strauss 1953:535). Unlike Lévi-Strauss, Dumézil has not sought to delineate a comprehensive model of human cognition per se, but instead has concentrated on a single, albeit widespread cognitive model, or "ideology," as he terms it, that was shared by the several ancient Indo-European speaking communities (cf. Littleton 1974, 1982). Moreover, the tradition he has focused on is not a primitive one; indeed, from Lévy-Bruhl's perspective, the Indo-European ideology Dumézil has spent half a century attempting to explicate is precisely the one which, in Greece at least, ultimately managed to transcend "prelogicality." Yet from a methodological standpoint there are some interesting similarities between the two scholars.

For one thing, both Dumézil and Lévy-Bruhl are committed cognitive relativists. In a brilliant series of books and essays Dumézil (e.g., 1941, 1958, 1977; see also Littleton 1982) has conclusively demonstrated that the ancient Indo-Europeans (Indians, Iranians, Greeks, Romans, Germans, Celts, etc.) viewed the world in terms of a tripartite "ideology" or cognitive model. That is, all phenomena—social, religious, mythological, natural, or whatever—were conceived in terms of three hierarchically ranked "functions": (1) cosmic and juridical sovereignty, (2) physical prowess, and (3) plant, animal, and human fertility. Endlessly replicated in triads of gods (e.g., the "archaic" Roman triad formed by Jupiter, Mars, and Quirinus [cf. Dumézil 1966], that is, the cosmic sovereign, the war god par excellence, and the incarnation of fertility and physical well-being, as well as the "mass" of the society), triads of social classes (e.g., the three Aryan *varṇa*, or castes, of ancient India: Brahmans, Kṣatriyas, and Vaiśyas, that is, the priests, the warriors, and the cultivators), triads of diseases and their cures, triads of calamities, tripartite conceptions of space, and threefold paradigms of almost every conceivable variety, these three "functions" were uniquely Indo-European.[8] Other ancient civilizations, such as those of the Near East, China, or Middle America, operated in terms of fundamentally different ideologies; the same can be said for contemporary primitive societies. In short, as Dumézil sees it, there is no overarching or universal human cognitive model—or at least none that can be described with any certainty—and the maximum cognitive "unit," as it were, seems to be the language family (see Littleton 1982:274).

While Lévy-Bruhl does not focus on the Indo-European tradition, ancient or modern, he is also aware of the importance of numbers and numerical sequences. For example, in the previously cited chapter on numeration he discusses in detail the importance of the number four among a great many North American Indians, something that had long since become common knowledge among anthropologists by 1910 (e.g., Tylor 1871 1:361-2), and goes on to assert that, "similar phenomena are to be found throughout the Far East, to say nothing of the Indo-European and Semitic peoples" (p. 191). To be sure, the context here is a discussion of the importance of the numbers five, six, and seven, and he betrays no awareness whatsoever of the overwhelming significance of the number three in the Indo-European tradition. Yet his clear emphasis on the sacred and "mystic" importance of numeration generally, and the extent to which numerical systems are replicated in almost every imaginable cultural context, is strikingly similar to Dumézil's approach.

A second and more fundamental similarity between the two French scholars is that both make effective use of the Durkheimian concept of collective representation. In Dumézil's case, this idea was absorbed indirectly, primarily as a result of his intense association with the eminent Durkheimian Sinologist Marcel Granet, as well as through his general awareness of the French School of sociology (Mauss was his senior colleague at the École Practique des Hautes Études for many years), and rarely if ever does he use the phrase itself. But like Lévy-Bruhl, who was, of course, very much a member of that School, at least in the early part of his career, the notion that social facts are intimately linked to religious "facts," and that the end result is a comprehensive model that constrains the way a people think about the world and their relationship to it, pervades his work. Thus, the tripartite ideology of the Indo-Europeans is but one of a great many such ideologies that might be elicited from the range of cultural and historical data confronting the anthropologist. By the same token, Lévy-Bruhl's "law of participation" is perhaps but one of several bases upon which a viable cognitive model can be constructed. Again, both scholars are firmly committed to the notion of cognitive relativity, and while it would certainly be unfair to suggest that Lévy-Bruhl anticipated Dumézil and the development of what has come to be known as "the new comparative mythology" (Littleton 1982), the latter's fundamental orientation—if not his discoveries—was at least to some extent foreshadowed in *How Natives Think*.

XI

The third contemporary sub-field which relates to Lévy-Bruhl, symbolic anthropology, has close ties with the new ethnography as well as with Lévi-Straussian (if not Dumézilian) structuralism. Indeed, as three of its leading practitioners, Colby, Fernandez, and Kronenfield, have recently pointed out (1981:422), the distinctions between symbolic and cognitive anthropology are today rapidly dissolving, and an increasing number of symbolic anthropologists, like Walter Edwards (1982), have found it convenient to adopt a Lévi-Straussian frame of reference. Nevertheless, the school has a separate history, the taproots of which can be traced back to Friedrich Max Müller, Wilhelm Mannhardt, and other nineteenth-century scholars who first attempted to come to grips with the role played by symbols and metaphors in religious texts and rituals.[9] Other pioneer contributors include Frazer, Durkheim, Freud, Jung, Joseph Needham, G. H. Mead, C. S. Pierce, Husserl, and Lévy-Bruhl himself, whose importance here is explicitly acknowledged by Colby et al. (1981:430).

However, the immediate roots of symbolic anthropology lie in the same subsoil that produced cognitive anthropology, namely, the disenchantment with materialism that surfaced in the mid-fifties, and the increasing awareness of the extent to which linguistic models could be applied to the analysis of cultural data as a whole. The chief contemporary exponents of this approach, such as Mary Douglas (1966, 1971), David Schneider (1968), Victor Turner (1967, 1975), Clifford Geertz (1973), James Fernandez (1974, 1977), and Sherry Ortner (1973), are all concerned with the extent to which a society's "key symbols," to use Ortner's apt phrase, form a *code*, a semiotic system which exercises a powerful force on both the world-view and the behavior of those who have internalized it. For the most part, symbolic anthropologists are less apt to be as rigorously "linguistic" in their interpretations as their cognitive anthropologist colleagues; as Dougherty and Fernandez (1981:414) put it: "The science-humanities debate is clearly present in the relation between cognitive and symbolic anthropology—the former given to analytical and formal methods of inquiry and concerned with planning and prediction, and the latter much more concerned with the artful enterprise of what Kroeber called the 'descriptive integration' of field materials." But even the most "artful" of symbolic anthropologists, as well as their adherents in other disciplines, such as Roland Barthes (1972), are constrained to look for a systematic logic within the "forest of symbols," as Victor Turner so eloquently phrases it in his well-known title.

Perhaps no symbolic anthropologist has been more prone to "descriptive integration" than Clifford Geertz. Throughout his work one finds a consistent respect for both competence (that is, a shared symbol system or code) and performance (the specific behavior patterns that are generated by the symbols). This complex integration of observed and elicited data, predicated on the interpretation of symbol systems, is the essence of what, following Gilbert Ryle, he has chosen to call "thick description." As Geertz (1983:49) puts it:

> If anthropological interpretation is constructing a reading of what happens, then to divorce it from what happens— from what, in this time or that place, specific people say, what they do, what is done to them, from the whole vast business of the world—is to divorce it from its applications and render it vacant. A good interpretation of anything—a poem, a person, a history, a ritual, an institution, a society— takes us into the heart of that of which it is the interpretation.

Thus a good interpretation, especially a symbolic interpretation, is necessarily rooted in concrete examples, and the symbolic code one elicits must never be construed as separate and apart from the domains it serves to integrate. Nor should it be considered *in vacuo*, as Lévi-Strauss is sometimes wont to do.

Another contemporary scholar who shares this concern, especially as it relates to metaphors and their relationship to behavior, is James Fernandez (1974, 1977, 1982), whose efforts to untangle the complex associations among metaphors (and metanyms) in what he calls "expressive culture," that is, the twin domains of ritual (performance) and sacred text (competence), must be ranked among the most elegant contributions so far made to symbolic anthropology.

As the reader will discover, much of the foregoing was anticipated by Lévy-Bruhl. *How Natives Think* is certainly characterized by "thick description" and a pervasive awareness of the extent to which symbols and metaphors are interconnected. It is from such interlocking "collective representations" that the author elicits the "law of participation" and its attendant mysticism. Lévy-Bruhl is thoroughly cognizant of the presence throughout the primitive cultures he compares of a semiotic code that generates specific "performances." A good example can be seen in his analysis (pp. 76-78) of the role played by the *Alcheringa*, or "Dream-Time," in Australian aboriginal culture. Drawing on the famous account by Spencer and Gillen (1899), he points out that the ceremonies associated with this concept, which involve a participatory interface, as it were, among the ancestors, the individual, and the totem animal or plant, serve to define both the way the world is and the way the world—and all that it contains—works. As Lévy-Bruhl puts it (p. 92), "To our minds, there are necessarily three distinct relationships here, however close the relationship may be. To the primitive minds, the three make but one, yet at the same time are three." This, then, is a manifestation of a participatory "competence model," one which indeed exercises a powerful influence on the behavior of those who subscribe to it. And the relationship between competence and performance here is also reciprocal. As he expresses it (p. 92): ". . . the influence which the ceremonies exercise over the totemic species is more than direct: it is *immanent*. How can the primitive doubt their effective power? The most invincible logical certitude gives way before the symbiotic feeling which is an accompaniment of collective representations thus lived and translated into action." That the semiotic code expressed in the *Alcheringa* complex is "prelogical" and therefore fundamentally different from the semiotic codes characteristic of "conceptual" societies, where the rule of non-contradiction holds sway, doesn't make it any less significant. Or any less worthy of respect.

Again, the terminology is different, and few if any contemporary symbolic anthropologists would attempt to generalize a common semiotic system for *all* non-Western societies—Turner's (1964) emphasis on the importance of liminality and its associated symbols is a partial exception, although his purview clearly includes Western as well as non-Western ritual behavior. But on balance Lévy-Bruhl's approach to the analysis of symbols and symbolic systems clearly anticipates the relativist approach shared by Geertz, Fernandez, and the rest, and his importance in the history (or better, perhaps, pre-history) of the sub-discipline, although recognized, is patently far greater than most symbolic anthropologists have heretofore been willing to admit.

XII

In sum, although for the most part dismissed and/or ignored by contemporary social scientists—and, indeed, eventually abandoned by Lévy-Bruhl himself—the central idea developed in *How Natives Think*, namely, that non-Western cultures are characterized by a "mentality" that is *wholly* different from the one generally associated with Western culture, is thoroughly congruent with one of the central assumptions of contemporary cultural anthropology: the rules underlying cognitive and/or symbolic systems are as arbitrary and as varied as the range of cultures that has produced them. And as we have just seen, much of what is now taken for granted by cognitive, structural, and symbolic anthropologists was in fact anticipated in Lévy-Bruhl's work, especially his early work.

To be sure, his rhetoric may often seem archaic, and the ethnographic data upon on which he relied has in many instances long since been superseded (for example, his conception of Australian totemism was predicated on the same incomplete data base that misled most of his more celebrated contemporaries, including Frazer, Freud, and Durkheim; see, for example, Radcliffe-Brown 1965 [1929]). Moreover, the notion that there is but a single primitive mentality has rightly been called into question, even by his more recent admirers. But all things considered, Lévy-Bruhl's insights into the relationship between cultural patterns and cognitive models, to say nothing of how this interface is reflected in the semiotic codes that govern the ways human communities make sense out of the world and their relationship to it, were truly remarkable for 1910. That he failed to recognize the often fundamental differences *among* primitive thought-modes, choosing, rather, to emphasize what he perceived to be the common denominator that linked such thought-modes into a single "mentality," that is, the "law of participation," should not be held against him. Indeed, few if any of his contemporaries were as atuned to the idea of cognitive relativity as he was, and it was not until well over a decade after his death that anthropologists really began to come to grips with the problems he had wrestled with so cogently—if not definitively—in *How Natives Think*.

What is more, Lévy-Bruhl was the first modern scholar to take non-Western modes of thinking seriously, and to accord them a modicum of intellectual respect. This was certainly not the case among his "intellectualist" contemporaries, including Freud, Frazer, and even Durkheim, whose attitudes toward these matters were at best patronizing and at worst ethnocentric in the extreme. However, to Lévy-Bruhl, the "law of participation" and the "mystical representations" of reality it engenders are neither aberrations, nor the infantile gropings of minds not yet fully formed.[10] Rather, in the final analysis, the primitive conception of reality is, as Carlos Castaneda (1970) has aptly phrased it, "a separate reality," and must be understood as such. Once again, Lévy-Bruhl emerges as a bona fide forerunner, as a true cognitive relativist in an age of scholars who, for the most part, dismissed primitive conceptions of the world as inherently absurd (cf. Littleton 1976:150-1).

In this connection it might be observed that if we discount the assumption that prelogicality is necessarily confined to the simpler end of the cultural spectrum—as we have seen, Lévy-Bruhl himself did so late in his career—it is perhaps possible to suggest that his most important single contribution was the discovery of a deep-seated dichotomy between two alternative reality-constructs, thought-modes, "logics," or whatever, one predicated on participation and the other on the rule of non-contradiction, which can be detected in varying proportions everywhere. Admittedly, the latter mode has generally been dominant in Western culture, at least among its elites, since well before Aristotle.

But the key word here is *dominant*. As Lévy-Bruhl points out in the all too often overlooked final paragraph of *How Natives Think* (p. 386), the participatory, or prelogical mode has lurked at the edges of Western culture since its inception, and at various times has all but displaced the rational thought-mode. One such time was the late Hellenistic and Roman period (ca. 100 B.C. to 400 A.D.), which was characterized by an obsession with mysticism and magic (cf. Seligmann 1968:23f., Wilson 1971:176f.). Gnosticism, the Kabbala, Manichaeanism, and a host of other esoteric cults and sects were spawned by this obsession, as was the inherently prelogical core of Christian theology itself—that is, the notion that God is at once singular and plural, and can manifest Himself simultaneously as Father, Son, and Holy Ghost. Indeed, many of the early Church Fathers, including the aforementioned Tertullian, would have been more at home intellectually with the participatory world-view shared by don Juan and his fellow *brujos* than Castaneda himself seems to have been at the outset of his spiritual odyssey![11] At the same time, the concept of the Trinity rapidly became one of the principal bones of contention among Christian theologians, from Arius and Athanasius to Thomas Aquinas, as they struggled to reconcile a universe predicated on the rule of non-contradiction with an idea rooted in a prelogical conception of reality.

Thus, embedded in all of us, it would seem, are the seeds of this "separate reality," this alternate way of looking at the world, and the current popularity of so-called New Age religions (cf. Adler 1979, Ellwood 1979) is eloquent testimony of the degree to which the "law of participation" is still to be reckoned with in Western thought, despite the overt dominance of the rule of non-contradiction and a "rational" world-view. But before we dismiss these occult manifestations—to say nothing of the fundamental tenets of Christianity and other mainstream religions—as inherently absurd, it would be well to remember that at least one thoroughly rational scholar, the author of *How Natives Think*, found himself constrained to conclude that the "logic" underlying these belief systems, as well as their counterparts in primitive cultures, may ultimately prove to be as valid—or at least as legitimate—as the one promulgated by Aristotle.

XIII

As I indicated at the outset, I began this project with some trepidation, having been conditioned by my teachers to regard Lévy-Bruhl as an intellectual curiosity unworthy of serious consideration. But as I became aware of the extent to which he had anticipated much that contemporary cognitive, structural, and symbolic anthropologists now take for granted, and as I digested what eminent scholars such as E. E. Evans-Pritchard and Rodney Needham have had to say about his intellectual achievements, I realized that my teachers had been wrong, and that Lucien Lévy-

Bruhl was in fact a true pioneer, worthy of being mentioned in the same breath with Frazer, Durkheim, Weber, and the others who, in that memorable decade and a half between 1900 and 1915, laid the foundations of modern social science.

To be sure, the book that follows, which, in retrospect, I now consider to have been a remarkable contribution to the growth of anthropological theory, is not without its faults. As we have seen, many of Lévy-Bruhl's assumptions about the nature of the primitive world can be called into question, and his assertion that there is but a single prelogical "mentality," in the strict sense of the word, is not supported by the ethnographic and historical data currently at our disposal; Dumézil's demonstration that the ancient Indo-Europeans possessed a unique, albeit essentially pre-rational ideology is a good case in point.

At the same time, the author's more fundamental conclusion that there are at least two antithetical thought-modes, or "logics," one of which is more likely, other things being equal, to be encountered in simple societies, is still problematical, at least in my opinion, and should someday be tested against the massive corpus of data we have amassed since 1910. Indeed, if it were to survive such a test, Lévy-Bruhl's central thesis might yet provide the foundation for a more profound understanding of how *human beings*—natives and non-natives alike—think. And it is for this reason, more than any other, that I commend *How Natives Think* to all serious students of both the growth and the potential of the anthropological enterprise.

NOTES

1. Lévy-Bruhl's close association with the psychologist-cum-philosopher Théodule Ribot is further evidence of the extent to which he was knowledgeable in that field. Indeed, he frequently contributed articles to the psychologically oriented *Revue philosophique*, which Ribot had founded, and in 1917 took over the administration of the journal (Cazeneuve 1972:xiii).

2. Lilian Clare's choice of an English title is puzzling, as it does not really convey the sense of the French original. I initially suggested that a new English title be substituted—perhaps something on the order of *Mental Configurations among Primitive So-*

cieties—that would more accurately reflect what Lévy-Bruhl meant by *Les fonctions mentales dans les sociétés inférieures*. But, as Clare's title has been inextricably associated with this book since 1926, it seems wise, in retrospect, to stay with the inaccurate, albeit in its own way classic, *How Natives Think*.

3. As Cazeneuve (1972:xi) observes, Lévy-Bruhl was much involved with left-wing causes and "did not hide his sympathy for socialism." Also, like many others of his generation, he was deeply concerned with the notorious Dreyfus Affair, and in 1931 published a retrospective account of this most unfortunate episode (Lévy-Bruhl 1931).

4. E.g., Frazer (1919 IV:63), who in large measure based his theory of totemism on this presumed ignorance of the role of the father in conception. Such theories have long since been discredited.

5. For example, in his otherwise comprehensive history of anthropological theory Marvin Harris (1968:413, 482) mentions Lévy-Bruhl but twice in peripheral contexts, and makes no attempt whatsoever to assess the importance of his ideas to the discipline. In short, like the great majority of contemporary anthropologists, he simply ignores him.

6. In February of 1929 Husserl gave two lectures at the Sorbonne which were later published in French translation under the title *Méditations cartésiennes* (1931; see also Husserl 1950 [1973]). It is not impossible to suggest that Lévy-Bruhl was a member of the audience, and that he sought out the German philosopher afterwards. It would certainly have been in character!

7. By "analogous" I do not mean to imply "identical." As Hoijer (1964:142) puts it, "The world of social reality characteristic of the Navaho, and reflected in their language, is no more like that of the Hopi than it is our own."

8. It should be noted that Dumézil's discovery has inspired a great deal of further research concerning specific manifestations of the tripartite ideology in a variety of Indo-European contexts: e.g., medical lore (Puhvel 1970), the calendar (Strutynski 1975), and the transposition from myth to epic in the Indian (Wikander 1947) and ancient Greek traditions (Littleton 1970).

9. Max Müller's specific contributions to semiotics, many of which were seminal, such as his brilliant analysis of the symbolism expressed by the Sanskrit word *ātman* ("breath" or "soul") in the

Upanishadic literature (Müller 1897:xxviii-xxxii), have unfortunately been obscured by the widespread rejection of his "solar
mythology"—itself a grand, albeit flawed attempt to elicit a semiotic code—shortly after the turn of the century (see Dorson
1958).

10. Leach's (1970:91) reference to "the Frazer-Lévy-Bruhl-
Sartre notion that primitive thought is characterized by naiveté,
childishness, superstition, and so on" to the contrary notwithstanding. However, in all fairness, Leach does seem to have a
better grasp of what Lévy-Bruhl means than do most of his critics.
Although seemingly put off by the latter's dichotomous approach
to cognition—he makes a point of saying that primitives are "no
more mystical than we are" (Ibid:88)—Leach nevertheless comes
close to the mark in characterizing the contexts in which the two
modes of thought are typically employed:

> The distinction . . . is between a logic which is constructed
> out of observed contrasts in the sensory qualities of concrete
> objects—e.g., the difference between raw and cooked, wet
> and dry, male and female—and a logic which depends upon
> the formal contrasts of entirely abstract entities—e.g., plus
> and minus or $\log_e x$ and e^x. The latter kind of logic, which
> even in our own society is used only by highly specialized
> experts, is a different way of talking about the same thing
> (Leach 1970:88-89).

It is in the latter, more abstract context that the "law of participation" competes with the rule of non-contradiction.

11. It should be noted that this "odyssey" has been called into
serious question by several of Castaneda's critics, who suggest
that the whole episode may be a grand hoax (cf. de Mille 1976,
1979, 1980). Be that as it may, the "separate reality" that he
describes is certainly consonant with Lévy-Bruhl's conception of
prelogicality, and the world-view he ascribes to don Juan is clearly
predicated on a participatory thought-mode that would also have
appealed to a great many Christian Gnostics, as well as to Simon
Magus, Apollonius of Tyana, Mani, and other adepts of the era
in question (see also Littleton 1976, Wilk 1977).

ACKNOWLEDGMENTS

I would like to thank James W. Fernandez, Gunar Freibergs, Kazuo Matsumura, Michael A. McAleenan, Jaan Puhvel, Ivan Strensky, Udo Strutynski, and other unnamed readers for their willingness to read a draft of this introduction and for their many valuable criticisms, comments, and suggestions. I would also like to thank Loren Hoekzema, of Princeton University Press, for his patience and consummate editorial expertise. However, my assessments of *How Natives Think*, as well as of Lévy-Bruhl's overall contributions to anthropological theory, are wholly my own, and I take full responsibility for them.

REFERENCES CITED

Adler, Margot
    1979   *Drawing Down the Moon: Witches, Druids, Goddess-Worshippers and Other Pagans in America Today.* Boston: Beacon Press.

Barthes, Roland
    1972   *Mythologies* (trans. Annette Lavers). New York: Hill and Wang.

Berlin, Brent, Dennis E. Breedlove, and Peter H. Raven
    1974   *Principles of Tzeltal Plant Classification: An Introduction to the Botanical Ethnography of a Mayan-Speaking People in Highland Chiapas.* New York: Academic Press.

Berlin, Brent, and Paul Kay
    1969   *Basic Color Terms: Their Universality and Evolution.* Berkeley: University of California Press.

Bunzel, Ruth V.
    1966   Introduction. *In* Lucien Lévy-Bruhl, *How Natives Think.* Pp. v-xviii, New York: Washington Square Press.

Cassirer, Ernst
    1953   *The Philosophy of Symbolic Forms.* New Haven: Yale University Press.

Castaneda, Carlos
    1968   *The Teachings of don Juan: A Yaqui Way of Knowledge.* Berkeley: University of California Press.
    1970   *A Separate Reality: Further Conversations with don Juan.* New York: Simon and Shuster.

Cazeneuve, Jean
    1972   *Lucien Lévy-Bruhl* (trans. Peter Rivière). Oxford: Basil Blackwell.

Colby, Benjamin N., James W. Fernandez, and David B. Kronenfield
    1981   Toward a Covergence of Cognitive and Symbolic Anthropology. *American Ethnologist* 8:422-50.

Conklin, Harold C.

   1964   Ethnogenealogical Method. In *Explorations in Cultural Anthropology*. Ward H. Goodenough, ed. pp. 25-55. New York: McGraw-Hill.

de Laguna, Frederica

   1940   Lévy-Bruhl's Contributions to the Study of Primitive Mentality. *The Philosophical Review* 49:552-66.

de Mille, Richard

   1976   *Castaneda's Journey: The Power and the Allegory*. Santa Barbara: Capra Press.

   1979   Explicating Anomalistic Anthropology with Help from Castaneda. *Zetetic Scholar* 1:69-70.

   1980   *The Don Juan Papers*. Santa Barbara: Ross-Erikson Publishers.

de Saussure, Ferdinand

   1916   *Cours de linguistique général*. Paris: Payot. [= *Course in General Linguistics*, 1966]

de Vries, Jan

   1977 [1961]   *Perspectives in the History of Religion* (trans. Kees W. Bolle). Berkeley: University of California Press.

Dorson, Richard M.

   1958   The Eclipse of Solar Mythology. In *Myth: A Symposium*. Thomas A. Sebeok, ed. pp. 25-63. Bloomington: Indiana University Press.

Dougherty, Janet W. D., and James W. Fernandez

   1981   Introduction [to a special issue on Symbolism and Cognition]. *American Ethnologist* 8:413-21.

Douglas, Mary

   1966   *Purity and Danger: An Analysis of Concepts of Pollution and Taboo*. New York: Praeger.

   1971   *Natural Symbols: Explorations in Cosmology*. New York: Pantheon Books.

Dumézil, Georges

   1941   *Jupiter, Mars, Quirinus: essai sur la conception indo-européenne de la société et sur les origines de Rome*. Paris: Gallimard.

   1958   *L'idéologie tripartie des Indo-Européens*. Brussels: Collection Latomus.

   1966   *La religion romaine archaïque*. Paris: Gallimard. [= *Archaic Roman Religion*, 1970]

1977   *Les dieux souvrains des Indo-Européens.* Paris: Gallimard.

Durkheim, Émile
1893   *De la division du travail social: étude sur l'organisation des sociétés supérieurs.* Paris: Felix Alcan. [= *The Division of Labor in Society*, 1933]
1896   *Les reglès de la méthode sociologique.* Paris: Felix Alcan. [= *The Rules of the Sociological Method*, 1938]
1912   *Les formes élémentaires de la vie religieuse: le système totémique en Australie.* Paris: Felix Alcan. [= *The Elementary Forms of the Religious Life*, 1915]

Durkheim, Émile, and Marcel Mauss
1903   De quelques formes primitives de classification: contributions à l'étude des représentations collectives. L'année sociologique 6:1-72. [= *Primitive Systems of Classification*, 1968]

Edwards, Walter
1982   Something Borrowed: Wedding Cakes as Symbols in Modern Japan. *American Ethnologist* 9:699-711.

Eliade, Mircea
1969   *The Quest: History and Meaning in Religion.* Chicago: University of Chicago Press.

Ellwood, Robert S.
1979   *Alternative Altars: Unconventional and Eastern Spirituality in America.* Chicago: University of Chicago Press.

Evans-Pritchard, E. E.
1934   Lévy-Bruhl's Theory of Primitive Mentality. *Bulletin of the Faculty of Arts* [Egyptian University, Cairo], Vol. 2.
1965   *Theories of Primitive Religion.* Oxford: Oxford University Press.
1981   *A History of Anthropological Thought* (André Singer, ed.). New York: Basic Books.

Feldman, Burton, and Robert D. Richardson
1972   *The Rise of Modern Mythology.* Bloomington: Indiana University Press.

Fernandez, James W.
1974   The Mission of Metaphor in Expressive Culture. *Current Anthropology* 15:119-45.
1977   The Performance of Ritual Metaphors. In *The Social Use of Metaphor: Essays on the Anthropology of Rhetoric.*

J. David Sapir and J. Christopher Crocker, eds. pp. 100-131. Philadelphia: University of Pennsylvania Press.

1982   *Bwiti: An Ethography of the Religious Imagination in Africa.* Princeton: Princeton University Press.

Frake, Charles O.

1962   The Ethnographic Study of Cognitive Systems. In *Anthropology and Human Behavior.* Thomas Gladwin and William Sturtevant, eds. pp. 72-85. Washington, D.C.: The Anthropological Society of Washington.

1964a   Notes on Queries in Anthropology. *American Anthropologist* 66:132-45.

1964b   A Structural Description of Subanum "Religious Behavior." In *Explorations in Cultural Anthropology.* Ward H. Goodenough, ed. New York: McGraw-Hill.

1977   Plying Frames Can Be Dangerous: Some Reflections on Methodology in Cognitive Anthropology. *Quarterly Newsletter of the Institute for Human Development* 1:1-7.

Frazer, Sir James G.

1919   *Totemism and Exogamy* (4 vols.). London: Macmillan and Co.

Geertz, Clifford

1973   *The Interpretation of Cultures: Selected Essays.* New York: Basic Books.

1983   Thick Description: Toward an Interpretive Theory of Culture. In *Contemporary Field Research.* Robert M. Emerson, ed. Pp. 37-59. Boston: Little, Brown.

1984   Distinguished Lecture: Anti Anti-Relativism. *American Anthropologist* 86:263-78.

Goldenweiser, Alexander

1933   *History, Psychology and Culture.* New York: Alfred A. Knopf.

Goodenough, Ward H.

1957   Cultural Anthropology and Linguistics. In *Report of the Seventh Annual Roundtable Meeting on Linguistics and Language Study.* Paul Garvin, ed. Pp. 167-73. Washington, D.C.: Georgetown University.

Gumperz, John J.

1964   Linguistic and Social Interaction in Two Communities. *American Anthropologist* 66:137-53.

Harris, Marvin
1968   *The Rise of Anthropological Theory*. New York: Thomas
Y. Crowell Co.
Hays, H. R.
1958   *From Ape to Angel: An Informal History of Anthropology*.
New York: Capricorn Books.
Hoijer, Harry
1964   Cultural Implications of Some Navaho Linguistic Cat-
egories. In *Language in Culture and Society*. Dell Hymes,
ed. pp. 142-60. New York: Harper and Row.
Honigmann, John J.
1976   *The Development of Anthropological Ideas*. Homewood,
Ill.: The Dorsey Press.
Horton, Robin
1973   Lévy-Bruhl, Durkheim and the Scientific Revolution.
In *Modes of Thought: Essays on Thinking in Western and Non-
Western Thought*. Robin Horton and Ruth Finnegan, eds.
Pp. 249-305. London: Faber.
Husserl, Edmund
1900-01   *Logische Untersuchungen*. Tübingen: M. Niemeyer.
[=*Logical Investigations*, 1970]
1913   *Ideen zu einen reinen Phänomenologie und phänomenolo-
gischen philosophie*. Haale: M. Niemeyer. [=*Ideas: A General Introduction to Pure Phenomenology*, 1931]
1931   *Meditations cartesiennes*. Paris: Armand Collin.
1950   Cartesianische Meditationen: Einleitung in die tran-
szendentale Phänomenologie. In *Husserliana*. S Strasser, ed.
The Hague: Martin Nijhoff. [=*Cartesian Meditations: Introduction to Phenomenology*, 1973]
Jensen, Adolf E.
1963 [1951]   *Myth and Cult among Primitive Peoples*. (trans.
by Marianna Tax Choldin and Wolfgang Weissleder) Chicago: University of Chicago Press.
Kay, Paul
1970   Some Theoretical Implications of Ethnographic Se-
mantics. *Current Directions in Anthropology* 3 (Part 2):19-
31.
Keesing, Roger M.
1972   Paradigms Lost: The New Ethnography and the New

Linguistics. *Southwestern Journal of Anthropology* 28:299-332.

1983   Theories of Culture. In *Language, Culture, and Cognition.* Ronald W. Casson, ed. Pp. 42-66. New York: Macmillan and Co.

Leach, Edmund

1970   *Claude Lévi-Strauss.* New York: The Viking Press.

Leenhardt, Maurice

1949   Preface to *Les Carnets de Lévy-Bruhl.* Paris: Presses Universitaires de France.

Lévi-Strauss, Claude

1953   Social Structure. In *Anthropology Today.* A. L. Kroeber, ed. Pp. 524-53. Chicago: University of Chicago Press.

1958   *Anthropologie structurale.* Paris: Plon. [=*Structural Anthropology*, 1963]

1962   *Le pensée sauvage.* Paris: Plon. [=*The Savage Mind*, 1966]

1964   *Le cru et le cuit.* Paris: Plon. [=*The Raw and the Cooked*, 1969]

1966a   *Du miel aux cendres.* Paris: Plon. [=*From Honey to Ashes*, 1973]

1966b   *The Savage Mind.* Chicago: University of Chicago Press. [=*La pensée sauvage*, 1962]

1967   The Story of Asdiwal. In *The Structural Study of Myth and Totemism.* E. R. Leach, ed. Pp. 1-48. London: Tavistock.

Lévy-Bruhl, Lucien

1903   *La morale et la science des moeurs.* Paris: Alcan. [=*Ethics and Moral Science*, 1905]

1910   *Les fonctions mentales dans les sociétés inférieures.* Paris: Alcan. [=*How Natives Think*, 1926]

1922   *La mentalité primitive.* Paris: Alcan. [=*Primitive Mentality*, 1923]

1927   *L'âme primitive.* Paris: Alcan. [=*The Soul of the Primitive*, 1928]

1930a   *Les carnets de Schwartzkoppen* (Preface by Lucien Lévy-Bruhl). Paris: Presses Universitaires de France.

1930b   *Le surnaturel et la nature dans la mentalité primitive.* Paris: Alcan. [=*Primitives and the Supernatural*, 1935]

1935　*La mythologie primitive.* Paris: Alcan.

1938　*L'expérience mystique et les symboles chez les primitifs.* Paris: Alcan.

1949　*Les carnets de Lévy-Bruhl.* Paris: Presses Universitaires de France.

Littleton, C. Scott

1970　Some Possible Indo-European Themes in the *Iliad.* In *Myth and Law among the Indo-Europeans.* Jaan Puhvel, ed. Pp. 229-46. Berkelely: University of California Press.

1974　"Je ne suis pas . . . structuraliste": Some Fundamental Differences between Dumézil and Lévi-Strauss. *Journal of Asian Studies* 34:151-58.

1976　An Emic Account of Sorcery: Carlos Castaneda and the Rise of a New Anthropology. *Journal of Latin American Lore* 2: 145-55.

1982　*The New Comparative Mythology: An Anthropological Assessment of the Theories of Georges Dumézil* (3rd ed.). Berkeley: University of California Press.

Lowie, Robert H.

1937　*The History of Ethnological Theory.* New York: Rinehart and Co.

Malefijt, Annmarie de Waal

1974　*Images of Man: A History of Anthropological Thought.* New York: Alfred A. Knopf.

Malinowski, Bronislaw K.

1948 [1925]　*Magic, Science and Religion and Other Essays.* New York: The Free Press.

Mauss, Marcel

1939　Lévy-Bruhl sociologue. *Revue philosophique* 127:251-3.

Müller, Friedrich Max

1897　Preface. *The Sacred Books of the East*, vol. 1. Pp. ix-xxxviii. New York: The Christian Literature Company.

Needham, Joseph

1925　*Science, Religion and Reality.* New York: Macmillan and Co.

Needham, Rodney

1972　*Belief, Language, and Experience.* Oxford: Basil Blackwell.

O'Keefe, Daniel Lawrence
    1982   *Stolen Lightning: The Social Theory of Magic*. New York: Random House.

Ortner, Sherry B.
    1973   On Key Symbols. *American Anthropologist* 75:1338-46.

Pike, Kenneth L.
    1954   *Language in Relation to a Unified Theory of the Structure of Human Behavior*. Glendale, Calif.: Summer Institute of Linguistics.

Puhvel, Jaan
    1970   Mythological Reflections of Indo-European Medicine. In *Indo-European and Indo-Europeans*. George Cardona, Henry M. Hoenigswald, and Alfred Senn, eds. Pp. 369-82. Philadelphia: University of Pennsylvania Press.

Radcliffe-Brown, A. R.
    1965 [1929]   The Sociological Theory of Totemism. In *Structure and Function in Primitive Society*. pp. 117-32. New York: The Free Press.

Radin, Paul
    1927   *Primitive Man as Philosopher*. New York: D. Appleton.
    1937   *Primitive Religion: Its Nature and Origin*. New York: The Viking Press.

Romney, A. Kimball, and Roy D'Andrade
    1964   Cognitive Aspects of English Kin Terms. *American Anthropologist* 66:146-70.

Sahlins, Marshall D., and Elman R. Service
    1960   *Evolution and Culture*. Ann Arbor: University of Michigan Press.

Schneider, David
    1968   *American Kinship: A Cultural Account*. Englewood Cliffs, NJ: Prentice-Hall.

Seligmann, Kurt
    1968 [1948]   *Magic, Supernaturalism, and Religion*. New York: Grosset and Dunlap.

Spencer, Sir Baldwin, and Francis James Gillen
    1899   *The Native Tribes of Central Australia*. London: Macmillan and Co.

Spradley, James P.

1970   *You Owe Yourself a Drunk: An Ethnography of Urban Nomads*. Boston: Little, Brown.

1972   Foundations of Cultural Knowledge. In *Culture and Cognition: Rules, Maps, Plans*. James P. Spradley, ed. Pp. 3-40. San Francisco: Chandler.

1979   *The Ethnographic Interview*. New York: Holt, Rinehart, and Winston.

Stanner, W. E. H.

1965 [1956]   The Dreaming. In *Reader in Comparative Religion* (2nd ed.). William A. Lessa and Evon Z. Vogt, eds. pp. 158-67. New York: Harper and Row.

Strensky, Ivan

n.d.   Marcel Mauss's Plan for the Structural Study of Myth. Unpublished ms.

Steward, Julian H.

1955   *Theory of Culture Change*. Urbana: University of Illinois Press.

Strutynski, Udo

1975   Germanic Divinities in Weekday Names. *The Journal of Indo-European Studies* 3:363-84.

1977   Claude Lévi-Strauss and the Study of Religion: A Reaction to *The Savage Mind*. *Epoche* 1:40-46.

Sturtevant, William C.

1964   Studies in Ethnoscience. *American Anthropologist* 66:99-131.

Turner, Victor

1964   Betwixt and Between: The Liminal Period in *Rites de Passage*. In *The Proceedings of the American Ethnological Society*. Pp. 4-20. Seattle: University of Washington Press.

1967   *The Forest of Symbols*. Ithaca, NY: Cornell University Press.

1975   Symbolic Studies. *Annual Review of Anthropology* 4:145-61.

Tylor, Sir Edward Burnett

1871   *Primitive Culture: Researches into the Development of Mythology, Philosophy, Religion, Language, Art and Custom* (2 vols.). London: John Murray.

Van der Leeuw, G.

1928   *La structure de la mentalite primitive*. Strasbourg: Imp. Alsacienne.

Wallace, Anthony F. C.
   1962   Culture and Cognition. *Science* 135:257-351.
Wallwork, Ernest
   1984   Religion and Social Structure in *The Division of Labor*.
   American Anthropologist 86:43-64.
Whorf, Benjamin Lee
   1956   *Language, Thought, and Reality* (John Carroll, ed.).
   Cambridge, Mass: The M.I.T. Press.
Wikander, Stig
   1947   Pāṇḍava-sagan och Mahābhāratas mytiska förutssätt-
   ningar. *Religion och Bibel* 6:27-39.
Wilk, Stan
   1977   Castaneda: Coming of Age in Sonora. *American Anthropologist* 79:84-91.
Wilson, Colin
   1973   *The Occult: A History*. New York: Vintage Books.

HOW NATIVES THINK

BOOKS BY LUCIEN LÉVY-BRUHL

La morale et la science des moeurs (1903)

Les fonctions mentales dan les sociétés inférieures (1910)

La mentalité primitive (1922)

L'âme primitive (1927)

Les surnaturel et la nature dans la mentalité primitive (1930)

La mythologie primitive (1935)

L'expérience mystique et les symboles chez les primitifs (1938)

Les carnets de Lévy-Bruhl (1949)

PREFACE

LA MENTALITÉ PRIMITIVE, which appeared in English in 1923, and *Les Fonctions Mentales dans les Sociétés Inférieures*, published in the same language to-day, really make one and the same work in two volumes. It was due to the accident of circumstances alone that the second was translated into English before the first. The volumes can certainly be read separately, but, as the critics have remarked, the essential theories I maintain and the principles upon which I rely are all contained in the earlier one, now available to the English reader, and undoubtedly the two volumes will be best understood if read in the order in which they were written.

The fact that at this date, after having been submitted to the tests of time and experience, the theories maintained in *Les Fonctions Mentales* still seem to me to hold good, would possibly not be sufficient guarantee of their truth—nor even the fact that my present researches in the same subject appear to confirm them. One is always fearful of being the dupe of flattering illusions concerning the cause he is pleading. Happily in this case I can appeal to other witnesses, less likely to be partial. Among those whose official functions, or vocations, bring them into constant relations with primitives, among the administrators and missionaries who share their everyday life, there are many who, hitherto strangers to me, have been good enough to write and tell me that these volumes have been of service to them. They say that the reading of *Les Fonctions Mentales* and *La Mentalité Primitive* helps them to comprehend much that had appeared both unintelligible and ridiculous in the way natives reason, and also in their customs, and that their relations with them are accordingly facilitated and improved.

In this I find the most valuable reward and the best encouragement that I can possibly receive, and this, too, emboldens me to present to-day to the English-reading public the translation of *Les Fonctions Mentales,* in the hope that it may be as well received as *Primitive Mentality* has been.

I also desire to express my thanks to Mrs. Clare for her excellent translation and for the care with which she has compiled the index.

L. LÉVY-BRUHL.

PARIS,
October 1925.

CONTENTS

  I. A brief definition of collective representations. The object of
this book. Its bearing upon the work of sociologists and upon
present-day psychology.

  II. Earlier theories. Comte and his teaching with regard to the
higher mental functions. The mind of the primitive, from the
point of view of ethnography, anthropology, and that of the
English school in particular.

 III. A postulate granted by all : the human mind is at all times and
everywhere true to type. The " animism " of Tylor and Frazer
and their school implies acceptance of this postulate.

 IV. A critical examination of the methods of this school. Examples
drawn from Frazer's work. 1. It leads to probabilities merely.
2. It disregards the social nature of the phenomena to be explained. The influence of this school upon associationistic psychology, and Herbert Spencer's philosophy of evolution.

  V. Types of mentality differ among themselves as do social types.
The paucity of documentary evidence, either contemporaneous
or earlier, in determining these differences. To what extent,
and by what methods, can this deficiency be made good ?

PART I

CHAPTER I

  I. Emotional and motor elements inherent in the collective
representations of primitives. Mystic properties attributed to
animals, plants, part of the human body, inanimate objects, the
soil, the shape of manufactured articles. The persistence of this
form and the danger of making any change in it whatever.
Primitives do not perceive things as we do. Our traditional
problems have to be reversed.

CONTENTS 9

PART II

CHAPTER IV

CHAPTER V

PART III

CHAPTER VI

CHAPTER VII

CONTENTS

CHAPTER VIII

PART IV

CHAPTER IX

INTRODUCTION

I

THE representations which are termed collective, defined as a whole without entering into detail, may be recognized by the following signs. They are common to the members of a given social group; they are transmitted from one generation to another; they impress themselves upon its individual members, and awaken in them sentiments of respect, fear, adoration, and so on, according to the circumstances of the case. Their existence does not depend upon the individual; not that they imply a collective unity distinct from the individuals composing the social group, but because they present themselves in aspects which cannot be accounted for by considering individuals merely as such. Thus it is that a language, although, properly speaking, it exists only in the minds of the individuals who speak it, is none the less an incontestable social reality, founded upon an ensemble of collective representations, for it imposes its claims on each one of these individuals; it is in existence before his day, and it survives him.

This fact leads at once to a very important result, one on which sociologists have rightly insisted, but which had escaped the notice of anthropologists. To be able to understand the processes by which institutions have been established (especially among undeveloped peoples), we must first rid our minds of the prejudice which consists in believing that collective representations in general, and those of inferior races in particular, obey the laws of a psychology based upon the analysis of the individual subject. Collective representations have their own laws, and these (at any rate in dealing with primitives [1]) cannot be discovered by studying the " adult,

[1] By this term, an incorrect one, yet rendered almost indispensable through common usage, we simply mean members of the most elementary social aggregates with which we are acquainted.

civilized, white man." On the contrary, it is undoubtedly the study of the collective representations and their connections in uncivilized peoples that can throw some light upon the genesis of our categories and our logical principles. Durkheim and his collaborators have already given examples of what may be obtained by following this course, and it will doubtless lead to a theory of knowledge, both new and positive, founded upon the comparative method.

This great task cannot be accomplished save by a series of successive attempts. Perhaps their inception will be rendered easier if we determine which are the most general laws governing collective representations in undeveloped peoples. To find out exactly what are the guiding principles of primitive mentality, and how these make themselves felt in the primitive institutions and customs, is the preliminary problem with which we have to deal in this volume. Without the labours of those who have preceded me—the anthropologists and ethnologists of various countries—and more particularly without the information afforded me by the French sociological school I have just mentioned, I could never have hoped to solve this problem, or even to present it in practical terms. The analysis by that school of numerous collective representations, and of the most important among them, such as the group ideas of what is sacred, of "mana," totem, magic and religious symbols, etc., has alone rendered possible this attempt to co-ordinate and systematize these representations among primitives. Basing my conclusions on those labours, I have been able to show that the mental processes of "primitives" do not coincide with those which we are accustomed to describe in men of our own type; I believe I have even been able to discover wherein the difference between them lies, and to establish the most general laws peculiar to the mentality of primitives.

I have received practical help, too, from the fairly large number of psychologists who, following Ribot, aim at showing the importance of the emotional and the motor elements of mental life in general and extending to the intellectual life, properly so called. To quote but two works, both Ribot's *Logique des Sentiments* and Heinrich Maier's *Psychologie des emotionalen Denkens* show how narrow were the limits within which traditional psychology, under the influence of formal logic, sought to confine the life of thought. Mental processes are infinitely more elastic, complex, and subtle, and they comprise more elements of the psychic life than a too " simplist " intellectualism would allow. Ribot's observations on psychology, therefore, have been very valuable to me. Nevertheless, the research I have undertaken differs widely from his. His analysis bears mainly upon subjects which are interesting from the emotional, passionate, or even pathological standpoint of our social aggregates, and hardly gives a glance at the collective phenomena to be found among other peoples. I, on the other hand, propose to determine which are the most general laws governing collective representations (including their affective and motor elements) in the most undeveloped peoples known to us.

II

That the higher mental functions should be studied by the comparative, that is, the sociological, method, is no new idea. Auguste Comte had already distinctly advocated it in his *Cours de Philosophie positive.* He would divide the study of these functions between biology and sociology. His well-known dictum : " Humanity is not to be defined through man, but on the contrary, man through humanity " is designed to show that the highest mental functions remain unintelligible as long as they are studied from the individual alone. If . we are to understand them we must take the development of the race into consideration. In a man's mental life everything which is not merely the reaction of the organism to the stimuli it receives is necessarily of a social character.

The idea was a fertile one, but it did not bear fruit immediately, either in Comte or in his more or less direct followers. In Comte it found the way barred, so to speak, by a sociology that he believed he had constructed in its entirety, but which actually was a philosophy of history. He thought he had shown that the law of the three stages exactly expresses the intellectual evolution of humanity considered as a whole, and also that of any particular community. In establishing the science of the higher mental functions, therefore, he does not consider it necessary to begin with a comparative study of these functions in different types of human societies. In the same way, when constructing his " cerebral chart," he is not guided by physiology, so sure is he that the work of the physiologists will confirm *a priori* his classification and location of the faculties. So too, when formulating the essential features of his theory of the higher mental functions, the law of the three stages suffices him, since the more special laws cannot fail to come into line with that one. Similarly, he constructed his theory according to the development of Mediterranean civilization, but without suspecting *a priori* that the laws thus discovered may not hold good of all the races of humanity. In one sense, then, Comte is the initiator of a positive science of the mental functions, and to a large extent the merit of having conceived it and of having shown it to be a sociological science ought to be accorded him. But he did not undertake the investigation of phenomena which such a science demands. He did not even attempt it, and at the time he wrote his *Politique positive*, he would doubtless have condemned it as " useless."

Nevertheless, the patient and meticulous study of mental phenomena in differing types of human societies, the necessity of which Comte had not perceived, had been begun by others, and they pursued it perseveringly, not as philosophers but as experts, with the straightforward aim of discerning and classifying facts. I mean the anthropologists and ethnologists and the English school of anthropology in particular. *Primitive Culture*, the important work of its head, E. B. Tylor, which appeared in 1871, and marks an epoch in the history of anthropological science, led the way for a large number of zealous and well-trained collaborators, whose work is not unworthy of their leader. Thanks to their zeal, an immense mass of documents dealing with the institutions, customs, and languages of so-called savage or primitive races, and with the group ideas governing these, has been accumulated. Work of a similar kind has been carried on in Germany and in France. In the United States, the Ethnological Bureau of the Smithsonian Institute published some excellent monographs on the Indian tribes of North America.

Now as the documents increased in number, a certain uniformity in the phenomena of which they treated became continually more evident. As fast as undeveloped peoples were discovered, or more thoroughly studied, in the most distant quarters of the globe, sometimes at the very antipodes of each other, extraordinary likenesses, sometimes even exact resemblances, down to the smallest details, were found to exist. There were the same institutions ; the same religious or magical ceremonies ; the same beliefs and customs relating to birth and death ; the same myths, and so on. Thus the comparative method established itself, as it were. Tylor makes continual and very felicitous use of it in his *Primitive Culture*; so, too, does Frazer in *The Golden Bough,* and so also do other representatives of the school, such as Sydney Hartland and Andrew Lang.

By so doing, these writers have been the necessary precursors of the positive science of the higher mental functions, but they did not originate it, any more than Comte, though the reasons in their case were not the same. Why did not the use of the comparative method lead them to it ? Was it for want of having regarded the problem as universal, and, having once compared primitive races with each other, comparing them with our own ? Not at all. The English school of anthropology, on the contrary, following the example of its head, is perpetually trying to show the relation between " savage " and " civilized " mentality, and to *explain* it. And it is just this *explanation* which has prevented their going any further. They had it ready-made. They did not look for it in the facts themselves, but imposed it on them. While testifying to the existence of primitive institutions and beliefs so entirely different from our own, they did not ask themselves whether, to account for them, they ought not to examine various hypotheses. They took it for granted that the facts could be explained *in one way only*. Do the collective representations of the communities in question arise out of higher mental functions identical with our own, or must they be referred to a mentality which differs from ours to an extent yet to be determined ? Such an alternative as the latter did not occur to their minds.

2

III

Without entering upon a critical discussion of the method employed and the results obtained by these experts [1]—a discussion to which I could not devote the space it demands— I should merely like to demonstrate in a few words the consequences to their theory of this belief in the identity of a " human mind " which, from the logical point of view, is always exactly the same at all times and in all places. Such an identity is admitted by the school as a postulate, or rather, an axiom. There is no need to demonstrate it, or even formally enunciate it : it is an understood principle, and too evident for any consideration of it to be necessary. Accordingly, the collective representations of primitives, so often foreign to our ideas, and the connections we find between them, which are no less strange, do not raise problems the solutions of which may either amplify or modify our conception of the " human mind." We know already that this mind of theirs is not different from our own. All we have to find out is the way in which mental functions exactly like ours have been able to produce these representations and their connections, and here comes in the general hypothesis which the English school of anthropology favours : it is animism.

Frazer's *Golden Bough*, for instance, clearly shows how animism accounts for many of the beliefs and practices found almost everywhere in primitive social aggregates, numerous traces of which survive in our own. We shall notice that the hypothesis comprehends two successive stages. In the first place, the primitive, surprised and moved by apparitions which present themselves in his dreams—where he sees once more the dead and the absent, talks and fights with them, touches them and hears them speak—believes in the objective reality of these representations. To him, therefore, his own existence is a double one, like that of the dead and absent who appear to him. He admits his actual existence as a living and conscious personality, and at the same time as a soul able to separate itself from him, to become external to him and

---

[1] On this point see Durkheim's articles in the *Revue Philosophique* of January and February 1909, entitled " Examen critique des systèmes classiques sur l'origine de la pensée religieuse."

manifest itself in a " phantom " state. This belief would be universal among primitives, because all would be subject to the psychological self-delusion in which it originated. In the second place, when they want to account for the natural phenomena which make an impression on their senses, and assign a cause to them, they immediately apply and generalize the explanation they have accepted of their dreams and hallucinations. In all forms of being, and behind all natural phenomena, they imagine " souls," " spirits," " intentions," similar to those they believe they have experienced in themselves and their companions, and in animals. It is a simple and artless logical process, but not less spontaneous nor less inevitable to the " primitive " mind, than the psychological illusion which preceded it and upon which it is based.

Thus without any attempt at reflection, by the mere influence of mental processes which are the same to all, the primitive develops a " philosophy " of his own, childish and clumsy, no doubt, but yet perfectly consistent with itself. It propounds no problem that it cannot immediately solve to its complete satisfaction. If it were anyhow possible for all the experience acquired and transmitted through the centuries to be suddenly obliterated—if we were brought face to face with nature like the real " primitives," we should be certain to construct for ourselves a " natural philosophy," which would also be primitive, and that philosophy would be a universal animism, quite correct from the logical point of view, considering the paucity of positive data we should have at command.

The hypothesis of animism in this sense, then, is a direct consequence of the axiom which dominates the researches of the English school of anthropology, and, according to our view, it is this that has prevented it from attaining to a positive science of the higher mental functions, to which the comparative method would seem to be leading. For while the resemblance in institutions, beliefs and practices in undeveloped peoples of the most varied kind is explained by such a hypothesis, it takes no trouble to demonstrate that their superior mental functions are identical with our own. The axiom serves them as demonstration. The fact that myths and collective representations like those on which totemism is based, such as the belief in spirits, in separate and external souls, and in sympathetic magic, are to be found in all human aggregates, is a necessary result of the structure of the " human mind." The laws governing the association of ideas, and the natural and irresistible application of the law of causality, combined with animism, would be certain to engender these collective representations and their connections. It is only the spontaneous working of an unvarying logical and psychological process. Nothing is easier to explain if we once admit, as the English anthropological school implicitly does, that this process is the same in undeveloped peoples as it is with us.

Must we admit this ? That is what I have to find out. But even at this point it is clear that if there be any doubt about this axiom, animism, based upon it, would also be matter of doubt and could in no case serve as a proof. We should find it impossible, unless we argued in a vicious circle, to account for the spontaneity of animism in primitives by a specific mental construction, and affirm the existence of the latter in them by relying upon this same spontaneity of animism for support. An axiom and its deduction cannot be proved by each other.

IV

It now remains to be seen whether the animist theory is borne out by the facts, and whether it is sufficient to account for the institutions and beliefs of primitive peoples. This is the point upon which Tylor, Frazer, Andrew Lang and many other representatives of this school have expended both knowledge and skill. The tremendous amount of documentary evidence they bring forward in support of their position is almost incredible to those who have not read it. In dealing with this vast collection, however, two things must be borne in mind. The first is that we may consider the presence of the same institutions, beliefs, practices in a great number of widely separated but typically analogous peoples, as established. From this we may legitimately conclude that the mental processes which produce these similar ideas are the same, for it is clear that resemblances of such a kind, which occur so frequently and are so exact, cannot be merely fortuitous. But the accumulated facts which are conclusive upon this point

are not equally valid when it is a case of proving that these
ideas have a common origin in the belief in animism, in a
spontaneous " natural philosophy " which would be the
earliest reaction of the human mind to the appeal of experience.

Undoubtedly the explanation of each belief or practice thus
obtained is usually plausible, and we can always imagine the
working of the mental process which led to it in the primitive :
but it is only plausible.   And is it not the first rule of any
prudent method never to take for granted that which is merely
probable ?   Savants have learnt in so many cases that the
apparently true is rarely the truth.   There is a like reserve, in
this respect, among philologists and natural philosophers.
Must not the sociologist be equally cautious ?   The very
language of the anthropologists and the form adopted by their
demonstrations show that they do not go beyond probability,
and the number of the facts brought forward adds nothing to
the conclusive force of the argument.

Uncivilized races have an almost universal custom of
destroying a dead man's weapons, his clothes, the things he
used, even his house, and occasionally they sacrifice his wives
and his slaves.   How are we to account for this ?   " The
custom," says Frazer, " *may* [1] have sprung from the idea that
the dead were angry with the living for dispossessing them. . . .
The idea that the souls of the things thus destroyed are dispatched to the spirit-land . . . is less simple and therefore
probably [1] later." [2]

Undoubtedly this custom *may* have arisen thus ; but it
may also be of different origin.   Frazer's theory does not
preclude any other, and his wording even acknowledges this.
As to the general principle upon which he relies, and which he
expressly formulates a little further on :   " In the evolution of
thought, as of matter, thè simplest is the earliest," it undoubtedly proceeds from Herbert Spencer's philosophy, but
that does not make it any the more certain.   I do not think
it can be proved in the material world, and in what we know
of the world of " thought," the facts would seem to contradict
it.   Frazer seems to be confusing " simple " and " undiffer-

---

[1] The italics are mine (L. L.-B.).
[2] " Certain Burial Customs as Illustrative of the Primitive Theory of the
Soul," *Journal of the Anthropological Institute* (henceforth *J.A.I.*), xv. p. 75
(note 1), (1885).

entiated" here. Yet we find that the languages spoken by peoples who are the least developed of any we know—Australian aborigines, Abipones, Andaman Islanders, Fuegians, etc.—exhibit a good deal of complexity. They are far less "simple" than English, though much more "primitive."

Here is another instance, taken from the same article by Frazer. It is a common practice in varying regions, and persistent from all time, to place in the mouth of a dead man either some grains of corn or a gold coin. Frazer quotes from a considerable number of documents in proof of this. Then he explains it thus. " The original custom may have been that of placing food in the mouth, for which in after times valuables (money or otherwise) were substituted, that the dead might buy his own food." [1] The explanation is a probable one, but in one case in which we can check it, it is incorrect. A similar custom has existed in China from time immemorial, and De Groot, following old Chinese documents, gives us the true reason. Gold and jade are substances which endure indefinitely. They are symbols of the celestial sphere, "which is unchangeable, indestructible, beyond the influences of decay. . . . Hence jade and gold (pearls too) naturally endow with vitality all persons who swallow them ; in other words, they intensify their souls or *shen*, which are, like the heavens, composed of Yang matter ; and they hold at a distance from the dead corruption and decay, thus furthering their return to life." [2] We must even go further. "Taoist and medical authors assert that, whoever eats jade, gold or pearls does not only prolong his life, but ensures also the existence of his body after death, saving it from putrefaction. This doctrine, by its mere existence, intimates that *sien*, who acquired immortality by eating such or other substances, were conceived to continue using their body after their earthly career, or removed to the region of the immortals, also corporally. A new light is thus shed on the custom of ancients and moderns to keep away corruption from the dead by placing the three precious things in their mouths or other apertures : it was an attempt to make *sien* of them." [3] Elsewhere the dead are given money with which to make their purchases in the next world, but it is

[1] *J.A.I.*, xv. pp. 77–9 (note).
[2] J. J. M. de Groot, *The Religious System of China*, i. p. 271.
[3] Ibid., ii. pp. 331, 332.

not put into their mouths. Here we have a belief similar to that which induces the Chinese to choose for their coffins woods distinguished for their durability, such as pine and cypress " both of which are possessed of great vitality, so that the wood, when placed around the dead, might facilitate their return to life." [1] These are cases, similar to so many others we read of, of participation through contact.

These two examples will doubtless suffice, although we could cite many similar ones. The " explanations " of the English school of anthropology, being never anything more than probable, are always affected by a co-efficient of doubt, which varies according to the circumstances of the case. They take it for granted that the ways which, to our minds, seem to lead naturally to certain beliefs and practices, are precisely those trodden by the members of the communities in which they are to be found. Nothing can be more risky than such a postulate, and it would possibly not be confirmed five times out of a hundred.

In the second place, the phenomena to be accounted for—institutions, beliefs, practices—are all pre-eminently social phenomena. Should not the representations and the connections between the representations be of the same nature ? Are they not necessarily " collective representations " ? But in such a case the animist theory becomes suspect, and with it the postulate upon which it was based, for both theory and postulate deal with the mental processes of *the individual human mind* only. Collective representations are social phenomena, like the institutions for which they account ; and if there is any one point which contemporary sociology has thoroughly established, it is that social phenomena have their own laws, and laws which the analysis of the individual *qua* individual could never reveal. Consequently any attempt to " explain " collective representations solely by the functioning of mental operations observed in the individual (the association of ideas, the naïve application of the theory of causality, and so on), is foredoomed to failure. Since some of the data which are essential to the problem have been omitted, its defeat is certain. We might just as well hope to make scientific use of the idea of a human individual mind imagined to be devoid of

[1] J. J. M. de Groot, *The Religious System of China*, i. p. 294.

all experience whatever.   Would it be worth while to try and reconstruct the method in which such a mind would represent the natural phenomena which occurred within and around him ?   As a matter of fact, we have no means of knowing what such a mind would be like.   As far back as we can go, however primitive the races we may study, we shall never find any minds which are not socialized, if we may put it thus, not already concerned with an infinite number of collective representations which have been transmitted by tradition, the origin of which is lost in obscurity.

The idea of an individual human mind absolutely free from all experience is, then, as fanciful as that of man prior to social life.   It does not correspond with anything that we can grasp and verify, and the hypotheses implying it could but be arbitrary.   If on the other hand, we start with collective representations as our data, as a reality which will bear scientific examination, we shall certainly not have probable and seductive " explanations " to oppose to those of the English school.   It will all be much less simple.   We shall find ourselves faced by complex problems, and very frequently we shall not have sufficient data to solve them ;   very frequently, too, the solutions we shall propose will be hypothetical.   But at least we may hope that by a positive study of collective representations we may arrive by degrees at a knowledge of the laws which govern them and thus obtain a more correct interpretation of the mentality of primitive peoples, and even of our own.

One example, perhaps, will suffice to show how complete is the contradiction between the standpoint of the English school of anthropology and the one we hope to see adopted.   Tylor writes : " Conformably with the early child-like philosophy in which human life seems the practical key to the understanding of nature at large, the savage theory of the universe refers its phenomena in general to the wilful action of pervading personal spirits.   It was no spontaneous fancy, but the reasonable inference that effects are due to causes, which led the rude men of old days to people with such ethereal phantoms their own homes and haunts, and the vast earth and sky beyond.   Spirits are simply personified causes." [1]   There is nothing simpler or

[1] *Primitive Culture* (4th edit.), ii. pp. 108, 109.

more acceptable than this "explanation" of an immense number of beliefs, provided we admit, as Tylor does, that they are the result of a "reasonable inference." But it is very difficult to grant this. When we consider the collective representations which, in undeveloped peoples, imply a belief in spirits pervading the whole of nature, which inspires the practices relating to these spirits, it does not seem as if these practices are the result of a mental curiosity seeking for causes. Myths, funeral rites, agrarian practices and the exercise of magic do not appear to originate in the desire for a rational explanation : they are the primitives' response to collective needs and sentiments which are profound and mighty and of compulsive force.

I do not maintain that this desire for an explanation does not exist. Like so many other potentialities which will be realized later when the social group develops, this curiosity is latent, and it may possibly be already manifest to a slight extent in the mental functioning of such peoples. But it is assuredly contrary to the facts to see in it one of the main directing controls of that functioning, and the origin of the collective representations relating to most of the natural phenomena. If Tylor and his followers are satisfied with such an "explanation," it is because they assume these beliefs to exist in individual minds similar to their own. As soon, however, as we take into consideration the collective nature of these ideas, the inadequacy of this explanation is apparent. Being collective, they force themselves upon the individual ; that is, they are to him an article of faith, not the product of his reason. And since the collective representations, as a rule, predominate most where the races are least advanced, the mind of the "primitive" has hardly any room for such questions as "how ?" or "why ?" The ensemble of collective representations which master him and excite in him an intensity of feeling which we cannot even imagine, is hardly compatible with that disinterested contemplation of a matter which a purely intellectual desire to probe into its cause would demand.

Without entering upon a detailed discussion of the theory of animism here—for we shall find room for it later—we are allowed to think that Tylor's dictum that "spirits are personified causes" does not suffice to account for the place held by spirits in the collective representations of primitives. To us, however, interested first of all in analysing these representations without any preconceived ideas about the mental processes upon which they depend, it may possibly be the " spirits," on the contrary, which will help us to understand what certain " causes " are. Perhaps we shall find that the effect of the efficient cause—*vexata quæstio* to the philosophers —is a sort of abstract precipitate of the mystic power attributed to spirits. This is a theory which we intend to examine, and in any case we shall be suspicious of categorical and comprehensive pronouncements. The English school of anthropology, with its lofty theory of animism and its preconceived ideas, always has at least a probable explanation of the phenomena it has collected. If new phenomena manifest themselves, its theory is plastic and general enough to permit of its explaining these too ; it only requires the exercise of a little ingenuity. It sees in these a confirmation of its theory. But this confirmation has precisely the same validity as the probable " explanations " of which it is but a fresh example.

We are sure to be asked how a savant such as Tylor, whose perspicacity is so marvellous and whose criticism is so acute in dealing with special phenomena, should have shown himself less exacting when a general theory was at stake, and how it is that his followers could have imitated his example in this matter. Perhaps we must take into account here the influence of contemporary English philosophy, and the theory of evolution in particular. At the time *Primitive Culture* appeared, and for some years after, the philosophy of associationism seemed to have a definite sway. The evolutionism of Herbert Spencer, then greatly in repute, exercised considerable fascination over many minds. They saw in it the expression of the most comprehensive philosophical synthesis : an expression which could at the same time be adapted to any class of natural phenomena whatever, and thus serve as a guiding line in scientific research. It could be applied to the history of the solar system as easily as to the genesis of organic matter, or that of the intellectual life. They might therefore anticipate that it would be extended to social phenomena, and Spencer did not disappoint them in this. He too, as we know, took as his governing hypothesis in explaining the mentality of primitives, a theory of animism based upon an associationistic philosophy.

At the present day, Herbert Spencer's evolutionism is somewhat severely judged. His generalizations appear hasty, presumptuous, and not well founded. Thirty years ago, however, they were considered both substantial and potent. Tylor and his school believed they saw in them a guarantee for the continuity in man's mental development which they formulate. Such a doctrine allowed them to present this development as an uninterrupted evolution, the stages of which could be noted, from the animistic beliefs of " primitives " to the Newtonian conception of the universe. At the same time, a little throughout his *Primitive Culture*, and especially in its concluding parts, Tylor takes the trouble to refute a theory according to which " savage " races are in reality degenerate ones—their representation of nature, their institutions and beliefs being the almost obliterated but yet recognizable remains of original revelation. But to oppose to this theory of a theological order, can Tylor find anything better than the theory of evolution which is, according to him, of a scientific order ? The latter provides him with a rational interpretation of the facts. That which has been presented as the vestiges of a more perfect antecedent state, Tylor readily explains, from the evolutionist point of view, to be the rudimentary germ of a succeeding state which shall be more differentiated.

Finally, when we remember how much apparent clearness and intelligibility the general theory of animism gives to the mass of evidence, we shall not be surprised at the success it has shared with the theory of evolution, nor wonder that the large majority of the English school of anthropology should have remained faithful to it until now.

V

The series of social phenomena are solidary with respect to each other, and they are placed in mutual relationship. A definite type of society, with its own institutions and customs, will therefore necessarily have its own mentality. Different mentalities will correspond with different social types, and all the more because institutions and customs themselves are at bottom only a certain aspect of collective representations, only these representations considered objectively, as it were. Thus we are led to perceive that the comparative study of the different types of human societies is linked up with the comparative study of the collective representations and the connections between these, which dominate such societies.

Similar considerations must have prevailed with the naturalists when, while retaining the idea of the identity of the essential functions in all living beings, or at any rate, of all animal nature, they decided to admit types differing fundamentally from each other. There is no doubt that the processes of nutrition, respiration, secretion, reproduction, do not vary in essentials, whatever the organism which manifests them may be. But they may be manifested in an ensemble of conditions which are totally different from the histological or anatomical or physiological point of view. General biology made a great advance when it recognized that it could not (as Auguste Comte believed) find in the analysis of the human organism the means of attaining a clearer understanding of the organism of a sponge. From that time forward, the study of biology proper was not complicated by preconceived ideas of the subordination of one entity to another, notwithstanding the possibility of forms originally of a common type, prior to divergence.

In the same way, there are features which are common to all aggregates of human beings, by which they may be distinguished from the rest of the animal world. Language is spoken, traditions are transmitted, and institutions maintained. The higher mental operations, therefore, have everywhere a basis of homogeneity. This being once admitted, however, human aggregations, like organisms, may differ profoundly in their construction and as a consequence their higher mental operations will also present corresponding differences. We must then reject beforehand any idea of reducing mental operations to a single type, whatever the peoples we are considering, and accounting for all collective representations by a psychological and mental functioning which is always the same. If it be true that there are aggregates of human beings who differ from each other in construction as invertebrate animals differ from vertebrates, a comparative study of the various types of collective mentality is just as indispensable to anthropology as comparative anatomy and physiology are to biology.

Is there any need to say that this comparative study, conceived thus as universal, presents difficulties which at the moment are insurmountable ? In the present state of sociology we could not dream of undertaking it. The differentiation of types of mentality is as difficult as that of types of society, and for similar reasons. What I am attempting here, by way of introduction, is a preliminary study of the most general laws to which collective representations in inferior races are subjected, and more especially those of the most primitive peoples of which we know anything. I shall endeavour to construct, if not a type, at any rate an ensemble of characteristics which are common to a group of neighbouring types, and in this way to define the essential features of the mentality peculiar to undeveloped peoples.

In order to bring out these features as clearly as possible, I shall compare that mentality with our own, i.e. with that of races which are the product of " Mediterranean " civilization, in which a rationalistic philosophy and positive science have been developed. For the first rough attempt at comparative study there is an evident advantage in making choice of the two mental types available, between which the difference is *greatest*. The essential dissimilarities between such will be most marked, and as a consequence they will be least likely to escape attention. Moreover, in starting with these we shall be most easily able to approach the study of the intermediary or transitional types.

Even when confined to such limits, the attempt will no doubt appear only too bold, and very uncertain as to result. It remains incomplete ; it opens up many more questions than it can answer ; and leaves unsolved more than one vast problem which it touches in a superficial way. I am not forgetting all this, but, in examining a mentality which is so obscure, I have thought it better to confine myself to that which seemed to stand out most distinctly. Besides, as far as the mentality peculiar to our society is concerned, since it is only to serve me as a state for comparison, I shall regard it as sufficiently well defined in the works of philosophers, logicians and psychologists, both ancient and modern, without conjecturing what sociological analysis of the future may modify in the results obtained by them up to the present. The real object of my researches, therefore, is the study, by means of the collective representations of primitives, of the mental processes which regulate them.

But we do not know these representations and their connections except by the institutions, beliefs, myths, customs of undeveloped peoples, and how do we obtain these? It is nearly always from the accounts of travellers, sailors, missionaries—in short, from documents to be found in the ethnographical records of the two hemispheres. Every sociologist ought to realize the value of these documents. It is a problem of capital importance, to which the ordinary rules of criticism apply, and one which I cannot broach here. I must, however, draw attention to the fact that the anxious care to observe undeveloped peoples scientifically, by means of a system as objective, precise and detailed as that which experts employ in determining natural phenomena, and as similar as it can be to this, is but of recent growth. And now that it does exist, a kind of irony ordains that it has scarcely any object. The last century has witnessed irreparable losses to the comparative study of human aggregates. The peoples whose institutions would have been of the greatest interest to this scientific study are rapidly becoming extinct in the most widely separated districts. The undeveloped peoples still remaining are doomed to disappear speedily, and it behoves careful observers to make haste.

The enormous accumulation of the older records by no means makes up for what we are losing in this way. With rare exceptions, the facts collected in passing by travellers who only go through a country are of very little value. Major Powell remarks with good reason that these people can no more make known to us the institutions of a tribal community than they can give an exact description of the flora of a country, the fauna of a district, or the geological formation of a continent.[1]

[1] *Report of the Bureau of Ethnology of the Smithsonian Institute, Washington* (henceforth cited as *E. B. Rept.*), iii. p. 62

In most cases, too, those who first saw these peoples from within, even if they lived among them for some time, were too much engaged otherwise to be able to give accurate and detailed accounts, as complete as possible, of the institutions and customs which came to their notice. They observed what seemed to them most noteworthy and singular, the things that piqued their curiosity ; they described these more or less happily. But the observations thus collected were always merely side-issues to them, never the main reason for their sojourn among these peoples. Moreover, they did not hesitate to interpret phenomena at the time they described them : the very idea of hesitation would have seemed quite unnecessary. How could they suspect that most of their interpretations were simply misapprehensions, and that " primitives " and " savages " nearly always conceal with jealous care all that is most important and most sacred in their institutions and beliefs ?

Nevertheless, as Tylor has clearly shown, many of these old observations are illuminated and corrected by the light of the knowledge we possess to-day. Some of them, indeed, are very valuable ; for instance, those made by certain missionaries who resided for a long time in the community they describe, who seem to have assimilated its spirit somewhat, and in whose accounts we can easily separate observation properly so-called from the preconceived ideas which have mingled with it. Such, among others, are the Jesuit fathers who were the first to come in contact with the Indian tribes of North America,—Dobrizhoffer with the Abipones, in the eighteenth century,—and more recently, missionaries like Turner in Samoa, Codrington in Melanesia, etc. The earliest of this class of observers had the advantage of knowing nothing of sociological theories, and it often happens that their accounts are of all the more importance to us precisely *because* they do not understand what they are relating. As a set-off to this, however, they are often irritatingly incomplete, and silent upon the most essential points.

Compared with these sketches, the correctness of which is never certain, which their designers have sometimes retouched or refashioned according to the taste of the period, the observations made to-day by professional ethnographers appear like good, clear photographs. In fact, the collaborators of the Ethnological Bureau of the Smithsonian Institute of Washington use both photographic and phonographic apparatus as part of their necessary equipment. It is from investigators aware of the difficulties of their task, and expert in the methods which admit of their attacking it with the best chances of success, that we look for documents. But even in such cases we must not overlook such precautions as a considered criticism demands. Many among them are missionaries, Catholic or Protestant, and they, like their predecessors of past centuries, are convinced that savages derive some kind of natural religion from God, and owe to the agency of the devil their most reprehensible customs. Many of them, both cleric and lay, have read the works of Tylor and Frazer, and have become their adherents. Since they have the self-imposed task of procuring fresh evidence in support of their masters' theories, they observe with prejudiced eyes. This becomes a serious disadvantage when they set out provided with a detailed set of questions drawn up in the spirit of a particular school. Their eyes seem to be screened in a way which prevents them from perceiving any fact not provided for in their catechism, and in relating what they do see, their preconceived interpretation can no longer be distinguished from the facts themselves.

PART I

3

CHAPTER I

COLLECTIVE REPRESENTATIONS IN PRIMITIVES' PERCEPTIONS AND THE MYSTICAL CHARACTER OF SUCH

I

BEFORE undertaking an investigation of the most general laws governing collective representations among undeveloped peoples, it may be as well to determine what the essential characteristics of these representations are, and thus avoid an ambiguity which is otherwise almost inevitable. The terminology used in the analysis of mental functions is suited to functions such as the philosophers, psychologists, and logicians of our civilization have formulated and defined. If we admit these functions to be identical in all human aggregates, there is no difficulty in the matter ; the same terminology can be employed throughout, with the mental reservation that "savages" have minds more like those of children than of adults. But if we abandon this position—and we have the strongest reasons for considering it untenable—then the terms, divisions, classifications, we make use of in analysing our own mental functions are not suitable for those which differ from them ; on the contrary, they prove a source of confusion and error. In studying primitive mentality, which is a new subject, we shall probably require a fresh terminology. At any rate it will be necessary to specify the new meaning which some expressions already in use should assume when applied to an object differing from that they have hitherto betokened.

This is the case, for instance, with the term " collective representations."

In the current parlance of psychology which classifies phenomena as emotional, motor, or intellectual, " representation " is placed in the last category. We understand by it a matter of cognizance, inasmuch as the mind simply has the image or idea of an object. We do not deny that in the actual mental life every representation affects the inclinations more or less, and tends to produce or inhibit some movement. But, by an abstraction which in a great many cases is nothing out of the ordinary, we disregard these elements of the representation, retaining only its essential relation to the object which it makes known to us. The representation is, *par excellence*, an intellectual or cognitive phenomenon.

It is not in this way, however, that we must understand the collective representations of primitives. Their mental activity is too little differentiated for it to be possible to consider ideas or images of objects by themselves apart from the emotions and passions which evoke these ideas or are evoked by them. Just because our mental activity is more differentiated, and we are more accustomed to analysing its functions, it is difficult for us to realize by any effort of imagination, more complex states in which emotional or motor elements are *integral parts* of the representation. It seems to us that these are not really representations, and in fact if we are to retain the term we must modify its meaning in some way. By this state of mental activity in primitives we must understand something which is not a purely or almost purely intellectual or cognitive phenomenon, but a more complex one, in which what is really " representation " to us is found blended with other elements of an emotional or motor character, coloured and imbued by them, and therefore implying a different attitude with regard to the objects represented.

Moreover, these collective representations are very often acquired by the individual in circumstances likely to make the most profound impression upon his sensibility. This is particularly true of those transmitted at the moment when he becomes a man, a conscious member of the social group, the moment when the initiation ceremonies cause him to undergo new birth,[1] when the secrets upon which the very life of the group depends are revealed to him, sometimes amid tortures which subject his nerves to the most severe tests. It would be difficult to exaggerate the intense emotional force of such

[1] Vide Chap. VIII. pp. 352-3.

representations. The object is not merely discerned by the mind in the form of an idea or image ; according to the circumstances of the case, fear, hope, religious awe, the need and the ardent desire to be merged in one common essence, the passionate appeal to a protecting power—these are the soul of these representations, and make them at once cherished, formidable, and really *sacred* to the initiated. We must add, too, that the ceremonies in which these representations are translated into action, so to speak, take place periodically ; consider the contagious effect of the emotional excitement of witnessing the movements which express them, the nervous exaltation engendered by excessive fatigue, the dances, the phenomena of ecstasy and of possession,—in fact everything which tends to revive and enhance the emotional nature of these collective representations. At any time during the intervals between the occurrences of these ceremonies, whenever the object of one of these representations once more arises in the consciousness of the " primitive," even should he be alone and in a calm frame of mind at the moment, it can never appear to him as a colourless and indifferent image. A wave of emotion will immediately surge over him, undoubtedly less intense than it was during the ceremonies, but yet strong enough for its cognitive aspect to be almost lost sight of in the emotions which surround it. Though in a lesser degree, the same character pertains to other collective representations—such, for instance, as those transmitted from generation to generation by means of myths and legends, and those which govern manners and customs which apparently are quite unimportant ; for if these customs are respected and enforced, it is because the collective representations relating to them are imperative and something quite different from purely intellectual phenomena.

The collective representations of primitives, therefore, differ very profoundly from our ideas or concepts, nor are they their equivalent either. On the one hand, as we shall presently discover, they have not their logical character. On the other hand, not being genuine representations, in the strict sense of the term, they express, or rather imply, not only that the primitive actually has an image of the object in his mind, and thinks it real, but also that he has some hope or fear connected with it, that some definite influence emanates from it, or is exercised upon it. This influence is a virtue, an occult power which varies with objects and circumstances, but is always real to the primitive and forms an integral part of his representation. If I were to express in one word the general peculiarity of the collective representations which play so important a part in the mental activity of undeveloped peoples, I should say that this mental activity was a *mystic* one. In default of a better, I shall make use of this term— not referring thereby to the religious mysticism of our communities, which is something entirely different, but employing the word in the strictly defined sense in which "mystic" implies belief in forces and influences and actions which, though imperceptible to sense, are nevertheless real.

In other words, the reality surrounding the primitives is itself mystical. Not a single being or object or natural phenomenon in their collective representations is what it appears to be to our minds. Almost everything that we perceive therein either escapes their attention or is a matter of indifference to them. On the other hand, they see many things there of which we are unconscious. For instance, to the primitive who belongs to a totemic community, every animal, every plant, indeed every object, such as the sun, moon, and stars, forms part of a totem, and has its own class and sub-class. Consequently, each individual has his special affinities, and possesses powers over the members of his totem, class, and sub-class ; he has obligations towards them, mystic relations with other totems, and so forth. Even in communities where this form does not exist, the group idea of certain animals (possibly of all, if our records were complete) is mystic in character. Thus, among the Huichols, " the birds that soar highest . . . are thought to see and hear everything, and to possess mystic powers, which are inherent in their wing and tail feathers." These feathers, carried by the shaman, " enable him to see and hear everything both above and below the earth . . . to cure the sick, transform the dead, call down the sun, etc." [1] The Cherokees believe that fishes live in companies like human beings, that they have their villages, their regular paths through the waters, and that they conduct

[1] C. Lumholtz, *Unknown Mexico*, ii. pp. 7–8.

themselves like beings endowed with reason.[1] They think, too, that illnesses—rheumatic affections in particular—proceed from a mystic influence exercised by animals which are angry with the hunters, and their medical practices testify to this belief.

In Malaya and in South Africa the crocodile, and in other places the tiger, leopard, elephant, snake, are the object of similar beliefs and practices, and if we recall the myths of which animals are the heroes, in both hemispheres, there is no mammal or bird or fish or even insect to which the most extraordinary mystic properties have not been attributed. Moreover, the magic practices and ceremonies which, among nearly all primitive peoples, are the necessary accompaniment of hunting and fishing, and the sacrificial rites to be observed when the quarry has been killed, are sufficiently clear testimony to the mystic properties and powers which enter into the collective representations relating to the animal world.

It is the same with plant life. It will doubtless suffice to mention the *intichiuma* ceremonies described by Spencer and Gillen, designed to secure, in mystic fashion, the normal reproduction of plants,—the development of agrarian rites, corresponding with the hunting and fishing ceremonial, in all places where primitive peoples depend wholly or partly on the cultivation of the soil for their subsistence—and lastly, the highly unusual mystic properties ascribed to sacred plants, as, for instance, the soma in Vedic India, and the *hikuli* among the Huichols.

Again, if we consider the human body, we shall find that each organ of it has its own mystic significance, as the widespread practice of cannibalism and the rites connected with human sacrifices (in Mexico, for instance) prove. The heart, liver, kidney, the eyes, the fat, marrow, and so on, are reputed to procure such and such an attribute for those who feed on them. The orifices of the body, the excreta of all kinds, the hair and nail-parings, the placenta and umbilical cord, the blood, and the various fluids of the body, can all exercise magic influences.[2] Collective representations attribute mystic power

[1] J. Mooney, " The Sacred Formulas of the Cherokee," *E. B. Rept.*, vii. p. 375.
[2] K. Th. Preuss, "Der Ursprung der Religion und Kunst," *Globus*, lxxxvi. p. 20; lxxxvii. p. 19.

to all these things, and many wide-spread beliefs and practices
relate to this power. So, too, certain parts of plants and
animals possess peculiar virtues. " *Badi* is the name given to
the evil principle which . . . attends (like an evil angel)
everything in his life. . . . Von de Wall describes it as the
' enchanting or destroying influence which issues from anything ; for example, from a tiger which one sees, from a
poisonous tree which one passes under, from the saliva of a
mad dog, from an action which one has performed.' " [1]

Since everything that exists possesses mystic properties,
and these properties, from their very nature, are much more
important than the attributes of which our senses inform us,
the difference between animate and inanimate things is not of
the same interest to primitive mentality as it is to our own.
As a matter of fact, the primitive's mind frequently disregards
it altogether. Thus rocks, the form or position of which
strike the primitive's imagination, readily assume a sacred
character in virtue of their supposed mystic power. Similar
power is ascribed to the rivers, clouds, winds. Districts in
space, direction (the points of the compass), have mystic
significance. When the Australian aborigines assemble in
large numbers, each tribe, and each totem of a tribe, has its
own place, a place assigned to it by virtue of its mystic affinity
with a particular spatial region. Facts of a similar nature
have been noted in North America. I shall not lay any stress
on the rain, lightning, or thunder, the symbols of which play
so important a part in the religious ceremonies of the Zuñi,
the Australian aborigines, and all aggregates where a prolonged drought is a serious menace to the very existence of the
group. Finally, in Loango, the soil " is something more to the
Bafioti than the scene upon which their lives are played out.
There is in the ground, and there issues from it, a vital influence which permeates everything, which unites the present
and the past. . . . All things that live owe their powers to the
soil. . . . The people regard their land as a fief from their
god . . . the ground is sacred." [2] The same belief obtains
among the North American Indians, who consider it sacrilege
to till the ground, for by so doing they would run a risk of

---

[1] W. W. Skeat, *Malay Magic*, p. 427.
[2] Dr. Pechuël-Loesche, *Die Loango-Expedition*, iii. 2, pp. 194 et. seq. (1907).

offending the mystic power and drawing down dire calamities upon themselves.

Even things made, and constantly used, by man have their mystic properties and can become beneficent or terrifying according to circumstances. Cushing, who had lived among the Zuñis, had made them adopt him, and whose unusual versatility of mind led him finally to think like them, says that they, "no less than primitive peoples generally, conceive of everything made . . . whether structure or utensil or weapon, . . as living . . . a still sort of life, but as potent and aware nevertheless and as capable of functioning not only obdurately and resistingly, but also actively and powerfully in occult ways, either for good or for evil. As for living things they observe every animal is formed, and acts or functions according to its form—the feathered and winged bird flying, because of its feathered form, the furry four-footed animal running and leaping, and the scaly and finny fish swimming—. . . So the things made or born in their special forms by the hands of man also have life and function variously according to their various forms." Even the differences in the claws of beasts, for example, are supposed to make the difference between the hugging of the bear and the clutching of the panther. "The forms of these things not only give their power, but also restrict their power, so that if properly made, that is made and shaped strictly as other things of their kind have been made and shaped, they will perform only such safe uses as their prototypes have been found to serve." It is therefore of the utmost importance that they shall be faithfully reproduced, so that one may not have to fear the unknown "powers" which a fresh form might possess.[1]

In this way, according to Cushing, we can account for the extraordinary persistence of the same forms among primitive peoples, including even the most minute details of the ornamentation with which they decorate the products of their industries and arts. The Indians of British Guiana, for instance, "show extraordinary skill in many of the things they manufacture but they never improve upon them. They make them exactly as their fathers did before them."[2] This is not,

[1] F. H. Cushing, "Zuñi Creation Myths," E. B. Rept., xiii. pp. 361-3.
[2] Bernau, Missionary Labours in British Guiana, p. 46 (1847).

as we have been told, merely the result of habit, and of a spirit of conservatism peculiar to these peoples. It is the direct result of active belief in the mystic properties of the things, properties connected with their shape, and which can be controlled through this, but which would be beyond the power of man to regulate, if there were the slightest change of form. The most apparently trifling innovation may lead to danger, liberate hostile forces, and finally bring about the ruin of its instigator and all dependent upon him.

In the same way, any change effected by manual labour in the state of the soil, building, digging, mining, the making of a pavement or the demolition of a building, or even a slight modification in its shape by the addition of a wing, may be the cause of the greatest misfortunes.

" Should anyone fall suddenly ill and die," says De Groot, " his kindred are immediately ready to impute the cause to somebody who has ventured to make a change in the established order of things, or who has made an improvement in his own property. . . . Instances are by no means rare of their having stormed his house, demolished his furniture, assailed his person. . . . No wonder Chinamen do not repair their houses until they are ready to fall and become uninhabitable." [1] The steeple to be placed on the Catholic church in Pekin raised such a storm of protestation that the erection of it had to be abandoned. This mystic belief is intimately associated with that which the Chinese call the *fungshui*. But we find similar instances in other places. Thus, in the Nicobar Isles, " some of the chief men of Mus, Lapati, and Kenmai came and requested me to postpone fixing the beacon until the arrival of their people from Chowra, for they said that in consequence of this new work, and of a tree that had been felled down by Mr. Dobie in their graveyard, near the object, the sea was annoyed and had caused high wind and big surf, until they supposed that their friends would be drowned at sea." [2]

In Loango, " the stranger who goes away must not demolish his buildings or lay waste his plantations, but leave them just as they are. That is the reason why the natives protest when Europeans take down whole houses which they

[1] *The Religious System of China*, i. p. 1041.
[2] Solomon, " Diaries Kept in Car Nicobar," *J.A.I.*, xxxii. p. 230.

had built, to transport them elsewhere. The corner-stones and pillars at least should not be taken out of the ground. . . It is even forbidden to carry away the trunks of trees, to make excavations for mines, and so forth. A contractor exposes himself to serious trouble if, consulting his own wishes, he is so presuming as to make a new path, even if much shorter and more convenient than the one in use." [1] This is not mere misoneism, the dislike of any change which breaks established custom. With the old road, they know how matters stand, but they are ignorant of the unforeseen consequences, possibly calamitous, which might ensue upon the abandonment of it and the opening up of a fresh one. A road, like everything else, has its own peculiar mystic properties. The natives of Loango say of an abandoned path that it is " dead." To them, as to us, such an expression is metaphorical, but in their case it is fraught with meaning. For the path, " in active existence " has its secret powers, like houses, weapons, stones, clouds, plants, animals, and men—in short, like everything of which the primitive has a group idea. " All things have an invisible existence as well as a visible one," say the Igorots of the Philippine Islands.[2]

From these facts and many similar ones which we might quote, we can draw one conclusion : primitives perceive nothing in the same way as we do. The social *milieu* which surrounds them differs from ours, and precisely because it is different, the external world they perceive differs from that which we apprehend. Undoubtedly they have the same senses as ours—rather more acute than ours in a general way, in spite of our persuasion to the contrary—and their cerebral structure is like our own. But we have to bear in mind that which their collective representations instil into all their perceptions. Whatever the object presented to their minds, it implies mystic properties which are inextricably bound up with it, and the primitive, in perceiving it, never separates these from it.

To him there is no phenomenon which is, strictly speaking, a physical one, in the sense in which we use the term. The

[1] Dr. Pechuël-Loesche, *Die Loango-Expedition*, iii. 2, pp. 209–12.
[2] Jenks, *The Bontoc Igorot*, p. 196 (Manila, 1905).

rippling water, the whistling wind, the falling rain, any natural phenomenon whatever, a sound, a colour,—these things are never perceived by him as they are by us, that is, as more or less compound movements bearing a definite relation to preceding and to subsequent movements. His perceptive organs have indeed grasped the displacement of a mass of material as ours do ; familiar objects are readily recognized according to previous experience ; in short, all the physiological and psychological processes of perception have actually taken place in him as in ourselves. Its result, however, is immediately enveloped in a state of complex consciousness, dominated by collective representations. Primitives see with eyes like ours, but they do not perceive with the same minds. We might almost say that their perceptions are made up of a nucleus surrounded by a layer of varying density of representations which are social in their origin. And yet such a simile seems somewhat clumsy and inexact, for the primitive has not the least feeling of such a nucleus and surrounding layer ; it is we who separate them ; we, who by virtue of our mental habits cannot help distinguishing them. To the primitive the complex representation is still undifferentiated.

The profound difference which exists between primitive mentality and our own is shown even in the ordinary perception or mere apprehension of the very simplest things. Primitive perception is fundamentally mystic on account of the mystic nature of the collective representations which form an integral part of every perception. Ours has ceased to be so, at any rate with regard to most of the objects which surround us. Nothing appears alike to them and to us. For people like ourselves, speaking the language familiar to us, there is insurmountable difficulty in entering into their way of thinking. The longer we live among them, the more we approximate to their mental attitude, the more do we realize how impossible it is to yield to it entirely.

It is not correct to maintain, as is frequently done, that primitives associate occult powers, magic properties, a kind of soul or vital principle with all the objects which affect their senses or strike their imagination, and that their perceptions are surcharged with animistic beliefs. It is not a question of *association*. The mystic properties with which things and beings are imbued form an integral part of the idea to the primitive, who views it as a synthetic whole. It is at a later stage of social evolution that what we call a natural phenomenon tends to become the sole content of perception to the exclusion of the other elements, which then assume the aspect of beliefs, and finally appear superstitions. But as long as this " dissociation " does not take place, perception remains an undifferentiated whole. We might call it " polysynthetic," like words in the languages spoken by certain primitive peoples.

In the same way, we shall find ourselves in a blind alley, whenever we propound a question in such terms as : How would the primitive's mind explain this or that natural phenomenon ? The very enunciation of the problem implies a false hypothesis. We are supposing that his mind apprehends these phenomena like our own. We imagine that he simply perceives such facts as sleep, dreaming, illness, death, the rise and decline of the heavenly bodies, rain, thunder, etc., and then, stimulated by the principle of causality, tries to account for them. But to the mentality of undeveloped peoples, there are no natural phenomena such as we understand by the term. Their mentality has no need to seek an explanation of them ; for the explanation is implied in the mystic elements of the collective representations of them. Therefore problems of this nature must be inverted. What we must seek is not the logical process which might have resulted in the interpretation of phenomena, for this mentality never perceives the phenomenon as distinct from the interpretation ; we must find out how the phenomenon became by degrees detached from the complex in which it first found itself enveloped, so that it might be apprehended separately, and how what originally was an integral part of it should later on have become an " explanation."

II

The very considerable part played by collective represen tations in the primitives' perceptions does not result alone in impressing a mystic character upon them. The same cause leads to another consequence, and these perceptions are accordingly *oriented* differently from our own. In that which our perceptions retain, as well as in that which is disregarded, the chief determining factor is the amount of reliance that we can place upon the unvarying reappearance of phenomena in the same given conditions. They conduce to effect the maximum " objective " validity, and, as a result, to eliminate everything prejudicial or merely unnecessary to this objectivity. From this standpoint, too, primitives do not perceive as we do. In certain cases where direct practical interests are at stake, we undoubtedly find that they pay great attention to, and are often very skilful in detecting differences in, impressions which are very similar, and in recognizing external signs of objects or phenomena, upon which their subsistence, and possibly even their lives, depend. (The shrewdness of the Australian aborigines in finding and profiting by the dew which has fallen during the night,[1] and other similar facts, are an example of this.) But, even setting aside that which these fine perceptions owe to training and memory, we still find that in most cases primitives' perceptive powers, instead of tending to reject whatever would lessen objectivity, lay special stress upon the mystic properties, the occult forces of beings and phenomena, and are thus oriented upon factors which, to us, appear subjective, although to primitives they are at least as real as the others. This characteristic of their perceptions enables them to account for certain phenomena, the " explanation " of which, when based solely upon mental or logical processes in the individual, does not appear adequate.

It is a well-known fact that primitives, even members of communities which are already somewhat advanced, regard artificial likenesses, whether painted, carved, or sculptured, as real, as well as the individual they depict. " To the Chinese," says De Groot, " association of images with beings actually becomes identification, both materially and psychically. An image, especially if pictorial or sculptured, and thus approaching close to the reality, is an *alter ego* of the living reality, an abode of the soul, nay it is that reality itself. . . . Such intense association is, in fact, the very backbone of China's inveterate idolatry and fetish-worship." [2] In support of his

---

[1] Eyre, *Journals of Expeditions of Discovery into Central Australia,* ii. p. 247.
[2] J. J. M. de Groot, *The Religious System of China,* ii. pp. 340-55.

statement, De Groot gives a long series of tales which seem wholly incredible, but which Chinese authors find perfectly natural. A young widow has a child by a clay statue of her husband; portraits are endued with life; a wooden dog starts running; paper animals, horses, for instance, act exactly like living animals; an artist, meeting a horse of a certain colour in the street, recognizes it as a work of his. . . . From these the transition to customs which are very general in China is an easy one.—Such customs as placing upon the tombs of the dead miniature figures of animals, burning paper money there, for instance.

In North America, the Mandans believe that the portraits taken by Catlin are alive like their subjects, and that they rob these of part of their vitality. It is true that Catlin is inclined to draw a long bow, and his stories must be taken with a grain of salt. In this respect, however, the beliefs and sentiments he attributes to the Mandans are exactly what we find noted elsewhere in similar circumstances. " I know," says one man, " that this man put *many of our buffaloes in his book*, for I was with him, and we have had no buffaloes since to eat, it is true." [1]

" They pronounced me the greatest medicine-man in the world," writes Catlin, " for they said I had made *living beings* —they said they could see their chiefs alive in two places— those that I had made were *a little* alive—they could see their eyes move—could see them smile and laugh, and that if they could laugh, they could certainly speak, if they should try, and they must therefore have some life in them." [1] Therefore, most Indians refused him permission to take their likenesses. It would be parting with a portion of their own substance, and placing them at the mercy of anyone who might wish to possess the picture. They are afraid, too, of finding themselves faced by a portrait which, as a living thing, may exercise a harmful influence.

" We had placed," say the Jesuit missionaries, " images of St. Ignatius and St. Xavier upon our altar. They regarded them with amazement; they believed them to be living persons, and asked whether they were *ondaqui*" (plural form of *wakan*, supernatural beings) : " in short, that which

[1] Catlin, *The North American Indians*, i. pp. 122-3 (Edinburgh, 1903).

they recognize as superior to humanity. They inquired whether the tabernacle were their dwelling, and whether these *ondaqui* used the adornments which they saw around the altar." [1]

In Central Africa, too, " I have known natives refuse to enter a room where portraits were hanging on the walls, because of the *masoka* souls which were in them." [2] The same author tells the story of a chief who allowed himself to be photographed, and who, several months later, fell ill. In accordance with his request, the negative had been sent to England, and " his illness was attributed to some accident having befallen the photographic plate."

Thus the similitude can take the place of the model, and possess the same properties. In Loango, the followers of a certain eminent wonder-worker used to make a wooden image of their master, imbued it with " power," and gave it the name of the original. Possibly even they would ask their master to make his own substitute, so that after his death, as well as during his life, they could use it in performing their miracles.[3] On the Slave Coast, if one of twins happens to die, the mother " . . . to give the spirit of the deceased child something to enter without disturbing the survivor, carries about, with the latter, a little wooden figure, about seven or eight inches long, roughly fashioned in human shape, and of the sex of the dead child. Such figures are nude, as an infant would be, with beads around the waist." [4] With reference to the Bororo of Brazil we read " they begged Wilhelm most earnestly not to let the women see the drawings he had made of the bull-roarers ; for the sight of the drawings would kill them as the real things would." [5] Many similar instances had already been collected by Tylor.[6]

Are these to be explained from a purely psychological point of view, as is so frequently the case, by the association of ideas ? Must we say, with De Groot, that it is impossible for

[1] Ed. Thwaites, *Relations des Jésuites*, v. p. 256 (1633).
[2] Hetherwick, " Some Animistic Beliefs of the Yaos," *J.A.I.*, xxxii. pp. 89–90.
[3] Dr. Pechuël-Loesche, *Die Loango-Expedition*, iii. 2, pp. 378–9 (1907).
[4] A. B. Ellis, *The Yoruba-speaking Peoples*, p. 80.
[5] K. von den Steinen, *Unter den Naturvölkern Zentralbräsiliens*, p. 386.
[6] *Primitive Culture*, ii. pp. 169 et seq.

them to distinguish a mere resemblance from identity, and admit that primitives suffer from the same illusion as the child who believes her doll to be alive ?   First of all, however, it is difficult to decide whether the child herself is quite sure of it. Perhaps her belief is part of the game and at the same time sincere, like the emotions of grown-up people at the theatre, shedding real tears about misfortunes which they nevertheless know to be but feigned.   On the contrary, it is impossible to doubt that the primitives' beliefs which I have just mentioned *are* serious ;   their actions prove it.   How then can a portrait be " materially and psychically " identified with its original ? To my mind, it is not on account of a childish trust in analogy, nor from mental weakness and confusion ;   it is not due to a naïve generalization of the animist theory, either.   It is because, in perceiving the similitude, as in looking at the original, the traditional collective representations imbue it with the same mystic elements.

If primitives view the pictured resemblance differently from ourselves, it is because they view the original otherwise also.   In the latter we note its objective and actual characteristics, and those only : the shape, size, and proportions of the body ;   the colour of the eyes ;   the facial expression, and so forth ;   we find these reproduced in the picture, and there, too, we find these alone.   But to the primitive, with his perceptions differently oriented, these objective features, if he apprehends them as we do, are neither the only ones nor the most important ;   most frequently, they are but the symbols or instruments of occult forces and mystic powers such as every being, especially a living being, can display.   As a natural consequence, therefore, the image of such a being would also present the mingling of characteristics which we term objective and of mystic powers.   It will live and prove beneficial or malevolent like the being it reproduces ;   it will be its surrogate.   Accordingly we find that the image of an unknown—and consequently dreaded—object often inspires extraordinary dread.   " I had," says Father Hennepin, " a pot about three feet high shaped like a lion, which we used for cooking our food in during the voyage. . . . The savages never ventured to touch it with their hands unless they had previously covered them with beaver skins.   They imparted such terror of it to their wives that the latter had it fastened to the branches of a tree, for otherwise they would not have dared to sleep or even enter the hut if it were inside. We wished to make a present of it to some of the chiefs, but they would neither accept it nor make use of it, because they feared that it concealed some evil spirit which might have killed them." [1] We know that these Indians in the valley of the Mississippi had never before seen a white man, or a lion, or a cooking utensil. The likeness of an animal they did not know awakened in them the same mystic fears that its appearance among them would have done.

This identification which appears so strange to us must therefore occur naturally. It does not arise out of gross mental hallucination or childish confusion of ideas. As soon as we realize *how* primitives view entities, we see that they view reproductions of them in exactly the same way. If their perceptions of the originals ceased to be mystic, their images would also lose their mystic properties. They would no longer appear to be alive, but would be what they are to our minds—merely material reproductions.

In the second place, primitives regard their names as something concrete and real, and frequently sacred. Here are a few of the many proofs of it.

" The Indian regards his name, not as a mere label, but as a distinct part of his personality, just as much as are his eyes or his teeth, and believes that injury will result as surely from the malicious handling of his name as from a wound inflicted on any part of his physical organism. This belief was found among the various tribes from the Atlantic to the Pacific." [2] On the East African coast, " there is a real and material connection between a man and his name, and . . . by means of the name injury may be done to the man. . . . In consequence of this belief the name of the king . . . is always kept secret. . . . It appears strange that the birth-name only, and not an alias, should be believed capable of carrying some of the personality of the bearer elsewhere . . . but the native

[1] L. Hennepin, *Nouveau Voyage de l'Amérique Septentrionale*, pp. 366–7.
[2] J. Mooney, " The Sacred Formulas of the Cherokees," *E. B. Rept.*, vii. p. 343.

view seems to be that the alias does not really belong to the man." [1]

Accordingly all kinds of precautions become necessary. A man will avoid uttering his own name [2] and the names of others, while the names of the dead, above all, will never be pronounced; very frequently, too, even ordinary words in which the name of a dead person is implied will fall into desuetude. Alluding to a name is the same thing as laying hands on the very person or being that bears the name. It is making an attack upon him, outraging his individuality, or again, it is invoking his presence and forcing him to appear, a proceeding which may be fraught with very great danger. There are excellent reasons, therefore, for avoiding such a practice. " When they (the Santals) are hunting and see a leopard or a tiger they will always call the attention of their companions to the fact by calling out 'a cat,' or some similar name." [3] With the Cherokees, too, " it is never said that a person has been bitten by a snake, but that he has been 'scratched by a brier.' In the same way, when an eagle has been shot for a ceremonial dance, it is announced that 'a snow-bird has been killed,' the purpose being to deceive the rattlesnake or eagle spirits which might be listening." [4] The Warramunga, instead of mentioning the snake *Wollunqua* by its name when speaking of it, call it *Urkulu nappaurima*, " because," say they, " if they were to call it too often by its right name, they would lose their control over it, and it would come out and eat them all up." [5]

At the beginning of a fresh epoch in his life,—at his initiation, for instance—an individual receives a new name, and it is the same when he is admitted to a secret society. A town changes its name to indicate that it is commencing a new era ; Yedo becomes Tokyo.[6] A name is never a matter of indifference ; it implies a whole series of relationships between the man who bears it and the source whence it is derived. " A name implies relationship, and consequently protection ;

---

[1] A. B. Ellis, *The Ewe-speaking Peoples*, pp. 98–9.
[2] Rivers, *The Todas*, p. 627.
[3] Bodding, " On Taboo Customs amongst the Santals," *Journal of the Asiatic Society of Bengal*, iii. p. 20 (1898).
[4] J. Mooney, *The Sacred Formulas of the Cherokees*, p. 352.
[5] Spencer and Gillen, *The Northern Tribes of Central Australia*, p. 227.
[6] Chamberlain, *Things Japanese*, p. 344 (1902).

favour and influence are claimed from the source of the name, whether this be the gens or the vision. A name, therefore, shows the affiliation of the individual ; it grades him, so to speak." [1] In British Columbia, " names, apart from the staz or nickname, are never used as mere appellations to distinguish one person from another, as among ourselves, nor do they seem to have been used ordinarily as terms of address. They are primarily terms of relation or affiliation, with historic and mystic reference. They were reserved for special and ceremonial occasions. The ordinary terms of address among the Salish tribes, as among other primitive peoples, were those expressive of age." [2] With the Kwakiutl, " each clan has a certain limited number of names. Each individual has only one name at a time. The bearers of these names form the nobility of the tribe. When a man receives the totem of his father-in-law, he at the same time receives his name, while the father-in-law gives up the name, and takes what is called ' an old man's name,' which does not belong to the names constituting the nobility of the tribe." [3] Finally, De Groot notes that " the Chinese have a tendency to identify names with the persons who bear them, a tendency which may be classed on a level with their inability, already illustrated by numerous instances, of clearly discriminating between semblances or symbols and the realities which these call to mind." [4]

This last comparison seems perfectly correct, to my mind, and I think as De Groot does, that the same cause may account for both tendencies. This cause is not to be found in a childish association of ideas, however. It is in the collective representations which, forming an integral part of their perception of entities, form an integral part also of their perception of the likeness and the name which betokens them. The reality of the similitude is of the same kind as that of the original—that is, essentially mystic, and it is the same with the reality of the name. The two cases are alike except in one point—that

---

[1] Dorsey, " Siouan Cults," *E. B. Rept.*, xi. p. 368.
[2] Hill Tout, " Ethnology of the StatlumH of British Columbia," *J.A.I.*, xxxv. p. 152.
[3] F. Boas, " The North-western Tribes of Canada," *Reports of the British Association*, p. 675 (1898).
[4] *The Religious System of China*, i. p. 212.

which appeals to the sight in the first case, appeals to the hearing in the second, but otherwise the process is identical. The mystic properties in the name are not separated from those in the beings they connote. To us the name of a person, an animal, a family, a town, has the purely external significance of a label which allows us to discern without any possibility of confusion who the person is, to what species the animal belongs, which family and which town it is. To the primitive, however, the designation of the being or object, which seems to us the sole function of the name, appears a mere accessory and of secondary importance : many observers expressly state that that is not the real function of the name. To make up for this, there are very important functions of which our names are deprived. The name expresses and makes real the relationship of the individual with his totemic group ; with the ancestor of whom he is frequently a reincarnation ; with the particular totem or guardian angel who has been revealed to him in a dream ; with the invisible powers who protect the secret societies to which he belongs, etc. How does this arise ? Evidently because beings and objects do not present themselves to the primitive's mind apart from the mystic properties which these relations involve. As a natural consequence, names derive their characteristics from the characteristics of these same beings and objects. The name is mystic, as the reproduction is mystic, because the perception of things, oriented differently from our own, through the collective representations, is mystic.

We can therefore extend also to names Cushing's acute reflections, already quoted, with regard to the forms of objects. Names condition and define the occult powers of the beings who participate in them. Hence are derived the feelings and fears they awaken, and the precautions to which these fears lead. The problem is not to discover how the simple term " is associated " with mystic elements which are never separable from it in the minds of primitives. What is given is the ensemble of collective representations of a mystic nature expressed by the name. The actual problem is to ascertain how these collective representations become gradually impaired and dissociated, how they have assumed the form of " beliefs " less and less closely " attached " to the name, until the moment arrives when, as with us, it serves but as a distinctive designation.

The primitive is, as we know, no less careful about his shadow than he is about his name or his counterfeit presentment. If he were to lose it he would consider himself hopelessly endangered. Should it come into the power of another, he has everything to dread. Folklore of all countries has made us familiar with facts of this kind ; we shall cite but a few of them only. In the Fiji Islands, as in many places inhabited by people of a similar stage of development, it is a mortal insult to walk upon anybody else's shadow. In East Africa, murders are sometimes committed by means of a knife or nail thrust through the shadow of a man ; if the guilty person is caught in the act he is executed forthwith. Miss Kingsley in reporting this fact, shows clearly to what extent the West African negroes dread the loss of their shadow. "It strikes one as strange," she writes, " to see men who have been walking, say, through forest or grass land, on a blazing hot morning quite happily, on arrival at a piece of clear ground or a village square, most carefully go round it, not across, and you will soon notice that they only do this at noontime, and learn that they fear losing their shadow. I asked some Bakwiri I once came across who were particularly careful in this matter, why they were not anxious about losing their shadows when night came down and they disappeared in the surrounding darkness, and was told that was all right, because at night all shadows lay down in the shadow of the Great God, and so got stronger. Had I not seen how strong and how long a shadow, be it of man or tree or of the great mountain itself, was in the early morning time ? " [1]

De Groot notes similar precautions in China. " When the lid is about to be placed on the coffin, most of the bystanders not belonging to the nearest kindred retire a few steps, or even make off for the side apartments, as it is dangerous to health and detrimental to good luck to have one's shadow enclosed in a coffin." [2] What then *is* the shadow ? It is not the exact equivalent of what we call the soul ; but it is of the nature of the soul, and where the soul is represented as multiple, the

[1] Mary Kingsley, *West African Studies*, p. 176.
[2] J. J. M. de Groot, *The Religious System of China*, i. pp. 94, 210.

shadow (according to Miss Kingsley) is sometimes one of the souls. On his side, De Groot says : " We find nothing in the books of China which points positively to an identification of shadows and souls." [1] But, on the other hand, ghosts have no shadows. And De Groot concludes by saying : that " the shadow is a part of the personality which has an immense influence on his destiny," a characteristic which applies equally, as we have seen, to a person's picture or his name.

I shall therefore refer it to the same theory. If we ask ourselves : how has the primitive come to associate with the idea of his shadow beliefs which we find to be almost universal ? we might reply by an ingenious explanation, and one which would be psychologically probable, but it would be unsound, because the problem cannot be propounded in such terms as these. To enunciate it thus would be to imply that the idea of his shadow to the primitive is the same as to us, and the rest is superimposed. Now it really is nothing like that. The perception of the shadow, as of the body itself, like that of the image or the name, is a mystic perception, in which that which we properly call the shadow,—the design upon the ground of a figure which recalls the form of a being or object lighted from the opposite side—is only one element among many. We have not to discover how the perception of the shadow has been placed in juxtaposition or united with such and such a representation : these indeed form an integral part of the perception, so far as we can trace it in past observations. For this reason I should be prepared to take up a counter-position to that of De Groot. " The Chinese," he says, " are even to these days without ideas of the physical causation of shadows. . . . They must needs see in a shadow something more than a negation of light." [2] I, on the contrary, should say : the Chinese, having a mystic perception of the shadow, as participating in the life and all the properties of the tangible body, cannot represent it as a mere " negation of light." To be able to see a purely physical phenomenon in the production of the shadow, it would be necessary to have an idea of such a phenomenon, and we know that such an idea is lacking to the primitive. In undeveloped communities, there

[1] J. J. M. de Groot, *The Religious System of China*, ii. p. 83.   [2] Ibid.

is no perception unaccompanied by mystic qualities and occult properties, and why should the shadow be any exception ?

Finally, the same considerations apply equally to another class of phenomena—dreams—which occupy an important place in the primitive mind. To primitives the dream is not, as it is to us, simply a manifestation of mental activity which occurs during sleep, a more or less orderly series of representations to which, when awake, the dreamer would give no credence, because they lack the conditions essential to objective validity. This last characteristic, though it does not escape the primitives, seems to interest them but slightly. On the other hand, the dream, to them, is of far greater significance than to us. It is first a percept as real as those of the waking state, but above all it is a provision of the future, a communication and intercourse with spirits, souls, divinities, a means of establishing a relation with their own special guardian angel, and even of discovering who this may be. Their confidence in the reality of that which the dreams makes known to them is very profound. Tylor, Frazer, and the representatives of the English school of anthropology have brought together a vast number of facts which bear witness to this, collected by investigators of primitive peoples of the most diverse types. Shall I, too, quote some ? In Australia " Sometimes a man dreams that someone has got some of his hair or a piece of his food, or of his 'possum rug, or indeed anything almost that he has used. If he dreams this several times he feels sure of it and calls his friends together, and tells them of his dreaming too much about ' that man,' who must have something belonging to him. . . . Sometimes natives only know about having their fat taken out by remembering something of it as in a dream." [1]

To the North American Indians, dreams, natural or induced, have an importance which it would be difficult to overestimate. " Sometimes it is the rational mind which is wandering, whilst the mind which feels continues to animate the body. Sometimes the familiar spirit gives wholesome advice upon what is about to happen ; and sometimes it is a visit from the soul of the object of which one dreams. But in

[1] Howitt, " On Australian Medicine-men," *J.A.I.*, xvi. 1, pp. 29–30.

whatsoever fashion the dream may be conceived, it is always
regarded as a sacred thing, and as the most usual method
employed by the gods of making their will known to men. . . .
Frequently it is an order from the spirits." [1] In Lejeune's
Relations de la Nouvelle France, it is stated that the dream is
" the god of the heathens " ; and an observer of our own
times says : " Dreams are to savages what the Bible is to us,
the source of Divine revelation—with this important difference
that they can produce this revelation at will by the medium
of dreams." [2] Consequently the Indian will at once carry out
what has been commanded or simply indicated to him in a
dream. Mooney tells us that among the Cherokees, when a
man dreams that he has been bitten by a snake, he must
follow the same treatment as if he had really been bitten, for
it is a witch-snake that has done the injury, and if he did not,
swelling and ulceration would ensue, possibly even many
years later.[3] In the *Relations de la Nouvelle France* we read
that " a warrior, having dreamed that he had been taken
prisoner in battle, anxious to avert the fatal consequences of
such a dream, called all his friends together and implored them
to help him in this misfortune. He begged them to prove
themselves true friends by treating him as if he were an enemy.
They therefore rushed upon him, stripped him naked, fettered
him, and dragged him through the streets with the usual shouts
and insults, and even made him mount the scaffold. . . .
He thanked them warmly, believing that this imaginary
captivity would ensure him against being made prisoner in
reality. . . . In another case, a man who had dreamed he saw
his hut on fire, did not rest till he had witnessed its burning in
reality. . . . A third, not believing that his dream would be
sufficiently realistic if he were burned in effigy insisted on
having fire applied to his legs, as is done with captives about
to undergo capital punishment. . . . It was fully six months
before he recovered from the burns." [4]

The Malays of Sarawak never doubt their blood-relation-

---

[1] Charlevoix, *Journal d'un Voyage dans l'Amérique Septentrionale*, iii.
pp. 353–5.

[2] A. Gatschet, *The Klamath Language*, p. 77 (Contributions to *North
American Ethnology*, ii. 1).

[3] " Myths of the Cherokee," *E. B. Rept.*, xix. p. 295.

[4] *Années*, pp. 46–8 (1661–2).

ship with a certain animal, if they have dreamed about it.
" Wan's great-great-grandfather became blood-brother to a
crocodile. . . . Wan had several times met this crocodile
in dreams. Thus in one dream he fell into the river where
there were many crocodiles about. He climbed on to the
head of one which said to him, ' Don't be afraid,' and carried
him to the bank. Wan's father had charms given him by a
crocodile and would not on any account kill one, and Wan
clearly regards himself as being intimately related to crocodiles
in general." [1]

In short, to conclude with a peculiarly happy dictum of
Spencer and Gillen : " What a savage experiences during a
dream is just as real to him as what he sees when he is awake." [2]

To explain these phenomena, are we to rely upon the
current theory which refers them to a psychological illusion
constantly obtaining among primitives ? They would be
unable to distinguish an actual perception from one which,
though powerful, is merely imaginary. In all cases of life-like
representation, the belief in the objectivity of this representation would appear. Accordingly, the apparition of a dead
person would induce the belief that he was actually present.
The representation of one's own self, in a dream, acting,
travelling, conversing with persons who are at a distance or
who have disappeared, would convince one that the soul does
indeed leave the body during sleep and travels whither it feels
conscious of going. " The supreme confusion in the thought
of non-civilized individuals," says Powell, " is the confusion of
the objective with the subjective."

Without disputing the general accuracy of the psychological law which is invoked here, I should like to point out
that it does not wholly account for the way in which primitives
represent their dreams, and the use to which they put them.
In the first place, they distinguish very clearly between perceptions which come to them through dreams from those they
receive in the waking state, however similar they may otherwise be. They even recognize different categories of dreams,

[1] Hose and Macdougall, " Relations between Men and Animals in Sarawak," *J.A.I.*, xxi. p. 191.
[2] Spencer and Gillen, *The Northern Tribes of Central Australia*, p. 451.

and attribute a varying degree of validity to them. " The Ojibbeways have divided dreams into various classes, and given each a special name. The excellent Bishop Baraga, in his lexicon of that language, has collected the Indian names for a bad dream, an impure dream, an ominous dream, as well as for a good or happy dream." [1] " The Hidatsa have much faith in dreams, but usually regard as oracular only those which come after prayer, sacrifice, and fasting." [2] It is therefore with full knowledge of the circumstances and due reflection that primitives accord the one kind of perception as complete a credence as the other. Instead of saying, as people do, that primitives believe in what they perceive in the dream, *although* it is but a dream, I should say that they believe in it *because* it is a dream. The " illusion " theory does not suffice. How do we account for the fact that, knowing well that the dream *is* a dream, they should nevertheless rely upon it ? This cannot be explained as a mere psychological process effected in the individual. Here again, we are obliged to take into account the collective representations which make both the perception and the dream something entirely different for the primitive from what they would be for us.

Our perception is directed towards the apprehension of an objective reality, and this reality alone. It eliminates all that might be of merely subjective importance, and in this it is in contrast with the dream. We do not understand how anything that is seen in a dream can be placed on a par with that which we see in the waking state : and if such a thing does occur we are forced to believe that it is the result of a very strong psychological illusion. But with the primitives there is no such violent contrast as this. Their perception is oriented in another fashion, and in it that which we call objective reality is united and mingled with, and often regulated by, mystic, imperceptible elements which we nowadays characterize as subjective. In this way, in fact, it is closely related to the dream. Or, if we prefer to put it thus, we may say that their dream is a perception like the others. It is a compound into which the same elements enter, which awakens

[1] Kohl, *Kitchi Gama : Wanderings round Lake Superior*, p. 236.
[2] Dorsey, " Siouan Cults," *E. B. Rept.*, xi. p. 516.

the same sentiments, and which even impels to action. Thus the Indian who has a dream and risks his existence upon its truth, is not ignorant of the difference between this dream and a similar perception which he might have in his waking state. But, since his perception in the waking state and in the dream are alike mystic, this difference means very little to him. In our eyes, the objective reality of the perception is the measure of its validity ; in his, such a consideration is only secondary, or rather, is of no importance at all.

That which to us is perception is to him mainly the communication with spirits, souls, invisible and intangible mysterious powers encompassing him on all sides, upon which his fate depends, and which loom larger in his consciousness than the fixed and tangible and visible elements of his representations. He has therefore no reason to depreciate the dream, and consider it as a subjective and dubious representation, in which he must place no trust. The dream is not a form of inferior and illusory perception. On the contrary, it is a highly favoured form, one in which, since its material and tangible elements are at a minimum, the communication with invisible spirits and forces is most direct and most complete.

This accounts for the confidence which the primitive has in his dreams, a confidence which is at least as great as that he accords his ordinary perceptions. It accounts also for his seeking after means of procuring dreams which shall be revelatory and, among the North American Indians, for instance, for the whole technique of securing the sincerity and validity of dreams. Thus the young man, arrived at the age of initiation, who is going to try and see in a dream the animal which will be his guardian angel, his personal totem, has to prepare himself for this purpose by carrying out a series of observances. " He first purifies himself by the *impi* or steam bath, and by fasting for a term of three days. During the whole of this time, he avoids women and society, is secluded in his habits and endeavours in every way to be pure enough to receive a revelation from the deity whom he invokes " . . . then he subjects himself to various tortures " until the deities have vouchsafed him a vision or revelation." [1]

[1] Dorsey, " Siouan Cults," *E. B. Rept.*, xi. pp. 436–7.

This, too, accounts for the deference and respect shown to dreamers, seers, prophets, sometimes even to lunatics. A special power of communicating with invisible reality, that is, a peculiarly privileged perception, is attributed to them. All these well-known facts naturally result from the orientation of the collective representations which obtains in primitive peoples, and which endows with mysticism both the real world in which the " savage " dwells, and his perception of it.

III

Further differences between the primitives' perception and our own arise out of this mystic character. To us one of the essential signs by which we recognize the objective validity of a perception is that the being or phenomenon perceived appears to all alike under the same conditions. If, for instance, one person alone among a number present hears a certain sound repeatedly, or sees an object close by, we say that he or she is subject to delusions, or has a hallucination. Leibniz, Taine, and many others have insisted upon the agreement between the subjects who are perceiving as a means of distinguishing between real " and imaginary phenomena." Current opinion on this point, too, is wholly on the side of the philosophers. With the primitives, on the contrary, it constantly happens that beings or things manifest themselves to certain persons to the exclusion of others who may be present. No one is astonished at this, for all regard it as perfectly natural. Howitt writes, for instance : " Of course, the Ngarang was invisible to all but the *wirarap* (medicine-man)." [1] A young medicine-man in training, who is telling of his initiation, remarks : " After that I used to see things that my mother could not see. When out with her I would say ' Mother, what is that out there yonder ? ' She used to say ' Child, there is nothing.' These were the *jir* (or ghosts) which I began to see." [2] The aborigines observed by Spencer and Gillen think that during the night the sun visits the place where it arises in the morning, " and that it might actually be seen at night times by . . . clever medicine-men, and the fact that it can

[1] Howitt, " On Some Australian Medicine-men," *J.A.I.*, xvi. i. p. 42.
[2] Ibid., p. 50.

not be seen by ordinary persons only means that they are not gifted with sufficient power, and not that it is not there." [1] In their case, as with many other aggregates of the same stage of development, the medicine-man extracts from the body of the sufferer a small object only visible to the operator. " After much mysterious searching he finds and cuts the string which is invisible to everyone except himself. There is not a doubt amongst the onlookers as to its having been there." [2] In the form of witchcraft which the Australian aborigines called " pointing the death bone," a complicated series of operations would be carried on without anyone's perceiving them. " The blood of the victim, in some fashion which is unperceived, flows from him to the medicine-man, and thence to the receptacle where it is collected ; at the same time, by a corresponding movement a bone, a magic stone proceeds from the body of the sorcerer to the body of his victim—still invisibly—and, entering there, induces a fatal malady." [3]

We find the same beliefs in Eastern Siberia. " In the Alarsk department of the Government of Irkutsk . . . if anyone's child becomes dangerously ill, the Buryats . . . believe that the crown of his head is being sucked by Onok-hoi, a small beast in the form of a mole or cat. . . . No one except the shaman can see this beast." [4]

In North America, among the Klamaths of Oregon, the *kiuks* (medicine-man) who is called to treat a case of disease must consult the spirits of certain animals. " Such persons only as have been trained during five years for the profession of conjurers can see these spirits, but by them they are seen as clearly as we see the objects around us." [5] " Dwarfs can be seen only by those initiated into the mysteries of witchcraft." [6] Among the Tarahumares " large serpents, which only the shaman can see, are thought to live in the rivers. They have horns and very big eyes." [7] " The great Hikuli " (a sacred plant personified) " eats with the shaman, who alone is able to

[1] *The Native Tribes of Central Australia*, pp. 561–2.
[2] Ibid., p. 532.
[3] W. E. Roth, *Ethnological Studies among the N.W. Central Queensland Aborigines*, No. 264.
[4] V. Mikhailovski, *Shamanism in Siberia and European Russia*, analysed in *J.A.I.*, xxiv. p. 99 ; cf. p. 133.
[5] A. Gatschet, *The Klamath Language*, p. xcviii.   [6] Ibid., p. xcix.
[7] C. Lumholtz, *Unknown Mexico*, i. p. 340.

see him and his companions." [1]   In one of the Huichol ceremonies, the heads of the does are placed with the heads of the
bucks, because they, too, have horns, " though only the
shaman sees them." [2]

All such phenomena are to be expected if it be true that
the perception of primitives is oriented differently from our
own, and not pre-eminently concerned, as ours is, with the
characteristics of the beings and manifestations which we call
objective. To them the most important properties of the
beings and objects they perceive, are their occult powers, their
mystic qualities. Now one of these powers is that of appearing
or not appearing in given circumstances. Either the power is
inherent in the subject who perceives, who has been prepared
for it by initiation, or else holds it by virtue of his participation in some superior being, and so on. In short, mystic
relations may be established between certain persons and
certain beings, on account of which these persons are exclusively privileged to perceive these beings. Such cases are
analogous to the dream. The primitive, far from regarding
the mystic perception in which he has no part, as suspect, sees
in it, as in the dream, a more precious, and consequently more
significant communication with invisible spirits and forces.

IV

Conversely, when collective representations imply the
presence of certain qualities in objects, nothing will persuade
the primitives that they do not exist. To us, the fact that we
do not perceive them there is decisive. It does not prove to
them that they are not there, for possibly it is their nature not
to reveal themselves to perception, or to manifest themselves
in certain conditions only. Consequently, that which we call
experience, and which decides, as far as we are concerned,
what may be admitted or not admitted as real, has no effect
upon collective representations. Primitives have no need of
this experience to vouch for the mystic properties of beings
and objects : and for the same reason they are quite indifferent
to the disappointments it may afford. Since experience is

[1] C. Lumholtz, *Unknown Mexico*, p. 372.
[2] Id., *Symbolism of the Huichol Indians*, p. 68.

limited to what is stable, tangible, visible, and approachable in physical reality, it allows the most important of all, the occult powers, to escape.   Hence we can find no example of the non-success of a magic practice discouraging those who believe in it.   Livingstone gives an account of a prolonged discussion which he had with the rain-makers, and ends by saying : " I have never been able to convince a single one of them that their arguments are unsound.   Their belief in these ' charms ' of theirs is unbounded." [1]   In the Nicobar Islands, " the people in all the villages have now performed the cere- mony called *tanangla*, signifying either ' support ' or ' pre- vention.'   Its object is to prevent illness caused by the north- east monsoon.   Poor Nicobarese !   They do the same thing year after year, but to no effect." [2]

Experience is peculiarly unavailing against the belief in the virtues of " fetishes " which secure invulnerability : a method of interpreting what happens in a sense which favours the belief is never lacking.   In one case an Ashanti, having pro- cured a fetish of this kind, hastened to put it to the proof, and received a gunshot wound which broke his arm.   The " fetish man " explained the matter to the satisfaction of all, saying that the incensed fetish had that moment revealed the reason to him.   It was because the young man had had sexual rela- tions with his wife on a forbidden day.   The wounded man confessed that this was true, and the Ashantis retained their convictions.[3]   Du Chaillu tells us that when a native wears an iron chain round his neck he is proof against bullets.   If the charm is not effectual, his faith in it remains unshaken, for then he believes that some maleficent wonder-worker has produced a powerful " counter-spell," to which he falls a victim.[4]   Elsewhere he says : " As I came from seeing the king, I shot at a bird sitting upon a tree, and missed it.   I had been taking quinine, and was nervous.   But the negroes standing around at once proclaimed that this was a fetish-bird, and therefore I *could* not shoot it.   I fired again, and missed again.   Hereupon they grew triumphant in their declarations, while I . . . loaded again, took careful aim, and to my own

[1] *Missionary Travels*, pp. 24–5 (1857).
[2] Solomon, " Diaries kept in Cap Nicobar," *J.A.I.*, xxxii. p. 213.
[3] Bowditch, *Mission to Ashanti*, p. 439.
[4] *Explorations and Adventures in Equatorial Africa*, p. 338.

satisfaction and their dismay, brought my bird down. Immediately they explained that I was a white man, and not entirely amenable to fetish laws ; so that I do not suppose my shot proved anything to them after all." [1]

It is the same in Loango. " I had been presented," writes Pechuël-Loesche, " with a very fine collar, made of hair from the tail of an elephant . . . and adorned with teeth from a sea-fish and a crocodile. These teeth were to preserve me from any danger connected with water. . . . It frequently happened that my boat was upset when I was crossing the bar, and one day I had great difficulty in reaching the shore. I was told quite seriously that it was the teeth alone that had saved me, for without them my swimming powers would not have sufficed to help me clear the heavy breakers. *I was not wearing the collar*, but its efficacy was in no manner of doubt from that fact." [2] The fetish and the medicine-man always have the last word.

Primitive man, therefore, lives and acts in an environment of beings and objects, all of which, in addition to the properties that we recognize them to possess, are endued with mystic attributes. He perceives their objective reality mingled with another reality. He feels himself surrounded by an infinity of imperceptible entities, nearly always invisible to sight, and always redoubtable : ofttimes the souls of the dead are about him, and always he is encompassed by myriads of spirits of more or less defined personality. It is thus at least that the matter is explained by a large number of observers and anthropologists, and they make use of animistic terms to express this. Frazer has collected many instances which tend to show that this phenomenon obtains everywhere among undeveloped peoples.[3] Is it necessary to quote some of them ? " The Oráon's imagination tremblingly wanders in a world of ghosts. Every rock, road, river, and grove is haunted." . . . Sometimes, too, there are " malignant spirits." [4] Like the Santals, Mundas, and the Oráons of Chota-Nagpur, " the Kadars believe themselves to be compassed about by a host of invisible powers, some of whom are thought to be the spirits

---

[1] *Explorations and Adventures in Equatorial Africa*, p. 179.
[2] *Die Loango-Expedition*, iii. 2, p. 352.
[3] *The Golden Bough* (2nd edit.), iii. pp. 41 et seq.
[4] Risley, *Tribes and Castes of Bengal*, ii. pp. 143–5.

of departed ancestors, while others seem to embody nothing more definite than the vague sense of the mysterious and uncanny with which hills, streams, and lonely forests inspire the savage imagination. . . . Their names are legion, and their attributes barely known." [1] In Korea, " spirits occupy every quarter of heaven and every foot of earth. They lie in wait for a man along the wayside, in the trees, on the rocks, in the mountains, valleys, and streams. They keep him under a constant espionage day and night. . . . They are all about him, they dance in front of him, follow behind him, fly over his head and cry out against him from the earth. He has no refuge from them even in his own house, for there they are plastered into or pinned on the walls or tied to the beams. . . . Their ubiquity is an ugly travesty of the omnipresence of God." [2] In China, according to the ancient doctrine, " the universe is filled up in all its parts with legions of *shen* and *kwei.* . . . Every being and every thing that exists is animated either by a *shen*, or by a *kwei*, or by a *shen* and a *kwei* together." [3] With the Fang of East Africa, " spirits are everywhere ; in rocks, trees, forests, and streams ; in fact, for the Fang, this life is one continual fight against spirits corporal and spiritual." [4] " In every action of his daily life," writes Miss Kingsley, " the African negro shows you how he lives with a great, powerful spirit world around him. You will see him before starting out to hunt or fight rubbing medicine into his weapons to strengthen the spirits within them, talking to them the while ; telling them what care he has taken of them, reminding them of the gifts he has given them, though these gifts were hard for him to give, and begging them in the hour of his dire necessity not to fail him. You will see him bending over the face of a river talking to its spirit with proper incantations, asking it when it meets a man who is an enemy of his to upset his canoe, or drown him, or asking it to carry down with it some curse to the village below which has angered him." [5]

Miss Kingsley lays great stress upon the homogeneity of the

[1] Risley, *Tribes and Castes of Bengal*, i. p. 369.
[2] G. H. Jones, " The Spirit Worship in Korea," *Transactions of the Korea Branch of the Royal Asiatic Society*, ii. i. p. 58.
[3] J. J. M. de Groot, *The Religious System of China*, iv. p. 51.
[4] Bennett, " Ethnographical Notes on the Fang," *J.A.I.*, xxix. p. 87.
[5] *West African Studies*, p. 110.

African native's representations of everything. " The African mind naturally approaches all things from a spiritual point of view . . . things happen because of the action of spirit upon spirit." [1] When the doctor applies a remedy " the spirit of the medicine works upon the spirit of the disease." The purely physical effect is beyond the power of conception unless it be allied with the mystic influence. Or rather, we may say that there is no really physical influence, there are only mystic ones. Accordingly it is almost impossible to get these primitives to differentiate, especially when it is a case of an accusation of murder through the practice of witchcraft, for instance. Here is a typical case. " I explain to my native questioner," says Nassau, " that if what the accused has done in fetich rite with intent to kill, had any efficiency in taking away life, I allow that he shall be put to death ; if he made only fetiches, even if they were intended to kill, he is not guilty of this death, for a mere fetich cannot kill. But if he used poison, with or without fetich, he is guilty."

" But even so," adds Nassau, " the distinction between a fetich and a poison is vague in the thought of many natives. What I call a ' poison ' is to them only another material form of a fetich power, both poison and fetich being supposed to be made efficient by the presence of an adjuvant spirit." [2] This means that to their minds the mere fetich kills as certainly as the poison does. More certainly even ; for the poison kills only by virtue of a mystic power of which, in certain circumstances, it may be deprived. The idea of its physical properties which is so clear to the European mind, does not exist for the African.

We thus have good authority for saying that this mentality differs from our own to a far greater extent than the language used by those who are partisans of animism would lead us to think. When they are describing to us a world peopled by ghosts and spirits and phantoms for primitives, we at once realize that beliefs of this kind have not wholly disappeared even in civilized countries. Without referring to spiritualism, we recall the ghost-stories which are so numerous in our folk-lore, and we are tempted to think that the difference is one of degree only. Doubtless such beliefs may be regarded in our

[1] *West African Studies*, p. 330.   [2] *Fetichism in West Africa*, p. 263.

communities as a survival which testifies to an older mental condition, formerly much more general. But we must be careful not to see in them a faithful, though faintly outlined, reflection of the mentality of primitives. Even the most uneducated members of our societies regard stories of ghosts and spirits as belonging to the realm of the supernatural : between such apparitions and magical influences and the data furnished by ordinary perception and the experience of the broad light of day, the line of demarcation is clearly defined. Such a line, however, does not exist for the primitive. The one kind of perception and influence is quite as natural as the other, or rather, we may say that to him there are not two kinds. The superstitious man, and frequently also the religious man, among us, believes in a twofold order of reality, the one visible, palpable, and subordinate to the essential laws of motion ; the other invisible, intangible, " spiritual," forming a mystic sphere which encompasses the first. But the primitive's mentality does not recognize two distinct worlds in contact with each other, and more or less interpenetrating. To him there is but one. Every reality, like every influence, is mystic, and consequently every perception is also mystic.

CHAPTER II

THE LAW OF PARTICIPATION

I

IF the primitives' collective representations differ from ours through their essentially mystic character ; if their mentality as I have endeavoured to show, is oriented in another direction than our own ; we must admit, too, that their representations are not connected with each other as ours would be. Must we then infer that these representations obey some other system of logic than the one which governs our own understanding ? That would be going too far, for such a hypothesis would exceed that which facts warrant us in affirming. Nothing proves that the connections of collective representations must depend solely upon laws of a logical kind. Moreover, the idea of a logic different from our own could only provide us with a negative concept, devoid of meaning. Now as a matter of fact we can at least endeavour to comprehend how representations are connected in the minds of primitives. We understand their language, we make bargains with them, we succeed in interpreting their institutions and their belief : all this shows that there is a possible transition, a practicable method of communication between their mentality and our own.

With these exceptions, however, the mentalities are different, and the disparity becomes the more perceptible as the comparative study advances, and the documentary evidence admits of its being extended. The explorer who travels rapidly through communities of an uncivilized type has no time to probe into this problem ; in fact, he scarcely ever thinks of it as such. First, he ascertains the curious persistence of certain traits of human nature, manifesting themselves in the most varied conditions, and he then expresses

his surprise when brought face to face with methods of thinking and acting of which both the origin and reason escape
him. He leaves to his reader the task of discovering how
these successive impressions may be reconciled, or else he con-
fines himself to some general " explanations " derived from
traditional psychology and logic, if he happens to possess a
smattering of either.

But when we listen to observers who have lived for a
longer time among primitives, and especially those who have
endeavoured to penetrate their method of thinking and
feeling, we hear something quite different. Whether it be
the North American Indians (of whom Cushing and Powell
tell us), the negroes of the French Congo (studied by Miss
Kingsley), the Maoris of New Zealand (known to Elsdon
Best), or any other " primitive " people whatever, a " civilized
being " can never expect to see his thought following exactly
the same course as that of the primitive, nor to find again
the path by which the latter has travelled. " The mentality
of the Maori is of an intensely mystical nature. . . . We
hear of many singular theories about Maori beliefs and Maori
thought, but the truth is that we do not understand either,
and, what is more, we never shall. We shall never know the
inwardness of the native mind. For that would mean retracing
our steps for many centuries, back into the dim past, far back
to the time when we also possessed the mind of primitive
man. And the gates have long closed on that hidden road." [1]

Cushing had acquired a kind of mental " naturalization "
among the Zuñis. Not content with living with, and like,
them for many years, he had made their religious rulers adopt
him and admit him to their secret societies ; in their sacred
ceremonies he, like their priests, had his own rôle, and carried
it out. The unfortunately rare works of his which have been
published give us, however, the feeling of a form of mental
activity with which our own would never exactly correspond.
Our habits of thought are too far removed from those of
the Zuñis. Our language, without which we can conceive
nothing, and which is essential to our reasoning, makes use
of categories which do not coincide with theirs. Lastly and

[1] Elsdon Best, " Maori Medical Lore," *Journal of the Polynesian Society,*
xiii. p. 219 (1904).

chiefly, the ambient social reality, of which the collective representations and, to a certain extent, the language, are functions, is with them too far removed from our own case.

Thus the mentality of inferior peoples, though not so impenetrable as it would be as if it were regulated by a logic different from our own, is none the less not wholly comprehensible to us. We are led to imagine that it does not exclusively obey the laws of *our* logic, nor possibly of any laws which are wholly logical. An analysis of some characteristic phenomena may perhaps serve to throw light on this point.

Observers have frequently collected the arguments, or rather, the connections between representations which have seemed strange and inexplicable to them. I shall quote but a few instances. " A certain drought at Landana was attributed to the missionaries wearing a certain kind of cap during the services : the natives said that this stopped the rain, a great outcry that the missionaries must leave the country was raised. . . . The missionaries showed the native princes their own garden, that their cultivation was being ruined for want of water, and asked if it was probable that they would spoil their own crops. The natives remained unconvinced, and only when the rains at length fell plentifully did the excitement subside." [1] Pechuël-Loesche relates an exactly similar case, and adduces enough analogous facts to allow of our generalizing on the matter. " After the Catholic missionaries had landed, there was a scarcity of rain, and the plantations were suffering from drought. The people at once took it into their heads that this was the fault of these clerics, and especially due to the long robes they wore, for such had never been seen before. There was besides a white horse which had recently been landed, and it had prevented trading, and occasioned many troublesome discussions. A contractor had a great deal of trouble because he had replaced the pole of native wood which was badly warped, upon which his flag was erected, by an upright mast which had just been imported. A shiny mackintosh coat, an unusual hat, a rocking-chair, any instrument whatever, can give rise to disquieting suspicions. The entire coast population may be disturbed at the sight of a sailing-ship with unfamiliar rigging, or a steamer which has

[1] Philips, " The Lower Congo," *J.A.I.*, xvii. p. 220.

one more funnel than the others. If anything vexatious should occur, it is at once attributed to something unusual that has taken place." [1]

In New Guinea, " at the time my wife and I took up our residence in Motumotu," writes Edelfelt, " a kind of pleurisy epidemic prevailed along the coast. . . . Of course my wife and I were accused of bringing the messenger of destruction, and for this loud rumours were about that we—including the Polynesian teachers—should suffer death. . . . Someone or something was still the cause of it, and they blamed a poor unfortunate sheep I had, that was killed to please them ; but the epidemic raged as violently as ever. Now our two goats were blamed ; these animals, however, lived it all out. Finally, they levelled their abuse and accusations against a large picture of Queen Victoria, which hung in our dining-room. Previous to the epidemic appearing people came in from long distances to see this picture, and . . . would . . . look at it several hours at a time. . . . The harmless image of our gracious Queen became eventually . . . an imaginary destroyer of health and life, and they requested me to take the picture down ; to this I did not concede." [2]

At Tanna, in the New Hebrides, " it can hardly be said that there is any sequence of ideas, properly so called. If a person were passing along a path, and some creature (say a snake) fell on him out of a tree, and next day, or the week after, he heard of the death of a son in Queensland, he would connect the two. A turtle came ashore one night and laid a nestful of eggs. It was captured in the act. Such a thing had never taken place in the memory of the people. The conclusion was that Christianity was the cause of the turtle coming ashore to lay its eggs, and the right thing to do was to offer the turtle to the missionary who had brought the worship of Jehovah." [3]

Ideas are linked up in the same way in North America. " One evening, when talking about the animals of the country, I wanted to let them know that we had rabbits and leverets

---

[1] *Die Loango-Expedition*, iii. 2, p. 83.
[2] " Customs and Superstitions of New Guinea Natives," *Proceedings of Royal Geographical Society of Australasia*, Queensland Branch, vii. p. 1 (1891–2).
[3] Gray, " Notes on the Natives of Tanna," *J.A.I.*, xxviii. p. 131.

in France, and I showed them to them by making the shadow on the wall in the firelight. It happened quite by chance that they caught more fish than usual the next morning ; they believed that the shadow pictures I had made for them were the cause of this, and they begged me to do this every evening and to teach them how, a thing which I refused to do, as I would not minister to this foolish superstition of theirs." [1]

Lastly, in New Guinea. " A man returning from hunting or fishing is disappointed at his empty game-bag, or canoe, and turns over in his mind how to discover who would be likely to have bewitched his nets. He perhaps raises his eyes and sees a member of a neighbouring friendly village on his way to pay a visit. It at once occurs to him that this man is the sorcerer, and watching his opportunity, he suddenly attacks him and kills him." [2]

The current explanation of such phenomena consists of saying that primitives apply the principle of causality undiscerningly, and that they confound cause and antecedent. This would be the very common logical fallacy known as the fallacy of *post hoc, ergo propter hoc*. The primitives, we are told, have not the least idea that this can be wrong. That the representations are consecutive in their minds is a sufficient guarantee that they are connected : or rather, they do not consider the connection needs any guarantee. The observers themselves frequently suggest this explanation. " To natives," says Pechuël-Loesche, " there is no such thing as chance. Occurrences which are close together in point of time, even if widely removed in space, readily appear to them to be linked by a causal relation." [3]

It is true, and later on we shall discover the reason for it, that there is no such thing as chance to the primitive. As for the rest, the explanation suggested, if not wholly incorrect, is assuredly incomplete. Primitives are undoubtedly prone, as much as, and possibly more than, civilized beings, to the fallacy of *post hoc, ergo propter hoc*. But in the facts I have quoted, some simple cases from a very large number

[1] Father Sagard, *Le Grand Voyage au Pays des Hurons*, pp. 256–7 (1632).
[2] Guise, " Wangela River, New Guinea," *J.A.I.*, xxviii. p. 212.
[3] *Die Loango-Expedition*, iii. 2, p. 333.

of instances there is something more and something different; it is not merely an artless and erroneous application of the principle of causality. It is not only direct anteriority in time which makes the connection between one fact and another. The sequence perceived or remarked may suggest the connection, but the connection itself is not in any way confused with this sequence. It consists in a mystic relation which the primitive represents to himself—and of which he is convinced as soon as he represents it to himself—between the antecedent and the consequent : the first having the power to produce the second and make it apparent. This is a result of the very facts related by Pechuël-Loesche, if we regard them in the light of what has already been established respecting the mystic properties in the forms taken by persons and things.[1] What effects may not the mystic virtues of a cassock, a steamer with three funnels, a mackintosh, a tent-pole, in short, any unusual object produce ? Who knows the consequences which may arise from their very presence ? "Anything strange is uncanny to the native," say Spencer and Gillen.[2] In the case of Queen Victoria's portrait, the fallacy *post hoc, ergo propter hoc* is obviously an inadequate explanation. The portrait was well known to the natives long before the epidemic broke out. They did not attach any blame to it except in the fourth place, after having successively imputed the outbreak to the missionary, his sheep, and his two goats. If, after that, they laid the trouble at its door, it was undoubtedly because of the magic power they believed to be attaching to this unusual object. The case of the Hurons, related by Sagard, can be similarly explained.

To comprehend facts such as these, and refer them to one common principle, we must go back to the mystic nature of the collective representations in the mentality of undeveloped peoples and look for the same characteristic in the connections between them. The sequence in time is one element of the connection, but it is not always a necessary element, and it is never all-sufficing. If it were otherwise, how could we explain the fact that the most unvarying and most evident

---

[1] Vide Chap. I. pp. 41–43.
[2] *The Northern Tribes of Central Australia*, pp. 31–2.

sequences in phenomena so often escape the notice of primitives ? For instance, " the Ja-Luo believe that the sun goes
back to the east overhead during the night, hidden behind
the heavens. They do not associate the daylight sky with the
light of the sun, but look upon it as something quite distinct,
and asked what became of it at night." [1]

Dobrizhoffer points out that the Abipones are often unable
to comprehend direct and self-evident relations between
cause and effect. " A wound inflicted with a spear often
gapes so wide that it affords ample room for life to go out and
death to come in ; yet if the man dies of the wound, they
really believe him killed, not by a weapon, but by the deadly
arts of the jugglers. . . . They are persuaded that the juggler
will be banished from amongst the living, and made to atone
for their relation's death, if the heart and tongue be pulled
out of the dead man's body immediately after his decease,
roasted at the fire, and given to dogs to devour. Though so
many hearts and tongues are devoured, and they never observe
any of the jugglers die, yet they religiously adhere to the
custom of their ancestors by cutting out the hearts and tongues
of infants and adults of both sexes, as soon as they have
expired." [2]

Thus not only does the time sequence in phenomena of
the most impressive kind often remain unperceived by the
primitive's mind, but he frequently believes firmly in an order
of succession which is not borne out by experience, for experience can no more undeceive primitives than it can teach
them. In an infinite number of cases, as we have seen, their
minds are impervious to experience. Therefore when they
make the cassocks of the missionaries responsible for the
drought, or attribute an epidemic to a portrait, it is not merely
the sequence in point of time which impresses their minds and
becomes a causal relation to them. The mental process
is a different and rather more complex one. That which we
call experience and the natural order of phenomena does not
find in primitives, minds prepared to receive and be impressed
by it. On the contrary, their minds are already preoccupied

[1] Hobley, " British East Africa, Kavirondo and Nandi," *J.A.I.*, xxxiii.
p. 358.
[2] *An Account of the Abipones*, ii. p. 223.

with a large number of collective representations, by virtue of which objects, whatever they may be, living beings, inanimate objects, or articles manufactured by man, always present themselves charged with mystic properties. Consequently while these minds are very often unheedful of the objective relations, they pay great attention to the mystic connections, whether virtual or actual. These preformed connections are not derived from the experience of the present, and experience is powerless against them.

II

Let us then no longer endeavour to account for these connections either by the mental weakness of primitives, or by the association of ideas, or by a naïve application of the principle of causality, or yet by the fallacy *post hoc, ergo propter hoc* ; in short, let us abandon the attempt to refer their mental activity to an inferior variety of our own. Rather let us consider these connections in themselves, and see whether they do not depend upon a general law, a common foundation for those mystic relations which primitive mentality so frequently senses in beings and objects. Now there is one element which is never lacking in such relations. In varying forms and degrees they all involve a " participation " between persons or objects which form part of a collective representation. For this reason I shall, in default of a better term, call the principle which is peculiar to " primitive " mentality, which governs the connections and the preconnections of such representations, *the law of participation*.

At the moment it would be difficult to formulate this law in abstract terms. It will be sufficiently defined in the course of this chapter, although that which we desire to define scarcely enters the ordinary framework of our thought. However, in default of a wholly satisfactory formula, we can make an attempt to approximate it. I should be inclined to say that in the collective representations of primitive mentality, objects, beings, phenomena can be, though in a way incomprehensible to us, both themselves and something other than themselves. In a fashion which is no less incomprehensible, they give forth and they receive mystic powers, virtues, qualities, influences, which make themselves felt outside, without ceasing to remain where they are.

In other words, the opposition between the one and the many, the same and another, and so forth, does not impose upon this mentality the necessity of affirming one of the terms if the other be denied, or vice versa. This opposition is of but secondary interest. Sometimes it is perceived, and frequently, too, it is not. It often disappears entirely before the mystic community of substance in entities which, in our thought, could not be confused without absurdity. For instance, " the Trumai (a tribe of Northern Brazil) say that they are aquatic animals.—The Bororo (a neighbouring tribe) boast that they are red araras (parakeets)." This does not merely signify that after their death they become araras, nor that araras are metamorphosed Bororos, and must be treated as such. It is something entirely different. " The Bororos," says Von den Steinen, who would not believe it, but finally had to give in to their explicit affirmations, " give one rigidly to understand that they are araras *at the present time,* just as if a caterpillar declared itself to be a butterfly." [1] It is not a name they give themselves, nor a relationship that they claim. What they desire to express by it is actual identity. That they can be both the human beings they are and the birds of scarlet plumage at the same time, Von den Steinen regards as inconceivable, but to the mentality that is governed by the law of participation there is no difficulty in the matter. All communities which are totemic in form admit of collective representations of this kind, implying similar identity of the individual members of a totemic group and their totem.

From the dynamic standpoint also, the creation of entities and phenomena, the manifestation of such and such an occurrence, are the result of a mystic influence which is communicated, under conditions themselves of mystic nature, from one being or object to another. They depend upon a participation which is represented in very varied forms : contact, transference, sympathy, telekinesis, etc. In many aggregates of an undeveloped type the abundance of game, fish, or fruit, the regularity of the seasons, and the rainfall, are connected

[1] K. von den Steinen, *Unter den Naturvölkern Zentralbrasiliens,* pp. 305-6.

with the performance of certain ceremonies by individuals destined thereto, or to the presence or to the well-being of a sacred personality who possesses a special mystic power. Or yet again, the newborn child feels the effects of everything its father does, what he eats, etc. The Indian, out hunting or engaged in warfare, is fortunate or unfortunate according to whether his wife, left behind in the camp, eats, or abstains from eating, certain foods, or is doing or not doing certain things. The collective representations abound in relations of this nature. What we call the natural relation of cause and effect passes unnoticed, or is of but slight importance. It is the mystic participations which are in the front rank, and frequently occupy the whole field.

On this account the mentality of primitives may be called *prelogical* with as good reason as it may be termed *mystic*. These are two aspects of the same fundamental quality, rather than two distinct characteristics. If we take the content of the representations more particularly into account, we shall call it mystic—and, if the connections are the chief consideration, we pronounce it prelogical. By *prelogical* we do not mean to assert that such a mentality constitutes a kind of antecedent stage, in point of time, to the birth of logical thought. Have there ever existed groups of human or pre-human beings whose collective representations have not yet been subject to the laws of logic ? We do not know, and in any case, it seems to be very improbable. At any rate, the mentality of these undeveloped peoples which, for want of a better term, I call *prelogical*, does not partake of that nature. It is not *antilogical*; it is not *alogical* either. By designating it " prelogical " I merely wish to state that it does not bind itself down, as our thought does, to avoiding contradiction. It obeys the law of participation first and foremost. Thus oriented, it does not expressly delight in what is contradictory (which would make it merely absurd in our eyes), but neither does it take pains to avoid it. It is often wholly indifferent to it, and that makes it so hard to follow.

As has been said, these characteristics apply only to the collective representations and their connections. Considered as an individual, the primitive, in so far as he thinks and acts independently of these collective representations where possible, will usually feel, argue and act as we should expect him to do. The inferences he draws will be just those which would seem reasonable to us in like circumstances. If he has brought down two birds, for instance, and only picks up one, he will ask himself what has become of the other, and will look for it. If rain overtakes and inconveniences him, he will seek shelter. If he encounters a wild beast, he will strive his utmost to escape, and so forth. But though on occasions of this sort primitives may reason as we do, though they follow a course similar to the one we should take (which in the more simple cases, the most intelligent among the animals would also do), it does not follow that their mental activity is always subject to the same laws as ours. In fact, as far as it is collective, it has laws which are peculiar to itself, and the first and most universal of these is the law of participation.

The very material upon which this mental activity is exercised has already undergone the influence of the law of participation, for we must realize that their collective representations are very different from our concepts. The latter, the material with which our logical thought works, are themselves the result, as we know, of previous operations of a similar kind. The mere expression of a general abstract term, such as man, animal, organism, virtually connotes a number of separate judgments which involve definite relations between many concepts. But the collective representations of primitives are not, like our concepts, the result of intellectual processes properly so called. They contain, as integral parts, affective and motor elements, and above all they imply, in the place of our conceptual inclusions or exclusions, participations which are more or less clearly defined, but, as a general rule, very vividly sensed.

Why, for example, should a picture or portrait be to the primitive mind something quite different from what it is to ours? Whence comes that attributing of mystic properties to it, of which we have just had an instance? Evidently from the fact that every picture, every reproduction " participates " in the nature, properties, life of that of which it is the image. This participation is not to be understood as a share—as if the portrait, for example, involved a fraction of the whole of the properties or the life which the model

possesses. Primitive mentality sees no difficulty in the belief
that such life and properties exist in the original and in its
reproduction *at one and the same time*. By virtue of the
mystic bond between them, a bond represented by the law
of participation, the reproduction *is* the original, as the Bororo
are the araras. Therefore one may obtain from the one what
one gets from the other ; one may influence the second by
influencing the first. For this reason, if the Mandan chiefs
let Catlin take their portrait, they will not sleep quiet in
their graves. Why is this ? Because, by virtue of an inevitable participation, anything that happens to their pictures,
delivered over to strange hands, will be felt by them after
their death. And why is the tribe so uneasy at the idea that
the repose of their chiefs should be thus disturbed ? Evidently
—though Catlin does not tell us so—it is because the welfare
of the tribe, its prosperity, its very existence depend, by
virtue of this same participation, upon the condition of its
chiefs, whether living or dead.

The same argument applies to the other collective representations, the mystic character of which we have already
demonstrated : those concerning a man's name and his
shadow, for instance. There is one which we should dwell
on particularly, however, because it serves as a rallying-
point for the entire theory of primitive mentality. It is
the representation of the " soul," the starting-point of the
doctrine known as animism, the principles of which Tylor
formulates thus : " It seems as though thinking men, as
yet at a low level of culture, were deeply impressed by two
groups of biological problems. In the first place, what is it
that makes the difference between the living body and the dead
one ? What causes waking, sleep, trance, disease, death ?
In the second place, what are those human shapes which
appear in dreams and visions ? Looking at these two groups
of phenomena, the ancient savage philosophers probably made
their first step to the obvious inference that every man has
two things belonging to him, namely, his life and his phantom.
These two are evidently in close connection with the body,
the life as enabling him to feel and think and act, the phantom
as being his image or second self ; both, also, are perceived
to be things separable from the body, the life as able to **go**

away and leave it insensible or dead, the phantom as appearing to people at a distance from it, The second step . . . merely the combining the life and the phantom. As both belong to the body, why should they not also belong to one another, and be manifestations of one and the same soul ? . . . This, at any rate, corresponds with the actual conception of the personal soul or spirit among the lower races, which may be defined as follows : a thin unsubstantial human image, in its nature a sort of vapour, film or shadow ; the cause of life and thought in the individual it animates, independently possessing the personal conscience and volition of its corporal owner, past or present ; capable of leaving the body far behind, to flash swiftly from place to place ; mostly impalpable and invisible, yet also manifesting physical power, and especially the appearing to men, waking or asleep, as a phantasm separate from the body to which it bears a likeness ; continuing to exist and appear to men after the death of that body ; able to enter into, possess, and act in the bodies of other men, animals, and even of things. . . . These are doctrines answering in the most forcible way to the plain evidence of men's senses, as interpreted by a fairly consistent and rational primitive philosophy." [1]

It is indeed a favourite idea of Tylor's that animism is a doctrine which is all the more consistent and satisfactory from the logical standpoint, the nearer to its source that we can view it, that is, in its most primitive form. Later, when complicated by new elements and endeavouring to resolve more subtle problems and to generalize, it becomes obscure and entangled. At its source, its clarity is absolute because it imposes itself, so to speak, on the naïve reflection of the " savage philosopher " when faced by the facts. And the satisfaction which this philosopher would find in his hypothesis is savoured by the savant of to-day in his turn, when he affirms that this hypothesis is the spontaneous and universal product of an intellectual activity which is always identical at bottom, and which, like his own, is impelled by the rational need for supplying an answer to the problems which the facts propound to the intelligence.

It is a very seductive theory, and it seems as if, were we

[1] *Primitive Culture*, i. pp. 428–9 (4th edit., 1903).

in the place of the " savage philosopher," we should reason as
he does—that is, as we make him reason. But have such
" savage philosophers " ever existed ? Do the collective
representations of the soul in the lower races constitute a sort
of doctrine born of the necessity for resolving biological
problems ? Nothing seems more unlikely. Nothing seems more
improbable even, if it be certain that the mentality of such
races is oriented differently from our own, and that their
collective representations are, above all, mystical by nature,
primitives being much more concerned about the mystic
virtues inherent in things than about the logical coherence
of their own thought. That is why, the more rational and
consecutive this primitive " philosophy " of the soul becomes,
the more reason will there be to fear that, in spite of the
amount of evidence collected and the skill of those who interpret it, it will still be very far removed from that which it
pretends to explain.

As a matter of fact, in almost every case where there has
been an adequately prolonged and careful investigation, we
must abandon the happy simplicity of " one and the same
soul " manifesting itself as "life on the one side and phantom
on the other." The collective representations offer something
much more complex and far less easy to " explain."

To take a few examples from the West Coast of Africa,
Ellis has found a number of collective representations which
do not tally in any way (as he himself expressly states) with
the idea of a soul such as Tylor has defined, quoted above.
The natives, says Ellis, distinguish the *kra* from the *srahman*.
" The *kra* existed before the birth of the man, probably
as the *kra* of a long series of men, and after his death it will
equally continue its independent career, either by entering a
newborn human body, or that of an animal, or by wandering
about the world as a *sisa* or *kra* without a tenement. The
general idea is that the *sisa* always seeks to return to a human
body and again become a *kra*, even taking advantage of the
temporary absence of a *kra* from its tenement to take its place.
. . . The *kra* can quit the body it inhabits at will, and return
to it again. Usually it only quits it during sleep, and the
occurrences dreamed of are believed to be the adventures of
the *kra* during its absence. The *srahman* or ghost-man only

commences its career when the corporeal man dies, and it simply continues in the Dead-land, the existence the corporal man formerly led in the world. Thus we must consider separately (1) the man ; (2) the indwelling spirit or *kra* ; (3) the ghost or *srahman*, though in another form the last is only the continuation of the first in shadowy form."

This differentiation is applied in every case. " When the bush is torn up and withers, the *kra* (so to speak) of the bush enters a seedling bush, or a seed, and the ghost-bush goes to Dead-land. Similarly, the *kra* (so to speak) of the sheep, when that sheep is killed, enters a newborn lamb, and the ghost-sheep goes to Dead-land for the use of ghost-men. . . . Dead-land itself, its mountains, forests, and rivers are, the Tshi-speaking negro holds, the ghosts of similar natural features which formerly existed in the world."

The *kra*, therefore, is not the soul. " The soul, in the accepted sense of the word, is the ' animating, separable, surviving entity,' the ' vehicle of individual personal existence ' (Tylor), whereas every *kra* has been the indwelling spirit of many men, and probably will be of many more. The *kra* in some respects resembles a guardian spirit, but it is more than that. Its close connection with the man is indicated by the fact of its nocturnal adventures during its absence from the body being remembered by that man when he awakes. The latter even feels physically the effect of his *kra's* actions, and when a negro awakes feeling stiff and unrefreshed, or with limbs aching from muscular rheumatism, he invariably attributes these symptoms to the fact of his *kra* having been engaged in some struggle with another, or in some severe toil. . . . It has, though doubtless in a shadowy form, the very shape and appearance of the man, and both the mind and the body of the latter are affected by, and register the results of, the *kra's* actions."

" When the *kra* leaves the body of the man it inhabits, that man suffers no physical inconvenience ; it goes out, when he is asleep, without his knowledge, and if it should leave him when he is awake, he is only made aware of its departure by a sneeze or a yawn. When, however, the soul, ' the vehicle of personal individual existence,' leaves the body, that body falls into a condition of suspended animation ;

it is cold, pulseless, and apparently lifeless. Sometimes, though rarely, the soul returns after such an absence, and then the man has been in a swoon or trance ; more generally it does not return ; then the man is dead." [1]

How therefore are we to regard the relations of a man with his *kra* which certainly, as Ellis tells us, is not his soul ? It is equally incorrect to say that his *kra* is himself and that he is not himself. It is not the individual, for it existed before him and survives him ; it is nevertheless not himself, for upon awaking the individual remembers what the *kra* has done, endured, and suffered during the night. If we persist in submitting these representations to the claims of logical thought, we shall not only not discover in them the " consistent and rational philosophy " which Tylor and his school expect, but they will remain unintelligible. On the other hand, we shall understand them to the extent to which they may be " understood," if we refer them to the general law of participation. The individual, while living, participates in the *kra* that inhabits him, that is, he to a certain extent is this *kra*, and at the same time he is not : for the actual contradiction does not disturb his prelogical mentality. At the moment of death, this participation comes to an end. [2]

Representations which are just as involved are to be found in most undeveloped aggregates. Since they did not suggest any meaning which investigators could accept (judging them as they did by the rules of logical thought) these writers frequently tried to guard against absurdity by supposing that primitives admitted of several souls. It thus became possible to distribute among these that which would have been irreconcilable and incompatible in a single one. Spencer and Gillen, for instance, refer frequently to multiple souls in dealing with the tribes of Central Australians. [3] Among the natives of the Torres Straits, Haddon speaks of parts of

[1] A. B. Ellis, *The Ewe-speaking Peoples*, pp. 15–21, 106. Cf. *The Tshi-speaking Peoples*, p. 149.

[2] Traces of representations of this kind were found among the Greeks who, according to Rohde (*Psyche*, i. pp. 4, 6, 257 ; ii. pp. 141, 157, 183–4, 304–5), distinguished between a vital principle, a soul or shade in Hades after death, and another principle, which inhabited the body during life, but which neither disease nor death could affect.

[3] *The Native Tribes of Central Australia*, p. 515 ; *The Northern Tribes of Central Australia*, p. 450.

the soul. " There was a belief that part of the *mari* left at death, and part remained until frightened away." [1] In North America, a plurality of souls seems to be the rule. " They distinguish four souls in the same body. An old man told us sometime ago that some natives had two or three souls, and that his own had left him more than two years before, to go away with his dead parents, and that he now only possessed the soul of his body, which would go down to the grave with him. By this we know that they imagine that the body has a soul of its own, which some call the soul of their nation (?) and that besides there are others which leave it sooner or later according to their fancy." [2] " It is believed by some of the Hidatsa that every human being has four souls in one. They account for the phenomenon of gradual death where the extremities are apparently dead while consciousness remains, by supposing the four souls to depart, one after another, at different times. When dissolution is complete, they say that all the souls are gone, and have joined together again outside of the body." [3]—" The Mandan believe that each person has several spirits dwelling within him ; one of which is black, another brown, and a third light-coloured, the last alone returning to the Lord of Life."[4] The Dacotans recognize four : " (1) a spirit of the body, which dies with the body ; (2) a spirit which always remains with or near the body ; (3) the soul which accounts for the deeds of the body and is supposed by some to go south or by others west. The fourth always lingers with the small bundle of the hair of the deceased, kept by the relatives until they have a chance to throw it into the enemy's country, when it becomes a roving spirit, bringing disease and death." [5] Some Sioux even admit of five souls. In British Columbia, " man is believed to have four souls. The main soul is said to have the shape of a mannikin, the others are the shadows of the first. In disease either the lesser souls or the main one leave the body. Shamans can easily return the shadows, but not the main soul. If the latter leaves the body the sick one must die. After death the main soul goes to the sunset, and here it remains. The

[1] " The Western Tribes of Torres Straits," *J.A.I.*, xix. p. 317.
[2] *Relations du Père Lejeune*, p. 146 (1630).
[3] Dorsey, " Siouan Cults," *E. B. Rept.*, xi. p. 517.
[4] Ibid., p. 512.   [5] Lynd, cited by Dorsey, ibid., p. 484.

shadows become ghosts. They revisit the places which the deceased frequented during lifetime, and continue to do the same actions which he did when alive." [1]

These reports, to which we might add many others, are far from being unanimous regarding the functions of the various souls. Nevertheless they all attest a multiplicity of souls in the same individual, and diversity in the functions of these souls. They indicate, too, though less regularly and clearly, that the fate of these souls is not the same after death. Is it not permissible to imagine that this multiplicity is pre-eminently expressive of the impossibility which the investigators found in reconciling what the " savages " had told them, with their own preconceived ideas upon the soul ? Gross misunderstanding and misconstruction were inevitable. The missionaries and explorers were making use of terms (soul, spirit, ghost, etc.) defined for them by prolonged evolution in religion, philosophy, and literature, and they found themselves dealing with collective representations which were essentially mystic and prelogical, not yet reduced to a conceptual form, and paying very little regard to logical laws. Consequently nearly all they report needs to be revised and corrected. As a general rule, an observer's report is the more suspect, the more readily it agrees with the current conception of the soul. On the other hand, observations frequently manifest a characteristic obscurity, or even present an inextricable confusion, which is a faithful reflection of the perplexity felt by their authors.

I shall quote but two instances. " It is difficult to say precisely what the Fijians believe to be the essence of the immortal part of a man. The word ' yalo ' has the following meanings. Yalo (with pronoun-suffixed) means Mind, as Yalo-ngu. Yalo (with possessive pronoun separated) means Shade or Spirit. Yaloyalo means Shadow. From the possessive pronoun being suffixed we may gather that the mind was regarded as being as intimately connected with a man's body as his arm, but that the spirit could be detached from it." [2] Among the Yakuts, " the elementary soul of the object in

[1] F. Boas, " The North-western Tribes of Canada," *Reports of the British Association*, p. 461 (1894).

[2] B. A. Thompson, " The Ancestor Gods of the Fijians," *J.A.I.*, xxiv. p. 354 (note).

general (*ichchi*) which, it appears, merely expresses the fact of existence, differs from the soul of living things (*sur*). Life begins when respiration begins (*ty*). Living objects have a double soul therefore—*ichchi* and *sur* ; animals when dead or even ill lose their *sur* and preserve their *ichchi* alone, and in the case of death this disappears also. Men, and among animals, horses alone, have a triple soul : *ichchi*, *sur*, and the ' *kut*.' The human *kut* is small, no larger than a little piece of coal. Sometimes the shaman summons from beneath the earth, in the left or female part of the house, the *kut* of those who are sick. . . . The *kut* sometimes abandons man during his sleep, and wanders afar. If some misfortune befalls it during its travels, its owner falls ill. The *kut* is like a faint picture, like the shadow. As the shadow has three parts, one large and faint, one small and darker, and the centre quite black, so man has three souls. When he loses one, he suffers from a feeling of uneasiness ; when he loses two, he becomes ill ; and when he loses all three, he dies." [1] The confusion in this report and the evident impossibility of reconciling the different parts with the definitions given are very significant : they may however help us to understand what this pretended plurality of souls really amounts to.

It is noteworthy that without thinking of a prelogical and mystic mentality, without even having made any research into the problem which occupies my mind, Pechuël-Loesche should have arrived at the same conclusion, touching the plurality of souls, as I do. " If we were generalizing hastily," he says in conclusion, " we might speak of a belief in two souls, or even in three or four. The first would be power (Potenz) the creative principle (the essence of the ancestors passing to their descendants), possibly also part of the universal soul. Then there would be the personal or individual soul ; finally the dream-soul, and the wandering or desert-soul (Wildnisseele). But such a conception would be incorrect." [2] In my opinion, these various souls express " participations," irreducible to logical intelligibility, but the most natural thing in the world to prelogical mentality. We

---

[1] Sieroshewiski, *Douze Ans chez les Yakoutes*, cited *J.A.I.*, xxxi. p. 108 (note).
[2] *Die Loango-Expedition*, iii. 2, pp. 296–300.

can find sufficient evidence upon the subject of the desert-soul, which is what Miss Kingsley calls the "bush-soul."

The negroes of Calabar, she says, suppose there to be four souls : " (a) the soul that survives death, (b) the shadow on the path, (c) the dream-soul, and (d) the bush-soul. This bush-soul is always in the form of an animal in the forest—never of a plant. Sometimes when a man sickens it is because his bush-soul is angry at being neglected, and a witch-doctor is called in, who, having diagnosed this as being cause of the complaint, advises the administration of some kind of offering to the offended one. . . . The bush-souls of a family are usually the same for a man and his sons, for a mother and her daughters. . . . Sometimes all the children take the mother's, sometimes all take the father's. . . ." [1] " This bush-soul may be in only an earth pig, or it may be in a leopard, and . . . no layman can see his own soul. It is not as if it were even connected with all earth pigs or all leopards, as the case may be, but it is in one particular earth pig or leopard or other animal. . . . If his bush-soul dies, the man it is connected with dies. Therefore if the hunter who has killed it can be found out—a thing a witch-doctor cannot do unless he happens by chance to have had his professional eye on that bush-soul at the time of the catastrophe ; . . . that hunter has to pay compensation to the family of the deceased. On the other hand, if the man belonging to the bush-soul dies, the bush-soul animal has to die too." [2] Miss Kingsley has collected very detailed information about the diseases of this bush-soul, as well as those of the dream-soul, and of the treatment that such diseases require.

There was an exactly similar idea existing in Central America. Of the Guatemaltecs Gage tells the following quaint story : " Many are deluded by the Devil to believe that their life dependeth upon the life of such and such a beast (which they take unto them as their familiar spirit) and think that when that beast dieth they must die ; when he is chased, their hearts pant ; when he is faint, they are faint . . ." [3] This evidently refers to a forest-soul.

[1] *Travels in West Africa*, pp. 459–60.
[2] *West African Studies*, pp. 209–10.
[3] Bancroft, *The Native Races of the Pacific States of North America*, iii. p. 129.

We accordingly find nothing among primitives which exactly corresponds with the single soul which, according to Tylor, can manifest itself in the double form of vital principle and of phantom. Undoubtedly they everywhere believe in the objective reality of what they see in dreams, and everywhere, too, they are convinced that the ghosts of the dead return, at least for some time, to haunt the places in which they dwelt while living. But what we have just learnt about this proves indeed that their collective representations on this matter do not proceed from any need to account for these apparitions by a uniform concept of the " soul." On the contrary, I should say that originally (to the extent that such a term is permissible) the idea of a soul is not found among primitives. That which takes its place is the representation, usually a very emotional one, of one or more co-existent and intertwined participations, as yet not merged into the distinct consciousness of an individuality which is really one. The member of a tribe, totem, or clan, feels himself mystically united with the animal or vegetable species which is his totem, mystically united with his dream-soul, his forest-soul, and so on.

These communions, the intensity of which is renewed and increased at certain times (the sacred ceremonies, rites of initiation, and so forth), by no means exclude each other. They have no need to be expressed in definite terms to be profoundly felt, and felt by every member of the group. Later, when these rites and ceremonies have gradually ceased to be understood, and then to be practised, such participations retained in customs and myths will fall, so to speak, into the form of " multiple souls," as has happened in the case of the Calabar negroes, so carefully studied by Miss Kingsley. And later still, nearer our own times, as the example of the Greeks show, these multiple souls will in their turn be crystallized into a single soul, not without the distinction between the vital principle and the spiritual inhabitant of the body still remaining apparent. In short, the " soul " properly so called, which serves as the starting-point, of Tylor's theory, and which is, according to him, the object of the savage's primitive philosophy, does not appear, according to my view of the matter, except in peoples of a relatively advanced type. If he has referred it so far back it is not because he did not know the facts, for Tylor himself quotes a number of cases in which the multiplicity of " souls " is expressly mentioned. But his interpretation of these facts was, as it were, imposed upon him by his postulate, according to which the mentality of lower races obeys the same logical laws as our own thought. Let us abandon this postulate, and at once the mystical and pre-logical nature of this mentality appears, and with it the law of participation which governs its collective representations. From this it follows too that the concept of the soul can no longer be considered save as the product of thought which is already somewhat advanced, and not yet known to primitive peoples.

III

It scarcely ever happens that the primitive mind acquires its collective representations in an isolated state, apart from the connections with which they are usually bound up. The mystic character which attaches to them necessarily involves relations, which are also mystic, between the various objects of their thought. We may then admit *a priori*, as it were, that the same law of participation which governs the formation of the collective representations, rules the connections existing between them. To establish this position, it will be necessary to study the method in which the main inter-relations between persons and things do actually occur in the prelogical mind.

In the first place, the very existence of the social groups, in its relations with that of the individuals which compose them, is most frequently represented (and felt at the same time) as a participation, a communion, or rather, a number of participations and communions. This characteristic is apparent in all the primitive societies about which we have fairly detailed and reliable information. It has been fully demonstrated in the two volumes on the tribes of Central Australia by Spencer and Gillen. Among the Aruntas " each individual is the direct incarnation of an Alcheringa ancestor or of the spirit part of some Alcheringa animal. . . . The totem of any man is regarded . . . as the same thing as himself. . . . Each totemic group is supposed to have a direct control over the numbers of the animal or plant the name of which he bears. . . ."[1] Lastly, each totem is mystically bound to a strictly defined locality or portion in space which is always occupied by the spirits of the totemic ancestors, and this is called " local relationship."[2]

The collective representation in this case is exactly like that which so astonished Von den Steinen when the Bororos " rigidly " maintained that they were araras, and the Trumai that they *were* aquatic animals. Every individual *is* both such and such a man or woman, alive at present, a certain ancestral individual, who may be human or semi-human, who lived in the fabulous age of the Alcheringa, and at the same time he *is* his totem, that is, he partakes in mystic fashion of the essence of the animal or vegetable species whose name he bears. The verb " to be " (which moreover is non-existent in most of the languages of undeveloped peoples) has not here the ordinary copulative sense it bears in our languages. It signifies something different, and something more. It encompasses both the collective representation and the collective consciousness in a participation that is actually lived, in a kind of symbiosis effected by identity of essence. This is the reason that the members of a definite totemic group alone have the power to carry out the *intichiuma* ceremonies, the aim of which is to secure a regular reproduction of a certain animal or plant species.[3] This explains, too, the performances, ceremonies, dances (with or without masks, painted decorations, costumes, tattooings) which are to be met with in many primitive peoples, and which are designed to attain the same end—the bison dances of the North American Indians, stag dances of the Huichol Mexicans, the serpent dances of the Zuñis and in other *pueblos*, for instance.

With the Australian tribes, we may say that Spencer and Gillen have put a finger on the very spot, not only revealing the mystic and at the same time utilitarian significance of the *intichiuma* ceremonies, but the intimate relation which exists between the individual, his totemic group and his totemic species, a relation which cannot be expressed by a concept,

---

[1] *The Native Tribes of Central Australia*, pp. 202–4.
[2] Ibid., pp. 303, 544. [3] Ibid., pp. 169–70

just because the wholly mystic relation consists of a participation which cannot be comprised within the limits of logical thought. "At the first glance it looks much as if all that they intended to represent was the behaviour of certain animals, but the ceremonies have a much deeper meaning, for each performer represents an ancestral individual who lived in the Alcheringa. . . . It is as a reincarnation of the never-dying spirit part of one of their semi-animal ancestors that every member of the tribe is born, and therefore, when born he, or she, bears of necessity the name of the animal or plant to which the Alcheringa ancestor was a transformation or a descendant." [1] The ceremonies and dances, therefore, are intended to revive and maintain, by means of the nervous exaltation and ecstasy of movement not wholly unlike that seen in more advanced societies, the community of essence in which the actual individual, the ancestral being living again in him, and the animal or plant species that forms his totem, are all mingled. To our minds, there are necessarily three distinct realities here, however close the relationship may be. To the primitive minds, the three make but one, yet at the same time are three.

In this way the influence which the ceremonies exercise over the totemic species is more than direct : it is *immanent*. How can the primitive doubt their effective power ? The most invincible logical certitude gives way before the symbiotic feeling which is an accompaniment of collective representations thus lived and translated into action.

Another aspect of this participation or rather communion is revealed by the part played in the life of the individual and of the community among the Aruntas, by the sacred objects known as *churinga*. These things (pieces of wood or stone of an oblong shape, and generally decorated with mystic designs) are most carefully preserved and deposited in a sacred place which women and children dare not approach. Every totemic group has its own, and from the standpoint of logical thought it would be very difficult to define exactly what *churinga* are, or are not. The external souls of individuals ; the vehicles of ancestral spirits and possibly the bodies of these ancestors themselves ; extracts of totemic essence ;

[1] *The Native Tribes of Central Australia*, p. 228.

reservoirs of vitality—they are all of these in turn and simultaneously. The recognition of their mystic power attains its highest intensity at the moment of the initiation ceremonies, which we shall examine in detail later.[1] At this stage, however, I may note, on Spencer and Gillen's authority, the deep religious respect which surrounds the *churinga*, the care taken to preserve them, and the veneration and precaution with which they are handled. " During the whole time the presence of the *churinga* " (which had been lent to a neighbouring tribe, and were being examined on their return) " seems to produce a reverent silence as if the natives really believed that the spirits of the dead men to whom they have belonged in times past were present, and no one, while they were being examined, ever spoke in tones louder than a whisper." [2] Everywhere, the very expressions used by investigators suggest the idea of participation. " A man who possesses such a *churinga* as the *churinga* snake one will constantly rub it with his hand, singing as he does so about the Alcheringa history of the snake, and gradually comes to feel that there is some special association between him and the sacred object —that a virtue of some kind passes from it to him and also from him to it." [3] Can we be surprised, therefore, that the *churinga* is represented, or rather, felt, to be a living being ? It is something very different from a piece of wood or stone. It is intimately connected with the ancestor ; it has emotions as we have, and these can be calmed when it is stroked with the hand, in the same way in which those of living people may be soothed.[4]

From a participation which is directly represented and actually felt, such as described by Von den Steinen and by Spencer and Gillen, it is an easy transition to the belief, which is so common in undeveloped races, in a relationship between men and animals, or rather, between certain groups of men and certain predetermined animals. Such beliefs are often expressed in myths. Among the Aruntas, Spencer and Gillen collected a number of legends relating to semi-human or semi-animal beings, which establish a living transition between

[1] Vide Chap. VIII. pp. 354–8.
[2] *The Native Tribes of Central Australia*, p. 303.
[3] *The Northern Tribes of Central Australia*, pp. 277–8.
[4] Ibid., p. 265 (note).

the two classes. Very frequently, too, the expressions used by the observers are significant. Thus, in describing a totemic ceremony, it is said : " The particular rat-man or man-rat—for, as already said, the identity of the human individual is sunk in that of the object with which he is associated, and from which he is supposed to have originated—to whom this ceremony referred, is supposed to have travelled to Walyirra, where he died, and where his spirit remained associated as usual with the *churinga*." [1] Spencer and Gillen find in these mythical ideas " a crude attempt to describe the origin of human beings out of non-human creatures who were of various forms ; some of them were representations of animals, others of plants, but in all cases they were to be regarded as intermediate stages in the transition of an animal or plant ancestor into the human individual who bears its name as that of his or her totem." [2]

Among the peoples who are more advanced in development, the idea of these mythical animals is slightly different. The ancestors of the totemic group are not exactly like animals that exist to-day, but they have a mystic share of both the animal and the human nature. The primitives project upon them, as it were, the participation which forms the union between the social group and its totemic animal. In British Columbia, for instance, " I sought to learn from him (i.e. the usual informant) whether his people were known as the otter-people, and whether they looked upon the otter as their relatives, and paid regard to these animals by not killing or hunting them. He smiled at the question and shook his head, and later explained that although they believed their remote ancestor to have been an otter, they did not think it was the same kind of otter as lived now. The otters from which they were descended were otter-people, not animals, who had the power to change from the forms of men and women to those of the otter. All the animals in the old-time were like that, they were not just common animals and nothing else ; they were people as well and could take the human or the animal form at will, by putting on or taking off the skin or other natural clothing of the animal. . . . Among the Thompsons they have a distinct term in their

---

[1] *The Native Tribes of Central Australia*, p. 231.   [2] Ibid., p. 392.

language by which these mystic beings are distinguished from ordinary animals." [1]

Here again mystic participations account for relationships that the lower races consider as natural and evident, however absurd and unimaginable they appear to European investigators. Du Chaillu tells us that the African " king Quengueza refused to eat the meat offered him. ' It is *roondah* for me.' He explained that the meat of the *Bos brachicheros* was forbidden to his family, and was an abomination to them, for the reason that many generations ago one of their women gave birth to a calf instead of a child. I laughed, but the king replied very soberly that he could show me a woman of another family whose grandmother had given birth to a crocodile, for which reason the crocodile was *roondah* to that family. . . . They are religiously scrupulous on this matter . . . scarce a man is to be found to whom some article of food is not *roondah*." [2] There is no need to lay stress on such beliefs, for they are excessively general, and experience, in the rare cases in which it can be appealed to, proves powerless against them Rajah Brooke tells of a man who had had his leg mutilated by an alligator, despite his mystic relationship with that animal. " I asked him if he had since retaliated on the alligator tribe. He replied, ' No ; I never wish to kill an alligator, as the dreams of my forefathers have always forbidden such acts ; and I can't tell why an alligator should have attacked me, unless he mistook me for a stranger, and that was the reason the spirits saved my life.' " [3]

When a social group or an individual thus considers itself solidary with, or related to, a totemic animal, when he or it objectifies this participation in the actual relations with the animal, does it signify the animal species considered in its entirety and, so to speak, in an abstract fashion, or all the members of the species considered collectively, or is it a certain animal in particular ? This question presents logical thought with hypotheses which are distinct and mutually exclusive, and we have to choose between them. Prelogical mentality, however, hardly ever separates them (except in the case of the

---

[1] Hill Tout, " The Halkomelem of British Columbia," *J.A.I.*, xxiv. p. 325.
[2] *Equatorial Africa*, pp. 308–9 ; *J.A.I.*, xxiv. p. 325.
[3] *Ten Years in Sarawak*, i. p. 235.

" forest-soul " given above) just because the law of participation, which mainly governs them, allows of his thinking of
the individual in the collective and the collective in the individual without any difficulty. Between the bear and bears,
and the bison and bisons, and one fish and fish in general,
such a mentality pictures a mystic participation, and neither
the species as a whole nor the individual existence of its representatives means the same to him as it would do to us.

Are the honours so frequently paid in ceremonious style
to an animal killed in the chase, meant for that animal in
particular, or for the spirit of the genus whose goodwill must
be secured ? There is no alternative in the case : such
honours are paid to both, as one and indivisible. " A Frenchman having one day thrown away a mouse which he had
just caught, a little girl picked it up, intending to eat it. The
child's father snatched it from her and began to caress the
dead animal affectionately. . . . ' I am doing this,' he said,
' so that the spirit of the mouse may not trouble my child
when she has eaten it.' " [1] This guardian spirit, interpreted
as a concept for rational thought, is a relation which in reality
can find no expression in its categories : it is the interpretation
of a participating relation between the individual animal
and the collective. And this participation does not find its
reason and its proof, as it seems to us, in the identity of
anatomical structure or physiological function, of external
characteristics which are apparent and can be verified by
experience : it is conceived and felt " in terms of spirit "
like every reality which the prelogical mind perceives. To
such a mind that which is of supreme interest in the animal
(setting aside the need of obtaining food from it ; and even
eating the flesh of an animal is above all participating mystically in its nature), is not its visible form or qualities ; it
is the spirit of which it is the manifestation, upon which the
mystic relations of this animal (whether regarded individually
or collectively, matters little), with the human groups in
question depend. Invisible and intangible, this " spirit "
is at once in each and all. Such " multipresence " proves
no stumbling-block to prelogical mentality.

[1] Charlevoix, *Journal d'un Voyage dans l'Amérique Septentrionale,* iii.
pp. 299–300.

Bancroft relates a Californian belief, which seems incredible to him, and which throws strong light upon the mystic participation between the individual and the species. " They called this bird (the buzzard) the *panes*, and once every year they had a festival of the same name, in which the principal ceremony was the killing of a buzzard without losing a drop of its blood. It was next skinned, all possible care being taken to preserve the feathers entire. . . . Last of all the body was buried within the sacred enclosure amid great apparent grief from the old women, they mourning as over the loss of relative or friend. Tradition explained this : the *panes* had indeed been once a woman, whom, wandering in the mountain ways, the great god Chinigchinich had come suddenly upon and changed into a bird. How this was connected with the killing of her every year anew by the people and with certain extraordinary ideas held relative to that killing is, however, by no means clear ; for it was believed that as often as the bird was killed it was made alive again, and more, and—faith to move mountains—that the birds killed in one same yearly feast in many separate villages were one and the same bird ! " [1]

IV

So far we have been considering especially, as far as the collective representations of primitives are concerned, what we might call the participating relations from the static point of view, that is, those which govern the existence of objects, natural phenomena, individuals or species. Let us now pass to the dynamic aspect, and consider the influence and sway which beings and objects mutually exercise. To tell the truth, it is one of the characteristic features of primitive mentality that in very many cases the difference between the two points of view tends to disappear. It is often impossible to decide whether an influence is transitive or immanent, and in spite of the difficulty which *we* feel in conceiving that which we consider contradictory, it is both at the same time. This is the case with the influence exercised by the totemic group upon the animal or plant which is its totem, by means of the

[1] *The Native Races of the Pacific States of North America*, iii. p. 168.

intichiuma ceremonies. In North America, again, the members of the wind totem are supposed to have a special influence on blizzards, and they are entreated to send a breeze when the mosquitoes become too troublesome.[1] In the Torres Straits, " an Umai man (having the dog as his totem) was credited with understanding the habits of dogs, and with ability to exercise special control over them."[2] Among the tribes of Central Australia " an euro man gives to a plum-tree man a ' sung-over ' *churinga* for the purpose of assisting him to hunt the animal."[3] In the Kaitish tribe, the headman of the water totem must religiously refrain from using a pointing stick or bone against an enemy, for if he did so, the water would become foul and infectious.[4]

These facts and many others which might be cited serve to show how insensibly prelogical mentality establishes a connection between the influence exercised upon oneself and the influence exercised on something else. When a certain act of the water totem chief makes the water undrinkable, it is impossible to decide whether the influence exercised is imagined as transient or as immanent : prelogical mentality does not differentiate. But that which we perceive clearly in the relations of the totemic groups with the being or object or species which is their totem, a profound and informed analysis of prelogical mentality would discover among an infinitude of other relations, which this same mentality would also picture as subject to the law of participation. Thus there exists a mystic participation between each totemic group and a certain spot which pertains to it, that is, between this totemic group and a certain point of the compass. The cardinal points, in their turn, are bound up (also by mystic participation) with colours, winds, mythical animals, and these with rivers, or sacred forests, and so on, almost to infinity. The natural environment of a certain group, tribe or family of tribes, for instance, thus appears in their collective representations, not as an object or a system of objects and phenomena governed by fixed laws, according to the laws of rational thought—but as an unstable ensemble of mystic

[1] Dorsey, " Siouan Cults," *E. B. Rept.*, xi. p. 410.
[2] Haddon, " The West Tribes of Torres Straits," *J.A.I.*, xix. p. 325.
[3] Spencer and Gillen, *The Native Tribes of Central Australia*, pp. 202-4.
[4] Id., *The Northern Tribes of Central Australia*, p. 463.

actions and reactions, of which persons, things, phenomena, are but the vehicles and manifestations, an ensemble which depends upon the group, as the group depends upon it.

Oriented differently from our own, and pre-eminently engaged with mystic qualities and connections, with the law of participation as its supreme guide and control, primitive mentality perforce interprets in a fashion other than ours what *we* call nature and experience. Everywhere it perceives the communication of qualities (through transference, contact, projection, contamination, defilement, possession, in short, through a number of varied operations) which, either instantaneously or in the course of time, bring a person or a thing into participation with a given faculty ; and these qualities have the power of consecrating him or it, or the contrary, at the beginning or end of a ceremony.[1] Later on, from a formal point of view, and to demonstrate the actual functioning of prelogical mentality, I shall pass in review a certain number of magical or religious practices derived from these ideas, and they will appear to be inspired and maintained by this belief in a participation. The beliefs relating to the different kinds of taboo fall under this head. When an Australian aboriginal or a Maori, terrified at the idea that he has unconsciously partaken of a food which is forbidden, dies from having infringed his taboo, it is because he feels himself hopelessly impregnated by a death-dealing influence which has entered his body with the food in question. This same influence was imparted to the food through participation : for example, it may have been the remains of a chief's repast which an unfortunate man of the common people has eaten inadvertently.

The same ideas are at the bottom of the universal belief which affirms that certain men become animals—tigers, wolves, bears, etc.—whenever they put on the skins of such. To the primitives, such an idea is wholly mystic. They are not concerned with knowing whether the man, in becoming a tiger, ceases to be a man, and later, when he becomes a man again, is no longer a tiger. That which is of paramount importance to them is the mystic virtue which makes these individuals " participable," to use Malebranche's term, of both tiger

[1] Cf. Hubert and Mauss, *Mélanges d'Histoire des Religions*, pp. 22-32, 66-7

and man in certain conditions, and consequently more formidable than men who are never anything but men, and tigers
which are always tigers only.

"How is this?" said the worthy Dobrizhoffer to the Abipones, "you daily kill tigers in the plain without dread,
why then should you weakly fear a false imaginary tiger in
the town?" "You Fathers don't understand these matters,"
they reply, with a smile. "We never fear, but kill, tigers
in the plain, because we can see them. Artificial tigers
we do fear, because they can neither be seen or killed
by us." [1]

So, too, the Huichol who adorns himself with the eagle's
feathers does not do so solely, or even mainly, for decoration.
He believes that he can, by means of these feathers, transfer
to himself some of the acute visual power, strength, and
shrewdness of the bird. Again it is participation which
is the basis of the collective representation that dictates this
action.

As a general rule, the processes employed by primitives
to obtain the results they desire afford enlightenment as to
their ideas of natural forces, and the manifestation of the
living beings and phenomena which surround them ; for we
may say that they either imitate the manifestation, such as
they suppose it to be, or else they imagine it as a symbol of
what they do themselves. Now these processes, as we shall
see in detail later on, are essentially mystic, and almost always
involve the elements of participation. Their idea of the
forces of ambient nature, then, presents the same characteristics. This is a fresh reason for abandoning the plausible
and seductive, yet incorrect theory according to which, by
spontaneous and inevitable application of anthropomorphic
analogy, primitives see everywhere in nature wills, spirits, souls
like their own. Far from sanctioning our attributing to
them previous reflection upon their own activity, or a generalization which is founded on the result of such reflection, the
facts forbid of our endowing them with that logical and consistent natural " philosophy " which, at any rate in its origin,
animism would be.

We must undoubtedly take into account the stupendous

[1] Dobrizhoffer, *An Account of the Abipones*, ii. pp. 77–8.

number of facts collected and classified by Tylor, Frazer, and their collaborators and disciples, and grant that, according to these facts, we never find in the collective representations of primitives anything that is dead, motionless, without life. There is abundance of evidence that all entities and all objects, even those which are inanimate and inorganic, even things manufactured by men's hands, are imagined capable of exercising and undergoing the most diverse influences.   The Malay miner believes that tin ore may have special affinities for certain people and cannot be discovered by others ; [1] and we have noted how very important, according to Cushing's account, is the exact shape to be given to familiar objects of manufacture. But it does not therefore follow that the tin ore or the domestic utensils have a soul conceived by analogy with the human soul.   It is only permissible to conclude that the primitive's ideas of entities and objects and all that relates to them are mystic, and governed by the law of participation.   It may be that at a certain stage in the development of the mentality, the members of a given social group tend both to acquire a more distinct consciousness of their own personality, and to imagine similar personalities outside themselves in animals, trees, rocks, etc., or in gods and spirits. But neither this representation, nor this generalized analogy, is a natural and original product of this mentality.

Pechuël-Loesche has made a detailed study of this matter, as far as the Bafioti of the east coast of Africa are concerned.[2] We cannot here reproduce or even summarize his arguments, which are based upon a very meticulous observance of beliefs and customs. His conclusion is that such words as " will " or " soul " or " spirit " should be altogether eliminated. There is indeed something in the beings and the phenomena, but it is neither soul nor spirit nor will. If it be absolutely necessary to give it expression, it would be best to use " dynanism " instead of " animism." Pechuël-Loesche quotes a traveller of the seventeenth century, according to whom " these people know neither God nor devil, for they cannot give either any proper name ; but they confine themselves to applying the term ' mokisie ' to everything in which they perceive

[1] Skeat, *Malay Magic*, p. 259.
[2] *Die Loango-Expedition*, iii. 2, pp. 356-7.

hidden force." He notes too that the wonder-workers have just as much fear of the souls of the dead as the laymen. " If one should ask a celebrated *nganga* by the help of whose soul or spirit he is performing, he will look at you without answering, with a glance full of fear. He has never had any idea of that sort of thing ; it is much too dangerous. . . . In short, the Bafioti do not know elementals. According to them there are forces of power and life existing everywhere (and to-day they regard them as proceeding from one supreme god)—then there are themselves, and between the two, the souls of the dead. There is nothing more. It is with these forces, and not with souls or spirits, that the black magic and its opponent, the white magic, operate." [1]

It is the same with the most undeveloped tribes of South America. " The most primitive animist idea consists in regarding nature as animate everywhere (*Allbeseelung*) ; an idea which is by no means derived as a result of a knowledge of the human soul, but which is formed at the same time as that by means of simple analogy." [2] Junod the missionary very aptly expresses the character of this idea of nature. " The Ba-Ronga," he says, " like their allied race, the Bantus, are animists. In their eyes, the world is full of spiritual influences, sometimes favourable but more often formidable, which must be warded off. Do they imagine these clearly ? No : their animist ideas are very vague. . . . On the other hand, there are two or three conceptions which are very familiar to them, and these figure more clearly on the vague background of their beliefs. These are their conceptions of *khombo* (misfortune), *nsila* (defilement), and *yila* (that which is forbidden)." [3]

Even investigators of the Tylor and Frazer school, in describing what they see, use expressions which tend to modify their masters' theory in the way I have indicated. Thus " the root idea," says Skeat, " seems to be an all-pervading animism, involving a certain common vital principle (*Semangat*) in man and Nature, which, for want of a more suitable word, has been here called the Soul." [4] In the island of Borneo,

[1] *Die Loango-Expedition*, pp. 276–7, 313.
[2] P. Ehrenreich, *Die Mythen und Legenden der Süd-Americanischen Urvölker*, p. 19.
[3] Junod, *Les Ba-Ronga*, p. 471.　　　[4] *Malay Magic*, p. 579.

the natives " may be said to attribute a soul or spirit to almost every natural agent and to all living things." But how are we to understand this animist doctrine ? " They feel themselves to be surrounded on every hand by spiritual powers, which appear to them to be concentrated in those objects to which their attention is directed by practical needs. Adapting a mode of expression familiar to psychologists, we may say that they have differentiated from a *continuum* of spiritual powers a number of spiritual agents with very various degrees of definiteness. Of these the less important are extremely vaguely conceived, but are regarded as being able to bring harm to men." [1]

This *continuum* of spiritual powers, antecedent to the definite individualities which are the result of differentiation, we find described in North America in almost exactly the same terms by Miss Alice Fletcher. " The Indians," she says, " regarded all animate and inanimate forms, all phenomena as pervaded by a common life, which was continuous and similar to the will power they were conscious of in themselves. This mysterious power in all things they called *Wakonda*, and through it all things were related to man, and to each other. In the idea of the continuity of life, a relation was maintained between the seen and the unseen, the dead and the living, and also between the fragment of anything and its entirety." [2] Would it be possible to bring more thoroughly home, in terms of animism, the mystic representations governed by the law of participation, which form the basis of prelogical mentality ? Finally, in his recent book,[3] A. C. Kruijt also admits that, instead of the traditional animism, the mentality of primitives first of all imagines a *continuum* of mystic forces, a principle of continuous life, an *Allbeseelung*, and that individualities or personalities, souls, spirits, only appear in the second place.

It is therefore permissible to believe that, the more carefully one collects data, the more one detaches them from the animist interpretation which observers have only too frequently

[1] Hose and Macdougall, " Men and Animals in Sarawak," *J.A.I.*, xxxi. p. 174.
[2] " The Signification of the Scalp-lock (Omaha Ritual)," *J.A.I.*, xxvi. p. 437.
[3] *Het Animisme in den Indischen Archipel*, pp. 1–2 (1906).

incorporated with them, even unconsciously, the more evident it will appear that the mentality of primitives, being mystic, is necessarily prelogical also : which means that, preoccupied above all with the mystic powers and properties of persons and things, it conceives of their relations under the law of participation without troubling about contradictions which rational thought cannot possibly tolerate.

CHAPTER III

THE FUNCTIONING OF PRELOGICAL MENTALITY

I

It would be idle to institute any comparison between the discursive processes of prelogical mentality and those of our thought, or to look for any correspondence between the two, for we should have no grounds on which to base a hypothesis. We have no *a priori* reason for admitting that the same process is used by both. The discursive operations of our rational thought—the analysis of which has been made familiar to us through psychology and logic—require the existence and the employment of much that is intricate, in the form of categories, concepts, and abstract terms. They also assume an intellectual functioning, properly so called, that is already well-differentiated. In short, they imply an ensemble of conditions which we do not find existing anywhere in social aggregates of a primitive type. On the other hand, as we have seen, prelogical mentality has its own laws, to which its discursive operations must necessarily submit.

In order to determine what these operations are, and how they are accomplished, our only resource is to describe and analyse them according to the direct connections we have observed between the collective representations. This is a most difficult task, both on account of the character of these same operations, and of the incompleteness of the documents at our disposal. The attempt I am about to make, therefore, will undoubtedly yield an imperfect and very unfinished outline only, but it will not have been useless if it shows that the operations of prelogical mentality depend upon the law of participation, and cannot be explained apart from it.

Before we begin to analyse these operations, we must first of all say something about the co-existence of the laws of contradiction and participation. Are we to suppose that certain operations are governed entirely by the first, and others just as exclusively by the second, of these laws ? Do we imagine, for instance, that every individual representation is the result of thought that is already logical, whilst collective representations alone submit to a law peculiar to prelogical mentality ? Water-tight compartments of this kind are inconceivable, if only because it is very difficult—indeed almost impossible—to trace a distinct line of demarcation between individual and collective representations. What can be more individual, to all appearances, than sense-perceptions ? Nevertheless we have noted the extent to which the primitive's sense-perceptions are enveloped in mystic elements which cannot be separated from them and which undoubtedly are collective in their nature. The same may be said of most of the emotions experienced and of most of the movements which take place almost instinctively at the sight of a certain object, even quite an ordinary one. In these communities as much as in our own, perhaps even more so, the whole mental life of the individual is profoundly *socialized*.

We must therefore expect to see the influence of the law of participation exercised, not only pre-eminently in what we have called collective representations, but also making itself felt more or less emphatically in all mental operations. Conversely, the effect of the law of contradiction is already more or less strong and constant, first of all in operations which would be impossible without it (such as numeration, inference, etc.) and then also in those which are governed by the law of participation. There is nothing but what is changing and unstable, and this is one of the greatest difficulties with which we have to contend. In the mentality of primitive peoples, the logical and prelogical are not arranged in layers and separated from each other like oil and water in a glass. They permeate each other, and the result is a mixture which is a very difficult matter to differentiate. Since the laws of logic absolutely exclude, in our own thought, everything that is directly contrary to itself, we find it hard to get accustomed to a mentality in which the logical and prelogical can be co-existent and make themselves equally perceptible in mental processes.

The prelogical element which our collective representations still contain is too small to enable us to reconstruct a mental state in which the prelogical, when dominant, does not *exclude* what is logical.

What strikes us first of all is that prelogical mentality is little given to analysis. Undoubtedly in a certain sense every act of thought is synthetic, but when it is a question of logical thought this synthesis implies, in nearly every case, a previous analysis. Relations are expressed by judgments only after the food for thought has first been well digested, and subjected to elaboration, differentiation, and classification. Judgment deals with ideas which have been rigidly defined, and these are themselves the proof and product of previous logical processes. This previous work, in which a large number of successive analyses and syntheses occur and are recorded, is received ready-made by every individual in our communities when he first learns to talk, by means of the education inseparably bound up with his natural development ; so much so indeed that certain philosophers have believed in the supernatural origin of language. In this way the claims of logical thought are urged, established, and then confirmed in each individual mind by the uninterrupted constraining force of his social environment, by means of language itself and of what is transmitted by language. This is a heritage of which no member of our community is deprived, and which none would ever dream of refusing. Logical discipline is thus imposed upon his mental operations with irresistible force. The fresh syntheses which it effects must submit to the definitions of the concepts employed, definitions which the previous logical operations have legitimatized. In short, his mental activity, in whatever form it may be exercised, must submit to the law of contradiction.

The conditions under which prelogical mentality operates are altogether different. There is no doubt that it, too, is transmitted socially by means of language and concepts without which it could not be exercised. It also implies work which has been previously accomplished, an inheritance handed down from one generation to another. But these concepts differ from ours,[1] and consequently the mental

[1] Vide Chap. III. pp. 126-7.

operations are also different. Prelogical mentality is essentially synthetic. By this I mean that the syntheses which compose it do not imply previous analyses of which the result has been registered in definite concepts, as is the case with those in which logical thought operates. In other words, the connecting-links of the representations are given, as a rule, with the representations themselves. In it, too, the syntheses appear to be primitive and, as we have seen in our study of perception, they are nearly always both undecomposed and undecomposable. This, too, explains why primitive mentality seems both impervious to experience and insensible to contradiction in so many instances. Collective representations do not present themselves separately to it, nor are they analysed and then arranged in logical sequence by it. They are always bound up with preperceptions, preconceptions, preconnections, and we might almost say with prejudgments ; and thus it is that primitive mentality, just because it is mystical, is also prelogical.

But, someone may object, if the mental operations of uncivilized peoples differ from logical thinking in their mode of functioning, if their paramount law is the law of participation, which *a priori* allows of these preconnections and participations of participations which are so infinitely varied, if their mentality does finally escape the control of experience, will it not appear to us unbridled and unregulated, and just as purely arbitrary as it is impenetrable ? Now in nearly all inferior races we find, on the contrary, that the mentality is stable, fixed and almost invariable, not only in its essential elements, but in the very content and even in the details of its representations. The reason is that this mentality, *although* not subordinate to logical processes, or rather, precisely *because* it does not submit to them, is not free. Its uniformity reflects the uniformity of the social structure with which it corresponds. Institutions fix beforehand, so to speak *ne varietur*, the combinations of collective representations which are actually possible. The number of the connecting-links between the representations and the methods by which they are connected are predetermined at the same time as the representations themselves. It is especially in the preconnections thus established that the predominance of the law of participation and the weakness of the strictly intellectual claims are made manifest.

Moreover, collective representations as a rule form part of a mystical complex in which the emotional and passionate elements scarcely allow thought, as thought, to obtain any mastery. To primitive mentality the bare fact, the actual object, hardly exists. Nothing presents itself to it that is not wrapped about with the elements of mystery : every object it perceives, whether ordinary or not, moves it more or less, and moves it in a way which is itself predestined by tradition. For except for the emotions which are strictly individual and dependent upon immediate reaction of the organism, there is nothing more *socialized* among primitives than are their emotions. Thus the nature which is perceived, felt, and lived by the members of an undeveloped community, is necessarily predetermined and unvarying to a certain extent, as long as the organized institutions of the group remain un- altered. This mystical and prelogical mentality will evolve only when the primitive syntheses, the preconnections of collective representations are gradually dissolved and decom- posed ; in other words, when experience and logical claims win their way against the law of participation. Then, in submitting to these claims, " thought," properly so called, will begin to be differentiated, independent, and free. Intellectual operations of a slightly complex kind will become possible, and the logical process to which thought will gradually attain, is both the necessary condition of its liberty and the indis- pensable instrument of its progress.

II

In the first place, in prelogical mentality memory plays a much more important part than it does in our mental life, in which certain functions which it used to perform have been taken from it and transformed. Our wealth of social thought is transmitted, in condensed form, through a hierarchy of concepts which co-ordinate with, or are subordinate to, each other. In primitive peoples it consists of a frequently enormous number of involved and complex collective repre- sentations. It is almost entirely transmitted through the memory. During the entire course of life, whether in sacred or profane matters, an appeal which without our active volition induces *us* to exercise the logical function, awakens in the primitive a complex and often mystic recollection which regulates action. And this recollection even has a special tone which distinguishes it from ours. The constant use of the logical process which abstract concepts involve, the, so to speak, *natural* use of languages relying upon this process, disposes our memory preferably to retain the relations which have preponderating importance from the objective and logical standpoint. In prelogical mentality both the aspect and tendencies of memory are quite different because its contents are of a different character. It is both very accurate and very emotional. It reconstructs the complex collective representations with a wealth of detail, and always in the order in which they are traditionally connected, according to relations which are essentially mystic. Since it thus, to a certain extent, supplements logical functions, it exercises the privileges of these to a corresponding degree. For instance, a representation inevitably evoked as the result of another frequently has the quality of a conclusion. Thus it is, as we shall see, that a sign is nearly always taken to be a cause.

The preconnections, preperceptions, and preconclusions which play so great a part in the mentality of uncivilized peoples do not involve any logical activity ; they are simply committed to memory. We must therefore expect to find the memory extremely well developed in primitives, and this is, in fact, reported by observers. But since they unreflectingly assume that memory with these primitives has just the same functions as with us, they show themselves both surprised and disconcerted by this. It seems to them that it is accomplishing marvellous feats, while it is merely being exercised in a normal way. " In many respects," say Spencer and Gillen of the Australian aborigines, " their memory is phenomenal." " Not only does a native know the track of every beast and bird, but after examining any burrow, he will at once, from the direction in which the last track runs, tell you whether the animal is at home or not. . . . Strange as it may sound . . . the native will recognize the footprint

of every individual of his acquaintance." [1] The earliest
explorers of Australia had already referred to this marvellous
power of memory. Thus Grey tells us that three thieves
were discovered by their footprints. " I got hold of an intelligent native of the name of Moyee-e-nan, and accompanied
by him, visited the garden whence the potatoes had been
stolen ; he found the tracks of three natives, and availing himself of the faculty which they possess of telling who has passed
from their footmarks, he informed me that the three thieves
had been the two wives of a native . . . and a little boy
named Dal-be-an." [2] Eyre is astonished at " the intimate
knowledge they have of every nook and corner of the country
they inhabit ; does a shower of rain fall, they know the very
rock where a little water is most likely to be collected, the
very hole where it is the longest retained. . . . Are there
heavy dews at night, they know where the longest grass grows,
from which they may collect . . . water in great abundance." [3]

W. E. Roth also draws attention to the exceptional memorizing powers of the North Queensland aborigines. He has
heard them " reciting a song the delivery of which takes
upwards of five nights for its completion (the Molonga set
of corroborees). . . . The wonder is increased when it is
remembered that the words are sung in a language of which
the singers of both localities (ninety miles apart) are entirely
ignorant. . . . A tribe will learn and sing by rote whole
corroborees in a language absolutely remote from its own,
and not one word of which the audience or performers can
understand the meaning of. That the words are very carefully committed to memory, I have obtained ample proof
by taking down phonetically the same corroborees as performed
by different-speaking people living at distances upwards of one
hundred miles apart." [4]

Von den Steinen has reported similar experiences in his
explorations of the Xingu basin. " Every tribe knew the
songs of the neighbouring tribes, without understanding their

[1] Spencer and Gillen, *The Native Tribes of Central Australia*, p. 25.
[2] Grey, *Journals of Two Expeditions of Discovery in North-western and
Western Australia*, ii. p. 351.
[3] Eyre, *Expeditions into Central Australia*, ii. p. 247.
[4] W. E. Roth, *Ethnographical Studies among the N.W. Central Queensland
Aborigines*, Nos. 191, 199.

exact meaning, a fact I was able to prove on numerous occasions." [1] In a large number of North American tribes we find incantations of a sacred character, faithfully transmitted from generation to generation, which are not understood, either by those who officiate or those who listen. In Africa, too, Livingstone likewise expressed surprise at the wonderful memory displayed by certain natives. " These chief's messengers have most retentive memories ; they carry messages of considerable length great distances, and deliver them almost word for word. Two or three usually go together, and when on the way the message is rehearsed every night, in order that the exact words may be kept to. One of the native objections to learning to write is that these men answer the purpose of transmitting intelligence to a distance as well as a letter would." [2]

One specially noticeable form of the memory so highly developed in natives is that which preserves to the minutest detail the aspect of regions they have traversed, and this permits of their retracing their steps with a confidence which amazes Europeans. Among the North American Indians this topographical memory "is something marvellous ; it is quite enough for them to have been in a place once only for them to have an exact image of it in their minds, and one which will never be lost. However vast and untravelled a forest may be, they cross it without losing their way, once they have got their bearings. The people of Acadia and the Gulf of St. Lawrence would often embark in the frail canoes to go to Labrador. . . . They would sail for thirty or forty leagues without a compass, and disembark at the precise spot at which they had decided to land. . . . Even when the sky is overcast, they will follow the sun for several days without making a mistake." Charlevoix is inclined to attribute this to an innate faculty. " This gift is inborn ; it is not the result of their observations, nor a matter of habit ; children who have scarcely ever left their village go about with as much confidence as those who have travelled the country." Like the Australian aborigines, " they have a marvellous gift for knowing whether anyone has passed a certain place. On

[1] K. von den Steinen, *Unter den Naturvölkern Zentralbrasiliens*, p. 268.
[2] Livingstone, *Zambesi and its Tributaries*, p. 267 (1865).

the shortest grass, the very hardest ground, and even on the stones they discover tracks, and by their direction and the outline of the foot and the way in which the person has stepped aside, they distinguish the footprints of different races, and the tracks of men from those of women." [1]

Pechuël-Loesche, who made a study of similar phenomena on the west coast of Africa, rightly distinguishes between what he calls the sense of locality (*Ortsinn*) and the sense of direction (*Richtsinn*). What we call sense of locality is simply a memory for places ; it is an acquired aptitude, founded on a very strong memorizing faculty, and on the recognition of an infinitude of detail which allows one to return to the same region in space. . . . Beyond and above this sense of locality is the feeling of direction (*Richtungsgefühl*), or the sense of direction (*Richtsinn*). It is not a special sense, it is the sense of locality carried to its highest degree of perfection, and therefore again a form of memory. He who has acquired it will never lose his way again. Undoubtedly, " he will not be certain of arriving without fail at a given point, but at any rate he will always start in the direction which leads to it . . . under the open sky, in the fog, rain, snow, or in the depths of night. Nevertheless I have noticed that this sense may be entirely at fault in violent storms. . . . Persons gifted with a strong sense of locality appear to be exempt from vertigo and sea-sickness." [2]

This analysis help us to understand similar observations made by other explorers when speaking of certain individuals belonging to primitive peoples. Thus an Australian named Miago " could indicate at once and correctly the exact direction of our wished-for harbour, when neither sun nor stars were shining to assist him. He was tried frequently, and under very varying instances, but strange as it may seem, he was invariably right. This faculty—though somewhat analogous to one I have heard attributed to the natives of North America—had very much surprised me when exercised on shore, but at sea, out of the sight of land, it seemed beyond belief, as assuredly it is beyond explanation." This same Miago " remembered accurately the various places we had

[1] Charlevoix, *Journal d'un Voyage dans l'Amérique Septentrionale*, iii. p. 239.
[2] *Die Loango-Expedition*, iii. 2, pp. 28-9.

visited during the voyage ; he seemed to have carried the
ship's track in his memory with the most careful accuracy." [1]

The same faculty has been noted in Fuegians. " Niqueaccas
was so well acquainted with all the coast between 47° and
the Straits of Magellan that upon being taken to a high hill,
immediately after landing from a cruise, in which they had
been far out of sight of land, he pointed out the best harbours
and places for seal then visible. . . . The boy Bob, when only
ten years old, was on board the *Adonea* at sea. As the vessel
approached land, Low asked him where a harbour could be
found. As soon as he understood what was meant, which
was an affair of some difficulty, for he could then speak but
very little English, he got up on the vessel's bulwark, and
looked anxiously around. After some hesitation, he pointed
to a place where the ship might go, and then went to the lead-
line, and made signs to Mr. Low that he must sound as he
approached the land . . . an extraordinary proof of the
degree in which the perceptive and retentive faculties are
enjoyed by these savages." [2]

It was evidently a case of thoroughly well-developed
" sense of locality " attaining the degree of superiority in
which it becomes, as Pechuël-Loesche calls it, a feeling of
direction, but there is nothing marvellous in it but a local
memory that is out of the common.

Von den Steinen has given us a good, though less surprising,
description of a similar case. " Antonio (a Bakairi) would see
and hear everything, and commit to memory the most insignificant details, and by means of such signs of locality he
exercised the faculty which educated people call the sense of
direction. If I had not convinced myself by frequently
questioning him I could scarcely have believed that anybody,
without written notes, could have acquired in a single voyage
on an ordinary river so exact a knowledge of the special
features of its course. Antonio not only remembered every
bend but he was able to tell me when I asked him, whether
there were two or three bends before we arrived at such and
such a place. He had the map of it in his head ; or, to

---

[1] Stokes, *Discoveries in Australia*, i. pp. 222–3 (1846).
[2] Fitzroy, *Narrative of the Surveying Voyages of the " Adventure " and the
" Beagle,"* ii. pp. 192–3.

express it more accurately, he had retained in their right order a number of apparently unimportant facts such as a tree here, a gunshot there, a little further on some bees, and so on." [1]

This extraordinary development of memory, and of a memory which faithfully reproduces the minutest details of sense-impressions in the correct order of their appearance, is shown moreover by the wealth of vocabulary and the grammatical complexity of the languages. Now the very men who speak these languages and possess this power of memory are (in Australia or Northern Brazil, for instance) incapable of counting beyond two or three. The slightest mental effort involving abstract reasoning, however elementary it may be, is so distasteful to them that they immediately declare themselves tired and give it up. We must admit therefore, as we have already said, that with them memory takes the place (at very great cost, no doubt, but at any rate it does take the place) of operations which elsewhere depend upon a logical process. With us, in everything that relates to intellectual functions, memory is confined to the subordinate rôle of registering the results which have been acquired by a logical elaboration of concepts. But to prelogical mentality, recollections are almost exclusively highly complex representations which succeed each other in unvarying order, and in which the most elementary of logical operations would be very difficult (since language does not lend itself thereto), supposing that tradition allowed of their being attempted, and granting that individuals possessed enough boldness to entertain the idea. Our thought, in so far as it is abstract, solves at one swoop a great number of problems implied in one single statement, provided that the terms employed are sufficiently general and definite. This is what prelogical mentality could not even imagine, and this accordingly makes it so difficult for us to reconstruct such a mentality. The amanuensis of the eleventh century who laboriously reproduced page by page the manuscript which was the object of his pious endeavour, is no further removed from the rotary machine of the great newspaper offices which prints off hundreds of thousands of copies in a few hours, than is prelogical mentality, in which

[1] K. von den Steinen, *Unter den Naturvölkern Zentralbrasiliens*, pp. 155-7.

the connections between the representations are preformed, and which makes use of memory almost entirely, from logical thought, with its marvellous stock of abstract concepts.

III

Are we to take it for granted, then, that this mentality, even in the very lowest social aggregates, makes no use of concepts whatever ? Certainly not : the ofttimes complicated language that it speaks, the institutions transmitted from generation to generation, are sufficient to prove the contrary. Yet the concepts that are used in such aggregates for the most part differ from our own. The mind that forms and employs them is not merely prelogical. It is essentially mystic, and if its mystic character determines, as we have already seen, the way in which it perceives, it exercises no less influence upon its methods of abstraction and generalization, that is, the way in which it creates its concepts. Especially in that which concerns representations which are strictly collective, prelogical mentality most frequently arrives at its abstraction by the law of participation. One can imagine that it is extremely difficult to give proof of this, the testimony afforded by observers being necessarily interpreted by concepts with which they are familiar, and which come within the limits of our logical thought. Nevertheless Spencer and Gillen have reported a certain number of facts which permit of our seeing fairly clearly how prelogical mentality practises abstraction.

" When asked the meaning of certain drawings . . . the natives will constantly answer that they are only play work, and mean nothing . . . but . . . similar drawings, only drawn on some ceremonial object or in a particular spot, have a very definite meaning. . . . The same native will tell you that a special drawing in one spot has no meaning, and yet he will tell you exactly what it is supposed to signify when drawn in a different spot. The latter, it may be remarked, is always on what we may call sacred ground, near to which the women may not come." [1]—" A *nurtunja* (a sacred pole), is symbolic of one, and only one, thing, though, as far as

---

[1] *The Native Tribes of Central Australia*, p. 617.

its appearance and structure are concerned, it may be precisely similar to a *nurtunja* which means something totally different. Suppose, for example, as on the last occasion, a large *churinga* or a *nurtunja* represented a gum-tree, then, in the mind of the native it becomes so closely associated with that object that it cannot possibly mean anything else ; and if a precisely similar *churinga* or *nurtunja* were wanted an hour afterwards to represent, say an emu, then a new one must be made." [1] Conversely, the same object, in different circumstances, may have very diverse meanings. " The various parts of the *waninga* " (a sacred symbol of a totemic animal or plant) " have very different meanings, but it must be remembered that the same structure will mean one thing when it is used in connection with one totem, and quite a different thing when used in connection with another." [2] Finally, with regard to designs which seem to have a geometric appearance, which have been collected from these same aborigines, Spencer and Gillen say : " The origin of these geometric drawings is quite unknown, and their meaning, if they have one, is a purely conventional one. Thus, for example, a spiral or series of concentric circles incised on the face of one particular *churinga* will signify a gum-tree, and a precisely similar design on another *churinga* will indicate a frog." [3]

Here we have very clear instances of what we shall call *mystic abstraction* which, different as it is from logical abstraction, is none the less the process which primitive mentality would frequently make use of. In fact, if exclusive attention be one of the primary conditions of abstraction, and if exclusive attention be necessarily paid to the features which are most interesting and important to the subject, we know which these features will be to a mentality which is mystic and prelogical. Beyond and above aught else, they are those which establish relations between the visible, tangible, concrete objects and the invisible and mysterious forces which compass them about, the spirits, phantoms, souls, etc., which secure to persons and things their mystic properties and powers. The attention of primitives, like their perception, is oriented differently from our own   Their abstraction accordingly is carried out differently, and dominated by the law of participation.

Such abstraction is very difficult for us to reconstruct effectively. How are we to understand the fact reported by Spencer and Gillen in the first of the observations just quoted : that two precisely similar drawings when found in different places may represent, in the one case, a certain definite object, and in the other, nothing at all ? To our minds, the most essential relation which a drawing bears is that of *resemblance*. Undoubtedly such a drawing may possess a symbolic and religious significance and at the same time arouse mystic ideas accompanied by strong emotions : such drawings, for instance, as the frescoes of Fra Angelico in St. Mark's, Florence. But those are features which are evoked by association of ideas and the resemblance remains the fundamental relation. On the contrary, that which interests prelogical mentality above all is the relation of the semblance, as of the object represented, to the mystic force within it. Without such participation, the form of the object or the design is a negligible factor.[1]

This is the reason that the design, when traced or engraved upon a sacred object, is more than a semblance ; it participates in the sacred nature of the object and is imbued with its power.

[1] Thus the European observer, when attempting to interpret the designs made by primitives, is nearly sure to go wrong. Von den Steinen proved this in Brazil. On his side Parkinson says : " We find ourselves faced with a difficult problem. The *Mitteilungen* sees in these drawings serpents, and in fact there is something that recalls the head and body of such ; but the Baining affirm that they represent pigs. . . . The figure that follows might if necessary pass for a face, but according to the natives, it represents a club, though it has not the remotest resemblance to such a thing. Certainly nobody in the wildest flights of imagination would have conceived of such an explanation. . . . I was inclined to regard the three circular forms which follow, as eyes, but the natives robbed me of this illusion, assuring me that eyes could not be reproduced. The explanations of the decorations have been given me by the Baining themselves ; there can be no doubt on this point therefore, since those who execute them associate a definite idea with their drawings, although in nearly every case we are unable to see the connection, for the design does not in any way resemble the object in question. We see how incorrect it is to interpret the ornamental decorations of a primitive people according to their resemblance to any object known to us. The Baining see in these conventional designs a shell, a leaf, a human form, etc. The idea is so firmly fixed in their minds that one can see the stupefied wonder on their faces when they are asked the meaning of these designs : they cannot conceive that anybody should fail to recognize at once the meaning of the decorations ". (Parkinson, *Dreissig Jahre in der Südsee*, pp. 621–7 ; cf. pp. 234, 235).

When this same design is found elsewhere, upon an object which possesses no sanctity, it is less than a semblance. Having no mystic signification, it has none of any kind.

The details which Catlin gives us in his tales of the portraits which he made of the Mandan chiefs confirms this view. Catlin talks incessantly of the surprise and fear which the sight of these portraits excited in the Mandans. Nevertheless these same Indians, from time immemorial, were accustomed to represent the most striking events in their history, and even rude traces of the chiefs' features, on their banners. How then are we to explain the terror which these portraits of Catlin's caused ? By their greater fidelity to the originals ? No. The truth was that the Mandans found themselves confronted by unwonted semblances, implying a mystic participation hitherto unknown to them, and consequently, like everything unknown, highly dangerous. Their own drawings also expressed participation, but it was a definite one, hence their security. Those made by Catlin expressed a different one, because the methods he used were strange to them, and his likenesses were " speaking." Thus in this case, as in the preceding ones, prelogical mentality makes its abstraction from the mystic standpoint. If there is no mystic participation felt, the form of the likeness is unperceived, or at any rate, does not arrest the attention. This is what the European observer interprets by saying that the design has then " no meaning whatever." It does not mean that the primitive fails to recognize the design, but that unless he abstracts mystically, he makes no abstraction at all.

The note which relates to the *nurtunja* is equally clear. The Aruntas cannot imagine that the same *nurtunja* figures first as a tree, and then as an emu : rather than that, they take the trouble of making a second *nurtunja*, otherwise exactly like the first, when they want to represent the emu. In this we might see a ritual observance which does not allow of the same object being used, with a religious significance, more than once. But Spencer and Gillen sweep away such an explanation. They explicitly state that the Aruntas attribute a different signification to two objects which are similar. It is an admirable instance of mystic abstraction. One of the two *nurtunja* participates mystically of the nature of the tree, the other of the emu's nature, and this suffices to render them totally different, so that one cannot be substituted for the other. Their identity in form does not interest the Aruntas any more than we should be interested in the identical sounds of " weigh " and "way," for instance. Just as we constantly use these words without paying any attention to that identity, so prelogical mentality remains indifferent to the resemblance in form between the two objects. Its attention is fixed on the mystic participation which gives each its sacred character.

Similarly, on a certain *churinga*, one design represents a gum-tree ; on another an absolutely similar design stands for a frog, and the observers conclude accordingly that to the Australian aborigines these designs bear a purely " conventional" meaning. They ought not to say " conventional," but " mystic " however. The design possesses no interest but in so far as it realizes a mystic participation, and this, in its turn, depends entirely upon the mystic nature of the *churinga* upon the surface of which the design has been traced. Their resemblance is no more noticed by the primitive than would the relative places of tonic and fifth in different scales be regarded by the musician when he looks at his score. Spencer and Gillen themselves say that an arrangement that signifies one thing when used in connection with a certain totem is something quite different when it relates to another. But the *churinga* have the same mystic character as the totems, and thus the same participations become possible.

From the first observation recorded above it follows that the place occupied by a person, an object, an image is of paramount importance, at any rate in some cases, to the mystic properties of such a person, object, or image. There is a corresponding participation between a definite place, as a place, and the objects and entities which are found there, and it thus possesses certain mystic properties peculiar to it. To the primitive mind space does not appear as a homogeneous unity, irrespective of that which occupies it, destitute of properties and alike everywhere. On the contrary, each social group among the tribes of Central Australia, for instance, feels itself mystically bound up with the portion of ground it occupies or travels over ; it has no conception that it might occupy another, or that some other group might inhabit the region it fills. Between the soil and the group participations exist, amounting to a kind of mystic property which cannot be transferred, stolen, or acquired by conquest. Moreover, in the region thus defined, each locality with its characteristic aspect and form, its own peculiar rocks and trees, springs and sand-heaps, etc., is in mystic union with the visible or invisible beings who have revealed their presence there, or dwell there, and with the individual spirits who there await their reincarnation. Between themselves and their locality there is reciprocal participation : without them it could not be what it is, and it is equally necessary to make them what they are. This it is which Spencer and Gillen designate "local relationship," [1] and it accounts for those "totemic pilgrimages" of which they have furnished so interesting a description.

But if it be thus, we have fresh reason for believing that the prelogical mind does not, in general, practise abstraction at all as ours are accustomed to do. The condition of our abstraction is the logical homogeneity of the concepts which permits of their combination. Now this homogeneity is closely bound up with the homogeneous representation of space. If the prelogical mind, on the contrary, imagines the various regions in space as differing in quality, as determined by their mystic participations with such and such groups of persons or objects, abstraction as we usually conceive of it becomes very difficult to such a mind, and we shall find that its place is taken by the mystic abstraction which is the result of the law of participation.

IV

The principles and processes peculiar to prelogical mentality appear to stand out more distinctly when it generalizes even than when it is a case of abstracting. I am not speaking of concepts which more or less resemble our own, the existence of which is testified by the linguistic vocabulary, and which

[1] *The Native Tribes of Central Australia*, pp. 14, 303, 544 ; *The Northern Tribes of Central Australia*, p. 29.

fairly represent what have been termed generic ideas, such as man, woman, dog, tree, and so on. In the following chapter we shall find that the element of generality in these concepts is usually restricted and counterbalanced by the very special determination of the classes of beings or objects they designate. With this exception such concepts correspond very fairly with certain of our general ideas. But in the collective representations, properly so called, of primitives, particularly in those relating to their institutions and religious beliefs, we find generalizations of quite a different kind, which it is extremely difficult for us to reconstruct, the analysis of which would probably allow us to seize the mystic and prelogical mind in the very act, as it were. We might endeavour to trace back such generalizations, starting, for instance, from certain myths and certain totemic beliefs which are attested by rites and ceremonies. But if it be possible it would be better still to apprehend them directly, and in the very combination of the elements which form them. In Lumholtz' excellent works upon *Unknown Mexico*, we find observations with respect to the Huichol Indians which throw strong light upon the way in which the prelogical mind generalizes.

" Corn, deer, and hikuli " (a sacred plant) " are, in a way, one and the same thing to the Huichol." [1] At first this identification seems absolutely inexplicable. To make it intelligible, Lumholtz explains it on utilitarian grounds : " Corn is deer (food substance) and hikuli is deer (food substance) and corn is hikuli . . . all being considered identical in so far as they are food substances." [1] This explanation is a probable one, and it undoubtedly becomes the one held by the Huichols themselves as the forms of their ancient faiths gradually lose their primitive meaning in their minds. But according to Lumholtz' own explanation, the Huichols who express themselves thus view the matter from another aspect : it is the mystic properties in these things, so differently regarded by us, that unites them in one and the same idea. The hikuli is a sacred plant which men (destined and prepared for this end by a series of very complicated rites) gather every year with great ceremonial, in a remote district, and at the cost

[1] C. Lumholtz, *Symbolism of the Huichol Indians*, p. 22.

of much fatigue and personal privation : the existence and the well-being of the Huichols are mystically connected with the harvesting of this plant.   Their corn harvest is absolutely dependent upon it.   If the hikuli were to fail, or were not gathered according to the obligatory rites, the cornfields would not yield their usual crops.   But deer, in their relations with the tribe, present the same mystic characteristics.   Deer-hunting, which takes place at a certain definite time of year, is an essentially religious function.   The welfare and preserva-tion of the Huichols depends on the number of deer killed at this time, just as they depend upon the quantity of hikuli which is gathered ; and the chase is accompanied by the same ceremonial practices and evokes the same collective emotions as the search for the sacred plant.   Hence results the identification of the hikuli, deer, and corn, which we find asserted several times over.

"A layer of straw had been spread outside of the temple at the right side of the entrance, and on this the deer was carefully deposited.   It was thus received in the same way as the corn-rolls, because in the Indian conception, corn is deer.   According to the Huichol myth, corn was once a deer." [1]—" To the Huichol so closely are corn, deer, and hikuli associated that by consuming the broth of the deer meat and the hikuli they think the same effect is produced, namely, making the corn grow.   Therefore, when clearing the fields they eat the hikuli before starting the day's work." [2]

It seems then that in these collective representations of the Huichols (representations which are inseparable, as we know, from intense religious emotions, which are also collec-tive), the hikuli, deer, and corn participate in mystic qualities of the highest importance to the tribe, and, for this reason, are considered as "the same thing."   This participation, *which is felt by them*, does not present the confusion which we, despite all our efforts, see in it.   Just because their collective representations are bound together by the law of participation, nothing seems simpler or more natural to them and, we may add, more necessary.   The prelogical and mystic mentality is exercised in this way without constraint or effort, and without being yet controlled by the claims of logical thought.

[1] C. Lumholtz, *Unknown Mexico*, ii. p. 45.   [2] Ibid , ii. p. 268.

But this is not all, and Lumholtz will show us how the participations just instanced are compatible with others of a like nature. "It has been pointed out," he writes, "that the deer is considered identical with hikuli and hikuli identical with corn, and certain insects identical with corn. The same tendency to consider heterogeneous objects as identical may be observed in the fact that a great variety of objects are considered as plumes. Clouds, cotton wool, the white tail of a deer, the deer's antlers, and even the deer itself are considered as plumes, and all serpents are believed to have plumes."[1] Here, then, we have the deer, which was already corn, and hikuli, which is also plumes. Lumholtz frequently lays stress upon this. "Hairs from the tail of a deer are tied round outside of the feathers" (on a ceremonial arrow). "It will be remembered that not only are deer-antlers plumes, but also the deer himself, and here is a striking illustration of the conception of the animal, his hair being employed in the place of feathers."[2]

Now we know from other passages that to the Huichol mind feathers possess mystic properties of a very special kind. "Birds, especially eagles and hawks . . . hear everything; and the same is the case with their plumes; they also hear, the Indians say, and have mystic powers. Plumes are to the Huichols health, life, and luck-giving symbols. By their help, the shamans are capable of hearing everything that is said to them from below the earth and from all the points of the world, and perform magic feats. The feathers of the vulture and of the raven are not considered as plumes. All plumes are desirable as attachments to ceremonial objects; therefore a Huichol has never too many of them. There is, however, one plume of special merit, and that is, strange to say, the deer. Everyone who kills a deer comes into possession of a precious plume, that insures him health and luck. . . . Not only the antler, but the whole body of the deer is, in the Huichol mind, a plume, just as a bird is called a plume; and I have met with instances where the hair from the tail of a deer actually served as plume attachments on ceremonial arrows."[3]

It is, then, the presence of mystic qualities both in birds

[1] C. Lumholtz, *Symbolism of the Huichol Indians*, p. 212.
[2] Ibid., p. 96.   [3] Ibid., p. 21.

(and their feathers) and the deer (and the hair of its tail) which makes the Huichol saying: "The deer is a plume" intelligible. Lumholtz accounts for this as due to "a strong tendency to see analogies; what to us are called heterogeneous phenomena are by them considered as identical."[1] But what really is this tendency? And how can the Huichols perceive any analogy between an eagle's feather, a grain of corn, the body of a deer, the hikuli plant, if it be not mystic analogies, and all the more so, because it is not merely a question of analogy or association, but of identity? Lumholtz is very emphatic on this point: to the Huichols, the deer *is* hikuli, the hikuli *is* corn, the corn *is* a plume.—Elsewhere we learn that most gods and goddesses *are* serpents, and so are the pools of water and the springs in which the deities live; so too are the staffs used by the gods. From the standpoint of logical thought, such "identities" are, and remain, unintelligible. One entity is the symbol of another, but not that other. But to the prelogical mind these identities are comprehensible, for they are identities of participation. The deer *is* hikuli, or corn, or plume, just as the Bororo *is* an arara, and as, in general, the member of a totemic group *is* his totem. The facts Lumholtz has related are of profound significance. It is by virtue of participation that the eagle's feather possesses the same mystic properties as the eagle itself, and the whole body of the deer the same as those in its tail; and it is by virtue of participation, too, that the deer becomes identified with the eagle's plume or the hikuli plant.

Without insisting further on this point, we have here the principle of a generalization which proves disconcerting to logical thought, but is quite natural to prelogical mentality. It is presented to our minds in the form of that which, for want of a better term, we have called the preconnections of the collective representations, since "identities" of the kind we have been considering always occur to each individual mind at the same time as the representations themselves, and this accounts for the profound difference between these "representations" and our own, even when it is a case of fairly general concepts which are somewhat similar. When a

[1] C. Lumholtz, *Unknown Mexico*, ii. p. 233.

primitive, an Australian or Indian, for instance, imagines
" deer " or " plume " or " cloud," the generic image presented
to his mind implies something quite different from the somewhat analogous image which the European mind would conjure
up in the same circumstances.

Our concepts are surrounded by an atmosphere of logical
potentiality. This is what Aristotle meant when he said
that we never think of the particular as such. When I imagine
Socrates as an individual, I think of the man Socrates at the
same moment. When I see my horse or my dog, I certainly
perceive their special characteristics, but these also as belonging to the species horse or dog. Strictly speaking, their image
may be imprinted on my retina and appear to my consciousness
as quite distinctive, as long as I am not paying attention
to it. But directly I apprehend it, it is inseparable from
everything connoted by the terms " horse " and " dog "—
that is, not only from an infinite number of other potential
images like the first, but also from the sustained consciousness
which I have both of myself and of a possible, logically ordered,
conceivable world of experience. And since each of my
concepts can be broken up into others which in their turn
can be analysed, I know that I can pass from these to others
by definite stages which are the same for all minds resembling
my own. I know that logical processes, if they be correct,
and their elements drawn from experience as they should be,
will lead me to definite results which experience will confirm,
however far I may pursue them. In short, logical thought
implies, more or less consciously, a systematic unity which is
best realizable in science and philosophy. And the fact that
it can lead to this is partially due to the peculiar nature of its
concepts, to their homogeneity and ordered regularity. This
is material which it has gradually created for itself, and
without which it would not have been able to develop.

Now this material is not at the command of the primitive
mind. Primitive mentality does indeed possess a language,
but its structure, as a rule, differs from that of our languages.
It actually does comprise abstract representations and general
ideas ; but neither this abstraction nor this generalization
resembles that of our concepts. Instead of being surrounded
by an atmosphere of logical potentiality, these representations

welter, as it were, in an atmosphere of mystic possibilities. There is no homogeneity in the field of representation, and for this reason logical generalization, properly so called, and logical transactions with its concepts are impracticable. The element of generality consists in the possibility—already predetermined —of mystic action and reaction by entities upon each other, or of common mystic reaction in entities which differ from each other. Logical thought finds itself dealing with a scale of general concepts varying in degree, which it can analyse or synthesize at will. Prelogical thought busies itself with collective representations so interwoven as to give the impression of a community in which members would continually act and react upon each other by virtue of their mystic qualities, participating in, or excluding, each other.

V

Since abstraction and generalization mean this for prelogical mentality, and its preconnections of collective representations are such, it is not difficult to account for its classification of persons and things, strange as it frequently appears to us. Logical thought classifies by means of the very operations which form its concepts. These sum up the work of analysis and synthesis which establishes species and genera, and thus arranges entities according to the increasing generality of the characters observed in them. In this sense classification is not a process which differs from those which have preceded or will follow it. It takes place at the same time as abstraction and generalization : it registers their results, as it were, and its value is precisely what theirs has been. It is the expression of an order of interdependence, of hierarchy among the concepts, of reciprocal connection between persons and things, which endeavours to correspond as precisely as possible with the objective order in such a way that concepts thus arranged are equally valid for real objects and real persons. It was the governing idea which directed Greek philosophical thought, and which inevitably appears as soon as the logical mind reflects upon itself and begins consciously to pursue the end to which it at first tended spontaneously.

But to the primitive mind this predominating concern for

objective validity which can be verified is unknown. Characteristics which can be discerned by experience, in the sense in which we understand it, characteristics which we call objective, are of secondary importance in its eyes, or are important only as signs and vehicles of mystic qualities. Moreover, the primitive mind does not arrange its concepts in a regular order. It perceives preconnections, which it would never dream of changing, between the collective representations; and these are nearly always of greater complexity than concepts, properly so called. Therefore what can its classifications be? Perforce determined at the same time as the preconnections, they too are governed by the law of participation, and will present the same prelogical and mystic character. They will betoken the orientation peculiar to such a mind.

The facts already quoted are sufficient proof of this. When the Huichols, influenced by the law of participation, affirm the identity of corn, deer, hikuli and plumes, a kind of classification has been established between their representations, a classification the governing principle of which is a common presence in these entities, or rather the circulation among these entities, of a mystic power which is of supreme importance to the tribe. The only thing is that this classification does not, as it should do in conformity with our mental processes, become compacted in a concept which is more comprehensive than that of the objects it embraces. For them it suffices for the objects to be united, and felt as such, in a complexity of collective representations whose emotional force fully compensates, and even goes beyond, the authority which will be given to general concepts by their logical validity at a later stage.

In this way the classifications to which Durkheim and Mauss have called our attention, noting their very different characteristics from those which distinguish our logical classifications, may again be explained. In many undeveloped peoples—in Australia, in West Africa, according to Dennett's recent book,[1] among the North American Indians, in China and elsewhere—we find that all natural objects—animals, plants, stars, cardinal points, colours, inanimate nature in general—are arranged, or have been originally arranged, in

[1] *At the Back of the Black Man's Mind* (London, 1906).

the same classes as the members of the social group, and if the latter are divided into so many totems, so, too, are the trees, rivers, stars, etc.   A certain tree will belong to such and such a class, and will be used exclusively to manufacture the weapons, coffins, etc., of men who are members of it.   The sun, according to the Aruntas, is a *Panunga* woman, that is, she forms part of the sub-group which can only intermarry with members of the *Purula* sub-group.   Here we have something analogous with that which we have already noticed about associated totems and local relationship, a mental habit quite different from our own, which consists in bringing together or uniting entities preferably by their mystic participations.   This participation, which is very strongly felt between members of the same totem or the same group, between the ensemble of these members and the animal or plant species which is their totem, is also felt, though undoubtedly to a lesser degree, between the totemic group and those who have the same location in space.   We have proofs of this in the Australian aborigines and in the North American Indians, where the place of each group in a common camping-ground is very precisely determined according to whether it comes from north or south or from some other direction.   Thus it is felt once more between this totemic group and one of the cardinal points, and consequently between this group and all that participates in it, on the one hand, and this cardinal point and all that participates in it (its stars, rivers, trees, and so forth), on the other.

In this way is established a complexity of participations, the full explanation of which would demand exhaustive acquaintance with the beliefs and the collective representations of the group in all their details.   They are the equivalent of, or at least they correspond with, what we know as classifications : the social participations being the most intensely felt by each individual consciousness and serving as a nucleus, as it were, around which other participations cluster.   But in this there is nothing at all resembling, save in appearance, our logical classifications.   These involve a series of concepts whose extent and connotation are definite, and they constitute an ascending scale the degrees of which reflection has tested. The prelogical mind does not objectify nature thus.   It *lives*

9

it rather, by feeling itself participate in it, and feeling these participations everywhere ; and it interprets this complexity of participations by social forms. If the element of generality exists, it can only be sought for in the participation extending to, and the mystic qualities circulating among, certain entities, uniting them and identifying them in the collective representation.

In default of really general concepts, therefore, primitive mentality is conversant with collective representations which to a certain extent take their place. Although concrete, such representations are extremely comprehensive in this respect, that they are constantly employed, that they readily apply to an infinite number of cases, and that from this point of view they correspond, as we have said, with what categories are for logical thought. But their mystic and concrete nature has often puzzled investigators. These did indeed note its importance and could not fail to draw attention to it, though at the same time they realized that they were face to face with a method of thinking which was opposed to their own mental habits. Some examples in addition to those already quoted will help to make us realize these representations, which are general without however being at the same time abstract.

In the Yaos,[1] Hetherwick notes beliefs which appear incomprehensible to him. He cannot understand how it is that the *lisoka* (the soul, shade or spirit) can be at once both personal and impersonal. In fact, after death the *lisoka* becomes *mulungu*. This word has two meanings : one, the soul of the dead, the other, " the spirit world in general, or more properly speaking the aggregate of the spirits of all the dead." This would be conceivable if *mulungu* meant a collective unity formed by the union of all the individual spirits ; but this explanation is not permissible, for at the same time *mulungu* signifies " a state or property inhering in something, as life or health inheres in the body, and it is also regarded as the agent in anything mysterious. ' It is *mulungu* ' is the Yao exclamation on being shown anything that is beyond the range of his understanding." This is a characteristic trait which we shall find

[1] Hetherwick, " Some Animistic Beliefs among the Yaos of Central Africa," *J.A.I.*, xxxii. pp. 89-95.

in all collective representations of this nature : they are used indifferently to indicate a person or persons, or a quality or property of a thing.

To get out of the difficulty, Hetherwick distinguishes between what he calls " three stages of animistic belief : (1) the human *lisoka* or shade, the agent in dreams, delirium, etc. ; (2) this *lisoka* regarded as *mulungu*, and an object of worship and reverence, the controller of the affairs of this life, the active agent in the fortunes of the human race ; (3) *mulungu* as expressing the great spirit agency, the creator of the world and all life, the source of all things animate or inanimate." It seems as if Hetherwick, like the French missionaries of old in New France, tends to interpret what he observes by the light of his own religious beliefs, but he adds, in good faith : " And yet between these three conceptions of the spirit nature no definite boundary line can be drawn. The distinction in the native mind is ever of the haziest. No one will give you a dogmatic statement of his belief on such points."

If Hetherwick did not get from the Yaos the answers he wanted, it may possibly have been because the Yaos did not understand his questions, but it was largely because he did not grasp their ideas. To the Yaos the transit from the personal soul, before or after death, to the impersonal soul or to the mystic quality which pervades every object in which there is something divine, sacred and mystic (not supernatural, for on the contrary nothing is more natural to primitive mentality than this kind of mystic power) is not felt. To tell the truth, there is not even such transit : there is " identity governed by the law of participation " such as we found in the case of the Huichols, entirely different from logical identity. And through the perpetual working of the law of participation, the mystic principle thus circulating and spreading among entities may be represented indifferently as a person or subject, or a property or power of the objects which share it, and consequently an attribute. Prelogical mentality does not consider there is any difficulty about this.

It is the same with the North American Indians, about whom we have abundant and definite information. Miss

Alice Fletcher,[1] in describing the mysterious power called
wakanda, writes of their idea of the continuity of life, by
which " a relation was maintained between the seen and the
unseen, the dead and the living, and also between the fragment
of anything and its entirety." Here continuity means what
we call participation, since this continuity obtains between
the living and the dead; between a man's nail-parings,
saliva, or hair and the man himself; between a certain bear
or buffalo and the mystic ensemble of the bear or buffalo
species.

Moreover, like the *mulungu* just spoken of, *wakanda* or
wakan may signify not only a mystic reality, like that which
Miss Fletcher calls " life," but a characteristic, a quality
belonging to persons and things. Thus there are *wakan*
men, who have gone through many previous existences.
" They arise to conscious existence in the form of winged
seeds, such as the thistle, . . . and pass through a series of
inspiration, with different classes of divinities, till they are
fully *wakanized* and prepared for human incarnation. They
are invested with the invisible *wakan* powers of the gods. . . ." [2]
Similarly, day and night are *wakan*. The term is explained
thus by an Indian : " While the day lasts a man is able to
do many wonderful things, kill animals, men, etc. . . . But
he does not fully understand why the day is, nor does he know
who makes or causes the light. Therefore he believes that it
was not made by hand, i.e. that no human being makes the
day give light. Therefore the Indians say that the day is
wakan. So is the sun. . . ." Here it is a property, a
mystic quality inherent in things that is meant. And the
Indian adds : " When it is night, there are ghosts and many
fearful objects, so they regard the night as *wakan*. . . .[3]
A yet earlier investigator, quoted by Dorsey, had already
remarked : " No one term can express the full meaning of
the Dacota's *wakan*. It comprehends all mystery, secret
power and divinity. . . . All life is *wakan*. So also is everything which exhibits power, whether in action, as the winds
and drifting clouds, or in passive endurance, as the boulder
by the wayside. . . . It covers the whole field of fear and

---

[1] " The Signification of the Scalp-lock," *J.A.I.*, xxvii. p. 437.
[2] Dorsey, " Siouan Cults," *E. B. Rept.*, xi. p. 494.   [3] Ibid., p. 467.

worship; but many things that are neither feared nor worshipped, but are simply wonderful, come under this designation." [1]

We may be inclined to ask, what, then, is *not wakan*? Such a question would in fact be urged by logical thought which demands the strict definition of its concepts, and a rigorously determined connotation and extent. But prelogical reasoning does not feel the need of this, especially when dealing with collective representations which are both concrete and very general. *Wakan* is something of a mystic nature in which any object whatever may or may not participate, according to circumstances. " Man himself may become mysterious by fasting, prayer and vision." [2] A human being is not necessarily *wakan* or not *wakan*, therefore, and one of the duties of the medicine-man in this matter is to avoid errors which might have fatal results. *Wakan* might be compared with a fluid which courses through all existing things, and is the mystic principle of the life and virtue of all beings. " A young man's weapons are *wakan* : they must not be touched by a woman. They contain divine power. . . . A man prays to his weapons on the day of battle."

If the observer recording these facts interprets them at the same time (as usually happens), and if he has not noted the difference between prelogical reasoning and logical thinking, he will be led direct to anthromorphic animism. Here, for instance, is what Charlevoix tells us about the same North American Indians : " If one is to believe the savages, there is nothing in nature which has not a corresponding spirit : but there are varying orders of spirits, and all have not the same power. When they fail to understand a thing, they attribute supreme virtue to it, and they then account for it by saying ' it is a spirit.' " [3] That means that this thing is " *wakan* " ; just as the Yaos say " it is *mulungu* ! "

Although Spencer and Gillen uphold the animistic theory, they are too keen observers not to have themselves noticed how very puzzling these collective representations are to our logical thinking. They remarked that certain words are some-

---

[1] Dorsey, " Siouan Cults," *E. B. Rept.*, xi. pp. 432–3.
[2] Ibid., p. 365.
[3] Charlevoix, *Journal d'un Voyage dans l'Amérique Septentrionale*, iii. p. 346.

times used as substantives, and then again as adjectives. For
instance, *arungquiltha* to the Aruntas is " a supernatural evil
power." " A thin ostrich or emu is either *arungquiltha* or is
endowed with *arungquiltha*. The name is applied indiscriminately either to the evil influence or to the object in which
it is, for the time being, or permanently, resident." [1] Elsewhere, Spencer and Gillen state that *arungquiltha* is sometimes
personal and sometimes impersonal. " They believe that
eclipses are caused by the periodic visits of the *arungquiltha*,
who would like to take up his abode in the sun, permanently
obliterating its light, and that the evil spirit is only dragged
out by the medicine-men." [2] Even the *churinga*, which these
aborigines regard as a sacred, living being and, according to
some observations made, as the body of a personal ancestor,
is on other occasions considered to be a mystic property
inherent in things. " *Churinga*," say Spencer and Gillen
explicitly, " is used either as a substantive, when it implies
a sacred emblem, or as a qualifying term, when it implies
sacred or secret." [3]

In the Torres Straits, also, " when anything behaved in a
remarkable or mysterious manner it could be regarded as a
zogo . . . rain, wind, a concrete object or a shrine can be
a *zogo* ; a *zogo* can be impersonal or personal ; it belonged in
a general way to particular groups of natives, but it was a
particular property of certain individuals, the *zogo le*, who alone
knew all the ceremonies connected with it, because the rites
were confined to them. . . . I do not know how the term
can be better translated than by the word ' sacred.' The
term *zogo* is usually employed as a noun, even when it might
be expected to be an adjective." [4]

Hubert and Mauss, in their acute analysis of the idea of
the *mana* of the Melanesians, described by Codrington, and
also that of the Huron *orenda*, have clearly brought out their
relation to the idea of *wakan*.[5] What we have just said about
the latter applies equally to these and to other similar con-

---

[1] *The Native Tribes of Central Australia*, p. 548 (note).
[2] Ibid., p. 566. Cf. *The Northern Tribes of Central Australia*, p. 629.
[3] Ibid., p. 139 (note).
[4] *The Cambridge Anthropological Expedition to Torres Straits*, vi. pp. 244-5.
[5] *Esquisse d'une théorie générale de la magie, Année Sociologique*, vii.
pp. 108 et. seq. (1904).

ceptions of which it would be an easy matter to find examples elsewhere, also interpreted as animistic. Such an idea is that of *wong*, which we find in West Africa. " The Guinea Coast negro's generic name for a fetish-spirit is *wong* ; these aerial beings dwell in temple-huts and consume sacrifices, enter into and inspire their priests, cause health and sickness among men, and execute the behests of the mighty Heaven-god. But part or all of them are connected with material objects and a native can say ' In this river, or tree or amulet, there is a *wong*.' . . . Thus among the *wongs* of the land are rivers, lakes and springs ; districts of land, termite-hills, trees, croco- diles, apes, snakes, elephants, and birds." [1]   It is from a mis- sionary's report that Tylor has borrowed this account, and it is by no means difficult to find in it, not only " the three stages of animistic belief " which Hetherwick noticed in the Yaos, but also a collective representation entirely similar to *wakan, mana, orenda*, and many others.

Collective representations of such a nature are to be found, more or less clearly indicated, in nearly all the primitive peoples who have been studied at all closely. They dominate, as Hubert and Mauss have well demonstrated, their religious beliefs and magic practices. It is possibly through them that the difference between prelogical mentality and logical thought can be best defined. When face to face with such repre- sentations the latter is always dubious. Are they realities which exist *per se*, or merely very general predicates ?   Are we dealing with one single and universal subject, with a kind of world-soul or spirit, or with a multiplicity of souls, spirits, divinities ?   Or again, do these representations imply, as many missionaries have believed, both a supreme divinity and an infinite number of lesser powers ?   It is the nature of logical thought to demand a reply to questions such as these. It cannot admit at one and the same time of alternatives which seem to be mutually exclusive. The nature of prelogical mentality, on the contrary, is to ignore the necessity. Essen- tially mystic as it is, it finds no difficulty in imagining, as well as feeling, the identity of the one and the many, the individual and the species, of entities however unlike they be, by means of

[1] Tylor, *Primitive Culture* (4th edit), ii. p. 205.

participation. In this lies its guiding principle ; this it is which accounts for the kind of abstraction and generalization peculiar to such a mentality, and to this, again, we must mainly refer the characteristic forms of activity we find in primitive peoples.

PART II

CHAPTER IV

THE MENTALITY OF PRIMITIVES IN RELATION TO THE LANGUAGES THEY SPEAK

THE essential characteristics of the mentality of a given social group should, it seems to me, be reflected to some extent in the language its members speak. In the long run the mental habits of the group cannot fail to leave some trace upon their modes of expression, since these are also social phenomena, upon which the individual has little, if any, influence. With differing types of mentality, therefore, there should be languages which differ in their construction. We could not venture very far upon the strength of so general a principle, however. In the first place, we do not know whether even in primitive peoples there is a single one who speaks *his own* language—that is, a language which exactly corresponds, according to the hypothesis suggested above, with the type of mind which his group ideas express. On the contrary it is probable that by reason of migration, intermingling and absorption of groups we shall nowhere encounter the conditions which such a hypothesis implies. Even in the period known to history a social group very often adopts the language of another group which has conquered it, or been conquered by it. We can therefore safely establish nothing more than a very general correspondence between the characteristics of the languages and those of the mentality of the social groups, confining ourselves exclusively to such characteristics as are to be found in the language and the mentality of all the groups of a certain kind.

In the second place, the languages of primitive peoples are still very little known. Of very many of them we possess no more than very imperfect vocabularies. They may perhaps allow of our placing them, provisionally, in a certain linguistic family, but they are wholly insufficient for the purpose of comparative study, and in the opinion of those best qualified to judge, a comparative grammar of the different families of spoken languages would be an impossible achievement.

Lastly, the construction of the languages spoken by primitive peoples conveys both that which is peculiar to their own mental habits and that which they have in common with ourselves. We have already found that *prelogical* does not mean *antilogical*. We cannot lay down a principle that these languages must have special grammars differing specifically from our own. We are compelled, therefore, to leave these too vast problems untouched, and discover by some more modest method how far an examination of their languages may confirm what I have already said about the mentality of primitives. Leaving grammar, properly so called, out of the question, I shall primarily search for what may be revealed of the mind of such peoples in the construction of their sentences and in their vocabulary, and I shall choose my examples preferably from the languages of the North American Indians, which have been specially studied by those who collaborate in the Washington Bureau of Ethnography. This does not, however, preclude me from quoting, for the purpose of comparison, from other tongues which may belong to quite different language groups.

I

Perhaps the most salient characteristic of most of the languages of the North American Indians is the care they take to express concrete details which our languages leave understood or unexpressed. " A Ponka Indian in saying that a man killed a rabbit, would have to say : the man, he, one, animate, standing (in the nominative case), purposely killed by shooting an arrow the rabbit, he, the one, animal, sitting (in the objective case) ; for the form of a verb to kill would have to be selected, and the verb changes its form by inflection or incorporated particles to denote person, number, and gender (as animate or inanimate) and gender again as sitting or lying, and case. The form of the verb would also express whether the killing was done accidentally or purposely, and whether it was by shooting . . . and if by shooting, whether by bow and arrow, or by gun." [1] So too, in the Cherokee tongue, "instead of the vague expression *we*, there are distinct modifications meaning I and thou, I and ye, I and ye two, I and he, I and they, etc., and in the plural I, thou, and he or they, I, ye, and he and they, etc., etc. In the simple conjugation of the present of the indicative, including the pronouns in the nominative and oblique cases, there are not less than seventy distinct forms. . . . Other nice distinctions ; the various forms of the verb denote whether the object be animate or inanimate, whether or not the person spoken of, either as agent or object, is expected to hear what is said, and in regard to the dual and plural numbers, whether the action terminates upon the several objects collectively, as if it were one object, or upon each object considered separately, etc." [2]

These languages, therefore, like our own, recognize a number category, but they do not express it in the same way. We oppose the singular to the plural : a subject or object is either singular or plural, and this mental habit involves a rapid and familiar use of abstraction, that is, of logical thought and the matter it deals with. Prelogical mentality does not proceed thus, however. "To the observing mind of the Klamath Indian," says Gatschet in his excellent Klamath grammar, "the fact that things were done repeatedly, at different times, or that the same thing was done severally by distinct persons, appeared much more important than the pure idea of plurality, as we have it in our language." [3] Klamath has no plural form, but it makes use of a distributive reduplication, and every time that this form indicates plurality, it is merely because this idea of distributive reduplication happens to coincide with the idea of plurality.

"Thus *nep* means hands as well as hand, the hand, a hand, but its distributive form *nénap* means each of the two hands or the hands of each person when considered as a separate individual. *Ktchō'l* means star, the stars, constellation or constellations ; *ktchóktchōl* means each star or every star

[1] Powell, " The Evolution of Language," *E. B. Rept.*, i. p. 16.
[2] Gallatin, *Transactions of the American Ethnological Society*, ii. pp. 130–1.
[3] A. Gatschet, *The Klamath Language*, p. 419.

or constellation considered separately. *Pádshaĩ* means you became blind of one eye ; *papádsha ĩ*, you are totally blind, you lost the use of each of your eyes." [1]

Does this mean that the Klamath language cannot express a plural ? By no means ; but it does so in varied forms. " The plural number of the subject of the sentence may be indicated in different ways : (1) analytically by adding to the noun a numeral or an indefinite pronoun (a few, some, all, many, etc.) ; (2) by the noun being collective, or one of the substantives designating persons, which possess a form for the real plural ; (3) the large majority of substantives having no real plural, their plurality is indicated in the intransitive verbs by the distributive form, and in a few transitive verbs by a special form which has *also* a distributive function ; (4) the dual form serves for two, three, or four subjects of certain intransitive verbs." [2]

To judge from these examples, which are by no means exceptional, if prelogical mentality primarily makes no use of the plural form it is because such a form is not sufficiently explicit, and does not specify the particular modality of the plural. The primitive's mentality needs to differentiate between two, three, a few, or many subjects or objects, to indicate whether they are together or separate. As we shall see later, it has no general terms for " tree " or " fish " but special terms for every variety of tree or of fish. It will therefore have methods of rendering, not the pure and simple plural, but the varying kinds of plural. As a general rule we shall find this peculiarity the more marked when we are considering languages spoken by the social groups in which prelogical mentality is still dominant.

In fact, in the Australian dialects, in those of the New Hebrides and Melanesia, and in those of New Guinea, we find used, sometimes as well as the plural form properly so called, sometimes without it, the dual, trial, and even what we might term the quadrial forms. Thus in the Papuan language of the island of Kiwai, " nouns are often used without any mark of number ; but when the noun is the subject of a verb, it is usual to distinguish number by means of a suffix. The singular is shown by the suffix *ro*, the dual by

A. Gatschet. *The Klamath Language*, pp. 262–3.   [2] Ibid., pp. 578–9.

the word *toribo*, the trial by the word *potoro*. The plural is shown by the word *sirio* preceding, or by the word *sirioro* following. The singular suffix *ro* is very commonly omitted. *Potoro* is used also for four, and its real meaning is therefore probably " a few." The *ro* suffixed in *potoro* and *sirioro* is probably the same as the singular *ro*, and suggests that *potoro* is a set of three, a triad, and *sirioro* a lot, a number." [1]

In this same language we find a multiplicity of verbal suffixes, simple and compound, the function of which is to specify how many subjects act upon how many objects at a given moment.   Here are examples of suffixes :

> *rudo* means the action of two on many in past time.
> *rumo* means the action of many on many in the past.
> *durudo*, the action of two on many in present time.
> *durumo*, the action of many on many in the present.
> *amadurodo*, the action of two on two in present time.
> *amarudo*, similar action in past time.
> *amarumo*, the action of many on two in past time.
> *ibidurudo*, the action of many on three in present time.
> *ibidurumo*, similar action in past time.
> *amabidurumo*, action of three on two in present time, etc.[2]

To my mind the desire for concrete specification could scarcely be expressed more clearly, as far as number is concerned.   Therefore we may say that these languages possess a whole system of plurals. " The dual number, and what is called the trial, are in Melanesian languages, with the exception of a very few words, really no distinct number, but the plural with a numeral attached." [3] This remark of Codrington's applies exactly to the languages of British New Guinea. It amounts to saying that these languages express as fully as possible a plural which is determinate in number, and not simply a plural.

The same phenomenon occurs frequently in the Australian languages. Thus, " in all the dialects having the Tyattyalla structure, there are four numbers, the singular, dual, trial, and plural.   The trial has also forms in the first person (inclusive

---

[1] *The Cambridge Expedition to the Torres Straits*, iii. p. 306.
[2] Codrington, *Melanesian Languages*, p. 111, quoted in *The Cambridge Expedition to Torres Straits*, iii. p. 428.
[3] Ibid.

and exclusive). The trial has also been found by me in the Thaguwurru and Woiwurru tongues. . . . The existence of trial was reported years ago in Aneityum and some other islands in the Pacific Ocean, and was observed to some extent in the pronouns of the Woddouro tribe in Victoria by Mr. Tuckfield." [1] " Although the dual is generally used, a trial is often met with in the Bureba language (Murray River)." [2] " The trial number, as existing in the native languages of Victoria, is different in character from that observed in some other countries. For example, in the New Hebrides, the case endings of the dual, trial and plural are independent and differ from each other in form. . . . But among the Victorian tribes, the trial number is formed by adding another case-ending to that of the plural." [3] In the Motu language of New Guinea, W. G. Lawes, the missionary, reports that the dual and the trial of pronouns is formed by additions to the plural. This is the fact which Codrington had noted.

In New Mecklenburg, in the Bismark Archipelago, forms of quadrial (*Vierzahl*) over and above the trial, had been encountered. These quadrial forms are to be found also in Nggao (Solomon Isles) and at Araga and Tanna, in the New Hebrides. They are the counterpart of the Polynesian " plurals," which in reality are trials.[4]

The diversity of these forms does not prevent our recognizing a common tendency in all. Sometimes we have the dual and trial as independent forms, co-existing with the plural, properly so called, in the New Hebrides ; sometimes there are plurals completed by a suffix which specifies a number, as in the languages of Melanesia and New Guinea, and some Australian tongues. Occasionally the distributive reduplication is prior to the plural proper and supplies its place ; or again, the plural seems to be wanting, and there are various ways of providing for it. For example, " In Dènè-dindjié there is no plural, and the idea of it is expressed by the addition of the word ' many ' to the singular. . . . The Peaux de lièvre and the Loucheux make use of the dual

[1] Mathews, " The Aboriginal Languages of Victoria," *Journal of the Royal Society of New South Wales*, pp. 72–3 (1903).
[2] Ibid., p. 172.
[3] Id., " Languages of the Kamitaroi," *J.A.I.*, xxxiii. pp. 282–3.
[4] P. W. Schmidt, *Anthropos*, ii. p. 905 (1907).

element and this form indiscriminately." [1] Occasionally, too, there is variety in the formation of the plural. Thus, in the Abipone language, " the formation of the plural number of nouns is very difficult to beginners, for it is so various that hardly any rule can be set down. . . . Moreover, the Abipones have *two* plurals : more than one, and many. *Joalei*, some men ; *Joaliripi*, many men." [2] This differentiation is a familiar one in Semitic languages also. We see in them the various methods (the list of which we have not exhausted) by which languages express the various modalities of numeration. Instead of indicating plurality in general, they specify what sort of plurality is intended : of two things together, or of three. Beyond three, a good many languages say " many." This is doubtless why we find no special forms for the plural, beyond the dual and the trial, in the tongues of the most primitive peoples we know of. Little by little, as the mental functioning is modified and representations necessarily become less concrete, there is a tendency to reduce plural forms to the simple plural. We lose the trial form first of all, and then the dual. Junod notes an isolated survival of the dual form in the Ronga language.[3] The history of Greek demonstrates a continuous decay of the dual form which is significant.[4]

II

It is not in the number category alone that the need for concrete expression manifests itself in the languages of primitives. There is at least the same wealth of forms which endeavour to render the varied modality of action denoted by a verb. For instance, in the language of the Ngeumba tribe of the Darling River, New South Wales, in the past and future tenses, terminations vary to indicate whether the action described occurred in the immediate, recent, or remote past, or will take place at once or in the near or remote future ; whether there has been, or will be, repetition or continuity of action ; and yet other modifications of verbal suffixes. These terminations are the same for all the persons in

[1] Petitot, *Dictionnaire de la Langue Dènè-dindjié*, p. lii.
[2] Dobrizhoffer, *An Account of the Abipones*, ii. p. 163.
[3] Junod, *Grammaire Ronga*, p. 135.
[4] Cuny, *Le Duel en Grec*, pp. 506–8.

the singular, dual, and plural. Therefore there are different forms to express—

I shall beat (indefinite).
I shall beat in the morning.
I shall beat all day.
I shall beat in the evening.
I shall beat in the night.
I shall beat again, etc.[1]

In the Kafir tongue, with the help of auxiliary verbs, we can obtain six or seven imperative forms, all with differing meanings:

1. *Ma unyuke e ntabeni*—Stand up to go up the hill.
2. *Ka unyuke e ntabeni*—Make one move to go up the hill.
3. *Suka u nyuke ntabeni*—Wake up to go up the hill.
4. *Hamb'o kunyuka*—Walk up to go up.
5. *Uz' unyuke e ntabeni*—Come to go up the hill, etc., etc.

Though all the above expressions may be rendered by "go up the hill," yet properly form (1) supposes a change of occupation, (2) may be used only of a momentary action ; (3) will best be said to one who is too slow to perform an order, (4) to one who has to go some way before beginning to go up the hill, and (5) conveys an order or prayer which allows delay in the execution, etc., etc.[2]

The extraordinary prolixity of the verbal forms in the languages of the North American Indians is well known, and in those known as Indo-European it seems to have been no less. In the Abipone language it creates, as Dobrizhoffer says, "a labyrinth most formidable." [3] In Northern Asia, "the Aléutian verb, according to Venianimof, can take more than four hundred endings, to indicate mood, tense, and person, without reckoning the tenses which may be formed with the help of auxiliaries. It is clear that originally each of these many forms corresponded with a definite shade of meaning, and that the Aléutian of former days, like the Turkish language of our times, was marvellously versatile in responding to the very minutest verbal modality." [4]

[1] Mathews, " Aboriginal Tribes of New South Wales and Victoria," *Journal of the Royal Society of New South Wales*, pp. 220–4 (1905). Cf. ibid., pp. 142, 151, 166 (1903).
[2] Torrend, *Comparative Grammar of the South African Bantu Languages*, p. 231.
[3] Dobrizhoffer, op. cit., ii. pp. 172–80.
[4] V. Henry, *Esquisse d'une Grammaire Raisonnée de la Langue Aléoute,*" pp. 34–5.

If the need for concrete expression and the accumulation of forms capable of expressing any peculiarities of action, or subject and object, are indeed features common to very many of the languages spoken by primitive peoples ; if these features tend to grow weaker or to disappear as communities advance in development, it is permissible to inquire what it is with which they correspond in that which we have called the mentality peculiar to these peoples. It is a mentality which makes little use of abstraction, and even that in a different method from a mind under the sway of logical thought ; it has not the same concepts at command. Will it be possible to go yet a little further and find, in examining the matter at its disposal—that is, the vocabulary of its languages—any positive indications of the manner of its functioning ?

The Klamath language, which may be taken to represent a very numerous family of languages in North America, obeys a well-marked tendency which Gatschet calls " pictorial," a tendency to delineate that which one desires to express. " A motion performed in a straight line is referred to differently from a motion performed sidewise or obliquely or at a distance from the one speaking, circumstances which it would seldon occur to us to express in European languages." [1] It is above all in its primitive form that the Klamath language displays this characteristic. At that time " it seems to have left unnoticed the expression of number in verbs, as well as in nouns and found no more necessity to define it than to define sex. Only a little more attention was paid to the categories of mode and tense, for what was done in all these belongs to later periods of linguistic development. Concrete categories alone were then accounted of importance ; for all relations bearing upon locality, distance, and individuality or severalty are distinguished with superior accuracy, and even tense is marked by means of particles which were originally locomotive." [2]

In short, it is especially spatial relations, all that can be retained and reproduced by visual and muscular memory, that the Klamath language aims at expressing, and this the more exclusively in the most remote period of its history.

[1] A. Gatschet, *The Klamath Language*, p. 460.   [2] Ibid., pp. 433–4.

Like nearly all the languages of primitive peoples, it has
no verb " to be." " The verb *gi* which takes the place of
it is, in fact, the demonstrative pronoun *ge*, *ke* (this one, this
here), in a verbified shape, and having assumed the verbal
form, it came to signify to be here, to be at this or that place,
to be at this time or at such a time." [1] In a general way,
that which relates to time is expressed by words which were
first of all applied to spatial relations. " In Klamath, as
in many other languages, there are only two tense-forms,
one for the completed and the other for the incompleted act or
state . . . and . . . both forms, whether appearing in the
verb or in some substantives, originally had a locative
character, now pointing to distance in time only." [2]

The spatial element predominates in the same way where
case is concerned. Setting aside the " three purely grammatical cases (subjective, direct objective, and possessive),
all the other cases, as instrumental, inessive, adessive, etc.,
are either locative, or take their origin in some locative relation
of the noun to the verb." [3] Even the possessive was originally locative, and the partitive also, which " is but another
form of the prefix *ta*, and originally both referred to objects
standing erect, as men, animals, trees, etc., the suffixed *i*
pointing to location *on*, *upon* something." [4] It is the same
with the inessive. " As the first of the five post-position
cases, I have placed the one formed of the pronominal element
i, *hi*. . . . It occurs in nominal inflection as a case-terminal
by itself, and also enters the composition of several others,
as *ti*, *χēni*, *ēmi*, *kshi*, *ksaki* . . . From its primary signification
upon the ground, have developed those of *within*, *at home*,
in the lodge, *for one's or another's benefit or disadvantage*, and
the temporal one *when*, *at the time when*." [5] Finally as to
the directive case : " this case post-position is a combination
of the two pronominal elements *ta* and *la*, which we find to
be the components of a large number of affixes. It is most
generally connected with verbs of motion, and corresponds
with our *to*, *toward*. . . . It is connected with the names
of the cardinal points of the horizon, and . . . the original

---

[1] A. Gatschet, *The Klamath Language*, pp. 430–1.
[2] Ibid., p. 402.   [3] Ibid., p. 467.
[4] Ibid., p. 476.   [5] Ibid., p. 485.

use made of this particle seems to have been that of pointing to objects visible at long distances." [1] We must refer to Gatschet's work for " a long series of locative case-endings." [2]

If we pass on to the demonstrative pronouns we shall find that there, too, we have a great many spatial pecularities most minutely expressed. Klamath is not content with distinguishing *this* from *that* ; it distinguishes, both in animate and inanimate kind :

> this (so near as to be touched)
> this (close by, right here)
> this (standing, being before you)
> this (present, visible, within sight)
>
> that visible (though distant)
> that absent
> that absent (departed)
> that (beyond sight)

All these forms are in use both for the subjective and the objective case,[3] and this is not, as we know, a peculiarity of the Klamath tongue. In most primitive languages, personal and demonstrative pronouns exhibit a large number of different forms, in order to express the relations of distance, relative position, visibility, presence or absence, between subject and object, etc. To quote but one or two examples taken from the languages of wholly undeveloped peoples, in the Wongai-bon tongue demonstrative pronouns are both numerous and varied, and represent divers grades of meaning which depend upon the position of the object with regard to the speaker as well as with regard to cardinal points. It is the same, too, with the Dyirrigan and Yota-yota languages.[4] In the case of the Yahgans, pronouns are very numerous . . . they have, the three numbers, and are declined like nouns. The Yahgans, when making use of pronouns, always indicate the position of the person spoken of. . . . For instance, they speak of him or her in relation to an object at the upper end of the

---

[1] A. Gatsch et, *The Klamath Language*, p. 489.
[2] Ibid., pp. 479 et seq.   [3] Ibid., pp. 538 et seq.
[4] Mathews, " Languages of . . . Queensland, New South Wales and Victoria," *Journal of the Royal Society of New South Wales*, pp. 151, 163, 170 (1903).

wigwam, or facing the door, or to a person at the bottom of
a creek or a valley—at the left or right of the wigwam or in
its interior—in the wigwam, near the threshold—outside the
house. All these pronouns are of three classes, according
to whether they refer to the position of the person who is
speaking, the person spoken to, or the one spoken of. . . . It
is the same with the demonstrative pronouns.[1]

The post-positions in Klamath are exceptionally numerous,
and nearly all express spatial relations. " Those of our
prepositions which are of an abstract nature, as about, on
behalf of, for, concerning, etc., are expressed by inflectional
suffixes, appended to the verb or noun, and all the post-
positions we meet are of a concrete, locative signification.
Even the few temporal post-positions are locative at the
same time." [2] In Gatschet's book the reader will find a list
of the " principal " of these, forty-three in number.

" Temporal adverbs have all evolved from locative
adverbs, and hence often retain both significations. . . .
Adverbs of space are very numerous and multiform, almost
all the pronominal radices having contributed to the list." [3]
Gatschet enumerates fifty-four of these which, he says, are
the most frequently met with. There are special ways of
expressing "close by," "in front," "here at the side," etc.

Without unduly prolonging the list of proofs, which it
would be quite easy to multiply, we may therefore regard
as established the conclusion formulated by Gatschet in the
following terms. " The concrete categories of position, location and distance are of such paramount importance to the
conception of rude nations as are to us those of time and
causality." [4] Every sentence in which concrete beings or
objects are in question (and in such languages there are
scarcely any others) must accordingly express their spatial
relation. This essential point may be compared with the
necessity of giving every noun in our language a gender.
" The student " (of language) says Powell, " must entirely
free his mind from the idea that gender is simply a distinction
of sex. In Indian tongues " (possibly, too, in Bantu and

---

[1] T. Bridges, " A few Notes on the Structure of the Yahgan," *J.A.I.*,
xxiii. pp. 53–80.
[2] A. Gatschet, *The Klamath Language*, pp. 554 et seq.
[3] Ibid., pp. 562 et seq., 583.   [4] Ibid., p. 306.

in Indo-European languages), " genders are usually methods
of classification primarily into animate and inanimate. The
animate may again be divided into male and female, but
this is rarely the case. Often by these genders all objects
are classified by characteristics found in their attitude or
supposed constitution. Thus we may have the animate and
inanimate, one or both, divided into the *standing, sitting, lying*
. . . or . . . into the *watery, mushy, earthy, stony, woody,
fleshy.*" [1]

In Klamath, for instance, "whenever an animate or inanimate subject or object is referred to as *being somewhere*, either
indoor or outdoor, around, below, between, or above somebody
or something, in the water or on the ground, the verb *gi*, to
be, is not employed, but the adverbial idea becomes verbified
in the form of some intransitive verb, so that below, e.g.
becomes *i-utila*, to be or lie below, underneath. The mode
of existence has also to be distinctly qualified in that verbified term ; it has to be stated whether the object or subject
was standing, sitting or lying, staying, living, sleeping.
Usually the idea of staying and living coincides with that of
sitting, and sleeping with that of lying on a certain spot." [2]
In other languages, modifications of the pronouns satisfy
this demand. With the Abipones, for example, if the object
of discourse is—

		MASCULINE.	FEMININE.
present,	it is designated by	eneha	anaha
if it be seated	it is designated by	hiniha	haniha
if it be lying	it is designated by	hiriha	hariha
if it be standing	it is designated by	haraha	haraha
if walking and visible	it is designated by	ehaha	ahaha
if walking and invisible	it is designated by	ekaha	akaha

If the object alone is—

seated	it is designated by ynitara
lying	it is designated by iritara
walking	it is designated by ekatara
absent	it is designated by okatara
standing	it is designated by eratara [3]

[1] Powell, " The Evolution of Language," *E. B. Rept.*, i. pp. 9–10.
[2] A. Gatschet, *The Klamath Language*, pp. 674–5.
[3] Dobrizhoffer, *An Account of the Abipones*, ii. p. 166.

Since facts like these are ascertainable in nearly all the languages of primitive peoples actually known to us, we may regard the necessity to which they bear witness as an essential element of primitive mentality.

III

But primitive mentality does not demand alone that the relative positions of things and persons in space, as well as their distance from each other, be expressed. It is not satisfied unless the language expressly specifies besides, the details regarding the form of objects, their dimensions ; way of moving about in the various circumstances in which they may be placed; and to accomplish this, the most divers forms are employed. The Klamath language, which will serve as a type once more, mainly has recourse to affixes, of which it possesses a surprising number. A few examples only will suffice to show the extent to which this meticulousness is prosecuted. I shall consider prefixes first.

(1) *Prefixes indicating form and dimensions.*

a, a verb and noun prefix, denoting long, high objects, such as poles, sticks, and also human beings when their stature is being considered. It differs from *tg, tk,* which are no longer met with save as part of a root syllable denoting the immobility of a subject placed upright, in that it denotes long objects which are not necessarily in an upright position. For instance :

> *aggédsha*—to describe a circle (the hand of a watch).
> *akátchga*—to break (poles and sticks).
> *alahia*—to show (a tree).

The prefix *a* is seen also in the initial syllable *ai* or *ei,* when referring to a movement made with the head, as *aika,* to move the head forward.

(2) *Prefixes denoting a special method of dealing with definite objects.*

iy, y, prefixes of transitive verbs and their derivatives, indicating an action performed with or upon a number of elongated persons or objects, or upon objects considered collectively, when not standing in an invariable upright position. If there be but one object, the prefixes are *a*, *e*, *ksh*, *u*. . . . For example :

> *idsah*—to cause to move, or carry away (a single object, *éna*).
> *itpa*—to fetch away, to remove (a single object, *átpa*).

(3) *Prefixes denoting movement in a certain direction.*

ki, *ke*, *ge*, *k*, *g*, prefixes of transitive and intransitive verbs and their derivatives, to indicate an action accomplished obliquely, from the side, or a lateral movement towards an object.

> *kiápka*—to lie down across (*ipka*, to be lying).
> *kimádsh*—an ant (anything which walks or moves sideways).

Km is a prefix formed from the combination of the prefix *k* (shortened form of *ki*) and *ma* (abbreviated to *m*), the latter indicating a curvilinear movement or object, *km* accordingly denotes a lateral or curvilinear movement, or the turning movement of an object, like a cord, thread, or wrinkle.

> *kmukóltgi*—to wrinkle (as the effect of moisture).

(4) *Prefixes denoting form and movement.*

l, prefixed to verbs and nouns which describe or indicate the outside of a round or spheroidal, cylindrical, discoid or bulbed object, or a ring ; also voluminous ; or again, an act accomplished with an object which bears such a form ; or a circular or semi-circular or waving movement of the body, arms, hands, or other parts. Therefore this prefix is to be found connected with clouds, celestial bodies, rounded slopes on the earth's surface, fruits rounded or bulbed in shape, stones and dwellings (these last being usually circular in form). It is employed, too, for a crowd of animals, for enclosures, social gatherings (since an assembly usually adopts the form of a circle), and so forth.

(5) *Prefix denoting a movement in a definite medium.*

tch, *ts*, a prefix which appears in terms exclusively denoting the movements observed in water and other liquids, the floating of objects on or in water, the flow or movement of liquids themselves.

> *tchéwa*—to float (from *éwa*, used of water-birds).
> *tchlā'lχa*—to sink (from *élχa*).

(6) *A compound prefix indicating a certain movement or form.*

shl, a prefix compounded of the prefixes *sh* and *l*, and indicating, in nouns, as in verbs (almost invariably transitive) objects of a slender, flexible shape, of the nature of leaves, such as linen, cloaks, hats, other articles of clothing or things in which one may be wrapped, and also other objects which may have folded surfaces; even baskets, because they are flexible.

> *Shlaniya*—to stretch (a skin, for instance).
> *Shlâ-ish*—a mat.
> *Shlápa*—to open, be in flower.
> *Shlápsh*—bud.

In summing up, Gatschet gives a recapitulation of the Klamath language-prefixes, which the question of space forbids me to quote. I shall indicate the most important at least, in order that a glance at the various functions of the prefixes may enable us to see the predominance of the function which serves to specify spatial relations, forms, and methods of moving and acting.

A. *Prefixes relating to verbs*, auxiliary, reflective, causative, transitive, and intransitive, etc.

B. *Prefixes relating to number :* singular, plural.

C. *Prefixes relating to the form and contour of subject or object :* (1) forms which are round or spherical or large ; (2) flat, smooth, flexible, like threads ; (3) forms like leaves, and like coverings for the body ; (4) long, elongated, and tall forms.

D. *Prefixes relating to the attitude and position ;* as upright, straight, rigid.

E. *Prefixes relating to movement,* (1) in the air ; (2) below ; (3) outside, in or on water and other liquids ; (4) performed by an oblique movement ; (5) in a zigzag on the ground ; (6) in the form of a wave ; (7) with the head ; (8) with the hands or arms ; (9) with the back or feet.

F. *Prefixes referring to relations expressed by adverbs* i.e. locative prefixes.[1]

The number of suffixes, and the variety of their functions is far greater even than those which our study of prefixes

---

[1] A. Gatschet, *The Klamath Language*, pp. 302–3.

has made manifest. I shall not enter into detail about the
relations they express. I shall merely note that they serve
to reproduce, among others, the following ideas : to begin,
continue, cease, return to, to be accustomed to do, either
frequently or at the beginning, to pass to, to move to a longer
or shorter distance, to move in a zigzag or in a straight line,
to go up, along the ground, or below, to describe circles in
the air, to come towards or go away from (the subject or
object being either visible or invisible), to change one's place
in the hut or outside it, on the water or below its surface,
and finally an infinity of other details, many of which would
be neither observed nor expressed by us, but which strike
the Indian mind more forcibly than they would our own.[1]

Gatschet notes that prefixes refer rather to the category
of form, while suffixes preferably relate to those of the way
of acting, movement, and repose. But it is not always easy
to maintain this difference, as we shall see from the following
list of suffixes, a list which is much abridged, only the headings
of which I reproduce here.

A. *Suffixes describing movement :* (1) in a straight line, or
for a short distance ; (2) towards the ground ; (3) towards
some other object, or towards the subject of the verb ;
(4) far away, to separate ; (5) above or below something ;
(6) on a horizontal plane ; (7) circular (whether inside or
outside the house) ; (8) around an object ; (9) turning or
winding ; (10) vibratory or oscillating ; (11) down ; (12) in
the water.

B. *Suffixes to denote staying, or remaining at rest :* (1) in
the interior of the hut or some other enclosed space ; (2) outside, beyond certain limits ; (3) on, above, or on the surface
of ; (4) around, encompassing something ; (5) below, beneath ;
(6) between ; (7) at a distance from ; (8) in the woods or
marshes or on the cliffs ; (9) in the water ; (10) around and
near the water.[2]

C. *Suffixes descriptive of acts accomplished by living beings
or by parts of their bodies :* (1) frequentative ; (2) iterative ;
(3) habitual ; (4) in movement ; (5) outside ; (6) above, on
the surface of ; (7) below, beneath ; (8) with a weapon or
instrument ; (9) with or on the body ; (10) with the mouth ;

---

[1] A. Gatschet, *The Klamath Language*, p. 305.   [2] Ibid., p. 396

(11) with the back ; (12) near or in the fire ; (13) in taking away ; (14) in making a gesture ; (15) in somebody's interest ; (16) in calling by name ; (17) with verbs expressing desire ; (18) as regarding the degree of accomplishment attained (inceptive, continuative, executed in part only, completely, lastingly).[1]

This method of specifying the details of the action expressed or the object denoted may be pursued almost indefinitely by the help of affixes. To take an example from Klamath, the verb *gálepka* means to raise oneself, to mount to. By adding an *h* it indicates mounting upon something by using one's hands. Then *ge'hláptcha* signifies doing this *en route*, while walking or travelling, and finally *ge'hláptchapka* expresses the fact that one does this at a distance from, and unseen by, others. In the passage quoted, the last of these expresses the act of a prisoner who escapes on horseback during the night.[2] " To carry a child " may be expressed in a variety of ways, the main differences being whether the infant is carried on its plank-cradle or without it ; on the arm or on the back ; whether borne to the hut, or outside it, etc.[3] Details which would be absolutely insignificant to us become the ground of fine distinctions between verbs which we should call synonymous, but which are not so to the Indian. Gatschet tells us that occasionally their reason for expressing the same act or the same condition by different verbs is not due to a difference in the act or condition, but to divergences in the subjects and objects of the verb as to shape, quality, and number. . . . They have eight terms to express seizing, twelve for separating, fourteen for washing. Many other instances illustrative of the niceties of perception and the wealth of descriptive terms in the language might be given.

This quality, however, as we know, is not the sole prerogative of the Klamath Indians. Such a characteristic is found, no less marked, among their neighbours, and it is common to most of the languages spoken by the North American tribes. In the Hurons' tongue, " in describing a journey, the expressions used differ according to whether it was accomplished by land or sea. The active verbs increase

[1] A. Gatschet, *The Klamath Language*, pp. 397–8.
[2] Ibid., p. 68.   [3] Ibid., pp. 698–9.

in proportion with the things which may be done ; for instance, the verb expressing eating varies with the number of comestibles in the case. Action is described differently for animate or inanimate objects ; to see a man, and to see a stone, requires two verbs. To use something which belongs to the user must be expressed differently from the verb which indicates the use of some other person's property.[1] With the Nez-percés, verbs assume different forms according to whether the subject or object is advancing or retreating.[2] In the language of the Yahgans, there are ten thousand verbs, the number of which is considerably increased by the use of prefixes and suffixes, to indicate whence one comes or whither one goes, to north, south, east, or west, above, below, outside, inside, and we are told that these differences are almost inexhaustible, even without reckoning the locative adverbs.[3] The Abipones, we are told, have an incredible number of synonyms, for they have different words to indicate wounding by the teeth of man or animal, by a knife, a sword, or an arrow ; to express fighting with a spear, arrows, the fists, or indulging in wordy warfare ; to indicate that the two wives of a man are fighting about him, etc. . . . Different particles are affixed to indicate exactly the place and varying positions of the subject of discourse ; above, below, around, in the water, in the air, on the surface, etc. There are many diverse forms of the verb " to follow," for example, and a person coming, going, following with his hand something below or above him, following with his .eyes, or with his mind, or following other people, may all be expressed.[4] In South Africa, Livingstone found that verbs possessed the same power of expressing delicate shades of meaning. " It is not the want, but the superabundance of names that misleads travellers, and the terms used are so multifarious that good scholars will at times scarcely know more than the subject of conversation. . . . We have heard about a score of words to indicate different varieties of gait—one walks leaning

[1] Charlevoix, *Journal d'un Voyage dans l'Amérique Septentrionale*, iii. pp. 196–7.
[2] Bancroft, *The Native Races of the Pacific States of North America*, iii. p. 622.
[3] T. Bridges, " Notes on the Structure of the Yahgan," *J.A.I.*, xxiii. pp. 53–80.
[4] Dobrizhoffer, op. cit., ii. pp. 186–90.

forward, or backward; swaying from side to side; loungingly or smartly; swaggeringly; swinging the arms, or only one arm; head down or up, or otherwise: each of these modes of walking was expressed by a particular verb. . . ." [1]

IV

From these and many similar facts which might be quoted, we see that the languages of primitive peoples "always express their ideas of things and actions in the precise fashion in which these are presented to the eye or ear." [2] They have a common tendency to describe, not the impression which the subject receives, but the shape and contour, position, movement, way of acting, of objects in space—in a word, all that can be perceived and delineated. They try to unite the graphic and the plastic elements of that which they desire to express. We may perhaps understand this need of theirs if we note that the same peoples, as a rule, speak another language as well, a language whose characteristics necessarily react upon the minds of those who use it, influencing their way of thought and, as a consequence, their speech. These peoples, in fact, make use of sign-language, at least in certain circumstances, and where it has fallen into disuse, there are still traces which show that it assuredly has existed. Very frequently, moreover, it is used without the explorers becoming aware of it, either because the natives do not employ it in their presence, or because the fact has escaped attention. One of them, according to Roth, took these gestures for masonic signs ! [3]

Nevertheless, in cases where the most undeveloped peoples are concerned, we have some explicit testimony. Spencer and Gillen have observed this in Australia. "Amongst the Warramunga, widows are not allowed to speak sometimes for as long a period as twelve months, during the whole of which time they communicate only by means of gesture language, in which latter they are so proficient that they

---

[1] Livingstone, *The Zambesi and its Tributaries*, p. 537.
[2] Schoolcraft, *Information*, ii. p. 341.
[3] W. E. Roth, *Ethnological Studies among the N.W. Central Queensland Aborigines*, No. 72.

prefer, even where there is no obligation upon them to do so, to use it in preference to speaking. Not seldom, when a party of women are in camp, there will be almost perfect silence and yet a brisk conversation is all the while being conducted on their fingers, or rather with their hands and arms, as many of the signs are made by putting the hands, or perhaps the elbows, in varying positions."[1] " In the case of the widows, mothers, and mothers-in-law " (of Northern tribes) " this ban " (of silence) " extends over the whole period of mourning, and even at the expiration of this the women will sometimes voluntarily remain silent. . . . There is a very old woman in the camp at Tennant Creek who has not spoken for more than twenty-five years."[2] In South Australia, " after a death . . . the old women may refuse to speak for two or three months, expressing what they want to say by gestures with the hands—a sort of deaf and dumb language which the men are as adept in as the women."[3] Like the Cooper's Creek natives, those of the Port Lincoln district make use of many signs which are very necessary to the chase, not uttering a word the while. By using their hands they can inform their companions what animals they have found, and exactly where these are. . . . They have, too, signs for all varieties of game.[4] Howitt collected a certain number of the signs used by the Cooper's Creek natives in their gesture-language.[5] Roth has given us a fairly detailed dictionary of it, and he was able to prove that the language he had thus formulated was understood and practised throughout the North of Queensland.[6] In the Dieyerie tribe, it was found that an extensive sign-language existed side by side with the oral one, and that all animals, natives, both men and women, the sky, the ground, walking, riding, jumping, flying, swimming, eating and drinking, and a vast number of other things or acts all possessed their

[1] *The Native Tribes of Central Australia*, pp. 500–1.
[2] *The Northern Tribes of Central Australia*, pp. 525, 527.
[3] " On the Habits of the Aborigines in the District of Powell Creek," etc., *J.A.I.*, xxiv. p. 178.
[4] Wilhelmi, *Manners and Customs of the Natives of the Port Lincoln District*, quoted by Brough Smyth, *The Aborigines of Victoria*, i. p. 186.
[5] Ibid., ii. p. 308.
[6] *Ethnological Studies among the N.W. Central Queensland Aborigines*, chap. iv.

own particular signs which enabled a conversation to be carried on without a single spoken word.[1]

In the Torres Straits, gesture-language was noted both in the eastern and western islands, and Haddon regrets that he did not collect its signs.[2] It has been met with in (German) New Guinea also.[3] To give but one instance in Africa, " the Masai have a sign-language which is well developed, as Fischer reports." [4]

Dobrizhoffer noticed an Abipone medicine-man who could communicate with others secretly, so that nobody should hear a sound, and this he did by means of gestures in which hands, arms, and head all played their part. His colleagues replied, and thus they were able to keep in touch with each other.[5] Language of this kind appears to be very general throughout the whole of South America. The Indians of the various tribes do not understand each other's speech, but they can communicate with each other by signs.[6]

Finally, it seems to be clear that in North America sign-language has been used everywhere : we have only to recall Mallery's monograph on the subject which appeared in the first volume of the *Reports of the Bureau of Ethnography.* It is a real language, possessing its own vocabulary, forms, and syntax. " We might," says one explorer, " formulate a complete grammar of this language by gesture. . . . We may judge of its prolixity from the fact that Indians of different tribes, who do not know a word of each other's oral language, can gossip together for half a day, and tell each other all manner of things merely by the movements of their fingers or heads and feet." [7] Boas relates that a language of this kind was still fairly prevalent in the interior of British Columbia in 1890.[8]

---

[1] S. Gason, *The Dieyerie Tribe,* in Woods, *The Native Tribes of South Australia,* p. 290.
[2] *The Cambridge Expedition to Torres Straits,* iii. pp. 255–62. Cf. *J.A.I.,* xix. p. 380.
[3] Hagen, *Unter den Papuas,* pp. 211–12.
[4] Dr. G. A. Fischer, quoted by Widenmann, " Die Kilimandjaro-Bevöl-kerung," *Petermann's Mitteilungen,* No. 129 (1889).
[5] Dobrizhoffer, op. cit., ii. p. 327.
[6] Spix and Martius, *Travels in Brazil,* ii. p. 252.
[7] Kohl, *Kitchi Gami : Wanderings round Lake Superior,* pp. 140–1.
[8] F. Boas, " The North-western Tribes of Canada," *Report of British Association,* pp. 291 et seq. (1890).

In most primitive societies, therefore, two languages, the one oral, the other by means of gesture, exist side by side. Are we to assume that they do so without exerting any mutual influence, or must we believe, on the other hand, that the same mentality expresses itself by both, and conversely is modelled upon them? The latter view appears the more acceptable, and it is indeed confirmed by the facts. In a very important work upon " manual concepts," F. H. Cushing [1] lays stress upon the relations between language expressed by manual movements and the spoken language. He demonstrated how the Zuñi order of the cardinal points and the formation of nouns of number originated in definite movements of the hands. At the same time he demonstrated in his own case, the resourcefulness of a method which belongs to him, and which his personal genius (the expression is not too strong) as well as the circumstances of his life, enabled him to apply very happily.

To understand the mentality of " primitives," we must endeavour to reconstitute in ourselves conditions which resemble theirs as closely as possible. On this point we are all agreed. Cushing lived among the Zuñis ; he lived with them, and like them ; he was initiated into their rites and ceremonies ; he became a member of their secret societies, and really was as one among the rest. But he did more than this, and herein lies the originality of his method. With infinite patience he revived the primitive functions of his own hands, living over again with them their experiences of prehistoric days, with the same material and under the same conditions as at that period, *when the hands were so at one with the mind that they really formed a part of it.* The progress of civilization was brought about by reciprocal influence of mind upon hand and *vice versa.* To reconstitute the primitives' mentality, he had to rediscover the movements of their hands, movements in which their language and their thought were inseparably united. Hence the daring yet significant expression " manual concepts." The primitive who did not speak without his hands did not think without them either. The difficulties which the application of the method suggested and employed by Cushing entail are considerable. He alone, probably,

[1] " Manual Concepts," *American Anthropologist,* v. pp. 291 et seq.

or men endowed with the same unusual tendencies and the same patience as he, would be able to put it into practice profitably, but it certainly led him to valuable results. For instance, Cushing shows how the extreme specializing of verbs, which we have noted everywhere in the languages of primitives, is a natural consequence of the part which the manual movements play in their mental activity. He declares this to have been a grammatical necessity, and says that in the primitive mind thought-expressions, expression-concepts, complex yet mechanically systematic, were effected more quickly than, or as quickly as, the equivalent verbal expression came into being.[1]

Speaking with the hands is literally thinking with the hands, to a certain extent ; therefore the features of these "manual concepts" will necessarily be reproduced in the verbal expression of thought. The general processes in expression will be similar : the two languages, the signs of which differ so widely as gestures and articulate sounds, will be affiliated by their structure and their method of inter-preting objects, actions, conditions. If verbal language, therefore, describes and delineates in detail positions, motions, distances, forms, and contours, it is because sign-language uses exactly the same means of expression.

In this respect there is nothing more instructive than the sign-language of N.W. Queensland, of which Roth has given us a detailed description. In this language, as in the other, the real vital unit is not primarily the isolated sign or gesture any more than the word, but the sentence or the complex ensemble, of varying length, which expresses in inseparable fashion a complete meaning. The significance of a gesture lies in the "context." Thus the gesture of a boomerang may express not only the object itself, but also, according to the context, the idea of reaching or killing something with it, or of making, or stealing, it. An interrogative gesture awakens the idea of a question, but the nature of the demand depends upon that which has preceded or is to follow.[2]

Moreover, the "ideograms" which serve to denote persons, things, and actions, are nearly always descriptive

---

[1] "Manual Concepts," *American Anthropologist*, pp. 310–11.
[2] W. E. Roth, op. cit., No. 72.

of movement. They reproduce either the attitudes or familiar movements of living beings (quadrupeds, birds, fishes, etc.) or the movements used in capturing them, or in creating or employing some object, etc. For instance, to denote the porcupine, manual movements exactly describe its quaint way of burrowing into the earth and throwing it aside, its quills, its manner of raising its little ears. To express *water*, the ideogram reproduces the way in which the native laps up the liquid he has taken in his hand. For *collar*, the two hands are put in the position of encircling the neck, with a gesture of closing them behind, and so forth. Weapons are minutely described to the eyes by the gestures employed in making use of them. In short, the man who speaks this language has at his disposal a great number of fully-formed visual motor associations and the idea of persons or things, when it presents itself to his mind, immediately sets these associations going. We may say that he imagines them at the moment he describes them. His verbal language, therefore, can but be descriptive also. Hence the importance given to contour, form, situation, position, method of movement, visual characteristics of persons and things in general ; hence the classification of objects according to whether they are standing, lying, seated, etc. Mallery tells us that the words of an Indian language which are synthetic and undifferentiated parts of speech are strictly analogous in this respect with the gestures which are the elements of sign-language, and that the study of the latter is valuable for the purpose of comparison with the words. The one language explains the other, and neither can be studied to advantage if the other be unknown.[1]

Mallery's study of the sign-language of the North American Indians was very searching, and he endeavoured to formulate syntax of it. Of this we have but to retain that which throws light upon the mental habits of those using it, and at the same time illustrates their verbal language. The latter *necessarily* descriptive. It may even happen that it is accompanied by gestures which are not only a spontaneous expression of emotion, but an indispensable element of the language itself. With the Halkomelem of British Columbia,

[1] Mallery, " Sign-language," *E. B. Rept.*, i. p. 351.

for instance, "it may boldly be affirmed that at least a third
part of the meaning of their words and sentences is expressed
in those aids to primitive language, gestures and tonal differences." [1] The Coroados of Brazil complete and perfect the
meaning of their sentences by their accent, the speed or
slowness of the pronunciation, and certain signs made with
hand or mouth, or other gestures. If the Indian wishes to
indicate that he is going to the wood, he says "wood go,"
and a movement of his mouth shows the direction that he
intends to take.[2]

Even among the Bantu peoples who, as a rule, belong to
a type of community which is fairly advanced, the oral
language, itself very descriptive, is constantly accompanied
by movements of the hand joined with the demonstrative
pronouns. It is true that such movements are no longer
actual signs, like those which constitute a language by gesture
but they are aids to the exact description which is given by
means of words. For instance, a native will scarcely ever
be heard to use a vague expression such as "he has lost an
eye"; but since he has noticed which eye it was, he will
say, pointing to one of his own, "this is the eye he has lost."
In the same way, he will not say that two places lie at a
distance of three hours' journey, but rather, "If you start
when the sun is there, you will arrive when it is there," at
the same time indicating different parts of the sky. So, too,
first, *second*, and *third* are not indicated by words, but by the
pronoun *this*, with the first, second or third finger extended.

It is not even essential that these "aids" to description
should be gestures and movements exclusively. The need
for description may seek its fulfilment by means of *Laut
bilder*, as the German explorers call them, i.e. delineations or
reproductions of that which they wish to express, obtained by
means of the voice. Westermann tells us that the language
of the Ewe tribes is richly endowed with the means of interpreting an impression received by direct sounds. Such
prolixity proceeds from the almost irresistible tendency to

---

[1] Hill Tout, "Ethnographical Reports . . . Halkomelem British Columbia,
J.A.I., xxxiv. p. 367.
[2] Spix and Martius, *Travels in Brazil*, ii. pp. 254–5.
[3] Torrend, *Comparative Grammar of the South African Bantu Language*.
p. 218.

imitate all one hears or sees, and in general, all one perceives, and to describe it by means of a sound or sounds, chiefly, of movements. But there are also imitations or vocal reproductions of these *Lautbilder* for sounds, odours, tastes, tactile impressions. There are some used in connection with the expression of colour, fulness, degree, grief, well-being, and so on. It does not admit of doubt that many words, properly so called (nouns, verbs, and adjectives), have their origin in these *Lautbilder*. Properly speaking, they are not onomatopœic words ; they are descriptive vocal gestures rather. An example will best explain them.

"In the Ewe language," says Westermann, "as in many related languages, we find a very special kind of adverb . . . which as a rule describes a *single* action or state, or a *single* property of objects, which therefore are applicable to a *single* verb only, and are never found in connection with any other. Many verbs, especially those descriptive of a transmission through the organs of sense, have a whole series of such adverbs to give more precision to the action, state or property they express. . . . These adverbs are actually *Lautbilder*, vocal imitations of sense-impressions. . . . For instance, the word *zo*, to walk, may be joined with the following adverbs, which are used only with it, and which describe various kinds of walking, or different gaits : [1]

Zo báfo bafo—the gait of a little man whose limbs shake very much while he is walking.

Zo béhe behe—to walk with a dragging step, like a feeble person.

Zo bia bia—the gait of a long-legged man, who throws his legs forward.

Zo boho boho—of a corpulent man, who walks heavily.

Zo búla bula—to walk in a dazed fashion, without looking ahead.

Zo dzé dze—an energetic and firm step.

Zo dabo dabo—a hesitating, feeble step, shaking.

Zo gõe gõe—to walk swinging the head and the buttocks.

Zo gowu gowu—to walk with a slight limp, the head bent forward.

Zo hloyi hloyi—to walk with many things, or with clothes floating around.

Zo ka kà—to walk proudly, upright, without moving the body unnecessarily.

Zo kódzo kodzo—the gait of a tall man or animal, with the head slightly bent.

Zo kondobre kondobre—like the last, but with a feeble and lifeless step.

---

[1] Cf. Livingstone's observation, quoted on pp. 157-8.

Zo kondzra kondzra—to walk with long steps, drawing in the abdomen
Zo kpádi kpadi—to walk with the elbows close to the sides.
Zo kpō kpō—to walk quietly and easily.
Zo kpúdu kpudu—the short hasty step of a little man.
Zo kundo kundo—like *kondobre kondobre*—but not in any unfavourable
   sense.
Zo lûmo lûmo—the quick gait of small animals like rats and mice.
Zo mōe mōe—like *gōe gōe*.
Zo pla pla—to walk with small steps.
Zo sî sî—the light step of small people who sway.
Zo taka taka—to walk carelessly and heedlessly.
Zo tyatyra tyatyra—a quick but rigid step.
Zo tyende tyende—to walk shaking the abdomen.
Zo tya tya—to walk quickly.
Zo tyádi tyadi—to walk with a limping or dragging step.
Zo tyô tyô—the well-poised and firm step of a very tall person.
Zo wúdo wudo—the quiet step (in a favourable sense), specially women's
Zo ẁla ẁla—a quick, light, unencumbered gait.
Zo ẁui wui—quick, rapid.
Zo ẁē ẁē—the walk of a fat man who advanced with a rigid step.
Zo ẃiata ẃiata—to advance with a firm and energetic step; said
   specially of people with long legs.

These thirty-three adverbs do not exhaust the list of those
used to describe the manner of walking. Moreover, most
of them may be met with in two forms : an ordinary and a
diminutive one, according to the stature of the subject of
discourse.[1] Naturally, there are similar adverbs or *Lautbilde*
for all the other movements, such as running, climbing, swimming, riding, driving, for instance.[2] Finally, these descriptiv
adverbs are not joined to the verb as if the idea occurred in
two points of time : firstly a conception of walking in general
and then the particular method being specified by means of
the *Lautbild*. On the contrary, to the minds concerned, th
conception of walking in general never presents itself alone
it is always a certain way of walking that they thus delineat
vocally. Westermann even notes that as the delineation b
degrees gives place to a real concept, the special adverb
tend to disappear, and other more general ones, such as very
much, to a great extent, etc., etc., are substituted.[3]

The same descriptive auxiliaries are noted in the Bant
languages. In Loango, for instance, " each man uses th

[1] Dr. Westermann, *Grammatik der Ewesprache*, pp. 83–4.
[2] Ibid., p. 130.   [3] Ibid., p. 82.

language in his own way, or . . . to speak more correctly, the language issues from the mouth of each according to the circumstances and his own mood at the time. This use of language is unrestrained and natural as the sounds uttered by the birds, and I cannot think of any more apt comparison." [1] To put it in another way, words are not something fixed and immutable once for all, but the vocal gesture describes, delineates, expresses graphically, in the same way as the gesture of the hands, the action or thing in question. In the Ronga tongue there are " certain words which the Bantu grammarians regard generally as interjections or onomatopœics. They are usually vocables of one syllable only, by means of which natives express the sudden and direct impression which a sight, sound, or idea, makes upon them, or describe a movement, an apparition, a noise. It is quite enough to have listened to some of the perfectly free and unrestrained conversations of negroes to note the immense number of expressions of this kind which they have at command. We may be inclined to say perhaps : ' It is merely a childish way of speaking, not worth the trouble of listening to.' The truth is quite the contrary, however. The naturally versatile and ready-witted mind of the race is reflected in this picturesque language. Through such words it succeeds in expressing shades of meaning which a more restrained language could not render. Again, these little words have been the origin of numerous verbs, and would deserve recognition on that account. . . . Nevertheless it must be owned that these descriptive adverbs vary very much with individuals. Some among them embellish their speech to an extent which makes it incomprehensible for the uninitiated, and even invent new expressions. Many of these words, however, are actually incorporated into the language understood by all." [2]

V

The plastic and essentially descriptive character of the languages, both verbal and sign-languages, confirms what we have already said with regard to the special form of

[1] Dr. Pechuël-Loesche, *Die Loango-Expedition*, iii. 2, pp. 91–5.
[2] Junod, *Grammaire Ronga*, pp. 196–7.

abstraction and generalization proper to primitive mentality
The primitive mind is well acquainted with concepts, bu
these are not at all like ours : it forms them in another way
and uses them in a method which differs from that of logica
thought. " It is our aim," says Gatschet, " to speak clearly
and precisely ; the Indian's is to speak descriptively ; while
we classify, he individualizes." The following example shows
the difference clearly. The Delaware word *nadholineen* i.
composed of *nad*, a derivative of the verb *naten*, to seek
of *hol*, from *amochol*, a boat, and *ineen*, which is the verba
termination for the first person plural. It means " Find the
boat for us." It is the imperative of a verb expressing
I am finding the boat for you, him, etc., which is conjugated
like any other verb . . . but is always used in a *special* sense
It always signifies : find *the* boat, and expresses a particula
act, having no general meaning ; it does not mean : " find
any boat." This is otherwise in classical languages. The
Latin *aedifico*, *belligero*, *nidifico*, do not mean build a specia
edifice, make war on a particular nation, construct a certaix
specified nest. . . . So too, φιλογραμματέω, φιλογραφέω
φιλοδοξέω, φιλοδεσποτεύομαι, φιλανθρωπέω, do not express
preference for a certain book, picture, etc. They express
general love of literature, painting, and so forth. Had the
a special meaning at some remote period of their history
There is nothing to tell us so, and we know nothing about
it. But what we do know is, that in the development c
primitive American languages, verbs taken in a special sens
appeared first of all, and that if one wanted to give them
general application, it was done by inserting an adverbia
particle which means " habitually." [1]

Again, while it cannot be denied that those who spea
these languages have a concept of hand, foot, ear, etc. ; thei
concepts do not resemble ours. They have what I shoul
call an " image-concept," which is necessarily specialized
The hand or foot they imagine is always the hand or foo
of a particular person, delineated at the same time. Powe
tells us that in many Indian tongues of North America the
is no distinct word for eye, hand, arm, or the other par

[1] Gallatin, in *Transactions of the American Ethnological Society,*
pp. 136-8.

or organs of the body ; but such are always found incorporated with or attached to a pronoun which signifies the possessor. If an Indian were to find an arm that had fallen from an operating-table, he would say " I have found *his arm* " (i.e. someone's), and such linguistic peculiarity, though not universal, is met with frequently.[1] It is to be found in many other languages, too. For instance, the Bakairi of Brazil do not say " tongue," but always add a pronominal adjective, my tongue, your tongue, etc. ; and this rule applies to the other parts of the body.[2] The same holds good for terms denoting relationship, father, mother, etc., which are very rarely used alone. In the Marshall Archipelago, " there is no generic term for ' father,' the word never being used save in conjunction, and applied to a particular person. It is the same for ' mother, brother, sister,' " etc.[3]

The language spoken by the natives of the Gazelle peninsular of the Bismark Archipelago, " like most of the Melanesian languages, and some of the Micronesian (of the Gilbert Islands) and of Papua, make use of the possessive pronoun as a suffix when expressing substantives denoting relationship, parts of the body, and some prepositions." [4]

Grierson had noted that in the north-eastern provinces of India, the word " father," as a general idea, not connected with any special person, and therefore requiring a certain amount of abstractive thought, was never used alone, but always in conjunction with a possessive pronoun. . . . A hand, also, could not be imagined save as belonging to somebody, and even when the possessive form of the sentence rendered the pronoun unnecessary, the tendency to specialization was so strong that it was still added, as " of my mother her hand." [5] In the Angami tongue, nouns denoting parts of the body, or expressing relationship, had to be preceded by a possessive pronoun.[6] The same held good for the Semā language.[7] This is a very common feature, and it helps us to understand how it is that in primitive societies we find those complicated

---

[1] " The Evolution of Language," *E. B. Rept.*, i. p. 9.
[2] K. von den Steinen, *Unter den Naturvölkern Zentralbrasiliens*, p. 82.
[3] " Die Ebon-Gruppe im Marshall's Archipel," *Journal des Muséum Godeffroy*, i. pp. 39–40.
[4] Parkinson, *Dreissig Jahre in der Südsee*, p. 730.
[5] Grierson, *Linguistic Survey of India*, iii. 3, pp. 16–17.
[6] Ibid., iii. 2, p. 208.   [7] Ibid iii 2, p. 223.

degrees of relationship which prove so confusing to the
European, and which he masters only with difficulty. He tries
to conceive of them *in abstracto*, but the native never envisages
them thus. In his childhood he learned that certain persons
stood in such and such a relation to certain others, and the
learning required no more trouble or thought than the rules
of his (frequently just as complicated) mother-tongue.

The nearer the mentality of a given social group approaches
the prelogical, the more do these image-concepts predominate.
The language bears witness to this, for there is an almost
total absence of generic terms to correspond with general
ideas, and at the same time an extraordinary abundance of
specific terms, those denoting persons and things of whom
or which a clear and precise image occurs to the mind as
soon as they are mentioned. Eyre had already remarked
upon this with the Australian aborigines. He states that
generic terms such as tree, fish, bird, etc., were lacking,
although specific terms were applied to every variety of tree,
fish or bird.[1] We are told that the natives of the Tyers Lake
district, Gippsland, have no words for these either, but all
the species such as bream, perch, mullet, are distinguished
in each class.[2] The Tasmanians had no words to represent
abstract ideas, and though they could denote every variety
of gum-tree or bush, by name, they had no word for tree.
They could not express qualities, such as hard, soft, hot,
cold, round, tall, short, etc. To signify " hard " they would
say : like a stone ; for tall, big legs ; round, like a ball ;
like the moon ; and so on, always combining their words
with gestures, designed to bring what they were describing
before the eyes of the person addressed.[3]

In the Bismark Archipelago " there are no names for
colours. Colour is always indicated in the following way.
The object in question is always compared with another,
the colour of which has been accepted as a kind of standard.
For instance, they will say : This looks like, or has the colour
of a crow. In the course of time, the substantive alone has
been used in adjectival sense. . . . Black is named after

---

[1] Eyre, *Journals of Expeditions of Discovery into Central Australia*, ii.
pp. 392–3.
[2] Bulmer, quoted by Brough Smyth, *The Aborigines of Victoria*, ii. p. 27.
[3] Ibid., ii. 2, p. 413.

the various things from which this colour is obtained, or else a black object is named. Thus the word "*kotkot*" (crow) is used to denote *black*. Everything that is black, especially things that are glossy black, is called thus. *Likutan* or *lukutan* also means black, but rather in the sense of *dark* ; *toworo* is the black colour derived from burnt candle-nuts ; *luluba*, the black mud in the mangrove swamps ; *dep*, the black colour obtained from burning canary-wood gum ; *utur*, the colour of burnt betel-nut leaves mixed with oil. All these words are used for black, according to the circumstances of the case : there are just as many for other colours, white, green, red, blue, and so forth." [1]

It is the same with the Coroados of Brazil. "Their languages extend only to the denomination of the objects immediately surrounding them, and often express the predominant quality of things by imitative sounds. They distinguish with great precision the internal and external parts of the body, the various animals and plants, and the relation of such natural objects to each other is frequently indicated in a very expressive manner by the words themselves ; thus the Indian names of monkeys and palms were guides to us in examining the genera and species, for almost every species has its particular Indian name. But it would be in vain to seek among them words for the abstract ideas of plant, animal, and the abstract notions colour, tone, sex, species, etc. Such a generalization of ideas is found only in the frequently used infinitive of the verbs to walk, eat, drink, dance, see, hear, etc." [2] In California, " there are no genera, no species : every oak, pine, or grass has its separate name." [3]

Everything being represented in these " image-concepts," i.e. delineations in which the slightest peculiarity is shown —and this not only for the natural species of all animate nature, but for objects of all kinds, whatever they be, all movements or actions, all states or qualities which language expresses—it follows that these " primitive " languages have

[1] Parkinson, *Dreissig Jahre in der Südsee*, pp. 143–5. Cf. *The Cambridge Expedition to Torres Straits*, ii. pp. 55–68.
[2] Spix and Martius, *Travels in Brazil*, ii. pp. 252–3. Cf. *The Cambridge Expedition to Torres Straits*, ii. 1, pp. 44, 64.
[3] Powers, *Tribes of California*, p. 419.

a wealth of vocabulary unknown to ours. This extensive vocabulary has been the source of wonder to many explorers. " They " (the Australian aborigines) " have names for almost every minute portion of the human frame ; thus, in asking the name for the arm, one stranger would get the name for the upper arm, another for the lower arm, another for the right arm, another for the left arm, etc." [1] " The Maoris have a most complete system of nomenclature for the flora of New Zealand. They are acquainted with the sex of trees, etc., and have distinct names for the male and female of some trees. Also they have different names for trees which change the form of their leaves, at the different stages of growth. In many cases they have a special name for the flowers of tree or shrub . . . different names for young unexpanded leaves and for the berries. . . . The *koko* or *tui* bird has four names ; two for the male and two for the female according to the seasons of the year. There are different names for the tail of a bird, of an animal, of a fish ; three names for the cry of the *kaka* parrot (in anger, fear, or in ordinary circumstances)." [2]

Speaking of the Bawenda tribe of South Africa, Gottschling says : " For every kind of rain there is a special name in their language. . . . There is not a single geographical fact of their country but they have given it a name of their own. Even geological features have not escaped their notice, for they have specific names for every kind of soil and also for every sort of stone or rock. . . . There is not a tree, shrub or plant that has not a name in their language. They distinguish even every kind of grass by a different name." [3] Livingstone found the Bechuana vocabulary a source of wonder. " He " (Dr. Moffat) " was the first to reduce their speech to a written form, and has had his attention directed to the study for at least thirty years, so he may be supposed to be better adapted for the task " (of translating the Bible) " than any man living. Some idea of the copiousness of the language may be formed from the fact that even he never spends a week at his work without dis-

[1] Grey, *Journals*, etc., ii. p. 209 (1841).
[2] Elsdon Best, " Maori Nomenclature," *J.A.I.*, xxxii. pp. 197–8.
[3] E. Gottschling, " The Bawenda," *J.A.I.*, xxxv. p. 383.

covering new words." [1]—With regard to India, Grierson
speaks of " the great number of terms for closely related ideas
in the Kuki-Chin language," making the comparison of the
vocabularies of different dialects a matter of some difficulty.
" Then in Lushei," he says, " there are ten terms for ants,
all probably denoting various kinds of ants ; twenty terms for
basket ; different words for different kinds of deer, but no general
word for deer." [2]—The North American Indians " have even
many expressions, which may be almost called scientific, for
frequently recurring forms of the clouds, and the characteristic
features of the sky physiognomy which are quite untranslatable,
and for which it is hopeless to seek an equivalent in European languages. Thus the Ojibbeways, for instance, have a
peculiar fixed name for the appearance of the sunshine between
two clouds. In the same way they have a distinct appellation
for the small blue oases which at times are seen in the sky
between dark clouds." [3]—The Klamath Indians have no
generic term for fox, squirrel, butterfly or frog ; but each
species has its own name. There is an almost countless
number of substantives in the language.[4]—The Lapps have
a great many terms to denote various kinds of reindeer,
according to their age. . . . There are twenty words for ice,
eleven for cold, forty-one for snow in all its forms, twenty-six
verbs to express freezing and thawing, and so on. Hence
they resist any attempt to exchange their language for
Norwegian, which is much more limited in this respect.[5]—
Finally, the Semitic languages, and even those we ourselves
use, have known such wealth of vocabulary. " We must
imagine every Indo-European language as resembling the
modern Lithuanian speech, poor in general terms, yet well
supplied with specific ones indicating all particular actions
and the details of familiar objects." [6]

The same tendency accounts for the vast number of
special names given to single objects, and particularly to
the least peculiarity in the soil. In New Zealand, with the

[1] Livingstone, *Missionary Travels*, pp. 113–14.
[2] Grierson, *Linguistic Survey of India*, iii. 3, p. 16.
[3] Kohl, *Kitchi Gami : Wanderings round Lake Superior*, p. 229.
[4] A. Gatschet, *The Klamath Language*, pp. 464, 500.
[5] Keane, " The Lapps: their Origin, etc.," *J.A.I.*, xv. p. 235.
[6] A. Meillet, *Introduction à l'Étude Comparative des Langues Indo-Euro-
péennes* (2nd edit.), p. 347.

Maoris, " everything has its name : their houses, canoes, weapons, and even garments have distinctive appellations given them. . . . Their lands and roads are all named ; so also the sea beaches round the islands, their horses, cows, and pigs, even their trees . . . rocks and fountains. Go where you will, in the midst of an apparently untrodden wilderness ; ask, has this spot a name ? and any native belonging to that district will immediately give one." [1] In Southern Australia " every range has its name ; likewise every mountain has its particular name ; so that blacks can state the precise mountain or hill in an extensive range they will meet. I have upwards of two hundred names of mountains in the Australian Alps . . . even every bend in the river Murray has a name. " [2] In Western Australia, the natives " have names for all the conspicuous stars, for every natural feature of the ground, every hill, swamp, bend of a river, etc., but not for the river itself." [3]—Lastly, not to prolong this list unduly, in the Zambesi district, " every knoll, hill, mountain, and every peak on a range has a name, and so has every watercourse, dell, and plain. In fact, every feature or portion of the country is so distinguished by appropriate names that it would take a lifetime to decipher their meaning." [4]

VI

On the whole, therefore, the characteristics of the languages spoken by primitives correspond with those we have noted in their mentality. The image-concepts, which are a kind of delineation, allowing of a limited generality and elementary abstraction only, yet involve remarkable development of memory, and thus give rise to the wealth of form and vocabulary. Where logical thought has obtained the upper hand the social treasure of acquired knowledge is transmitted and preserved by means of concepts. Each generation in instructing that which succeeds teaches it to analyse these concepts, to draw out what is included in them, to recognize and make use of the resources of abstract reasoning. In the

---

[1] R. Taylor, *Te Ika a Maui*, pp. 328–9.
[2] Quoted by Brough Smyth, in *The Aborigines of Victoria*, ii. p. 122 (note).
[3] Ibid., p. 266.
[4] Livingstone, *The Zambesi and its Tributaries*, pp. 537–8.

peoples whom we are considering, on the contrary, this treasure
is still entirely, or almost entirely, explicit in the language
itself. It cannot fail to be transmitted, because the children
try to imitate their parents' speech, without any teaching,
properly so called, without any intellectual effort, simply by
memory. It is accordingly not susceptible to progress.
Supposing that the *milieu* and the institutions of a social
group do not change, its general mentality not changing either,
its wealth of image-concepts would be transmitted from
generation to generation without any great variation. When
it does change, other changes are at work also, and usually
it becomes impoverished.

Advance in conceptual and abstract thought is accompanied by a diminution in the descriptive material which
served to express the thought when it was more concrete.
The Indo-European languages have undoubtedly evolved in
this sense. In British Columbia, " on the coast, when a
masculine or a feminine article is used, the same terms serve
for male and female relations. Here " (among the Salish)
" where there is no grammatical distinction between the sexes,
separate terms are used. It is worth remarking that the
Bilqula, who have grammatical distinction of sex, distinguish
between but a few of these terms   This may indicate that the
separate forms have been lost by the tribes who use grammatical sex." [1] The increasing generality of the concepts causes
them by degrees to lose the exactness which characterized
them when they were at the same time, and primarily, images,
delineations, and vocal gestures. " Little by little," says
Victor Henry, " the idea of these finer shades of meaning
becomes obscured, so that the present-day Aleutians make
use of one single verbal form with many different meanings,
or several forms with one acceptation impartially, and the
native who is questioned about the reason which makes him
prefer one form to another will usually be unable to account
for his preference." [2]

This gradual impoverishment, which is the general rule,
shows clearly that the specializing terminology, and the

[1] F. Boas, " The North-western Tribes of Canada," *British Association
Reports*, pp. 690–1 (1890).

[2] V. Henry, *Esquisse d'une Grammaire Raisonnée de la Langue Aléoute*,
p. 34.

meticulous attention to detail, were not the result of desired and conscious effort, but merely of the necessity which the mode of expression demanded. Image-concepts could only be rendered and communicated by a kind of delineation, either by means of actual gestures, or oral expressions which are a species of vocal gesture, of which the " auxiliary descriptive adverbs " have provided a very clear example. As soon as the development of general ideas and abstract concepts permitted men to express themselves more easily, they did so, without troubling about the loss of the graphic precision which resulted. In fact, the ingenuity, extent and delicacy of the distinctions perceived and expressed, between the varieties of the same species of plants or animals, for example, must not lead us to believe that in them we have a mentality oriented like our own, towards the recognition of objective reality. We know that their mentality is otherwise oriented. In the reality of persons and things as their collective representations suggest them, the mystic, invisible factors, the occult powers, the secret participations, hold an incomparably higher place than the elements we consider objective. We need no other proof of this than the part played by notions like *mana*, *wakan*, *orenda*, *taboo*, contamination, and so forth. It is even sufficient to consider the classifications of entities that have been established. With primitive peoples, the principle of classification, disdaining the most striking objective traits, is founded preferably upon a mystic participation. The sum total of all entities is divided up as are the individuals of the social group ; trees, animals, stars, belong to this or that totem or clan or phratry. In spite of appearances, then, these minds, which evidently have no idea of genera, have none of species, families, or varieties either, although they are able to delineate them in their language. Their classification is something purely pragmatic, born of the necessity for action and expression, in which reflection has no part. So little of knowledge is therein that, for real knowledge to be formed, this material of thought and expression must first give place to another, and the image-concepts, which are at once both general and particular, must be superseded by concepts which are really general and abstract.

The language, too, will have been forced to lose the mystic

character which it necessarily assumes among primitive peoples. To their minds, as we already know, there is no perception unaccompanied by a mystic complex, no phenomenon which is simply a phenomenon, no sign that is not more than a sign : how then could a word be merely a word ? Every form that an object assumes, every plastic image and every delineation has mystic virtues : verbal expression, which is an oral delineation, must perforce possess them also. And this power does not pertain to proper nouns alone, but to all terms, whatever they may be. Moreover, names which express very specialized image-concepts do not differ from proper nouns nearly as much as our common nouns do.

Hence it follows that the use of words can never be a matter of indifference : the mere fact of uttering them, like the tracing of a drawing or the making of a gesture, may establish or destroy important and formidable participations. There is magic influence in the word, and therefore precaution is necessary. Special languages for certain occasions, languages reserved for certain classes of persons, begin to take shape. Thus, in a great many aggregates, we meet with a different language for men and women. Frazer collected many examples of this.[1] " It is a feature common to all the American nations," says Gallatin, " that women use different words from men for those purposes " (to express relationship) ; " and that the difference of language between men and women seems in the Indian languages to be almost altogether confined to that species of words . . . and to the use of interjections." [2] At the time when the young men are initiated and become full members of the tribe, it often happens that the seniors teach them a secret language unknown by and unintelligible to the uninitiated. " I have on several occasions reported the existence of a secret or cabalistic language used only by the men at the initiation ceremonies of several native tribes in New South Wales. While the novitiates are away in the bush with the elders of the tribe, they are taught a mystic name for surrounding natural objects, animals, parts of the body, and short phrases of

[1] J. G. Frazer, " Men's Language and Women's Language," *Fortnightly Review*, January 1900. Cf. *Man*, No. 129 (1901).
[2] Gallatin, *Transactions of the American Ethnological Society*, ii. pp. 131-2.

general utility." [1] Frequently, too, the members of the secret societies which are so common a feature in social groups of a primitive type, are initiated into a language spoken and understood by themselves alone; their introduction to the society, or their promotion to a sufficiently exalted rank therein, gives them the privilege of using this mystic language. Among the Abipones, " persons promoted to the rank of nobles are called *Hecheri* and *Nelereycati*, and are distinguished from the common people even by their language. They generally use the same words, but so transformed by the interposition or addition of other letters, that they appear to belong to a different language. . . . Moreover, they have some words peculiar to themselves, by which they supersede those in general use." [2]

In hunting it is essential to avoid uttering the name of the animals hunted, and in fishing, that of the fish that one desires to capture. Accordingly silence is enjoined, or the use of sign-language, and this accounts for the appearance of a special language when they are looking for camphor, or going fishing, or starting on a warlike expedition. A great many words are taboo, when the person of the king is in question : to eat or sleep or sit may not be expressed in the ordinary Malay words; special terms are essential. Moreover, when the king is dead, his name must be uttered no more.[3] We know that this was a very common custom in Madagascar. " There are many words which are used in a certain sense to the king (or queen) and these words cannot be used in this special sense with the common people ; especially those which have reference to the state or health of the living king. . . . Other words are common to kings and chiefs only. . . . The king has power to make certain words *fady*, viz. to prohibit their use, it may be for a time or entirely." [4] In many primitive societies, a woman and her son-in-law must avoid each other and not enter into con-

---

[1] Mathews, " Languages of Some Native Tribes," *Journal of the Royal Society of New South Wales*, pp. 157–8 (1903). Cf. Webster, *Primitive Secret Societies*, pp. 42–3.

[2] Dobrizhoffer, *An Account of the Abipones*, ii. pp. 204–5.

[3] Skeat, *Malay Magic*, pp. 35, 212, 315, 523. Cf. Skeat and Blagden, *Pagan Races of the Malay Peninsula*, ii. pp. 414–31.

[4] Last, " Notes on the Languages Spoken in Madagascar," *J.A.I.*, xxv p. 68.

versation. Nevertheless, "throughout the central and south-west districts of Victoria and in the south-east corner of South Australia there is a hybrid tongue or jargon in use, comprising a short code of words, by means of which a mother-in-law can carry on a limited conversation in the presence of her son-in-law respecting some events of daily life." [1]

That which finally proves the mystic worth and power in words as words, is the widespread custom, in magic ceremonies and even in ritual and religious ceremonies, of using songs and formulas which are unintelligible to those who hear them, and sometimes even to those who utter them. For these songs and these formulas to be effective, it is enough that they have been transmitted by tradition in a sacred language. For instance, with the tribes of Central Australia, Spencer and Gillen say : "As usual, in the case of sacred ceremonies, the words have no meaning known to the natives, and have been handed down from the Alcheringa." [2] In myths it appears that a change of language is frequently mentioned ; for instance, "at this spot the Achilpa changed their language to that of the Arunta people." [3] Another part of the tribe "camped apart and then moved on to Ariltha, where they changed their language to the Ilpirra language." [4] "Somewhere out west of the river Say the women (Unthippa) changed their language to Arunta." [5] So, too, in Fiji, Banks Islands, Tanna, New Guinea, the songs used in the sacred ceremonies are unintelligible to those who are singing. [6]

Throughout North America similar facts come to light. Jewitt noted, though without understanding, them in the Indians of Nootka Sound. "They have," he says, "a number of songs which they sing on various occasions : war, whaling, fishing, marriages and feasts, etc. The language of most of these appears to be very different, in many respects, from that used in their common conversation, which leads me to believe, either that they have a different mode of expressing

[1] Mathews, "Aboriginal Tribes of New South Wales and Victoria," *Journal of the Royal Society of New South Wales*, p. 305 (1905).
[2] *The Northern Tribes of Central Australia*, pp. 286, 462, 460, 606.
[3] *The Native Tribes of Central Australia*, p. 410.
[4] Ibid., p. 416.   [5] Ibid., p. 442.
[6] Sidney H. Ray, "Melanesian and New Guinea Songs," *J.A.I.*, xxvi. pp. 436-45.

themselves in poetry, or that they borrow their songs from their neighbours." [1] Catlin fully realized the mystic meaning of this. " Every dance has its peculiar step, and every step has its meaning ; every dance also has its peculiar song, and that is so intricate and mysterious oftentimes, that not one in ten of the young men who are dancing and singing it know the meaning of the song which they are chanting over. None but the medicine-men are allowed to understand them ; and even they are generally only initiated into these secret arcana on the payment of a liberal stipend for their tuition, which requires much application and study." [2] " A great portion of the phraseology of the Ojibwa ritual is in an archaic form of language, and is thus unintelligible to the ordinary Indian, and frequently to many members of the society. This archaic phraseology naturally appears impressive and important to the general populace, and the shamans delight to dwell on such phrases, not only to impress their hearers, but to elevate themselves as well." [3] Of the Klamath Indians, " many . . . do not understand all these songs, which contain many archaic forms and words, and the conjurors themselves are generally loth to give their meaning, even if they should understand them." [4] What we call the meaning of the words or the form matters little. The people remain indefinably attracted by them, because their mystic virtue and magic efficacy have been known from time immemorial. The most accurate and intelligible translation could not take the place of these incomprehensible songs, for they could not fulfil the same office.

[1] Jewitt, *Adventures and Sufferings*, p. 97.
[2] Catlin, *The North American Indians*, i. p. 142 ; ii. p. 181.
[3] Hoffman, " The Memomini Indians," *E. B. Rept.*, xiv. p. 61.
[4] A. Gatschet, *The Klamath Language*, p. 160.

CHAPTER V

PRELOGICAL MENTALITY IN RELATION TO NUMERATION

It is quite possible future works dealing with linguistics may confirm the theory I have suggested in the preceding chapter. Nevertheless, in what follows I shall confine myself to proving it in one particular point, upon which our documentary evidence is fairly complete and accessible : that is, the way in which different peoples, especially those of the most primitive type we know, practise numeration. The various methods of counting and calculating, of forming and using the names for numbers, will possibly enable us to see, actually at work, the mentality of primitives where it differs specifically from logical thought. This will serve as a specimen of proofs which I cannot enter upon in detail.

I

In a great many primitive peoples—those in Australia, South America, etc.—the only names for numbers are one and two, and occasionally three. Beyond these, the natives say " many, a crowd, a multitude." Or else, for three, they say two, one ; for four : two, two ; for five : two, two, one. Hence the opinion has frequently been formed that mental inaptitude or extreme indolence prevents them from discriminating any number higher than three. This is a hasty conclusion, however. It is true that these " primitives " form no abstract concept of four, five, six, etc. ; but we cannot legitimately infer from this that they do not count beyond two or three. Their minds do not readily lend themselves to operations familiar to us, but by the processes which are peculiar to them they can obtain the same results to a certain extent. Where synthetic representations are not analysed, there is more demand upon memory. Instead of the generalizing abstraction which provides us with our concepts, properly so called, and especially with those of number, their minds make use of an abstraction which preserves the specific characters of the given ensembles. In short, they count and even calculate in a way which, compared with our own, might properly be termed concrete.

Since we count by means of numbers and hardly ever count in any other way, we admit that in primitive societies which have no names for any number beyond three, it would be impossible to count further. But are we obliged to take it for granted that the apprehension of a definite plurality of objects can take place in one way only? Is it impossible for the mentality of primitive peoples to have its own peculiar operations and processes to attain the end we reach by numeration? As a matter of fact, if a well-defined and fairly restricted group of persons or things interests the primitive ever so little, he will retain it with all its characteristics. In the representation he has of it the exact number of these persons or things is implied: it is, as it were, a quality in which this group differs from one which contained one more, or several more, and also from a group containing any lesser number. Consequently, at the moment this group is again presented to his sight, the primitive knows whether it is complete, or whether it is greater or less than before.

A capability of this nature has already been noted, in very simple cases, among certain animals.[1] It does happen that a domestic animal, a dog, ape, or elephant, perceives the disappearance of an object in a restricted ensemble with which it is familiar. In many species, the mother shows by unmistakable signs that she knows that one of her little ones has been taken from her. If we remember that according to most observers the primitives' memory is " phenomenal," as Spencer and Gillen express it, or " miraculous," as Charlevoix pronounces it, we have stronger reason for believing that they can easily do without numerals. With the help of custom, each sum-total which matters to them is retained in their memory with the same exactness as that which makes them

---

[1] Ch. Leroy, *Lettres sur les Animaux*, p. 123.

recognize unerringly the track of such and such an animal or person. If anything is missing from the sum-total, they instantly perceive it. In the representation so faithfully preserved, the number of persons or things is not differentiated : nothing allows of its being expressed separately. It is none the less perceived qualitatively, or, if you prefer it, *felt*.

Dobrizhoffer has testified to this fact with the Abipones. They refuse to count as we do, i.e. by means of numerals. They are not only ignorant of arithmetic, but they dislike it. Their memory generally fails them (because they are required to make use of processes with which they are not familiar). "They cannot endure the tedious process of counting : hence to rid themselves of questions on the subject, they show as many fingers as they like, sometimes deceived themselves, sometimes deceiving others. Often," says Dobrizhoffer, "if the number about which you ask is more than three, an Abipon, to save himself the trouble of showing his fingers, will cry ' *Pop*,' which means ' many,' or *Chic leyekalipi*, ' innumerable.' " [1]

Yet they have their own way of accounting for numbers. "When they return from an excursion to hunt wild horses, or to shoot tame ones, none of the Abipones will ask them ' how many horses have you brought home ? ' but ' how much space will the troop of horse which you have brought home occupy ? ' " [2] And when they are about to start on an excursion, "as soon as they are mounted, they all look round, and if one dog be missing out of the many which they keep, begin to call him. . . . I often wondered how, without being able to count, they could so instantly tell if one were missing out of so large a pack." [3] This last is a very characteristic reflection of Dobrizhoffer's. It explains why it is that the Abipones and peoples like them, who do not make use of numerals, are at a loss to deal with them when they are first taught them.

So, too, the Guaranis have no numerals above four (although they have terms corresponding with the Latin : *singuli, bini, trini, quaterni*).[4] They, "like the Abipones,

---

[1] Dobrizhoffer, *An Account of the Abipones*, ii. p. 170.
[2] Ibid   [3] Ibid., ii. pp. 115–16.
[4] So, too, the Australian aborigines, who have no numerals above three are yet able to conjugate in the singular, dual, trial, and plural numbers.

when questioned respecting things exceeding four, immediately reply: 'innumerable.' . . . Generally speaking we found the art of music, painting, and sculpture easier learnt than numbers. They can all pronounce the numbers in Spanish, but are so easily and frequently confused in counting that you must be very cautious how you credit what they say in this matter." [1] Numeration is an instrument, the need for which they do not recognize, and the use of which is unfamiliar to them. They do not want numbers, apart from the totals which they can count so easily in their own way.

But, we may ask, if this be so, is not the only thing possible for primitives to represent these totals and preserve them in their memory? Are not the very simplest additions or sub-tractions beyond their powers? Not at all; they can perform such operations, for the prelogical mind in this respect (as in its language in general) proceeds in a concrete fashion. It has recourse to the representation of the movements which add units to the original whole or else subtract them from it. In this it has an instrument much less effective though more complicated than abstract numbers, but which permits it to perform the simple operations. It associates a regular series of movements and of the parts of the body connected with such movements with successive totals in such a way as to recall any of these at need by repeating the series from the beginning. If it be a case of fixing the day upon which a number of tribes are to meet for the common celebration of certain ceremonies, it will have to be several months ahead, because so much time is needed to tell all who are interested, and allow them to reach the spot agreed upon. How do the Australian aborigines start about it? "To indicate the precise time upon which the people should assemble . . . could be done by counting the different stages or camps to be made on the journey, or the number of ' moons.' If the number to be counted was large, recourse was had to the various parts of the body, each of which had a recognized name, and an understood position in this method of enumera-tion. So many parts thus enumerated, counting from the little finger of one hand, meant so many stages, or days, or months, as the case might require." (One side of the body

[1] Dobrizhoffer, op. cit., ii. pp. 171–2.

would be gone over, and then the other if necessary.)   Howitt
rightly observes that " this method of counting fully disposes
of any belief that the paucity of numerals in the language
of the Australian tribes arises from any inability to conceive
of more numbers than two, three, four." [1]

Whence does this paucity arise, indeed, if not in the habits
peculiar to the prelogical mind ?   As a matter of fact, in
nearly every case in which we note this scarcity of numerals—
a scarcity which *we* should consider dependent upon the
number not being differentiated from that which is being
enumerated—we find also this concrete method of numbering.
In the Murray Islands, Torres Straits, " the only natives'
numerals are *netat* (1) and *neis* (2). Any higher numbers
would be described either by reduplication ; e.g. *neis-netat*
= 2, 1 = 3 ; *neis neis* = 2, 2 = 4, etc., or by reference to
some part of the body. By the latter method a total of 31
could be counted.   The counting commenced at the little finger
of the left hand, thence counting the digits, wrist, elbow, armpit, shoulder, hollow above the clavicle, thorax, and thence in
reverse order down the right arm, ending with the little finger
of the right hand.   This gives 21.   The toes are then resorted
to, and these give 10 more." [2]   " Dr. Wyatt Gill says : ' Anything above ten the Torres Straits Islanders count *visibly*,[3]
thus : touch each finger, then the wrist, elbow, and shoulder
joint on the *right* side of the body ; next touch the sternum
and proceed to the joints of the *left*, not forgetting the fingers
of the left hand.   This will give 17.   If this suffice not, count
the toes, the ankle, knee, and hip joints (right and left).   This
will give 16 more, the entire process yielding 33.   Anything
beyond can be enumerated only by help of a bundle of
sticks.' " [4]

Haddon clearly recognized that there were no numerals,
nor even numbers properly so called, to be seen, but simply
a method, an " aid to memory " to recall a given total at need.
" There was," he says, " another system of counting by com-

[1] Howitt, " Australian Message Sticks and Messengers," *J.A.I.*, xviii.
pp. 317–19.
[2] Hunt, " Murray Islands, Torres Straits," *J.A.I.*, xxviii. p. 13.
[3] This is a striking expression, which reminds us of the language of
primitives, in which verbal utterance seems like a " tracing " of visual and
motor images.
[4] A. Haddon, " The West Tribes of Torres Straits," *J.A.I.*, xix. pp. 305–6.

mencing at the little finger of the left hand, then following on with the fourth finger, middle finger, index, thumb, wrist, elbow joint, shoulder, left nipple, and ending with the little finger of the right hand (19 in all). The names are simply those of the parts of the body themselves and are not numerals. In my opinion, this system could only have been used as an aid in counting, like using a knotted string, and not as a series of actual numbers. The elbow joint (*kudu*) might be either 7 or 13, and I could not discover that *kudu* really stood for either of those numbers, but in a question of trade a man would remember how far along his person a former number of articles extended, and by beginning again on the left little finger he could recover the actual number." [1]

So, too, in British New Guinea, we find the following system used in reckoning :

1 = *monou*—little finger of the left hand;
2 = *reere*—next finger ;
3 = *kaupu*—middle finger;
4 = *moreere*—index ;
5 = *aira*—thumb;
6 = *ankora*—wrist;
7 = *mirika mako*—between wrist and elbow;
8 = *na*—elbow;
9 = *ara*—shoulder;
10 = *ano*—neck;
11 = *ame*—left breast;
12 = *unkari*—chest;
13 = *amenekai*—right breast;
14 = *ano*—right side of the neck, etc. [2]

We notice that the same word, *ano*, for the neck, either on the right or left side, does for 10 and for 14, which would be quite impossible if it were a question of numbers and numerals. Yet there is no ambiguity here, for it is the naming of the parts of the body in a fixed order that eliminates confusion.

A British scientific expedition to the Torres Straits brought to light a certain number of facts which fully confirm the preceding. I shall quote but a few of them. At Mabuiag, " counting is usually performed on the fingers, beginning with the little finger of the left hand. There was also a system of

[1] " The West Tribes of Torres Straits," *J.A.I.*, xix. p. 305.
[2] James Chalmers, " Maipua and Namau Numerals," *J.A.I.*, xxvii. p. 141.

counting on the body, by commencing at the little finger of
the left hand : 1. *kutadimur* (end finger) ; 2. *kutadimur
gurunguzinga* = a thing following the end finger (fourth
finger) ; 3. *il get* = middle finger ; 4. *klak nitui get* (index
finger) = spear-throwing finger ; 5. *kabaget* = paddle finger
(thumb) ; 6. *perta or tiap* = wrist ; 7. *kudu* = elbow joint ;
8. *zugu kwuick* = shoulder ; 9. *susu madu* = breast flesh, sternum ; 10. *kosa dadir* = right nipple ; 11. *wadogam susu madu*
= other side breast flesh ; and so on, in reverse order, preceded
by *wadogam* (other side) ; the series ending with the little finger
of the right hand. . . . The names are simply those of parts
of the body themselves, and are not numerals." [1]

Manus, a native of the Murray Islands, counted as follows :

1. *kebi ke*—little finger ;
2. *kebi ke neis*—little finger two ;
3. *eip ke*—middle finger ;
4. *baur ke*—spear finger (index) ;
5. *au ke*—big finger (thumb) ;
6. *kebi kokne*—little bone joint (wrist) ;
7. *kebi kokne sor*—little bone back (back of the wrist) ;
8. *au kokne*—big bone joint (inner part of the elbow) ;
9. *au kokne sor*—bone joint back (elbow) ;
10. *tugar*—shoulder ;
11. *kenani*—armpit ;
12. *gilid*—pit above clavicle ;
13. *nano*—left nipple ;
14. *kopor*—navel ;
15. *nerkep*—top of chest ;
16. *op nerpek*—front of throat ;
17. *nerut nano*—other nipple ;
18. *nerut gilid* ;
19. *nerut kenani*, etc., up to
29. *kebi ke nerute*—little finger another.[2]

In British New Guinea also, counting is accomplished by
enumerating certain parts of the body, in a way that differs
slightly from the preceding, but also going back on the right
side after having begun on the left. " This is done in the Elema
district. 1 = *haruapu*, 2 = *urahoka*, 3 = *iroihu*, 4 = *hari*
(index), 5 = *hui* (thumb), 6 = *aukava* (wrist), 7 = *farae*
(forearm), 8 = *ari* (elbow), 9 = *kae* (armlet), 10 = *horu*
(shoulder), 11 = *karave* (neck), 12 = *avako* (ear), 13 = *ubuhae*

[1] *The Cambridge Expedition to Torres Straits*, iii. p. 47.
[2] Ibid., iii. pp. 86-7.

(eye), 14 = *overa* (nose), 15 = *ubwauka* (eye), 16 = *avako kai* (other eye), 17 = *karave haukai* (neck, other side), etc., etc., up to 27, *ukai haruapu.* . . . In the numbers from 15 onwards, *kai, ukai, haukai,* probably mean *other* or *second.*" [1]

Here is a final example, from a Papuan language spoken in the north-east of British New Guinea. " According to Sir William MacGregor, the practice of counting on the body is found in all the lower villages on the Musa river. They begin with the little finger of the right hand, use the fingers of that side, then proceed by the wrist, elbow, shoulder, ear, and eye of that side, thence to the left eye and shoulder, and down the left arm and hand to the little finger. Many of them in count-ing become greatly confused on reaching the face." [2] " Here is an example of this method : 1 = *anusi* (little finger of the right hand), 2, 3, 4 = *doro* (are the ring, middle, and index fingers respectively of the right hand), 5 = *ubei* (thumb), 6 = *tama* (right wrist), 7 = *unubo* (elbow), 8 = *visa* (shoulder), 9 = *denoro* (right ear), 10 = *diti* (right eye), 11 = *diti* (left eye), 12 = *medo* (nose), 13 = *bee* (mouth), 14 = *denoro* (left ear), 15 = *visa* (left shoulder), 16 = *unubo* (left elbow), 17 = *tama* (left wrist), 18 = *ubei* (thumb), 19, 20, 21 = *doro* (the index, middle, and ring fingers of the left hand), 22 = *anusi* (little finger of the left hand)." [3]

Here we see very clearly that the terms used are *not* numerals. How could the word *doro* stand for 2, 3, 4 and 19, 20, 21 alike, if it were not differentiated by the gesture which indicates the special finger of the right or left hand ?

Such a process admits of the counting to fairly high numbers, when the parts of the body enumerated in a fixed order are themselves associated with other objects more easily handled. Here is an instance taken from the Dayaks of Borneo. It was a case of announcing to a certain number of insurgent villages which had been conquered, the amount of fine which they would have to pay. How would the native messenger accomplish his task ? " He brought a few dry leaves, which he tore into pieces ; these I exchanged for paper, which served better. He arranged each piece separately on a table, and used his fingers in counting as well, until he reached 10, when he lifted his foot on the table, and took each toe to accord

---

‡ Op. cit., p. 323.   ² Op. cit., p. 364.   ³ Ibid.

with each bit of paper answering to the name of a village, name of chief, number of followers, and amount of fine ; after having finished with his toes, he returned to his fingers again, and when my list was completed, I counted forty-five bits of paper arranged on the table. He then asked me to repeat them once more, which I did, when he went over the pieces, his fingers and toes, as before. 'Now,' he said, 'this is our kind of letter ; you white men read differently to us.' Late in the evening he repeated them all correctly, placing his finger on each paper, and then said : ' Now, if I recollect them to-morrow morning it will be all right ; so leave these papers on the table,' after which he mixed them all in a heap. The first thing in the morning he and I were at the table, and he proceeded to arrange the papers as on the evening before, and repeated the particulars with complete accuracy ; and for nearly a month after, in going round the villages, far in the interior, he never forgot the different amounts, etc." [1] The substitution of pieces of paper for the fingers and toes is particularly noteworthy, for it illustrates a clear case of abstraction, still really concrete, with which the prelogical mind is familiar.

The inhabitants of Torres Straits, who have very few numerals, have " a custom of purchasing canoes on the three-years-hire system," and at the end of that period they are supposed to have paid for them. This method necessitates a fairly complicated method of counting and some elementary calculation.[2] Even Australian natives, who have no numeral above two, find some way of adding. " The Pitta-Pitta aboriginal has words for the first two numerals only. . . . Beyond 4, the savage will generally speak of ' a lot, a large number.' He certainly has visible conceptions of higher numbers " (this expression recalls that used by Haddon, already quoted), " and I have often had a practical demonstration of the fact by asking him to count how many fingers and toes he has, and telling him to mark the number in the sand. He commences with the hand open, and turns his fingers down by two, and for every two he will make a double stroke on the sand. . . . The strokes he makes . . . are

[1] Brooke, *Ten Years in Sarawak*, i. pp. 139–40.
[2] A. Haddon, " The West Tribes of Torres Straits," *J.A.I.*, xix. pp. 316, 342.

parallel one beside the other, and when the numeration is complete, he calls *pakoola* (2) for every two of them. This method of counting is common throughout the district, and often practised by the elders of the tribe *to ascertain the number of individuals in camp.*" [1]

Without describing concrete numeration so precisely as in the cases just cited, it frequently happens that observers allow us to perceive it in that which they report. The missionary Chalmers, for instance, tells us that "among the Bugilai of British New Guinea, he has found the following numerals : 1 = *tarangesa* (small finger of the left hand), 2 = *meta kina* (next finger), 3 = *guigimeta* (middle finger), 4 = *topea* (next to middle), 5 = *manda* (thumb), 6 = *gaben* (wrist), 7 = *trank-gimbe* (elbow), 8 = *podei* (shoulder), 9 = *ngama* (left breast), 10 = *dala* (right breast)." [2]

From the facts we have just quoted it is allowable to suppose that a more searching observation would have revealed that these are names for parts of the body used in concrete numeration rather than numerals. Moreover, such numeration may unconsciously become half-abstract and half-concrete, as the names (especially the first five) gradually bring before the mind a fainter representation of the parts of the body and a stronger idea of a certain number which tends to separate itself and become applicable to any object whatever. However, nothing proves that numerals are formed thus. The contrary seems even to be the rule for the numbers 1 and 2.

In the western tribes of Torres Straits, Haddon notes names for numbers up to six, and adds : " Beyond that they usually say *ras* or ' a lot.' . . . I also obtained at Muralug *nabiget* = 5, *nabiget nabiget* = 10, *nabikoku* = 15, *nabikoku nabikoku* = 20. *Get* means hand, and *koko* foot." But he adds : "*Nabiget* can hardly be said to be the name of the number five, but that there were as many objects referred to as there are fingers on one hand." [3] In other words, the number is not yet an abstract one.

In the Andaman Isles, in spite of the " wealth of formative particles, the numerals are limited to 1 and 2. Three really

[1] W. E. Roth, *Ethnological Studies Among the N.W. Central Queensland Aborigines*, No. 36. (The italics are the author's.)
[2] James Chalmers, " Maipua and Namau Numerals," *J.A.I.*, xxvii. p. 139.
[3] " The Western Tribes of Torres Straits," *J.A.I.*, xix. pp. 303-5.

means 'one more,' 4 = some more, 5 = all, and here their
arithmetic may be said to stop altogether. In some groups,
however, 6, 7 and perhaps even 10 may be reached by the
aid of the nose and fingers. First the nose is tapped with
the little finger of either hand to score 1, then with the next
finger for 2, and so on up to 5, each successive tap being
accompanied with the word *anka* (and this). The process is
then continued with the second hand, after which both hands
are joined together to indicate 5 + 5, the score being clenched
with the word *ardura* (all). But few get as far as this, and
the process usually breaks down at 6 or 7." [1]

When it is possible to trace them back to their original
meaning, numerals proper frequently reveal the existence of
concrete numeration similar to, if not identical with, that of
which we have given some instances. But instead of going
over the different parts of the upper half of the body with an
ascending movement to return on the other side in descending,
this concrete enumeration is connected with the movements
made by the fingers while counting. Thus are produced those
concepts which Cushing has very aptly called "manual"—
concepts of which he has made an original and exhaustive
study, and one which we might term experimental, since an
essential part of his system consisted in recalling the psychological condition of the primitives by forcing himself to accomplish exactly the same movements as theirs. Here are the
"manual concepts" which serve the Zuñis for counting the
earlier numbers :

1 = *töpınte*—taken as a starting-point;
2 = *kwilli*—raised with the preceding one;
3 = *ha'i*—the finger which divides equally;
4 = *awite*—all the fingers raised except one;
5 = *öpte*—the one cut off;
6 = *topalïk'ya*—another added to what is already counted;
7 = *kwıllik'ya*—two raised with the rest;
8 = *hailïk'ya*—three raised with the rest;
9 = *tenalik'ya*—all except one raised;
10 = *ästem'thila*—all the fingers;
11 = *ästem'th la topayäthl' tona*—all the fingers and one more
raised, etc. [2]

---

[1] Portland, " The Languages of the South Andaman Tribes," *J.A.I.*, xix.
pp. 303–5.
[2] *American Anthropologist*, p. 289 (1892).

In his book entitled *The Number Concept*, Conant quotes similar systems of "manual concepts." Here is a final instance, reported of the Lengua Indians of Chaco in Paraguay : " *Thlama* (1) and *anit* (2) are apparently rootwords ; the rest appear to depend upon them, and upon the hands. *Anta-thlama* (3) appears to be made by these two words joined ; 4 = ' two sides alike,' and 5 = ' one hand'; 6 = ' arrived at the other hand, one ' ; 7 = ' arrived at the other hand, two,' and so on. 10 = ' finished the hands ' ; 11 = ' arrived at the foot, one ' ; 16 = ' arrived at the other foot, one ' ; 20 = ' finished the feet.' Beyond that comes ' many,' and if a very large number is required, the ' hairs of the head ' are called into requisition." [1] But we must note that cases vary according to the state of development attained. The Zuñis count up to a thousand at least, and there is no doubt that they have real numerals, although the concrete enumeration of former times still appears under these. The Chaco Indians of Paraguay, on the other hand, like the Australian aborigines, do indeed seem to make use of a regular and constant series of concrete terms in which numbers are implied, though not yet differentiated.

II

It is usually admitted as a natural fact, requiring no examination, that numeration starts with the unit, and that the different numbers are formed by successive additions of units to each of the preceding numbers. This is, in fact, the most simple process, and the one which imposes itself upon logical thought when it becomes conscious of its functioning. *Omnibus ex nihilo ducendis sufficit unum.* Prelogical mentality, however, which has no abstract concepts at command, does not proceed thus. It does not distinctly separate the number from the objects numbered. That which it expresses by speech is not really numbers, but "number-totals," the units of which it has not previously regarded singly. To be able to imagine the arithmetical series of whole numbers, in their regular order, starting from the unit, it must have separated the number from that which the number

[1] Hawtrey, " The Lengua Indians of the Paraguayan Chaco," *J.A I,* xxxi. p. 296.

totals, and this is precisely what it does not do. It imagines, on the contrary, collections of entities or objects which are familiar to it both by nature and by number, the latter being felt and perceived, though not conceived in the abstract.

Accordingly, Haddon says of the western tribes of Torres Straits, that " they have a decided tendency to count by twos, or couples." And Codrington says : " In counting by couples in the Duke of York Island they give the couple different names, according to the number of them there are. The Polynesian way was to use numerals with the understanding that so many pairs, not so many single things, was meant ; *hokorua* (20) meant 40 (20 pairs)." In this instance, again, we might suppose that the natives start with the unit 2, agreeing to regard it as equal to 1. But Codrington adds : " In Fiji and the Solomon Islands there are collective nouns signifying tens of things very arbitrarily chosen, neither the number nor the name of the thing being expressed." (This is what we have just termed "number-totals," perfectly definite, but not differentiated.) " Thus in Florida *na kua* is ten eggs ; *na banara*, ten baskets of food. . . . In Fiji *bola* is a hundred canoes, *koro* a hundred coco-nuts, and *salavo* a thousand coco-nuts. . . . In Fiji four canoes in motion are *a waqa saqai va*, from *qai*, to run. In Mota two canoes sailing together are called *aka peperu* (butterfly—two canoes), from the look of the two sails, etc." [1]

As these " number-totals " may be varied indefinitely, the prelogical mind will find itself possessed of a very small number of numerals, properly so called, and of a surprisingly vast multiplicity of terms in which number is implied. Thus, in the Melanesian tongues, " when persons or things under certain circumstances are reckoned, the numeral is not simply used, but is introduced by a word which more or less describes the circumstances. If ten men are spoken of regarded as in a company together, it would not be *o tanun sanaval*, but *o tanun pul sanaval*, *pul* meaning to be close together; ten men in a canoe are *tanun sage sanaval* ; etc." [2]

In this respect we have a very noteworthy observation regarding the natives of New Pomerania. " Counting above 10 was far more trouble to them than our little ones find in

[1] *Melanesian Languages*, pp. 241–2.   [2] Ibid , pp. 304–5.

' once one is one, twice one is two.' They did not use their toes. After many attempts, it was found that they do not differentiate between 12 and 20 ; both are called *sanaul lua*, 10 plus 2 as well as 10 multiplied by 2. It is clear that they feel no need to distinguish them in speech, for they never count in abstract numbers, using numbers only in connection with substantives (number-totals) : for instance, 12 coco-nuts, 20 taro roots, a heap of 10 serving as the unit in the latter case. Then one can *see* whether it is a case of 10 coco-nuts and 2 more, or of 2 heaps of 10." [1]

Very frequently different names are given to totals composed of different things, even though the number may be the same. Then the languages seem to possess multiple lists of numerals ; but we must note that the number is wholly differentiated. In his very serviceable book, Conant has collected a good many facts of this kind, of which I shall quote a few only.

In the Carrier tongue, one of the Dènè dialects of Western Canada, the word *tha* means 3 things ; *thane*, 3 persons ; *that*, 3 times ; *thatoen*, in 3 places ; *thauh*, in 3 ways ; *thailtoh*, 3 things together ; *thahultoh*, the 3 times considered as a whole.[2] In the Tsimshian language of British Columbia, we find seven distinct series of numbers used to count different classes of objects. The first serves for counting when there is no definite object referred to, the second for flat objects and animals, the third for round objects and the divisions of time, the fourth for men, the fifth for long objects, the numbers being combined with the word *kan* (tree) ; the sixth for canoes, and the seventh for measures. This last seems to comprise the word *anon* (hand). Boas gives a table of the first ten numbers in the seven classes (see page 195).

We shall note that the first class, that of the words which are used for counting in general, is almost identical with the second, with the exception of a slight difference in 1 and 8. It is therefore allowable to suppose that the first class is not formed at the same time as the others, or independently of them, but, on the contrary, that there were special numerals

[1] Dr. Stephan, " Beiträge zur Psychologie der Bewohner von Neu-Pommern," *Globus*, lxxxviii. p. 206 (1905).

[2] Morice, *The Dènè Languages*, quoted by Conant in *The Number Concept*, p. 86.

	Counting in general.	Flat objects.	Round objects.	[Human beings.	Long objects.	Canoes.	Measures.
1	gyak	gak	g'erel	k'al	k'awutskan	k'amaet	k'al
2	t'epqat	t'epqat	goupel	t'epqadal	gaopskan	g'alp̃eeltk	gulbel
3	guant	guant	gutle	gulal	galtskan	galtskantk	guleont
4	tqalpq	tqalpq	tqalpq	tqalpqdal	tqaapskan	tqalpsqk	tqalpqalont
5	kctōñc	kctōñc	kctōñc	kcenecal	k'etcentskan	kctoōnsk	kctonsilont
6	k'alt	k'alt	k'alt	k'aldal	k'aoltskan	k'altk	k'aldelont
7	t'epqalt	t'epqalt	t'epqalt	t'epqaldal	t'epqaltskan	t'epqaltk	t'epqaldeont
8	guandalt	yuktalt	yuktalt	yuktleadal	ek'tlaedskan	yuktaltk	yuktaldelont
9	kctemac	kctemac	kctemac	kctemacal	kctemaetskan	kctemack	kcteasmilont
10	gy'ap	gy'ap	kp̃eel	kpal	kp̃eetskan	gy'apsk	kpeont

for certain categories of objects before there were any for simple counting. This is confirmed by an examination of the neighbouring languages in British Columbia. The number of numeral series there is almost "unlimited." Here are some in the Heiltsuk dialect.

OBJECT COUNTED.	1.	2.	3.
animated being	menok	maalok	yutuk
round object	menskam	masem	yutqsem
long object	ments'ak	mats'ak	yututs'ak
flat object	menaqsa	matlqsa	yutqsa
day	op'enequls	matlp'enequls	yutqp'enequls
fathom	op'enkh	matlp'enkh	yutqp'enkh
united	—	matloutl	yutoutl
group	nemtsmots'utl	matltsmots'ult	yutqtsmots'utl
full cup	menqtlala	matl'aqtlala	yutqtlala
empty cup	menqtla	matl'aqtla	yutqtla
full box	menskamala	masemala	yutqsemala
empty box	menskam	masem	yutqsem
loaded canoe	mentsake	mats'ake	yututs'ake
canoe and its crew	ments'akis	mats'akla	yututs'akla
all on the shore	—	maalis	—
all in the house	—	maalitl	— etc.[1]

Of the Kwakiutl, Boas says : " Besides the class-suffixes for animated beings, round, flat, long objects, days, fathoms, the numerals may take any of the noun suffixes. . . . The number of classes is unlimited. They are simply compounds of numerals and the noun-suffixes." [2] This is unusual copiousness, but it can be readily understood when we look back upon the general character of these languages, which are but slightly abstract, and pre-eminently " pictorial." It is hardly surprising that the numerals do not stand alone.

This accounts, too, for a peculiarity of the Micmac tongue of North America, which Conant pronounces " extremely noteworthy." In it, he says, numerals are really verbs instead of being adjectives or, as we occasionally find, nouns. They are conjugated in all the divers forms of mood, tense, person, and number. For instance, *naiooktaich* means " there is one " (now) ; *naiooktaichcus*, " there was one " (imperfect) ;

[1] F. Boas, " The North-western Tribes of Canada," *Report of the British Association for the Advancement of Sciences*, p. 658 (1890).
[2] Ibid., pp. 655–6.

and *encoodaichdedou*, " there will be one " (future). The various persons are shown by the following inflections :

Present.

1st person	*tahboosee-ek*	we are two
2nd person	*tahboosee-yok*	you are two
3rd person	*tahboo-sijik*	they are two

Imperfect.

1st person	*tahboosee-egup*	we were two
2nd person	*tahboosee-yogup*	you were two
3rd person	*tahboosee-sibunik*	they were two

Future.

3rd person	*tahboosee-dak*	they will be two, etc.

There is a negative conjugation also : *tahboo-seekw*, they are not two ; *mah tahboo-seekw*, they will not be two ; and so on, *naiookt* meaning one, and *tahboo* two.[1]

Conant explains these forms by saying that the numbers are *verbs* here, and they are being conjugated. But he might just as reasonably have said that these verbs are numerals, numerative verbs. We who know that primitive languages are not divided into parts of speech corresponding exactly with our own, and that it is better to consider that they contain words " functioning as verbs," although under other aspects they may be nouns, adjectives, etc., shall simply say that in the case under review, that which we call numerals in our languages are here " functioning as verbs."

It is not only in North America that we find facts of this kind. In India, Grierson collected similar instances. Thus in the Kuki Chin group of the Tibeto-Burman family of languages, " the numerals are, in this way, restricted in their sphere so as to apply to some special kind of objects." And he reports that these languages show a " tendency to specialize and individualize." [2] For example, in the Rāng Khōl tongue, the prefix *dar* is used when the numerals refer to money, and *dong* when they refer to houses.[3] These prefixes vary,

---

[1] Schoolcraft, *Archives of Aboriginal Knowledge*, v. p. 587, quoted by Conant, *The Number Concept*, p. 160.
[2] *Linguistic Survey of India*, iii. 3, p. 19.
[3] Ibid., iii. 3, p. 184.

too, with the form of objects : " *pūm*, which is used for round things ; *pŏrr*, for loads or bundles. Thus, *mai pūm kat* means one pumpkin ; *thing pŏrr kat*, a load of wood." [1] Sometimes there are special prefixes for definite classes of things. " Thus *sak* is used when human beings are counted, *ge* when inanimate things are counted, *māng* when animals, and *bol* when trees. These nouns are prefixed to the numerals. *Mānde sāk gūi* signifies two men. The prefix *ge* is also employed in simple counting : *gē sa, gé gui, gé gitam*—1, 2, 3. After 20, these particles are added between the tens and the units." [2] In the Mikir language of the Nāgā group of the Tibeto-Burman family, generic prefixes are used with numbers, such as—

With persons	hang
With animals	jón
With trees and things standing up	rong
With houses	hum
With flat things	pàk
With globular things	pūm
With parts of the body, as also rings, bangles and other ornaments	hong

Finally, according to observations quoted by Conant, the same multiplicity prevails, " to a certain extent," with the Aztecs. It is in current use by the Japanese, and Crawfurd found fourteen different classes of numbers without exhausting the list.[3]

According to our view these facts are traceable to the general trend of primitive mentality, for as its abstractions are always specializing rather than generalizing, it does, at a certain degree of development, form numerals ; but they are not abstract numbers such as we use. They are invariably the number-names of certain classes or persons or things, and these classes most frequently depend upon the conformation, attitude, position and movement of the objects. Now we have already seen how much importance these primitive languages accord to everything that expresses the contour and the relative position and movement of objects in space. This is carried to such a point that it would frequently be possible to superpose the detail of that which the words signify, upon

---

[1] *Linguistic Survey of India*, iii. 3, p. 118.
[2] Ibid., iii. 2, p. 71.   [3] *The Number Concept*, p. 89.

the delineation which translates it into a reality for the eyes, and the gesture-language which expresses it by movement.

In this way we can account for a phenomenon which occurs fairly frequently, and which is closely connected with the preceding. In certain languages numeration consists not only of numerals, more or less differentiated, but also of auxiliary terms, which are added to certain numbers to mark or range the stages of the numeration. English and American authors call such terms " classifiers." " These verbs," says Powell, " express methods of counting and relate to form ; that is, in each case they present the Indian in the act of counting objects of a particular form and placing them in groups of ten." [1] Boas has collected many examples of this kind among the dialects of British Columbia. They clearly show that the function of these auxiliaries is to make visible, as it were, the successive stages of the arithmetical process. " The appended verbs," says Powell, " used as classifiers signify *to place* ; but in Indian languages we are not apt to find a word so highly differentiated as *place*, but in its stead a series of words with verbs and adverbs undifferentiated, each signifying to place with a qualification, as *I place upon, I lay alongside of, I stand up, by,* etc."

Thus these appended verbs are doubly specialized : firstly, in that which concerns the movements executed by the subject counting, and secondly in respect of the form of the objects to be counted. " The verbs serving as classifiers," says Gatschet, " differ according to the shape of the counted objects, but all agree as to their common signification of *depositing, placing on the top of.*" [2] And he adds : " The fact that the units from one to nine are not accompanied by these terms must be explained by some peculiarity of the aboriginal mode of counting. . . . The first ten objects counted (fish, baskets, arrows, etc.) were deposited on the ground in a file or row ; and with the eleventh a new file was commenced . . . or a new pile."

Moreover, we are told, " these appended verbs *are not used for* 10 *or for multiples of* 10. Such suffixes classify only the unit or units following the 10, not 10 itself. This detail

[1] " The Evolution of Language," *E. B. Rept.*, i. p. xxi.
[2] A. Gatschet, *The Klamath Language*, p 534.

throws light upon their origin and the reason for using them.
The very number which follows directly after the 10 or its
multiples, 11, 31, 71, 151, etc., is sometimes accompanied
by other classifiers than the numbers 32 to 39, 72 to 79, etc. ;
because in the first case it applies to a single object, whilst
in the others it relates to plurality. When I say 21 fruits—
láp ni ta unepanta nā'sh lutish líkla—it literally means :
above the 20 fruits one is placed on the top. When I say 26
fruits—*lápĕna ta unepanta na'dshkshapta lutish péula*—I
understand : upon the top of twice 10 fruits I place 6
more. (The words *líkla* and *péula* are only used in speaking,
of globular objects.) But the 20 fruits which had been previously counted are not recalled by the classifier, which relates
only to the units mentioned by the number. The classifying
verb may be rendered by the indefinite expression ' counted,
numbered ' ; and before it the pronoun is omitted, but not
before its participles *líklato, péulatko*. The simple verbal
form, absolute or distributive, is used when the person speaking,
or another person, is about to count the objects : the past
participle placed in the direct or oblique cases in its absolute
or distributive forms, is used when the objects have been
previously counted, or the number is recalled." It should be
added that these appended verbs are not always used correctly
by the Indians, and they often omit them, seeming to perceive, as Gatschet says, that they are " a useless and cumber-
some addition." But they are *not* an addition at all. Nothing
favours the belief that the prelogical mind would have been
more sparing in its counting than in expressing in language
the sum-totals of its ideas. Its numeration merely presents
the same quality of minute specialization and " pictorial "
description that we found in the general construction of the
languages of primitives.

Codrington made a very careful study of numeration in
the Melanesian languages. I have already tried to explain
some of the data which he collected. Here I shall call attention
to the following fact : the same term may signify different
numbers successively. Codrington is thinking of what may
be termed the number-limit, the point at which enumeration
stops short. " A word," he says, " which in itself, though

we may not be able to trace its original meaning, is used to signify the end of the counting, naturally rises as the process of counting advances, to the signification of a higher number than it expressed at first. Thus in Savo *tale* or *sale* is 10, which in the Torres Islands = 100 ; the word, no doubt, is the same. As *tini* may possibly have signified the complete numeration as 3 in Mengone, and have advanced to 10 in Fiji, and even to 10,000 in Maori, so *tale* may have signified the end of counting when no number beyond 10 was counted, and have retained the meaning of 10 in Savo, while it has been advanced, as numeration improved, to signify 100 in Torres Islands. 'Many' means more in a later generation than in an earlier ; the Lakona *gapra* (10) means nothing but ' many ' ; *tar*, which in some languages is vaguely ' many,' is in one 100, in several 1,000." [1]

Clearly in its original form this number-limit is not a number, and the word expressing it is not a numeral either. It is a term containing the more or less vague idea of a group of objects exceeding the " number-totals," of which the primitive's mind has a clear and familiar intuitive grasp. But as numeration advances this term becomes a number, and moreover one that increases in value. When at last numeration is carried on by means of abstract numbers such as our own, the number-series is regarded as indefinite and the limiting term ceases to exist. The number is now absolutely differentiated from the things numbered, and the processes of logical thought supersede the functionings of prelogical mentality.

III

The result of all that we have just learnt seems to be a transformation of the traditional problems and a new method of treating them. Conant, for instance, after having collected the numerals employed by many primitive peoples in different parts of the world, is frankly puzzled by the diversity he finds in the numerical systems. Whence have the systems in use, differing so widely from each other, derived their bases ? How is it that the quinary system—the most natural

[1] Codrington, *Melanesian Languages*, p. 249.

of all, and one which would seem to be suggested to, and even imposed upon, man as soon as he begins to count—has not been universally adopted ? What is the reason of there being so many binary, quaternary, vigesimal, mixed and irregular systems ? Counting on his fingers, would not man have inevitably been led to 5 as a basis of reckoning ? Conant finds the basic 4, which is met with fairly often, the most puzzling of all. It seems incredible to him that men capable of counting up to 5 (with the help of their fingers) and beyond 5, could have gone back to 4, to make it the basis of their numerical system. It is an enigma to which, he frankly admits, he has found no clue.

Yet it is an artificial enigma. In formulating it one has to assume that individual minds like our own—that is, functioning in the same way, and accustomed to the same logical processes—have manufactured a system of numeration with these processes in view, and that they have been obliged to choose for it the basis which was most in accordance with their experience. Now such a supposition is unwarranted. As a matter of fact, numerical systems, like the languages from which they must not be disjoined, are social phenomena which depend upon the collective mentality. In every aggregate this mentality is strictly dependent upon the type of the aggregate and its institutions. In primitive societies the mentality is mystic and prelogical ; it expresses its thought in languages in which abstract concepts, such as we employ, are practically unknown. These languages do not possess numerals, properly so called, either, or at least, hardly ever. They make use of words " functioning as numbers," or else they have recourse to " number-totals," concrete representations in which the number is still undifferentiated. In short, however paradoxical the statement may appear, it is nevertheless true that for long ages primitive man counted before he had any numbers.

If this be so, how can we regard one special basis of a numerical system as more " natural " than any other ? Every basis actually adopted has been founded upon the collective representations of the social group in which we discover it. In the lowest class in which we are able to make observations, where the numeration is almost wholly concrete, there is no

basis at all, neither is there any numerical system. The
succession of movements going from the little finger of the
left hand to the little finger of the right, traversing successively
the fingers of the left hand, then ascending the wrist, elbow,
etc., to descend again in the inverse order on the right side
of the body, has no one time that is more stressed than any
other. It does not pause longer on the part of the body
which corresponds with 2 or 5 or 10 than with any other
part, for instance. Therefore Haddon is quite right in saying
that the words pronounced are the names of the parts
of the body and not the names of numbers. Numerals do
not appear until a regular periodicity begins to inform
the series.

This periodicity is in fact most frequently regulated by
the number of fingers and toes : in other words, the quinary
system is the most usual. It is not yet certain that, wherever
we meet with it, its origin is that which seems so natural to
us. Nearly all primitives use their fingers to count with,
and often too, those who know nothing of the quinary system
as well as those who use it. On this point the study of the
" manual concepts " is very instructive. Here is the method
of counting by a Dènè-Dindjié in Canada, for instance.
" Extending the left hand, the palm turned towards his face,
he bends his little finger, saying, 1 ; then he bends the ring
finger, saying 2, and bends the end again. The middle finger
is bent for 3. He bends the index and says, showing the
thumb, 4 ; there are no more but this. Then he opens the
hand and says 5 ; it is finished with my (or one, or the) hand.
The Indian, holding his left hand stretched out, three fingers
of it fastened together, separates the thumb and index, which
he brings near to the thumb of the right hand and says 6 ;
i.e. there are three on each side, three by three. He joins
four fingers of the left hand, brings the left thumb near the
thumb and index finger of the right hand, and says 7 ; (on
one side there are four, or else, there are still three folded,
or again, three on each side and the point in the middle).
He brings the three fingers of the right hand to touch the
left thumb, and thus obtaining two sections of four fingers,
he says 8 ; (four on four, or four on each side). Then showing
the little finger of the right hand, which alone remains folded,

he says 9 ; (there is still one below, or—one is still wanting, or—the little finger is lying down). Finally, clapping the hands in joining them, the Indian says 10 : i.e. each side is finished or, it is counted, reckoned, it is a count. Then he begins the same manœuvre once more, saying : one filled plus one, one counted plus one, etc." [1]

Thus the Dènè-Dindjié, whilst using his fingers to count with, has no idea of a quinary basis. He does not say, as we often find in other cases, 6 is a second one ; 7 is a second two ; 8 is a second three, etc. On the contrary, he says : 6 is 3 + 3, coming back to the hand whose fingers he has exhausted, and separating them to add two to the thumb of the other hand. This proves that in counting 5, in "finishing a hand," he has not marked any time more strongly than in counting 4 or 6. Therefore in this case and in the many others which resemble it, it is not in the method of counting itself, it is not in the movements accomplished that we find the principle of periodicity, that is, that which will be the basis of the numerical system.

A basis may be imposed for reasons which have absolutely nothing to do with convenience in reckoning, and the idea of the arithmetical use of numbers may not enter the question at all. Prelogical mentality is mystic, and oriented differently from our own. Accordingly it is often indifferent to the most evident objective qualities, and contrariwise concerned with the mysterious and secret properties of all kinds of entities. For instance, it may happen that the basic 4, and the quaternary system of numeration, arise out of the fact of the four cardinal points and the four winds, of the four colours and four animals, etc., which participate in these four points, and play an important part in the collective representations of the peoples under consideration. Therefore we do not need to tax our psychological insight in speculating why this basis should have been chosen by men who nevertheless reckoned with their five fingers. Where we find it used, it has not been selected from choice. It, as well as numbers, had a pre-existence, in that long period when they were as yet undifferentiated, and when the " number-totals " took the place of numeration proper. It is a mistake to picture

---

[1] Petitot, *Dictionnaire de la Langue Dènè-dindjié*, p. lv.

the human mind making numbers for itself in order to count, for on the contrary men first of all counted, with much effort and toil, before they conceived of numbers as such.

IV

When the numbers have names given to them, and a group has a numerical system at command, it does not follow that the numbers are *ipso facto* conceived abstractly. On the contrary, they usually remain connected with the idea of the objects most frequently counted. The Yorubas, for instance, have a somewhat noteworthy numerical system, to judge by the use of subtraction in it.

$$11, 12, 13, 14, 15 = 10 + 1, + 2, + 3, + 4, + 5;$$
$$16, 17, 18, 19 = 20 - 4, - 3, - 2, - 1;$$
$$70 = 20 \times 4 - 10;$$
$$130 = 20 \times 7 - 10, \text{ etc.}$$

This phenomenon is explained by the Yorubas' constant use of cowrie shells as money, and these are always arranged in parcels of 5, 20, 200, etc. " Numerals," says the observer who has noted this fact, " convey to the Yoruba ear and mind two meanings: (1) the number, and (2) the thing the Yorubas especially count, and this is money (shells). . . . Other objects are only counted in comparison with an equal number of cowries, for a nation without literature and without a school knows nothing of abstract numbers "[1] This conclusion is equally true of all social groups of the same level of development. The number, despite its being named, still adheres more or less to the concrete representation of a certain class of objects which are, *par excellence*, the objects counted, and other objects are counted only, as it were, by superposition on these.

But while admitting that this adherence yields by degrees, and numbers unconsciously come to be represented for themselves, this does not yet occur in a way that is abstract, and it is precisely *because* each has its name. With primitive

[1] Mann, " On the Numeral System of the Yoruba Nation," *J.A.I.*, xvi. p. 61.

peoples nothing, or at any rate, scarcely anything, is perceived in the way that seems natural to us. To their minds there is no physical phenomenon which is purely a phenomenon, no image which is nothing but an image, nor form that is wholly form. Everything perceived is compassed about by a complexity of collective representations in which the mystic elements predominate. In like manner, there is no name which is purely and simply a name ; neither is there any numeral which is nothing but a numeral. Let us disregard the practical use the primitive makes of numbers when, for instance, he reckons what is due for so many hours' work, or how many fish he has caught on a certain day. Every time he imagines a number *qua* number, he necessarily pictures it with the mystic property and value appertaining to that number, and to it alone, by virtue of participations which are equally mystic. The number and its name are indifferently the vehicle of these participations.

Thus each number has its own individual physiognomy, a kind of mystic atmosphere, a " field of action " peculiar to itself. Every number, therefore, is imagined—we might also say, felt—especially for itself, and without comparison with the others. From this standpoint numbers do not constitute a homogeneous series, and they are accordingly quite unsuited to the simplest logical or mathematical operations. The mystic personality contained in each makes them unable to be added, subtracted, multiplied or divided. The only processes they admit of are themselves mystic processes and not, like arithmetical operations, subject to the law of contradiction. In short, we might say that in the primitive's mind from two standpoints, number is undifferentiated, to a varying extent. In its practical use it still more or less adheres to the objects counted. In the collective representations the number and its name still participate so closely in the mystic qualities of the ensembles represented that they are indeed mystic realities themselves, rather than arithmetical units.

It is to be noted that the numbers which are thus enveloped in a mystic atmosphere hardly exceed the first ten. They are the only numbers known to primitive peoples, and to which they have given a name. In peoples who have risen to an abstract conception of number, the value and mystic power of numbers may indeed be preserved for a very long time, when it is a case of those which formed part of the very earliest collective representations : but they are not extended to their multiples, nor as a rule to the higher numbers. The reason for this is evident. The earlier numbers, to about ten or twelve, which are familiar to the prelogical, mystic, mentality, participate in its nature, and become purely arithmetical numbers at a very late epoch. Possibly there is not even yet any aggregate in which they bear that aspect alone, save to mathematicians. On the contrary, the higher numbers, very slightly differentiated in the primitive's mind, have never, *with their names*, been merged in its collective representations. They at once became arithmetical numbers and, with some exceptions, they have been nothing else.

This limits the extent to which I subscribe to the conclusions reached in Usener's fine book entitled *Dreiheit* (or Trinity).[1] After having adduced exhaustive evidence establishing the mystical nature of the number three, and the mysterious value and power attributed to it from remote antiquity, Usener accounts for it by concluding, as Diels does, that this mystic character had its origin in times when human societies counted no further than three. Three, then, would have signified the ultimate number, the absolute total, and thus for a long period it would have held the place given to infinity in more advanced aggregates. It is undoubtedly possible that with certain primitive races the number three may have enjoyed such prestige, but Usener's interpretation cannot be accepted as entirely satisfactory. As a matter of fact, in the first place, we do not find that numeration actually stops short at three anywhere. Even in the social groups inhabiting Australia, Torres Straits, and New Guinea, who have no numerals above one, two and occasionally three, prelogical mentality has methods of its own which permit of counting more than this. Nowhere is three the " ultimate " number. Moreover, the list of numbers named or used never stops short at a certain number which is distinctly the last, and expresses totality. On the contrary, all the data collected, not only in the primitive races just mentioned, but in Melanesia and both the Americas, as well as among the Dravidians

<hr>

[1] Rheinisches Museum, *N.F.*, lviii. pp. 1–48, 161–208, 324–364.

of India, etc., prove that the number-series always terminates in a vague term meaning "many" or "plenty," or "multitude," which afterwards becomes a definite numeral—five, six, or whatever it may be.   Finally, as Mauss rightly observes,[1] if Usener's theory were correct—if, for many centuries, the human mind, stopping short at the number three, had impressed an almost indelible character of mysticism upon it, such a character would pertain to the number in all social groups everywhere.   Now there is nothing of this sort with the peoples of North and Central America.   The numbers four and five, and the multiples of these, are constantly met with in their group ideas, and the number three plays a very insignificant part, or none at all.

These objections are not only effective against Usener's theory, but at the same time they overthrow all similar attempts at interpretation.   The otherwise extremely ingenious theory of MacGee,[2] for instance, which is based on the observation of North American natives, cannot account for data which have been collected among other primitive peoples. The common mistake of all such hypotheses is that of generalizing from a psychological process which their advocates believe they have analysed in this or that *milieu*, and which serves to account for the mystic worth attributed to certain numbers in these social groups.   Facts do not bear out this generalization, and this sort of " explanation " leads nowhere.   Must we not rather regard the collective representations of primitive races as prelogical and mystic by virtue of their constitution and their mental solidarity, and is not this true of the numbers they imply as well as of their other content ?   There is *no* number which possesses a name and appears in their representations which has not a mystic value.   That being granted, why should it be here the three, or there the four, or elsewhere the two or seven or any other number, which assumes a special importance and has a wholly individual virtue ?   The reason must be sought, not in purely psychological motive, for these would apply to all human aggregates, whatever their nature, but in the conditions peculiar to the group or collection of groups under consideration.   In this respect there

---

[1] *Année Sociologique*, vol. vii. p. 310 (1904).
[2] " Primitive Numbers," *E. B. Rept.*, xix. pp. 821-51.

is nothing more instructive than the facts revealed by Dennett in his book entitled *At the Back of the Black Man's Mind*.[1]

The classification of the various types of social groups is not yet advanced enough to provide the guiding thread we need here. But what we can even now establish is that there is no number among the first ten that does not possess supreme mystic importance for some social group or other. It is quite unnecessary to bring forward evidence of this, as far as the first three numbers are concerned. Even among the most advanced nations, there are traces of this mystic character still discernible both in religion and metaphysics. The " unit " has maintained a prestige upon which the monotheistic religions and the monistic philosophies plume themselves. " Duality " is often the antithesis of unity by qualities which are diametrically opposite, since it signifies, implies, and produces the exact contrary of that which unity signifies, implies and produces. Where unity is a principle of good, order, perfection and happiness, duality is a principle of evil, disorder, imperfection ; a sign, that is, a cause, of misfortune.[2] Many languages still preserve in their vocabulary traces of this opposition ; and we speak of " a double life," " duplicity," etc. I shall not lay further stress upon the mystic character of the number three : it is sufficient to remind you of Usener's monograph on the subject, mentioned above. I will confine myself to recalling some facts relative to the number four and those which follow it.

These facts, naturally, cannot be ascertained among the *most* primitive peoples we know, for such have not yet given names to the number four and those above it. The majority of the Indian groups of North America, however, attach to the number four a mystic virtue that surpasses that of any other. " Amongst almost all the Red Indian tribes, four and its multiples had a sacred significance, having special reference to the cardinal points and to the winds which blow from them, the sign and symbol of this quadruple nature-worship being the Greek or equal-armed cross." [3] In the great Navajo epic, " the gods are all four in number, and all range them-

[1] London, 1906.
[2] MacGee, " Primitive Numbers," *E. B. Rept.*, xix. pp. 821–51.
[3] Buckland, " Four as a Sacred Number," *J.A.I.*, xxv. pp. 96–9.

selves one at each cardinal point, being painted in the colour appropriate to that point. There are four bear gods, four porcupines, four squirrels, four long-bodied goddesses, four holy young men, four lightning birds, etc. The hero is allowed four days and four nights to tell his story, and four days are employed in his purification." So, too, we constantly find evidence of the mystic functioning of the number four in the Zuñi myths which Cushing has so admirably annotated for us, as well as in their rites and customs, as described by Mrs. Stevenson. "Choose then, four youths, so young that they have neither known nor sinned aught of the flesh. . . Them four ye shall accompany. . . . Ye shall walk about the shrine four times, once for each region and the breath and season thereof. . . . They carried the painted arrows of destiny, like the regions of men, four in number." [1]   Among the Sioux, "Takuskanskan, the moving deity, is supposed to live in the four winds, and the four black spirits of night do his bidding. . . . The four winds are sent by the 'something that moves.'" [2]   Again, with them there are four thunder-beings, or at any rate, "four varieties of their external manifestation. In essence, however, they are but one." (In this we recognize the effect of the law of participation.)   "One is black, another yellow, scarlet, blue, etc. They live at the end of the world upon a high mountain. The dwelling opens towards each of the four quarters of the earth, and at each doorway is stationed a sentinel: a butterfly at the entrance, a bear at the west, a deer north, and a beaver south." [3]

It is nowadays the fashion to give a psychological interpretation to facts of this kind, which are innumerable. An association between the number four and the cardinal points which are exactly four, the winds coming from these four regions, the four gods presiding over them, the four sacred animals which dwell there, and the four colours symbolizing them, is supposed to have been set up. The prelogical mind, however, was never conversant with these as isolated ideas. It did not first of all conceive of the north as a spatial region having the east on the right and the west on the left, and

[1] F. H. Cushing, "Zuñi Creation Myths," *E. B. Rept.*, xiii. p. 442.
[2] Dorsey, "Siouan Cults," *E. B. Rept.*, xi. p. 446.
[3] Dorsey, ibid., p. 442.

then combine with it the idea of a cold wind, snow, the bear, the colour blue. . . . All such ideas on the contrary were originally enveloped in a complex representation which is of a collective and religious nature, in which the mystic elements conceal those which we should consider the real ones. As one such element we find the number four, the vehicle on mystic participation, playing in this way a very important part, and one which, though indispensable to the prelogical mind, is very difficult for logical thought to reconstruct. When mystic participations are no longer felt, they leave behind, as it were, a residuum composed of these associations which still obtain to some extent everywhere. They are no longer anything but associations, because the internal bond which held them together has disappeared : but they were originally something very different. Such, for instance, are the associative correlation between cardinal points, seasons, colours, etc., so frequently met with in China. De Groot gives us the following :

East	Spring	Blue	Dragon
South	Summer	Red	Bird
West	Autumn	White	Tiger
North	Winter	Black	Tortoise [1]

The mystic participation realized by means of the number four in the minds of the North American tribes, is brought out in many instances. Catlin tells us that with the Mandans " there were also four articles of great veneration and importance lying on the floor of the lodge, which were sacks containing in each some three or four gallons of water . . . objects of superstitious regard, made with great labour and much ingenuity ; . . . sewed in the form of a large tortoise lying on its back, with a bunch of eagle's quill appended to it as a tail. . . . These four sacks of water have the appearance of great antiquity, and by inquiring . . . the medicine-man very gravely told me that ' those four tortoises contained the waters from the four quarters of the world—that those waters had been contained therein since the settling down of the world,' " an explanation which amused Catlin very much. He tells us, too, that the buffalo dance (intended to *oblige*

[1] J. J. M. de Groot, *The Religious System of China*, i. p. 317.

the buffaloes to come near the hunters) is repeated four times during the first day, eight on the second day, twelve on the third and sixteen on the fourth day, and that the dance is given *once* to each of the cardinal points, and the medicine-man smokes his pipe in those directions. On the second day it is given twice to each, three times on the third day, and four times on the fourth.[1]

We note the same mystic character attributed to the number four in the magic formulas of the Cherokees. Mooney lays considerable stress upon this. " The Indian," he says, " has always four as the principal sacred number, with usually another only slightly subordinated. The two sacred numbers of the Cherokees are four and seven. . . . The sacred four has direct relation to the four cardinal points, while seven, besides these, includes also ' above,' ' below,' and ' here, in the centre.' In many tribal rituals, colour and sometimes sex are assigned to each point of direction. In the sacred Cherokee formulas the spirits of the East, South, West and North are respectively Red, White, Black and Blue, and its colour has also its symbolic meaning of Power (War), Peace, Death and Defeat." [2] Mooney speaks too of " the veneration which their physicians have for the numbers four and seven. They say that after man was placed upon the earth four and seven nights were instituted for the cure of diseases in the human body. . . ." [3]

In British Columbia, with the StatlumH tribe, four is *par excellence* the sacred number. After birth " the mother and child remained in the lodge for at least four days, and if the weather permitted, this period would be extended to eight or twelve or twenty days, or to some other multiple of four, the Salish mystic number." [4] In Vancouver, during the initiation ceremonies of the medicine-man, " when he rises, he must turn round four times, turning to the left. Then he must put forward his foot four times before actually making a step. In the same way, he has to make four steps before

---

[1] *The North American Indians*, i. pp. 185-6.
[2] " Myths of the Cherokee," *E. B. Rept.*, xix. p. 431.
[3] Heywood, quoted by J. Mooney, " The Sacred Formulas of the Cherokee," *E. B. Rept.*, vii. p. 322.
[4] Hill Tout, " The Ethnology of the StatlumH of British Columbia," *J.A.I.*, xxxv. p. 140.

going out of the door. . . . He must use a kettle, dish, spoon and cup of his own, which are thrown away at the end of four months. . . . He must not take more than four mouthfuls at one time, etc." [1]

This same number four appears to form the basis of the complicated and obscure mysticism of numbers which became manifest in the southern and western parts of North America, and in Central America. " The nine days of ceremony . . . have a nomenclature suggestive of divisions into two groups of four each. . . . On this basis it will be seen that the number four, so constant in Pueblo ritual, is prominent in the number of days in the Snake ceremonial. I will call attention also to the fact that the nine days of ceremonies plus the four days of frolic make the mystic number thirteen. It may likewise be borne in mind that the period of twenty days, the theoretical length of the most elaborate Tusayan ceremony, was also characteristic of other more cultured peoples in Mexico, and that thirteen ceremonials, each twenty days long, make a year of 260 days, a ceremonial epoch of the Maya and related peoples." [2] I shall not enter into a discussion of this complicated question, but am content to have pointed out the significant place occupied by the number four, as we find it again in the Agrarian rites of the Cherokees.[3] Lastly, I shall quote a remark made by Hewitt, apropos of an Iroquois myth, in which four children—two boys and two girls—are mentioned. " The use of the number four is here remarkable. It seems that the two female children are introduced merely to retain the number four, since they do not take any part in the events of the legend." [4]

The mystic number thus assumes the aspect of a category in which the content of the collective representations must be arranged. This is a feature which is found, well marked, in the Far East. " European languages," says Chamberlain, " have such expressions as ' the four cardinal virtues ' or ' the seven deadly sins '; but it is no part of our mental disposition to divide up and parcel out almost all things visible

[1] F. Boas, " The North-west Tribes of Canada," *Reports of the British Association*, p. 618 (1890).
[2] Fewkes, " Tusayan Snake Ceremonies," *E. B. Rept.*, xvi. p. 275.
[3] J. Mooney, " Myths of the Cherokee," *E. B. Rept.*, xix. p. 423.
[4] Hewitt, " Iroquoian Cosmology," *E. B. Rept.*, xxi. p. 233 (note).

and invisible into numerical categories fixed by unchanging custom, as is the case among the natives from India eastwards." [1] In North America this "category" seems very closely bound up with the cardinal points or the spatial regions. We must not imagine, however, that prelogical mentality imagines these points or regions in any abstract way, and that it detaches the number four from its idea of these, for its mystic purposes. In this, as in all else, such a mentality obeys the law of participation ; it imagines spatial directions, cardinal points and their number only in a mystic complex to which the number four owes its categorical character, which is not logical, but mystic. " The breath-clouds of the gods are tinted with the yellow of the North, the blue-green of the West, the red of South, and the silver of the East." [2]

This complex naturally contains elements which are of social origin. The division of space into regions corresponds with the division of the tribe into groups. Durkheim and Mauss opine that the latter determine the former, and that it is the general principle of what they call classifications.[3] They quote facts observed in Australia especially, but also in China, and from the Pueblos of North America, particularly the Zuñis. I have already laid stress upon that which Spencer and Gillen term " local relationship," kinship by community of position, and participation between a group and a given region. When a tribe stays in a place, for instance, whether its stay be provisional or permanent, the different clans or totems do not take up their positions at their own discretion. Each has its predetermined site, settled by virtue of the mystic connection between the clans or totems and the points of the compass. We have found that facts of the same kind were noted in North America, and other observations made betoken this mystic connection. The Kansa, for instance, as Dorsey tells us, were accustomed to cut out the heart of an enemy they had killed, and throw it on the fire as a sacrifice to the four winds. The Yata men, i.e. those who camped on the left side of the tribal circle, would raise their left hands, and bow to the east, south, west, and north winds succes-

---

[1] *Things Japanese*, pp. 353-4.
[2] Stevenson, " The Zuñis," *E. B. Rept*, xxiii. p. 23.
[3] *Année Sociologique*, vi. pp. 1-72.

sively.[1] The ritual order is regulated by the mystic tie which unites the clans with the position in space which they occupy, and Dorsey further says that every time the Osage and Kansa tribes permanently established themselves in a village, there was a certain consecration of the dwellings, before the people could install their belongings, and this was associated with the cult of the four winds. " The symbol of the earth, *U-ma-ne*, in Dakota, has never been absent from any religious exercise I have yet seen or learned of from the Indians. It is a mellowed earth space, and represents the unappropriated life or power of the earth. . . . The square or oblong, with the four lines standing out, is invariably interpreted to mean the earth or land with the four winds standing towards it. The cross, whether diagonal or upright, always symbolizes the four winds or four quarters." [2]

The numbers five, six and seven also sometimes possess a sacred character among the North American tribes, although not so constantly so as the number four. Gatschet writes, for instance : " Here we have again the sacred number five occurring so often in the traditions, myths and customs of the Oregonian tribes." [3] " Many of the deified animals appear collectively, as five to ten brothers, or five sisters, sometimes with their old parents." [4] The number of cardinal points or spatial regions is not necessarily *four* ; with the North American tribes it is sometimes five (reckoning the zenith), six (then adding the nadir), and lastly seven, terminating in the centre or the place occupied by the one counting. With the Mandans, for instance, the medicine-man " took the pipe, and after presenting the stem to the North, to the South, to the East and the West—and then to the sun that was over his head . . ." [5]—With the Sia, " the priest, standing before the altar shook his rattle for a moment, and then waved it in a circle over the altar. He repeated this motion six times, for the cardinal points. . . . The circle indicated that all the cloud people of the world were invoked to water the earth. . .

[1] Dorsey, " Siouan Cults," *E. B. Rept.*, xi. p. 380.
[2] Ibid., p. 451.
[3] *The Klamath Language*, p. 86.
[4] Ibid., p. 101.
[5] Catlin, *The North American Indians*, i. p. 258.

This sprinkling of the cardinal points was repeated four times." [1] —"The Omaha and Ponka used to hold the pipe in six directions while smoking towards the four winds, the ground, and the upper world." [2]—" The snake chief made a circle of sacred meal about twenty feet in diameter . . . and drew in it six meal radii corresponding to the six cardinal points." [3] Finally, among the Cherokees, the sacred number four signifies the cardinal points, and the sacred seven signifies them also, by adding the zenith, nadir and centre.[4]

We find these numbers five, six and seven, involved in the same complex mystic participations as the number four. Among the Zuñis, Mrs. Stevenson has collected several examples relating to *six*. To quote but one of them, " these primitive agriculturists have observed the greatest care in developing colour in corn and beans to harmonize with the six regions : yellow North, blue West, red South, white East, variegated zenith, and black nadir." [5]

Similar phenomena are to be found throughout the Far East, to say nothing of the Indo-European and Semitic peoples. In China the complexity of correspondences and participations involving numbers is infinite. They intersect and even contradict each other without the Chinese sense of logic being at all disturbed. In Java the native week lasts five days, and the Javanese believe that the names of these days bear a mystical relation to colours and to the divisions of the horizon. " The 1 means white and East ; the 2, red and South ; the 3, yellow and West ; the 4, black and North ; the 5, mixed colour and forms the centre. . . . In an ancient manuscript found in Java, the week of five days is represented by five human figures, two female and three male." [6] In India the number five is lucky or formidable, according to the district, or according to the special participation concerned. " In 1817 a terrible epidemic of cholera broke out at Jessore. The disease commenced its ravages in August, and it was at once discovered that the August of this year had five Saturdays

[1] Stevenson, " The Sia," *E. B. Rept.*, xi. pp. 79, 93.
[2] Dorsey, " Siouan Cults," *E. B. Rept.*, xi. p. 375.
[3] Fewkes, " Tusayan Snake Ceremonies," *E. B. Rept.*, xvi. pp. 285, 295.
[4] J. Mooney, " Myths of the Cherokee," *E. B. Rept.*, xix. p. 431.
[5] Stevenson, " The Zuñis," *E. B. Rept.*, xxiii. p. 350.
[6] Skeat, *Malay Magic*, p. 545 (note).

(a day under the influence of the ill-omened Sani). The number five being the express property of the destructive Siva, a mystical connection was at once detected, the infallibly baleful influence of which it would have been sacrilege to question." [1] In another place the number five possesses favourable powers. " The peasant digs up five clods of earth with his spade. This is a lucky number, as it is a quarter more than four. . . . He then sprinkles water five times into the trench with the branch of the sacred mango. . . . Then a selected man ploughs five furrows. . . . In Mirzapur, only the northern part of the field, that facing the Himalaya, is dug up in five places with a piece of mango wood." [2] Agrarian rites and practices of this nature occur very frequently.

There are peculiarly important mystic virtues attaching to the number seven, especially in places where the influence of Chinese or Assyro-Babylonian beliefs obtains.[3] In Malaya, " every man is supposed . . . to possess seven souls in all, or perhaps, I should more accurately say, a sevenfold soul. This 'septenity in unity' may perhaps be held to explain the remarkable importance and persistence of the number seven in Malay magic (seven twigs of the birch, seven repetitions of the charm in soul abduction, seven betel leaves, seven blows administered to the soul, seven ears cut for the Rice soul in reaping)." [4] The animism which inspires Skeat's work evidently suggests this theory : I incline to think that it presents the matter the wrong way round. It is not because they conceive of seven souls or a sevenfold soul for every one that the Malays use seven everywhere. It is on the contrary because the number seven possesses magic virtues on their eyes that it becomes a kind of " category," upon which not only their magic practices, but also their ideas, not excepting their conception of the soul, are regulated. This is so true that Skeat himself adds : " What these seven souls were it is impossible without more evidence to determine." If each of the seven souls is so little differentiated that we may

[1] Crooke, *The Folklore of Northern India*," i. p. 130.
[2] Ibid., ii. p. 288.
[3] Vide Von Adrian, " Die Siebenzahl im Geistesleben der Völker," *Mitteilungen*, pp. 225–271 (Vienna, 1901). ; W. H. Roscher, " Die Siebenzahl," *Philologus*, pp. 360–74 (1901).
[4] Skeat, *Malay Magic*, pp. 50, 509.

speak equally well of one sevenfold soul, it is difficult to admit
that the value attached to the number seven in general has
its origin in this idea.

" When Hindus have removed the ashes from a burning-
ground they write the figures 49 on the spot where the corpse
was cremated. The Pandits explain this by saying that when
written in Hindi the figures resemble the conch-shell or wheel
of Vishnu ; or that it is an invocation to the 49 winds of heaven
to come and purify the ground. It is more probably based on
the idea that the number seven, as is the case all over the world,
has some mystic application." [1]—" In India, the water of seven
wells is collected on the night . . . of the feast of lamps,
and barren women bathe in it as a means of procuring children.
. . . Hydrophobia, all over Northern India, is cured by
looking down seven wells in succession." [2]—" The goddess of
smallpox, Sitala, is only the eldest of a band of seven sisters
by whom the pustular group of diseases is supposed to be
caused. . . . Similarly in the older Indian mythology we
have the seven mâtris, the seven oceans, the seven Rishis,
the seven Adityas, and Dānavas, and the seven horses of the
sun, and numerous other combinations of this mystic number." [3]—In Japan, " seven, and all the numbers into which
seven enters (seventeen, twenty-seven, etc.), are unlucky." [4]
It is the same with the Assyro-Babylonian people, who consider
the seventh, fourteenth, twenty-first and twenty-eighth
days ill-omened.[5]—Among the Hindus, medical prescriptions,
like all magic formulas in general, attach the greatest importance to numbers on account of their mystic virtues. For
example, " one favourite talisman is the magic square,
which consists in an arrangement of certain numbers in a
special way. In order to cure barrenness, for instance, it is
a good plan to write a series of numbers which added up
make 73 both ways, on a piece of bread, and with it feed a
black dog. . . . To cure a tumour a figure in the form of a
cross is drawn, with three cyphers in the centre and one at
each of the four ends. This is prepared on a Sunday and
tied round the left arm. The number of these charms is

[1] Crooke, *The Folklore of Northern India*, ii. p. 51.
[2] Ibid., i. pp. 50–1.   [3] Ibid., i. p. 218.
[4] Chamberlain, *Things Japanese*, p. 439.
[5] Jastrow, *The Religion of Babylonia and Assyria*, p. 377.

legion," [1] adds Crooke ; but it is not only in India that this
is so. An infinite number of similar ones can be found in
the magic and medicine of antiquity in Arabia and in the
Middle Ages, in Europe and among all peoples who have
numerals at command. The study of folk-lore affords abundant evidence of this.

Among more developed peoples, with whom large numbers
are of current usage, certain multiples of numbers of mystic
value participate in their peculiar properties. In India, for
instance, " when the new moon falls on Monday, pious Hindus
walk one hundred and eight times round it (the fig-tree)." [2]
Possibly 108 possesses special virtue as a common multiple
of 9 and 12, themselves multiples of 3 and 6. In the North-
west Provinces, the numbers 84 and 360 are of extraordinary
importance. *Chaurasi* (84), for instance, is the subdivision
of a *parganah* or district, amounting to 84 villages. " But it
is not with respect to the occupation of land only that the
numbers 84 and 360 are regarded with such favour. We
find them entering into the whole scheme of the Hindi, Buddhist
and Jaïn religions, cosmogonies, rituals, and legendary tales ;
so much so, as to show that they are not taken by mere chance,
as arbitrary numbers to fill up some of their extravagant
fictions, but with a designed purpose of veiling a remote
allusion under a type of ordinary character." [3] The use of
such mystic numbers is more systematic with the Buddhists
than with the Hindus.

May not this arise out of the fact that 84 is a multiple of
both 7 and 12 ; and 360 a multiple of 4, 6, 9, 5 and 12 ? There
would thus be a combination in 84 and 360, in which all the
properties of the respective numbers would participate.

On several occasions Bergaigne has laid stress upon the
nature of the mystic numbers in Vedic poetry, and the
mystic processes applied to these. Multiplication seems to
be effected chiefly by applying to the different parts of a whole
a system of division first applied to itself. For instance,
the division of the universe into three—heaven, earth, and
atmosphere—may be repeated for each of these three—

---

[1] Crooke, op. cit., i. pp. 159–60.   [2] Ibid., ii. p. 100.
[3] Elliot, *Memoirs of the Races in the North-west Provinces of India.* ii.
pp. 47 et seq.

three heavens, three earths, and three atmospheres—that is, nine worlds in all. Then, too, various systems of division having been applied to the universe, the figures given by two of them may also be multiplied together, thus : $3 \times 2 = 6$ worlds, three heavens and three earths.[1] Or again, to form a new magic number, we can add the unit to a given mystic number : $3 + 1$, $6 + 1$, $9 + 1$, etc. " The usual object of this is to introduce into any system of the universe whatever the idea of an invisible world, or into any group whatever, of persons or things the idea of a person or thing of the same kind, but distinguished from the rest by a sort of mystery which surrounds him or it."[2] The number 7, for instance, may possibly have independent mythological value ; but it is certain that the Rishis have at least divided it into $6 + 1$, the addition of the unit to the number of the six worlds. These mythological numbers derive their virtue from their mystic relation to the spatial regions : the septenary division of the universe, for example, (seven worlds, i.e. $6 + 1$) coincides with the mythological heptads, the seven places, races, ocean depths, rivers, and so forth.

That prelogical mentality is at work in these already systematized collective representations can be proved by the way in which the one and the many are identified. It is thus, says Bergaigne, that " most groups of mythological beings or objects may be reduced to a single being or object with many forms, which sums up the group as a whole. The elements of each group are in this way revived as so many manifestations of a single principle ; and the multiplicity of these manifestations is accounted for by the multiplicity of the worlds. . . . The seven prayers are only the seven forms of the prayer which, considered both in its unity and in its different manifestations, becomes the prayer or hymn with seven heads. . . . The seven cows of the master of the prayer are naturally the seven prayers issuing from his seven mouths. . . . A male has two or three mothers, two or three wives, etc."[3]

This leads to a conclusion which at first appears extraordinary ; different numbers are nevertheless equal numbers.

[1] Bergaigne, *La Religion Védique*, ii. p. 115.
[2] Ibid., ii. pp. 123 et seq   [3] Ibid., ii. pp. 147–8.

" The simultaneous and impartial use of three and seven . . . proves but one thing : their complete equivalence. . . . The various numbers we have found used for one another, because they all express, in different systems of division, the sum of the parts of the universe, have for the same reason been capable of being used, by a kind of pleonasm, side by side with each other. In fact, this has frequently been done. In this way, three is the same as seven, or as nine." This equivalence, an absurdity to logical thought, seems quite natural to prelogical mentality, for the latter, preoccupied with the mystic participation, does not regard these numbers in an abstract relation to other numbers, or with respect to the arithmetical law in which they originate. The primitive mind considers each as a reality grasped by itself, and not needing for its definition to be regarded as a functioning of other numbers. Thus every number has an inviolate individuality which allows it to correspond exactly with another number, itself equally inviolate. " Most of the mythological numbers of the Rig-Veda, especially 2, 3, 5 and 7, express, not merely an indefinite plurality, but a totality, and this totality answers in principle to the ensemble of the worlds." [1] Let it be, for instance, the mythical bull, having " four horns, three feet, two heads, seven hands ; bound with a threefold cord, the bull bellows, etc." (Here we have two, three, seven, worlds, and four cardinal points.)   The different characteristics in the description all indicate, by their allusion to the different divisional systems of the universe, that the personage in question is present everywhere.[2]   We know from other sources that the idea of omnipresence, or of " multipresence," according to Leibnitz' expression, is absolutely familiar to prelogical, mystical mentality.

Finally, to complete the delineation of these mystic numbers, Bergaigne says further : " The numbers three and seven, in the general system of Vedic mythology, should be regarded as frameworks prepared beforehand, independently of the personalities which may be summoned to occupy them." [3] *Frameworks prepared beforehand* : that is to say, categories, according to the expression used by Chamberlain,

[1] Bergaigne, *La Religion Védique*, ii. p. 156.
[2] Ibid., ii. p. 151.   [3] Ibid., iii. p. 99.

quoted above, and dealing with this precise subject. There is no better way of emphasizing the difference between these mystic numbers and those which serve the purpose of arithmetical calculation. Instead of the number depending on the actual plurality of the objects perceived or pictured, it is on the contrary the objects whose plurality is defined by receiving its form from a mystic number decided upon beforehand. Thus the properties of numbers predetermine, as it were, what the multiplicity will be in the collective representations.

How does it happen, we may ask, that the mystic nature of numbers is not most clearly manifest where the representations are themselves most profoundly mystic, that is, in the peoples of the most primitive type familiar to us ? How is it that this mystic character seems, on the contrary, more strongly marked in cases where logical thinking is already somewhat developed, and knows how to use numbers in a really arithmetical method—in the races of North America and the Far East, for instance, whilst it is not noticed in the Australian aboriginals, or in the South American or Indian primitives ? It may seem as if our theory does not take all the facts of the case into account, and that if we are to explain the mystic virtues attributed to numbers, we must have recourse to other principles than the participations of which these numbers are the vehicles in the collective representations.

This objection may be answered in the following ways :

(1) Among peoples still wholly primitive, numbers (above two or three) are as yet undifferentiated, and consequently they do not figure as actual numbers in the collective representations. As they have not been the object of an abstraction, not even of that isolating but not generalizing abstraction peculiar to prelogical mentality, they are never imagined *per se*. And above all, *having no names*, they can never act as condensers of mystic virtues, a part attributed to them in the collective representations of more advanced peoples.

(2) Above all, however, it is possibly in this undifferentiated and unnamed state that the mystic efficacy of the number is greatest. The divisions of the social group into totems, clans, phratries, which are themselves subdivided, although not expressed numerically, nevertheless comprehend definite

numbers ; and have we not found that these divisions and
their numbers extend to all reality represented, to animals,
plants, inanimate objects, stars, spatial directions ? Institutions, beliefs, religious and magical practices—do not all
these constantly imply, through these same divisions and
" classifications," the numbers which are comprised therein
without being expressed ? Yet it is precisely because the
mentality which is mystic and prelogical moves thus in an
element natural to it, that we find it so difficult to reconstruct
it. Whatever the effort we may make, a number which is
purely intricate, undifferentiated, felt and not conceived, is
unimaginable to us. A number is not a number to us unless
we imagine it and as soon as we picture it we imagine it
logically and with a name. There is no doubt that, once
named, we can very well conceive of it, either from the abstract
point of view, without any qualifying attribute, and absolutely
homogeneous with other numbers, or as a sacred vehicle of
mystic qualities. Our religions, and sometimes our metaphysics, still tell us of such numbers, and our myths, legends,
and folklore have familiarized us with them. But it is far
more difficult to go back to a number *which has no name*, and
to discover the function it fulfils in the collective representations of primitive peoples.

PART III

CHAPTER VI

INSTITUTIONS IN WHICH COLLECTIVE REPRESENTATIONS GOVERNED BY THE LAW OF PARTICIPATION ARE INVOLVED (I)

INTRODUCTION

OUR study of the collective representations and their inter-relations among primitives has led us to conclude that these people possess a mystic, prelogical mentality differing in many essentials from our logical thinking. This conclusion, moreover, seems to have been confirmed by our examination of certain characteristics in the languages spoken by primitives and the system of numeration used. A counter-proof, however, is necessary. We therefore have to show that primitives' ways of acting do indeed correspond with their ways of thinking, as analysed in this volume, and that their collective representations express themselves in their institutions with the mystic, prelogical characteristics already noted. Such a demonstration would not only yield a valuable verification of my theory, but would lead the way to a better interpretation of these institutions than any of the psychological and merely probable " explanations " so often urged, can afford, for this interpretation must above all take into account the mentality that is peculiar to the social groups under consideration.

By way of example I have selected a certain number of institutions, preferring either the simplest or else those which, as far as our knowledge goes at present, seem best suited to show the nature of prelogical mentality most clearly. In no case, however, have I ventured to suggest an " explanation," nor to reduce these examples to a general principle which would account equally well for all. To " explain " these customs or institutions properly would require a detailed monograph in each case, and I need hardly say that not even the first faint outline will be found here. My object is something quite different, and its scope is much more general. I only desire to show that if we are to understand these institutions and these practices we must refer them to that prelogical, mystic mentality, the chief laws of which I have endeavoured to determine, the mentality which is peculiar to primitives. Admitting these laws to have been established, the savant has still to inquire into the conditions in which each of these special institutions and practices has made its appearance and maintained its existence in any given community, but at any rate he will henceforth have at his disposal, to minimize the risk of his going astray, a clue which only too often was lacking to his predecessors

I

Let us first of all consider the operations by means of which the social group procures its sustenance—hunting and fishing, more particularly. Here, success is dependent upon a number of objective conditions : the presence of the game or the fish in a certain place, the necessary precautions in approaching it unperceived, the traps set to entice it to the desired spot, the projectiles required to bring it down and so forth. To the mind of the primitive, however, these conditions, although necessary, are by no means sufficient, and unless others be fulfilled, all the means employed will fail, whatever the skill of the hunter or fisherman. These means must possess magic virtue, must be endowed, so to speak, through the performance of special rites, with mystic power, just as the objective elements which are perceived are surrounded by a mystic complex. Without such magic performance, the most experienced hunter or fisherman will fail to find game or fish, or if he does perceive it, it will escape the snare or the hook. Or again, his bow or his gun will miscarry. He may even attack his prey, and prove it invulnerable ; or, having wounded it he may fail to find it. Thus the mystic operations are not mere preliminaries of the chase or the fishing, like St. Hubert's Mass, for example, when the effectual pursuit of game or fish remains the essential feature of the occasion. On the contrary, this effectual pursuit is not the most important factor to the primitive mind ; the really essential part is the mystic process which alone can bring about the presence, and secure the capture, of the prey. If such a process does not take place, there is no object in making any effort in the matter.

Processes of such a kind are manifold and often complex. For the sake of clearness I shall distinguish between those which must be carried out before, during, and after the chase ; and also those exercised upon the agent, (or the members of his group) to ensure his striking a successful blow, and those which have his prey as their aim, either to render it unable to escape or to defend itself, or else to pacify it and obtain pardon for its death. Accordingly we shall see action dominated by an ensemble of definite mystic relations, dependent upon the collective representations of the social group and, like these collective representations themselves, governed by the law of participation.

A. In hunting, the very first essential is to exert a magic influence upon the game pursued, to secure its presence, willingly or unwillingly, and to constrain it to come from a distance if need be. With most primitive people this process is considered indispensable. It consists mainly of dances, incantations and fasts. Catlin has given a detailed description of the buffalo dance, " held for the purpose of making ' buffalo come ', as they term it. . . . About ten or fifteen Mandans at a time join in the dance, each one with the skin of the buffalo's head (or mask) with the horns on, and in his hand his favourite bow or lance, with which he is used to slay the buffalo. . . . These dances have sometimes been continued for two or three weeks without stopping an instant, until the joyful moment when buffaloes make their appearance." (They represent the capture and the killing of the buffalo.) " When an Indian becomes fatigued of the exercise, he signifies it by bending quite forward, and sinking his body towards the ground ; when another draws a bow upon him and hits him with a blunt arrow, and he falls like a buffalo, is seized by the bystanders, who drag him out of the ring by the heels, brandishing their knives about him ; and having gone through the motions of skinning and cutting him up, they let him off, and his place is at once supplied by another, who dances into the ring with his mask on ; and by this taking of places, the scene is easily kept up night and day, until the desired effect, that of making ' buffalo come,' has been produced." [1]

It is a kind of drama, or rather pantomime, representing the prey and the fate that awaits him at the hands of the Indians. Since the primitive mind does not recognize an image, pure and simple ;—since to him the image participates of the original, and the original of the image, to be conversant with the image already, to some extent, ensures the possession of the original. This mystic participation constitutes the virtue of the operation.

In other places, this participation assumes a slightly different form. To secure the presence of the animal, it is essential to conciliate it. With the Sioux, for instance, " the bear-dance . . . is given several days in succession, previous to their starting out, and . . . they all join in a song to the Bear Spirit which, they think, holds somewhere an invisible existence, and must be consulted and conciliated before they can enter upon their excursion with any prospect of success. . . One of the chief medicine-men placed over his body the entire skin of a bear. . . . Many others in the dance wore masks on their faces, made of the skin from the bear's head ; and all, with the motions of their hands, closely imitated the movements of that animal, some representing its motion in running, and others the peculiar attitude, and hanging of the paws, when it is sitting up on its hind feet, and looking for the approach of an enemy." [2] Occasionally, the operations have undergone a kind of simplification of an abstract kind, which nevertheless allows their real nature to be perceived. " In order to cause the deer to move towards the locality where they may be desired, the shaman will erect, on a pole placed in a favourable position, an image of some famous hunter and conjurer. The image will represent the power of the person as conjurer, and the various paraphernalia attached to the image assist in controlling the movements

---

[1] Catlin, *The North American Indians*, i. pp. 127–8.
[2] Ibid., i. pp. 245–6.

of the animals." [1]—In West Africa, Nassau tells us, the native appeals to his fetich in hunting, warfare, trading, love-making, fishing, tree-planting, and starting upon a journey. " The hunter or hunters start out, each with his own fetich hanging from his belt or suspended from his shoulder . . . or if the hunt includes several persons, a temporary charm may be performed by the witch-doctor, or even by the hunters themselves. Such ceremonies preliminary to the chase are described by W. H. Brown as performed in Mashonaland," [2] and their object appears to be that of obliging the animals to appear. Conversely, certain acts are forbidden, because they would produce the contrary effect. " To name even the word deer when searching for one is ' mali ' or ' tabooed,' and now they thought it was useless my going to look for them any more. . . . They listen to omens religiously whenever on a hunting or fishing expedition, and never name the animal for fear that the spirits should carry information to the object of pursuit." [3] In British Columbia, " should a pubescent girl eat fresh meat, it was believed her father's luck as a hunter would be spoiled thereafter. The animals would not permit him to kill them ; for it was held that no animal could be killed against its own wish and will. Indeed the Indian looked upon all his food, animal and vegetable, as gifts voluntarily bestowed upon him by the ' spirit ' of the animal or vegetable, and regarded himself as absolutely dependent upon their good will for his daily sustenance." [4]

B. The magic operations to which the hunter himself must submit aim at securing for him mystic power over the game. These are often lengthy and complicated. In Canada, " the hunters observe a week's fast, during which time they may not drink a drop of water . . . they do not cease their incantations while the daylight lasts . . . many of them cut themselves in various parts of the body . . . and all this is done to induce the spirits to reveal where bears are to be found in large numbers. . . . With the same end in view, they offer prayers to the spirits of the beasts they have slaughtered in previous hunts. . . . Before they set out, all,

[1] Turner, " The Hudson Bay Eskimo," E. B. Rept., xi. pp. 196–7.
[2] Nassau, Fetichism in West Africa, p. 173.
[3] Brooke, Ten Years in Sarawak, ii. pp. 90–1.
[4] Hill Tout, " The Ethnology of the StatlumH," J.A.I., xxxv. p. 136.

or at any rate, most of them, must have seen bears in the same district in their dreams. . . . Later on, they bathe, whatever the weather may be, and a feast is given by the head hunter, who eats nothing himself, but recounts his hunting exploits.   There are renewed invocations to the spirits of the dead bears, and then they begin their march, besmeared with black, equipped as for war, and acclaimed by the whole village." [1]   So too, Nicolas Perrot relates : " This festival is always preceded by a week's fast, neither food nor drink being allowed, so that the bear may be favourable to him and to his party, and this means that he desires to find and kill bears without any disastrous consequences to him or any of his people. . . . When the day of departure arrives, he calls them all together, and they blacken their faces with charcoal as he does ; they all fast until evening, and then eat but very little." [2]

It is almost universal among primitive peoples that the hunter, about to start upon an expedition, should abstain from sexual relations, take careful note of his dreams, cleanse his person, fast, or at any rate, eat certain foods only, paint and adorn himself in a special manner ; and all of these are practices which will have mystic effects upon the game he desires to capture.   Boas tells us that " the mountain-goat hunter fasts and bathes for several nights.   Then early in the morning he paints his chin with red paint, and draws a red line over his forehead down to the point of his nose.   Two tail feathers of the eagle are fastened to his hair.   These ornaments are believed to enable him to climb well.   The elk hunter adorns his hair with coal, red paint, and eagle down, etc." [3]   The special aim of such adornment is to gain the animal's favour.   A bear-hunter assured Boas that he himself had received instructions from a bear regarding what he was to wear.

Mooney describes the magic preparations for the hunt made by the Cherokees, and in explaining them he reproduces the formulas which reveal their signification.   He tells us that

[1] Charlevoix, *Journal d'un Voyage dans l'Amérique Septentrionale*, iii. pp. 115–16 (1721).
[2] *Mémoire sur les Mœurs . . . de l'Amérique Septentrionale*, pp. 66–7.
[3] F. Boas, " The North-west Tribes of Canada," *Reports of the British Association*, p. 460 (1894).

ιe night before the departure the hunter " goes to the water "
ιd recites the appropriate formula. In the morning he leaves
ʻithout breaking his fast, and he neither eats nor drinks
ιuring the day's march. At sunset he again goes to the water
ιd repeats his incantation, and then he encamps, lights his
ʻe, eats his supper and, after having rubbed his breast with
ʒhes, he lies down for the night. Next morning his quest
ᵉgins . . . and in all hunting expeditions it is the rule, and
Ⅰmost a religious injunction, to abstain from food until
ɪnset. . . . The hunter addresses his supplications to the
ʻe whence he draws his omens, to the reeds of which he
ιakes his arrows, to Tsu'lkala the great lord of the game,
ιd finally he addresses in songs the very animals he is seeking
ɔ slay.[1]

In British Guiana, " before an Indian sets out to hunt, he
ɔes through one or more strange performances to ensure
ιccess. Round his house he has planted various sorts of
ʻbeenas ' or plants, generally caladiums, which he supposes
ɔˏact as charms to make the capture of game certain. These
ʻe for his dogs, which are made to swallow pieces of the roots
ιd leaves. Sometimes the poor brutes have to undergo
ιore painful operations. . . . The hunter inflicts tortures on
ɪmself . . . he submits to the bite of ants of a large and
ᵉnomous kind . . . and rubs himself with caterpillars which
ʻritate his skin, etc.[2] Finally, the weapons and implements
f the chase must also be endowed with special virtue by
ιeans of magical operations. To give but one example only,
-it is customary among the Fang in West Africa to make,
ʻevious to the expedition, *biang nzali*, which is a charm for
ιe guns, and to place the weapons upon it : this will enable
ιem to go direct to their mark." [3]

C. Let us now assume that all the operations have attained
ιeir end and the prey is in sight : will it now suffice to attack
ιd strike it down ? By no means ; here again, everything
ᵉpends upon the practice of magic. For instance, with the
ʒoux, " on coming in sight of the herd, the hunters talk
ɪndly to their horses, applying to them the endearing

---

[1] J. Mooney, "The Sacred Formulas of the Cherokee," *E. B. Rept.*,
i. pp. 370, 372, 342.
[2] Im Thurm, *Among the Indians of Guiana*, pp. 228–31.
[3] Bennett, "Ethnographical Notes on the Fang," *J.A.I.*, xxix. p. 94.

names of father, brother, uncle, etc. . . . The party having
approached near to the herd, they halt to give the pipe bearer
an opportunity to perform the ceremony of smoking, which
is considered necessary to their success. He lights his pipe
and remains a short time with his head inclined, and the
stem of the pipe extended towards the herd. He then smokes
and puffs the smoke towards the bisons, and the earth, and
finally to the cardinal points successively." [1] This rite is
evidently intended to bring the animals into mystic relation
with the hunters and with certain spatial positions which will
prevent their escaping. It is magic enchantment, designed
to make sure of them. We find something similar in Malaya.
" When the hiding-place (of the deer) is discovered, all the
young men of the *kampong* assemble, and the following ceremony is performed." . . . (A description is here given.) " It
is believed that the absence of this ceremony would render
the expedition unsuccessful, the deer would prove too strong
for the ropes. . . ." [2] So, too, in South Africa, Livingstone
relates of one of his men that he was considered the leader
of the hunting expedition, by virtue of his having a knowledge
of " elephant medicine." He would go in front of the rest
and examine the animals, everything depending upon his
verdict. " If he decided to attack a herd, the rest went
boldly on, but if *he* refused, none of them would engage.
A certain part of the elephant belonged to him by right. . . ." [3]
Lastly, in South Australia, in hunting emus, it is not enough
to have discovered their whereabouts ; they must be rendered
powerless by means of magical operations. " A mineral stone
about the size of a pigeon's egg . . . is found in the quarries
and called ' emu eye ' by the natives. These stones are
wrapped in feathers and fat, and when within a few hundred
yards of the birds they commence throwing them towards
the emus, believing there is a charm about the stones and
that it prevents the emus from running." [4]

In New South Wales, " when a man went out hunting
he took with him a charmed *wommera* or spear-lever, the hook

[1] Dorsey, " Siouan Cults," *E. B. Rept.*, xi. pp. 375-6.
[2] Skeat, *Malay Magic*, p. 172.
[3] Livingstone, *Missionary Travels*, pp. 599-600.
[4] Gason, " Manners, Customs, etc., of the Dieri, Auminie Tribes," *J.A.I.*
xxiv. p. 172

f which consisted of a bone from a dead man's arm, ground
o a point. The fat of the corpse was mixed with the gum
sed in lashing the hook to the shaft of the weapon. When
he hunter espied an emu, kangaroo, turkey or similar game,
e held up the *wommera* in sight of the animal, which would
hereby be spellbound, and unable to run away. . . . When
, clever man is out hunting and comes across the tracks of,
ay, a kangaroo, he follows them along and talks to the foot-
rints all the time for the purpose of injecting magic into the
nimal which made them. He mentions in succession all
he parts of the foot, and then names the different parts of the
eg right up to the animal's back. As soon as he reaches the
ackbone, the creature becomes quite stupid and is an easy
rey. . . ." Or again, " a hunter takes some fat, or skin, or
iece of bone, of a dead man, and puts it into a little bag.
Ie then goes to some place in the bush frequented by kanga-
oos, emus, etc. . . . Here he selects a tree belonging to the
roper phratry, and hangs his little bag on one of the spreading
ranches. When an animal gets within ' shooting distance '
f this magical artillery, it becomes stupid, and wanders about
eedlessly until the hunter gets an opportunity of spearing
t." Or yet again, " as soon as some emus or kangaroos
ppeared in sight, the men commenced chewing human hair
nd spitting towards the animals, accompanied by magical
ncantations. This was expected to work a charm on the
ame and cause them to remain quiet and sluggish, so that
 man could steal upon them. . . . In following along the
racks of an emu, kangaroo, wild dog, etc., if the hunter at
ntervals drop hot coals in the footmarks of the animal, this
ill have the effect of making it hot and tired, or induce it
o come round again towards its pursuer." [1] Similarly, near
ort Lincoln, " the superstitious simplicity of these natives
 strikingly apparent in their manner of hunting. . . . There
ave been transmitted to them, by their early ancestors,
everal short rhymes of two lines, which now are known to
he adults only, and these, on pursuing an animal, or when
n the point of spearing it, they constantly repeat with great

[1] Mathews, " Aboriginal Tribes of New South Wales and Victoria,"
ournal and Proceedings of the Royal Society of New South Wales, vol. xxxviii.
p. 254-7 (1905).

rapidity. The literal meaning is totally unknown to them
and they are quite unable to give an explanation of them, . .
but they faithfully believe them to possess the power, either
to strike with blindness the animal which they are pursuing
or to create in it such a feeling of security and carelessness
that it cannot perceive its enemies or to weaken it so that i
cannot effect its escape." [1]

These are very significant facts. They show clearly that
hunting is an essentially magical operation, and in it every
thing depends, not on the skill or strength of the hunter, bu
on the mystic power which will place the animal at his mercy

With many peoples success depends, too, upon certai
inhibitions to be observed during the hunters' absence b
those who did not accompany them, and particularly by thei
wives. In Indo-China, for instance, "the Laotian hunter
. . . set out after having recommended their women t
practise strict abstinence during their absence ; they forbad
them to cut their hair, anoint themselves with oil, to plac
the pestle and mortar for the rice out of doors behind th
house, or to make light of the marriage contract, for suc
practices would prejudice the result of the hunt. . . . If th
captured elephant in its struggles succeeds in overthrowin
the mounts engaged in subduing it, it is because the wife lef
at home is unfaithful to her husband. If the rope that bind
it breaks, she must have cut her hair ; and if the rope slip
so that the beast escapes, she must have smeared hersel
with oil." [2]

"When setting out they make offerings of rice, spirit
ducks, fowls, to the spirits of the long ropes with a runnin
noose which are to be used in capturing the elephants. Ye
more, the hunters command their wives to abstain from
cutting their hair or offering the hospitality of their homes t
a stranger. Should these commands be disobeyed, the animal
captured would escape, and the incensed husband would hav
the right to a divorce on his return. On his side, the hunte
must abstain from sexual relations and, in accordance with
a custom very common in Further India, must give conven

---

[1] Wilhelmi, "Manners and Customs of the Australian Natives, in Par
ticular of the Port Lincoln District," *Royal Society of Australia*, v. p. 17
1860).

[2] Aymonier, *Voyage dans le Laos*, i. pp. 62-3.

ional names to all ordinary things, which has the effect of
reating a special 'hunter's language.' In the hunting-field
he chief chants certain formulas, handed down from father
o son." [1] So, too, with the Huichols during the hunting of
he deer, a matter of the greatest significance to them, " the
important thing is that the chiefs, and the woman who has
officiated, do not infringe the law of fasting. They follow
he hunters in their thoughts all the time, and pray to the fire
and the sun and all the other gods to give success, and thus,
happiness to all. . . . Now and then some of the fasters
vould rise and pray aloud, and with so much fervour that
hey and all the rest were moved to tears." [2] From Schoolcraft
ve learn that if an Indian is unlucky in the chase he at once
declares that someone must have broken their laws.[3]

D. Even when the game has been shot down and retrieved,
all is not over. Fresh magical operations are necessary to
conclude the cycle that the initial ones have begun ; just in
he same way as in the sacrifice, the opening rites, as Hubert
and Mauss have demonstrated, correspond with the concluding
rites. These operations are of two kinds, and it is sometimes
difficult to distinguish between them. The object of the
earlier ones is to stultify the animal's vengeance—and at the
same time that of the spirit which represents all the animals
of the species ; for prelogical mentality, governed by the law
of participation, does not recognize any distinct difference
between the individual and the substance of the species.
The later ones tend to pacify the victim (or its spirit). Death
does not bring about entire disappearance in the case of
animals any more than it does with men. On the contrary
hey continue to live, that is, to participate in the existence
of their group, although in slightly different conditions, and,
again like men, they are destined to be born again. Accordingly it is of the greatest importance to remain on friendly
terms with them.

Mooney tells us that the Cherokees have formulas for
appeasing the animals which have been slaughtered, and that
the hunter, when returning to camp, lights a fire on the road

[1] Aymonier, *Voyage dans le Laos*, i. p. 311.
[2] C. Lumholtz, *Unknown Mexico*, ii. p. 43.
[3] Schoolcraft, *Information*, etc., ii. p. 175.

behind him so that the deer chief cannot follow him to his home,[1] (and inflict him with illness, particularly a rheumatic affection). In Canada, " when a bear has been killed, the hunter puts the bowl of his pipe between the animal's teeth, blows down it, and thus filling its mouth and throat with smoke, entreats its spirit not to harbour resentment for what its body has suffered, and not to injure his prospects in any succeeding chase he may undertake." [2]—Among the Indians of Nootka Sound, " after well cleansing the bear from the dirt and blood with which it is generally covered when killed, it is brought in and seated opposite the king, with a chief's bonnet wrought in figures on its head, and its fur powdered over with white down. A tray of provision is then set before it, and it is invited by words and gestures to eat." [3] Nothing is more common than the rendering of such honours to animals slain in the chase. Sometimes the ceremony assumes a mysterious character, and must be carried out away from the presence of the unbeliever. In West Africa, for instance, " even my presence," writes Nassau, " was objected to by the mother of the hunter ; (he, however, was willing). After the animal had been decapitated, and its quarters and bowels removed, the hunter, naked, stepped into the hollow of the ribs, and kneeling in the bloody pool contained in that hollow, bathed his entire body with that mixture of blood and excreta, at the same time praying the life-spirit of the hippo that it would bear him no ill-will for having killed it, and thus cut it off from future maturity ; and not to incense other hippo-potami that they should attack his canoe in revenge." [4] It was evidently rites of this kind to which Du Chaillu was referring when he wrote : " Before the *manga* (a kind of mamatee) was cut up, the *manga* doctor went through some ceremonies which I did not see, and nobody was permitted to see the animal while he was cutting it up." [5] In the case of the Huichols, it is a public ceremony, and a very complicated one. " The animal was laid so that its legs were turned toward the east, and all sorts of food and bowls of *tesvino*

[1] J. Mooney, "The Sacred Formulas of the Cherokee," *E. B. Rept.*, vii. p. 347.
[2] Charlevoix, op. cit., iii. p. 118.
[3] Jewitt, *Adventures and Sufferings*, p. 133.
[4] Nassau, *Fetichism in West Africa*, p. 204.
[5] *Equatorial Africa*, pp. 402-3.

were placed in front of it. Everyone in turn stepped up to the deer, stroking him with the right hand from the snout to the tail, and thanking him because he had allowed himself to be caught. ' Rest thyself, elder brother ' (if it be a doe they call her elder sister). A shaman may talk to the dead animal for a long time. . . . ' Thou hast brought us plumes, and we are profoundly thankful.' " [1] We know that antlers are akin to plumes. By means of such ceremonies normal relations between the social group to which the hunter belongs and the group of the slaughtered animal, are re-established once more.   The murder is cancelled, and there is no longer any reason to dread vengeance. Fresh hunting expeditions again become possible in the future, provided that they are accompanied by the same mystic practices.

II

The primitive peoples whose main sustenance is derived from fishing proceed in just the same way as those who depend upon hunting for their food supply. They exercise magic influence upon the fish by means of dances similar to those I have just cited. " The dances of the Torres Straits islanders are practised at night, and have for their object success in hunting and fishing. It is on these occasions that the extraordinary masks of tortoise-shell are used, and I assume that the forms of the masks to be worn would have relation to the particular sport to be engaged in ; for example, in the dance to ensure success in fishing, the mask would represent a fish, and so on." [2]—In the Nicobar Isles, " during the whole of the day, the people were engaged in preparing torches for the ceremony of Ki-alah for ' multiplying the fish in the sea,' and then started their fishing at night." [3]

The fisherman, like the hunter, must previously undergo fasts, rites of purification, periods of abstinence, in short, he must submit to mystic preparation. " When a man was going to hunt sea-otter he fasted and kept away from his wife for a month. He kept his chamber box behind the door, always

[1] C. Lumholtz, *Unknown Mexico*, ii. p. 45.
[2] C. H. Read, " Stone Spinning Tops from Torres Straits," *J.A.I.*, xvii. p. 87.
[3] Solomon, " Diaries kept in Car Nicobar," *J.A.I.*, xxxii. p. 2 8.

urinated into it, and let no one else touch it.　At the end of
the month he started out after an eagle, and having killed
one cut off the foot and tied a certain flower to it.　Then he
made a miniature canoe with figures of himself and perhaps
others inside, and he represented himself in the act of aiming
at a sea-otter.　He made the eagle's talon clasp the seat so
that he could have a sure aim and secure the animal.　When
at length he went out and was beginning to approach the sea
otter he blew some of his urine towards it.　This would confuse
it, so that it would swim in his direction.　Sometimes he tied
a piece of wood to the eagle's talon so that the sea-otter would
stand right up in the water like a buoy, and be easily shot."

"Those who go to catch sturgeon bathe in a pond early
in the morning."[2]　Jewitt says of the Indians of Nootka
Sound, "the king makes a point of passing a day alone on the
mountain, whither he goes very privately early in the morning
and does not return till late in the evening.　This is done for
the purpose of singing and praying to his god for success in
whaling the ensuing season. . . . The next two days he appears
very thoughtful and gloomy, scarcely speaking to anyone
and observes a most rigid fast. . . . In addition to this, for
a week before commencing their whaling, both himself and
the crew of his canoe observe a fast, eating but very little,
and going into the water several times in the course of each
day to bathe, singing and rubbing their bodies, limbs and
faces, with shells and bushes . . . they are likewise obliged
to abstain from any commerce with their women for the like
period."[3]

Sometimes these mystic observances are concentrated upon
a single individual who thus becomes, as it were, the vehicle
of the magic relation established between the human social
group and the fish group.　A very fine example of participation of this sort is to be found among the New Guinea
natives.　"The preparation for dugong and turtle fishing are
most elaborate, and commence two months before the fishing
is started.　A headman is appointed who becomes *belaga*
(holy).　On his strict observance of the laws of the dugong

[1] Swanton, "The Tlingit Indians," *E. B. Rept.*, xxvi. p. 447.
[2] F. Boas, "The North-west Tribes of Canada," *Reports of the British
Association*, p. 460 (1894).
[3] Jewitt, *Adventures and Sufferings*, pp. 154-5.

net depends the success of the season. He lives entirely
secluded from his family, and is only allowed to eat a roasted
banana or two after the sun has gone down. Each evening
at sundown he goes ashore and bathes on the point of land
overlooking the dugong feeding-ground . . . meanwhile throwing into the sea some *mula-mula*, i.e. medicine to charm the
dugong. While he is undergoing these privations all the able-
bodied men of the village are employed in collecting bark . . .
and making nets." [1]

Among the Ten'a Indians of the Yukon territory, when
the fishing season is beginning, a medicine-man is reputed to
penetrate beneath the ice to the place where the salmon, in
large numbers, spend the winter. This is evidently with the
purpose of securing their goodwill.[2] So too with the Hurons,
" in each fishing hut there is generally a ' fish preacher,'
accustomed to exhort the fishes by a sermon : if these are
clever men, they are greatly sought after, because the Hurons
believe that the exhortations of an able man have much power
to entice fish into their nets. The one we had was held to
be one of the best ; and it was a fine sight to witness his
efforts, both by word of mouth and by gesture when he
preached, as he used to do every evening after supper, after
having first enjoined silence, and arranged everyone in his
place, lying at full length around him. . . . His argument
was that the Hurons never burned fish-bones, and then he
proceeded, in the most affectionate terms, exhorting the fish,
entreating and conjuring them to appear, to allow themselves
to be caught, to take courage and not be afraid, since they
were serving their *friends*, who honoured them, and never
burned their bones. . . . To secure a good haul, they also
burn snuff sometimes, using certain expressions which I do
not understand. They throw some, too, with a like intention,
into the water for particular spirits whom they believe to be
presiding there, or rather, for the soul of the water, (since they
believe all material and inanimate things to possess a soul
that can hear) and they entreat it, in their customary fashion,
to be of good courage, and allow them to take a goodly number
of fish." [3]

[1] Guise, " Wangela River Natives," *J.A.I.*, xxviii. p. 218.
[2] Fr. Jetté, " On the Medicine-men of the Ten'a," *J.A.I.*, xxxvii. p. 174.
[3] Fr. Sagard, *Le Grand Voyage au pays des Hurons*," pp. 257-9 (1632).

The fisherman's canoe and all his implements must, like his own personality, be invested with magic virtue to ensure success. In Malay, " each boat that puts to sea has been medicined with care ; many incantations and other magic observances having been had recourse to. . . . After each take the boat is ' swept ' by the medicine man with a tuft of leaves prepared with mystic ceremonies which is carried at the bow for the purpose." [1] Just as the hunter prays to his horse and his weapons, so too, does the fisherman entreat the good-will of his nets. " One day, when I was about to burn at the camp fire the skin of a squirrel which a native had given me, the Hurons would not suffer me to do so, but made me burn it outside, because there were some nets in the camp at that time, saying that if I burned it there, these would tell the fish. I told them that the nets could not see, but they assured me they could, and that they also saw and ate. . . . I was once scolding the children of the district for some very bad behaviour, and the next day it happened that the men caught very few fish ; they attributed the fact to this repri-mand, which the nets had reported to the fishes." [2]

Many investigators have thought, too, that the form given to the fishing apparatus was designed to the same end as the ceremonies already described. " It is extremely probable that the carvings formerly inserted at the stern of most Torres Straits canoes had a magical significance . . . such were . . . the head of the frigate-bird, and occasionally that of the sea-eagle . . . the tail of a king-fish. . . . All these creatures are voracious fishers. The indication of a head at the butt-end of the dugong harpoons . . . was doubtless magical in signi-ficance." [3] In British Columbia, " almost all the clubs that I have seen," says Boas, " represent the sea-lion or the killer-whale—the two sea-animals which are most feared by the Indians, and which kill those animals that are to be killed by means of the club. The idea is . . . to give it a form appro-priate to its function, and perhaps, secondarily, to give it, by means of its form, great efficiency." [4]

With the Cherokees, " the fisherman must first chew a

[1] Skeat, *Malay Magic*, p. 193.
[2] Fr. Sagard, op. cit., p. 256.
[3] *The Cambridge Expedition to Torres Straits*, v. p. 338.
[4] F. Boas, op. cit., p. 679.

small piece of the Venus' flytrap and spit it upon the bait and also upon the hook. Then, standing facing the stream, he recites the formula and puts the bait upon the hook. . . . This . . . will enable the hook to attract and hold the fish as the plant itself seizes and holds insects in its cup. . . . The prayer is addressed directly to the fish, who are represented as living in settlements." [1]

During the fishing magical observances must be practised, and these correspond closely with those performed by the Sioux when the game comes in sight. For instance, in the case of the Baganda, " when the net is let down the chief fisherman takes some of the herbs they have obtained from the priest of Mukasa, which are kept in a special pot, and smokes them in a clay pipe ; the smoke he puffs from his pipe over the water, and it causes the fish to get into the net. . . . This pot has a special place where it resides ; it is supposed to be animate, and resents being put anywhere but in its place of honour, and vents its anger by causing the fish to escape. . . . The canoes, too, which are used in fishing, have fish offered to them." [2]—In New Zealand, we are told, " the religious ceremonies connected with fishing were very singular. The day before they went to sea, the natives arranged all their hooks around some human excrement, and used a *karakia* (magic incantation) which will not bear repetition. In the same evening there were incantations. . . . When they reached the sea, and all the hooks were duly arranged, the *tohunga* set apart for fishing commenced to pray . . . standing up and stretching out his arms. . . . The first fish caught was returned to the sea, a *karakia* being previously uttered over it, to cause it to bring abundance of fish to their hooks." [3]

Finally, after fishing as after hunting, mystic observances are necessary for the purpose of appeasing the " spirit " of the creature (and of its tribe) of stultifying its resentment and regaining its goodwill. " As soon as a sturgeon is caught," says Boas, " the ' sturgeon hunter ' sings, and by means of his song pacifies the struggling sturgeon, who allows himself to be killed." [4]   From his study of the Salish and other tribes,

[1] J. Mooney, " The Sacred Formulas of the Cherokee," *E. B.Rept.*, vii. p. 83.
[2] Roscoe, " Manners and Customs of the Baganda," *J.A.I.*, xxxii. pp. 55–6.
[3] R. Taylor, *Te Ika a Maui*, pp. 83–6.
[4] F. Boas, op. cit., p. 460 (1894).

Hill Tout has been led to the conclusion that these rites are always propitiatory. "They were intended to placate the spirits of the fish, or the plant, or the fruit, as the case may be, in order that a plentiful supply of the same might be vouchsafed to them. The ceremony was not so much a thanksgiving as a performance to ensure a plentiful supply of the particular object desired; for if these ceremonies were not properly and reverently carried out, there was danger of giving offence to the 'spirits' of the objects, and of being deprived of them." [1]

III

Is it necessary to demonstrate that most of the customs relating to war betray the same characteristics as those we have already studied? To the primitive mind there is no essential difference between fighting and hunting. In this pursuit also, we find the opening and the closing rites, the mystic ceremonies which mark the beginning of the campaign, dances, fasts, abstinence, purification, the consultation of dreams, the inhibitions imposed upon non-combatants, incantations directed against the enemy, charms, amulets, fetishes, medicines of all kinds to secure immunity from wounds, prayers to entreat the favour of the spirits; then, when the action commences, supplications addressed to the horses and weapons, the guardian spirits of the individual and the group, magical operations and formulas to bring about the blindness of the enemy, to incapacitate him from defending himself and paralyse his efforts; and lastly, after the battle, the ceremonies, often very complicated, by which the conqueror endeavours either to ward off the vengeance of his slaughtered foes (by mutilating or destroying their corpses) or else to conciliate their spirits,[2] to cleanse himself from the contamination he may have suffered during the struggle, and finally to

---

[1] "Ethnological Reports of the Halkomelem," *J.A.I.*, xxxiv. p. 331.
[2] They adopt the same attitude with regard to living prisoners. The North American Indians would either torture and kill their prisoners of war, *or else* they would adopt them. In the latter case they gave them the name of some dead warrior, whom they would represent henceforth. Thus they became merged in the very being of the social group, and from that time forward were subject to the same duties and enjoyed the same privileges as its other members. Cf. Catlin, *The North American Indians*, ii. p. 272.

make his superiority a lasting reality by the possession of
trophies, such as heads, skulls, jawbones, scalps, weapons, etc.
From the instant that war is seriously contemplated until the
moment when it becomes a thing of the past there are always
mystic relations to establish or to rupture, as the case may
be, and upon these relations and the necessary operations
involved the success of the campaign depends above all.
Gallantry, finesse, superior weapons, numbers, tactics are
certainly not matters of indifference, but they remain secondary conditions only. If the birds of augury refused to eat
and the Roman soldiers knew it, they believed that their
army would be beaten, but among primitive peoples, if the
dreams are unfavourable they do not even think of fighting.

Again, our method of presenting these facts, a method
necessarily in accordance with our mental habit of thought
and subject to the laws of a language which reflects this habit,
distorts them in the attempt to explain them. We cannot
avoid putting the mystic operations on the one side, and the
actions which combine to bring about the desired results on
the other. But it is inherent in the very nature of prelogical
mentality (and this makes it so difficult for us to reconstruct
it), that there is no difference between these. The operations
of both kinds form one inseparable method of acting. On
the one hand, all actions, even those of a most positive character, are mystic in their essence. The bow, gun, fishing-net,
the horse of the hunter or warrior, all these participate in
mysterious forces brought into action by these ceremonies.
And on the other hand, these ceremonies are not *only* the
indispensable preliminaries of the chase or of the fight : they
are, themselves, both hunting and fighting. In short, in these
forms of activity as in perception, primitive mentality has
another orientation than ours ; its character is essentially
mystic, and its collective representations are governed and
regulated by the law of participation.

IV

We understand, or at any rate we believe we understand,
without any difficulty the customs of the primitive relating
to hunting, fishing, and fighting, because we recognize that

there are, among our own peoples, customs which are apparently somewhat similar. Such are the agrarian rites still so persistently practised. Such, again, are those of a religious rather than mystical character, which intercede with a benevolent and powerful intermediary, for the success of an undertaking. The Icelandic fishing fleet, for instance, does not leave Paimpol without having received a priestly blessing ; without it, many of the sailors would dread returning with a scarcity of fish, or that they might nor return at all. So, too, a Spanish admiral, before setting out to sea, consecrates his fleet to the Virgin, and his crews believe that the Mother of Jesus will assure them the victory. But among primitive peoples other ceremonies of a similar kind take place, and these we do not understand, because the effect expected is not among those we should look for. Then we miss the analogy, and we realize that the explanation it furnished was superficial and inadequate. These are precisely the ceremonies which best enable us to penetrate the real character peculiar to a mentality which is prelogical and mystic.

Among them are the ceremonies which have for their aim the securing the regularity of the seasons, the normal production of the harvest, the usual abundance of fruit and of animals used for food, etc. Here we recognize one of the essential differences between their mentality and our own. To *our* way of thinking, " Nature " constitutes an objective order which is unchangeable. The savant, no doubt, has a clearer and more rational idea of it than the unlettered ; but as a matter of fact, the idea obtrudes in familiar fashion on all minds even without their reflecting upon it. And it matters little whether this order is conceived as having been created and maintained by God, since God Himself is regarded as unchanging in His decrees. Action is regulated therefore by the idea of an order of phenomena subject to certain laws and exempt from any arbitrary interference.

To the primitive's mind, however, " Nature," in this sense, is non-existent. The reality surrounding the social group is felt by him to be a mystic one : in it everything relates, not to laws, but to mystic connections and participations. Doubtless these do not, in general, depend any more upon the goodwill of the primitive than the objective order of Nature in our case depends upon the individual who imagines it. Nevertheless, this objective order is *conceived* as based upon a metaphysical foundation, whilst the mystic connections and participations are simultaneously imagined and felt as solidary with the social group, and dependent upon it as it depends upon them. We shall not be surprised, therefore, to find this group concerned in maintaining what is, to us, the natural order, and that it may succeed in this, making use of ceremonies similar to those which secure for it its supply of game or fish.

The most characteristic of these are undoubtedly the *intichiuma* ceremonies, which Spencer and Gillen have described in detail, and which they define thus : " sacred ceremonies performed by the members of a local totemic group with the object of increasing the number of the totem animal or plant." [1] I cannot give even a brief analysis of them here. As a rule, they consist of a series of very complicated rites : dances, paintings, special ornaments of the members of the totem exclusively concerned with the celebration of the ceremony, the imitation of the movements of the totemic animal and efforts to realize their communion with it. To minds of this kind, the individuals forming part of a totemic group, the group itself, and the totemic animal, plant, or object, are all the same thing. We must understand " the same " by virtue, not of the law of identity, but of the law of participation. We have already seen proofs of this.[2] The British Scientific Expedition to the Torres Straits affords others. " A . . . mystic affinity . . . is held to obtain between the members of a clan and their totem. This is a deeply ingrained idea and is evidently of fundamental importance. More than once we were told emphatically : ' Augud (the totem) all same as relation, he belong same family.' A definite physical and psychological resemblance was thus postulated for the human and animal members of the clan. There can be little doubt that this sentiment reacted on the clansmen and constrained them to live up to the traditional character of their respective clans. . . . We were told that

[1] *The Native Tribes of Central Australia*, p. 650.
[2] Vide Chap. II. pp. 91 et seq.

the following clans like fighting : the cassowary, crocodile, snake, shark . . . the ray and sucker-fish are peaceable. . . . The Umai (dog) clan was sometimes peaceable and at other times ready to fight, which is very characteristic of actual dogs." [1] And, in fact, in nearly all the islands of the Straits, the inhabitants would celebrate, with the help of costumes, masks, and dances, etc., ceremonies which were absolutely similar to the *intichiuma* ceremonies described by Spencer and Gillen.[2]

In the *intichiuma* ceremony of the witchetty grub totem, the actors reproduce the actions of the mythical ancestor, the intermediary through which the group participates in its totem, and which, as a consequence, exerts a mystic influence upon it.[3] Sometimes, even, the physical modality of this mystic influence can be apprehended. For instance, in the course of the *intichiuma* ceremony of the kangaroo totem, it may happen that the men of the totem cause their blood to flow over a certain rock. The effect of this proceeding is to drive in all directions the spirits of the kangaroos which used to inhabit this ground, and consequently to increase the number of living animals, for the kangaroo spirit enters into the living kangaroo just as the spirit of the male animal enters into the body of the female (when she is impregnated).

This close solidarity (which finds no satisfactory expression in our language, because it is something more than solidarity ; it is, so to speak, a mystic participation in the same essence) may be extended to all the members of a given social group, and thus realize that which we, for want of a better term, shall call " mystic symbiosis." In the Tjingilli tribe, Spencer and Gillen noted the following ceremony. " To make both young men and women grow strong and well-favoured, the men perform, at intervals of time, a long series of ceremonies . . . dealing with the various totems. There is no special reference to the young men or women in them, but they are performed solely with the idea and object of increasing the growth of the younger members of the tribe who are not, of

---

[1] *The Cambridge Expedition to Torres Straits*, v. p. 184. Cf. Skeat and Blagden, *Pagan Races of the Malay Peninsula*, ii. p. 120.
[2] Ibid., v. pp. 347-9.
[3] Spencer and Gillen, *The Native Tribes of Central Australia*, pp. 171 et seq.

course, allowed either to see them or take any part in them." [1]

There is some mystic participation between the rain and the members of the rain totem, between the water totem and its members, and as a result the *intichiuma* ceremonies will be performed in order to assure the regular rainfall, or the usual amount of water in the pools. These bear a striking resemblance, down to the most minute detail, to the ceremonies carried out, with the same end in view, by the Zuñis, Arapahos, and the *pueblos* of North America as a whole; ceremonies which the collaborators of the Ethnological Bureau in Washington have so carefully described. In Australia, as in New Mexico, we may see " a curved band supposed to represent a rainbow, a drawing also of one or more of these on his (the actor's) own body, and a special one on a shield which he brings with him. . . . This shield is also decorated with zigzag lines of white pipeclay which are supposed to represent the lightning." [2] Here, no doubt, we have another "motif," familiar to prelogical mentality : the mystic value residing in the likeness, and the power exercised over a person or thing by the possession of this likeness (a sympathetic magic which utilizes the participation between the one and the other). But in the *intichiuma* ceremonies, at any rate those celebrated by Australian aborigines, the appeal is simultaneously and specially to another yet more profound participation, I mean the essential communion between the totemic group and its totem. As Spencer and Gillen tell us, " the members of a totem, such as the rain or water totem, will hold their *intichiuma* when there has been a long drought, and water is badly wanted ; if rain falls in a reasonable time, then of course it is said to be influenced by the *intichiuma*. . . . The performance of these ceremonies is not associated in the native mind with the idea of appealing to the assistance of any supernatural being." [3] We know, moreover, that these investigators were never able to discover, in the aboriginals they studied, any idea of gods, properly so called, and " in no case is there the slightest indication or leaning to

[1] *The Northern Tribes of Central Australia*, p. 295.
[2] *The Native Tribes of Central Australia*, p. 170.
[3] Ibid.

anything which may be described as ancestor-worship. . .
These Alcheringa ancestors are constantly undergoing reincarnation so that this belief . . . practically precludes the
development of anything like a worship." [1]

Here we are confronted with a method of acting in which
the prelogical mystic mentality betrays itself in a different
fashion from that seen in most of the similar practices noted
in primitives of a more highly developed type than the
Australian aborigines. Nothing is more widespread than practices having as their object the cessation of drought, and the
assurance of rain : (we see this even yet in our own Rogations)
but such practices usually take the form of supplications or
prayers. Even when including, as they nearly always do,
recourse to sympathetic magic, they are at the same time
addressed to one or more divine beings or spirits or souls
whose intervention will produce the desired phenomenon.
They feel themselves further removed from the rain than
they do from souls or spirits or deities and they feel that
they can influence these last and communicate with them, by
means of prayers, fasting, dreams, sacrifices, dances, and
sacred ceremonies of all kinds : and they do not feel that they
can communicate directly with the rain in this way. In
certain parts of China, for instance, as De Groot tells us, the
people maintain the convents solely because they are convinced that they are able to regulate the winds and the rains,
and thus assure the crops, since these are so exposed to
drought in the treeless regions of China. . . . They subscribe
liberally to erect and maintain the buildings, in return for
which the monks are expected to bring about the cessation
of the drought by means of their ceremonies, when occasion
requires it.[2] The monks, in their turn, address themselves
to the divinities concerned, and regulate the *fung-shui*. Among
the Australians, on the contrary, we find no priests or intermediaries of any kind. The *intichiuma* ceremony manifests
the direct solidarity and mystic participation between the
rain-totem and the rain, as it does between the members of
the kangaroo totem and the kangaroos, and however strange
it may seem to us, this solidarity and this participation are

[1] *The Northern Tribes of Central Australia*, p. 494.
[2] J. J. M. de Groot, *La Code du Mahāyāna en Chine*, p. 100.

not only imagined but *felt* collectively by the members of the totemic group.

But, we may ask, supposing the rain falls without the ceremonies having taken place ? The aborigines have quite unconsciously provided for such an objection. They have given, beforehand, the most natural and decisive answer, regarded from the point of view of mystic mentality. The *intichiuma* ceremony has not been celebrated by the totemic group, it is true, but since the rain has fallen, it has nevertheless taken place, for it has been celebrated by well-disposed spirits (*iruntarinia*). " The *iruntarinia* are supposed frequently, but not always or of necessity, to commend in dreams to the *Aluntaja* " (an old man who acts as religious chief) " of any group the time at which it is right to perform the ceremony of the *intichiuma*. They themselves perform similar ceremonies, and after a plentiful supply of, say, witchetty grub or emu appears without the performance of *intichiuma* by the peoples of the respective totems, then the supplies are attributed to the performance of *intichiuma* by friendly *iruntarinia*." [1] At Mabuiag, in Torres Straits, a similar belief is to be found. " The *madub* was a wooden image of human shape. . . . The business of the *madub* was to take charge of the garden beside which it was placed, and to give good crops of yams, etc. . . . At night time the *madub* became animated and went round the garden, swinging the bull-roarers to make the plants in the garden grow, and they danced and repeatedly sang. . . Indeed, the *mari* (spirits) of the *madub* do what men do." [2] According to Bergaigne, the Vedic sacrifice is performed in heaven as on earth, and with the same results.[3]

There is an analogous belief which maintains that ceremonies having the same object as the *intichiuma*, are also performed by animals. " As a matter of fact the Tarahumares assert that the dances have been taught them by the animals. Like all primitive peoples they are close observers of nature. To them, animals are by no means inferior creatures ; they understand magic and are possessed of much knowledge, and

[1] Spencer and Gillen, *The Native Tribes of Central Australia*, pp. 519–21.
[2] *The Cambridge Expedition to Torres Straits*, v. pp. 345–6.
[3] *La Religion Védique*, i. pp. 12–13.

may assist the Tarahumares in making rain. In spring, the singing of the birds, the cooing of the dove, the chirping of the cricket, all the songs uttered by the denizens of the greensward, are to the Tarahumares appeals to the deities for rain. For what other reason should they sing or call? And as the gods grant the prayers of the deer expressed in its antics and dances, and of the turkey in its curious playing, they easily infer that to please the gods they, too, must dance as the deer and play as the turkey. . . . Dance, with these people is a very serious and ceremonious matter, a kind of worship and incantation rather than an amusement. . . . The very word for dancing, *nolávoa*, means literally to work." [1] So too, according to a Hopi tradition, cockroaches dying of thirst dance to obtain rain. [2]

In most primitive peoples rather more developed than the Australian aborigines, it is no longer the whole totemic group of the locality which secures, by the celebration of appropriate ceremonies, the desired result. Frequently *one* member of the group, possessing special qualifications, is the forced or the voluntary vehicle of the participation which is to be established. We noted a case of this kind in New Guinea, with respect to the dugong fishing. Sometimes it is an individual chosen expressly for this end, and doubtless indicated as the choice of the members of the group for some mystic reason or other. Sometimes he is qualified for this function by a special initiation which has rendered him more ready to receive and exercise magic influence than his fellows. And finally he is sometimes indicated beforehand by his birth and the participations it implies, since to these peoples a man actually *is* the same as his ancestors have been, and he really *is*, at times, the reincarnation of a certain ancestor. Thus it is that chiefs and kings, by virtue of their origin, are very often the intermediaries required. By the rites which they perform, and which they alone are qualified to perform, they secure the regularity of natural phenomena and the very life of the group.

It is in this way that we must interpret the numerous

---

[1] C. Lumholtz, *Unknown Mexico*, i. pp. 330–2.
[2] Voth, *The Traditions of the Hopi*, pp. 238–9 (*Field Columbian Museum, Anthrop.*, viii. 1905).

instances collected by Frazer in *The Golden Bough*, which show the social group almost as solicitous about the person of their king as a hive of bees is about the safety of its queen. The welfare of the group depends upon the king's welfare. To the Ba-Ronga, " royalty is a venerable and a sacred institution. Respect for the chief and obedience to his orders are universal, and it is not the display of wealth or power which maintains his prestige, but the mystic belief that the nation lives through him as the body does through the head." [1] We noted that the Mandans, according to Catlin, were very uneasy at the thought that their chiefs' portraits might be in the hands of strangers, and this might interfere with their repose in the grave. In Bengal, the Banjogis and Pankhos affirm that " in the time of one of the rajahs, Ngung Jungnung, they were the dominant and most numerous of all the tribes in this part of the earth. . . . They attribute the declension of their power to the dying out of the old stock of chiefs, to whom divine descent was attributed." [2]

The king, more particularly, often secures a regular rainfall and the abundant harvest which is its natural result. " In the good old times, when there was still a Ma Loango, the Bafoti were certainly more prosperous. The king enjoyed considerably more power than others. He did not urge on the clouds or direct the winds : . . . he did better than that, for he made the rain fall direct from heaven, as soon as his subjects needed it." [3] In Malaya, " the king is firmly believed to possess a personal influence over the works of nature, such as the growth of the crops and the bearing of the fruit-trees." (The same power is attributed to the British Residents.) " I have known (in Selangor) the success or the failure of the rice crops attributed to a change of district officers, and in one case I even heard an outbreak of ferocity which occurred among man-eating crocodiles laid at the door of a most zealous and able, though perhaps occasionally somewhat unsympathetic, representative of the government." [4]

The mystic power of the king sometimes persists after his death. Thus, with the Ba-Ronga people, " the death of

[1] Junod, *Les Ba-Ronga*, p. 139.
[2] Quoted by Grierson, *Linguistic Survey of India*, iii. p. 145.
[3] Dr. Pechuël-Loesche, *Die Loango-Expedition*, iii. 2, p. 449.
[4] Skeat, *Malay Magic*, p. 36.

Mapunga must have taken place in the course of the year 1890, but no one ever spoke of it. When the news was made public, however, Manganyeli, a young native from the Ribombo district said to me : ' When the *miphimbi* trees were so full of fruit last season (about Christmas, 1890)—we had an exceptional crop—we thought that the chief *must* be dead, and that he had sent us this wonderful abundance.' " [1]

It is, therefore, of the greatest importance that the tribe should remain in communication, or rather, in communion, with its dead kings. Junod has very clearly shown how such participation between the social group and its deceased chief is realized both physically and mystically, and the passage is worth quoting in full. " In every little Ba-Ronga clan . . . there is a sacred object which one might be inclined to take for an idol, but which is in reality something quite different. It is called the *mhamba* (a word which denotes any kind of offering or sacrifice, but which is especially applied to such an object as this). It even seems as if they had such a respect for it that they hesitate to give it an official name. They prefer to call it *nhlengoué* (treasure, wealth). But what *is* this *mhamba*, this holy and mysterious kind of ark ? When a chief dies, the nails of his hands and feet are cut off, and his hair and beard, and all the parts of his body which can be preserved are hardened with the manure formed from the oxen killed at the time of his death. Thus there is formed a sort of pellet which is afterwards wrapped round with strips of hide. When the successor of this chief dies, a second pellet is manufactured and added to the first, and thus it goes on for generations. At the present time the *mhamba* of the Tembé tribe is about a foot long, according to the account of one who has often seen it (since it is guarded by a cousin of his). The guardian of the sacred relic is very carefully selected. He must be a man of particularly calm temperament, not addicted to bad language or to intemperance. As a kind of high priest . . . he stands in a very responsible relation to the whole country. . . . The mysterious object is preserved in a building erected for the purpose, behind the village to which the guardian belongs. When the keeper of the *mhamba* knows that he is to make use of it for a religious

[1] Junod, *Les Ba-Ronga*, p. 128 (note).

ceremony, he lives in a state of entire continence for the previous month. As for the solemn sacrifice performed with the aid of this object, it is usually a goat. . . . The priest traces circles in the air with the *mhamba*. The prayer is then pronounced and it is of course addressed to all the former chiefs whose nails and hair the officiating priest holds in his hands : a strange and striking way of entering into communion with the gods. . . . The sacrifice with the *mhamba* is carried out (in the Tembé clan, at any rate), at the beginning of the *bokagne* season, before offering the firstfruits to the ghosts of the departed. In times of national danger, doubtless, they have recourse to this solemn practice.

" This amulet, therefore, of incalculable efficacy, is the nation's most treasured possession. . . . Consequently it is the very last object which would be allowed to fall into the hands of an enemy. If the army is vanquishèd and put to flight, the depositary of the *mhamba* starts first of all. . . . The sacred emblem will not be wrested from him until the entire forces of the tribe have been destroyed. Such a misfortune did occur, it seems, some years ago, to the Tembé clan. . . . Then a terrible drought ensued, and for a whole year the sky was of a fiery colour. . . ." And the worthy pastor concludes : " Is there not something profoundly logical in the idea of preserving some physical part of the mighty dead who have become the gods of their country, in order to exercise influence upon their will, and power over them ? " [1]

This account of his shows very clearly that to the collective consciousness of the social group, its welfare, its very existence and the regular order of nature are connected, by means of a mystic participation, with the kings and chiefs of the group. We know that to the prelogical mind, governed by the law of participation, part of a living whole is equal to the whole, *is*, in fact, the whole, in the prelogical sense of the verb " to be," and thus we can understand the part played by the nails and hair of the dead kings in the *mhamba*.

This recognized power, whether in the totemic groups, the medicine-men or the chiefs, living or dead, of consolidating or even of effecting, through appropriate ceremonies, the order of nature and the regular recurrence of generation, has a certain

[1] Junod, *Les Ba-Ronga*, pp. 398–401.

analogy with the continuous creation which theologians and certain metaphysicians have defined by saying that without the Divine intervention created beings could not subsist for a single instant. It is indeed a participation of the same kind that the prelogical mind imagines, though in a more gross fashion. According to its view the natural order only endures by virtue of periodical renewals, obtained through the special ceremonies performed by those possessing the requisite mystic powers. And the social order frequently disappears when the king dies, until his successor has assumed the power : every interregnum becomes anarchy. But there is this difference that, according to the doctrine of continuous creation, though the world subsists only through God, God would exist without the world if the latter were to disappear ; whereas in the case of prelogical mentality there is complete reciprocity. As a rule there is absolute action and reaction between the totemic group and its totem, and, in a higher type of society, between the nation and the succession of kings. It is the " mystic symbiosis " of which we have already spoken, and which our logical thought cannot clearly conceive save in a distorted form.

V

The community of essence, the mystic participation, is not conceived and sensed between the members of the same totemic group merely. It exists, too, in many primitive peoples, between the child and its father, the child and its mother, and the child and both parents ; and, once its principle has been recognized, it is translated into customs which express it very clearly. Of these customs the couvade is often the only one which claims the attention of explorers. Its apparent strangeness has struck them. In reality, however, it is but part of a sum-total of taboos or precautions which are imposed, sometimes on the father, sometimes on the mother, and sometimes on both, which begin as soon as the pregnancy is announced, and continue long after the birth of the child. We shall note but the chief of these only.

" When the wife of a Braman is in the family way, as soon

as her husband knows it, he cleans his teeth, and eats no
more betel nor trims his beard, and fasts until his wife gives
birth to her child." [1] "In Loango, the *nganga* (medicine-
man) imposes upon the future parents, or upon the mother
only, a taboo either simple or complicated, which they must
observe until the child has uttered its first cry, or taken its
first step, or even much later, until the child walks well, or
has brothers and sisters. It may happen therefore that a
father's conduct is somewhat strange before, as well as after,
the birth of his offspring." [2] Du Chaillu tells us that "while
she (a female gorilla) was alive, no woman who was enceinte
nor the husband of such woman dared approach her cage.
They believe firmly that should the husband of a woman with
child, or the woman herself, see a gorilla, even a dead one,
she would give birth to a gorilla, and not to a man child.
This superstition I have noticed among other tribes too, and
only in the case of the gorilla." [3]

At Amoy in China, the husband must be extremely cautious
in his movements during his wife's pregnancy. "If the soil
is disturbed, the repose and growth of the embryo in the womb
of women is, by the law of sympathy, disturbed also. . . .
Especially perilous is it to drive a nail into a wall, as it might
nail down the earth-spirit that resides in it, and cause the
child to be born with a limb stiff or lame, or blind of one eye ;
or it might paralyse the bowels of a child already born, and
give it constipation with fatal results. The dangers which
threaten a pregnant woman increase as her pregnancy advances. In the end, nothing that is heavy may be displaced
in the house, it being well known that the earth-spirits are
wont to settle preferably in things which, owing to their
weight, are seldom moved. But even the shifting of light
objects is a source of danger. Instances are known of fathers
who had rolled up their bed-mat after it had long lain flat,
being frightened by the birth of a child with a rolled-up ear.
One day I saw a boy with a hare-lip, and was told by the
father that his wife when pregnant of this child, had thought-
lessly made an incision in an old coat of his, while repairing

[1] Duarte Barbosa, " A Description of the Coast of East Africa and Malabar
in the Beginning of the Sixteenth Century," *Hakluyt Society*, xxxv. p. 123;
[2] Dr. Pechuël-Loesche, *Die Loango-Expedition*, iii. 2, p. 462.
[3] Du Chaillu, *Equatorial Africa*, p. 262 ; cf. p. 305.

it." [1]—In New South Wales, " certain foods are forbidden to women during portions of their pregnancy and lactation." [2] —In New Guinea, during pregnancy, the Jabim women abstain from the flesh of iguanas, cuttlefish, dogs, in short of all fat and rich foods, " for fear that the child may be born dead or deformed." A man of the Jabim tribe is equally bound by certain inhibitions. During his wife's pregnancy he is forbidden to go to sea ; " the fish avoid him, and the sea becomes rough." [3]

In Brazil, " many Indian tribes have a custom that when a pregnancy is declared, the husband and wife must rigorously observe a fast. They must abstain from everything but ants, mushrooms, and water with which a little guaranà powder has been mixed." [4]

In the Admiralty Isles, " when a pregnant woman feels her confinement approaching, she stays at home, and eats fish and sago only. She does not eat yams lest her child should be long and thin ; she does not touch taro, lest he should be short and stocky, and she abstains from pork, for fear that he should have bristles instead of hair." [5]

During the accouchement certain practices show that the idea of the solidarity between father and child is still felt. For instance, in the tribes studied by Spencer and Gillen, when labour has begun, the father's girdle is taken off and transferred to the mother. " Not a word is spoken, but if after a time the birth of the child is not announced, the husband, still quite unadorned, walks once or twice slowly, at a distance of about fifty yards, up and down past the *erlukwirra* (women's camp) with a view to inducing the unborn child to follow him." [6] In the more northerly tribes, " when the father of the newborn child goes out into the scrub for three days, away from his camp, he leaves his waist-girdle and arm-bands behind him, so that he has nothing tied tightly round any part of his body, a state of affairs which is supposed to be beneficial to the lubra." [7]

[1] J. J. M. de Groot, *The Religious System of China*, i. pp. 538–9.
[2] Mathews, " Aboriginal Tribes of New South Wales and Victoria," *Journal of the Royal Society of New South Wales*, p. 219 (1905).
[3] Hagen, *Unter den Papuas*, p. 229.
[4] Von Martius, *Beiträge zur Ethnographie Süd-Amerika's*, i. p. 402.
[5] Parkinson, *Dreissig Jahre in der Südsee*, p. 398.
[6] *The Native Tribes of Central Australia*, pp. 466–7.
[7] *The Northern Tribes of Central Australia*, p. 607.

Now we come to the couvade practices, properly so called, which have often been described. Upon examining them in detail, however, we see that in the majority of cases, the inhibitions and the observances are imposed upon both parents. Explorers have laid more stress upon the father's part in them, either because it is greater, as is frequently the case, or because the fact seems in their opinion more extraordinary and worthy of mention. And if the rules to be observed by the father are more important and more rigorous, it is because the community of substance between the child and himself are imagined and felt more vividly than that between the child and the mother. This participation has been well illustrated by Dobrizhoffer, who has described the couvade in detail : the abstinence from food, from all violent exercise, etc. Otherwise, if the child dies, it is the father's fault. An Indian refuses snuff, because he might injure his newborn child by sneezing. In short, the Abipones believe " that any discomfort whatever, suffered by the father, influences the child, on account of the close sympathy existing between them." [1]—Von den Steinen, too, has given us a detailed description of the couvade, as noted by him in Brazil. " The married pair did not leave their hut save to relieve the necessities of nature. They lived exclusively upon *pogu* boiled into a pap, and mandioc cakes crumbled and mixed with water. Any other food would have been injurious to the child ; it would have been as bad as if the child itself ate meat, fish, or fruit. . . . The Indians despise those who do not conform to this custom. . . . The father is weak and sickly, since he feels himself to be one with the newborn child. . . . Among the Bororos, not only does the father fast, but if the child is ill, it is the father who swallows the medicines, as we learnt from the dispenser to the Brazilian Military Colony, who was immensely astonished at this." [2]

According to Von Martius, inhibitions are placed upon the father and mother alike. " After the birth the father hangs his hammock beside his wife's, to await, as she does, the fall of the umbilical cord. During this time, the mother is regarded as unclean, and the beds of the pair are separated

[1] Dobrizhoffer, *Historia de Abiponibus*, ii. pp. 231 et seq.
[2] K. von den Steinen, *Unter den Naturvölkern Zentralbräsiliens*, pp. 289–94.

by a partition of palm-leaves, if they do not occupy separate
huts. For the whole period, neither father nor mother can
do any work, and the father cannot leave his hut save for a
moment in the evening. His habitual bath is forbidden. . . .''
(There are certain taboos with regard to food.) " Still more
strange is the forbidding of the scratching of the head or the
body with the finger-nails. . . . A breach of these regulations
would bring about the death of the nursling, or at any rate
make him sickly for the rest of his life." [1]

So too, in New Guinea, " until the child can walk and
begins to talk, the mother must follow the diet prescribed for
her pregnancy. After her accouchement, she must not smoke
tobacco, "because the child would be all blackened within,
and would die." The father, too, must abstain from tobacco
and betel-nut for a time ; however, according to what Vetter,
who tells us this, says about it, this rule is not very strictly
observed.[2] With the people of Goa, " during this period of
three weeks, not only the mother but also the father is deemed
to be impure, and is required to abstain from all his ordinary
occupations." [3]—In South India, " it was noted by the Rev.
S. Mateer, that, after the confinement of a Paraigan women
in Travancore, the husband is starved for seven days, eating
no cooked rice or other food, only roots and fruits, and drinking
only arrack or toddy." [4]—Among the Klamaths of Oregon,
" on account of a childbirth, the father and the mother eat
no meat for ten days." [5]

These facts, to which we might easily add many similar
instances, will doubtless suffice to show that all the customs
relating to the connection between the newborn child and
its parents, including the couvade, as well as the taboos
affecting pregnancy, imply, at any rate originally, the idea of
a close participation between the child just born, or about
to be born, and its father or mother, or both.

The case of the Bororo taking his sick child's medicine is
perhaps the most characteristic, because it marks the parti-

[1] Von Martius, op. cit., i. p. 643.
[2] Hagen, *Unter den Papua's*, p. 234.
[3] Risley, *Castes and Tribes of Bengal*, i. p. 289.
[4] E. Thurston, *Ethnographic Notes in South India*, p. 550.
[5] A. Gatschet, *The Klamath Language*, p. 91.

cipation most clearly. But the other customs proceed, at least primitively, from the same collective representations. As certain of these customs persist—the actual couvade, for instance—while others perish, as their meaning is lost, one seeks, and naturally will find, an explanation of the extraordinary custom which obliges a man to go to bed as soon as his wife is confined. These more or less probable explanations do not hold good, however, when the couvade is once relegated to the sum-total of the practices to which it belongs.

Even for a long time after the birth, even when at a distance from each other, the participation between father and child can still be strongly felt. Thus, in Borneo, " the war-coats of the men are often made of goat- or deer-skin, and any man may wear such a coat. But when a man has a young son he is particularly careful to avoid contact with any part of a deer, lest through such contact he should transmit to his son in any degree the timidity of the deer. On one occasion when we had killed a deer, a Kenyah chief resolutely refused to allow its skin to be carried in his boat, alleging the above reason." [1]

It is at the time of the initiation of the young men—an initiation, as we shall presently see, which is a kind of new birth—that the participation between them and their respective mothers becomes felt once more, and there are many customs which betray this. For instance, among the Aruntas, when the young man who has been circumcised is out in the bush, his mother " may not eat opossum, or the larger lace lizard, or carpet snake, or any fat, as otherwise she would retard her son's recovery. . . . Every day she rubs her body all over with grease, as in some way this is supposed to help her son's recovery." [2] In other tribes, " while the boy is out in the bush, the mother wears *alpita* in her hair . . . and is careful also never to let her fire go out. The object of the former is to assist the boy to be watchful at night-time. . . . The *alpita* is the tail tip of the rabbit-bandicoot, a small animal which is very lively during the night, so that, of course, the wearing of the *alpita* is a sure stimulus to wakefulness.

[1] Hose and Macdougall, " Men and Animals in Sarawak," *J.A.I.*, xxxi. p. 187.
[2] Spencer and Gillen, *The Native Tribes of Central Australia*, p. 250.

(The deprivation of sleep is one of the initiation tests.) Not only is it efficacious in the case of the actual wearer, but it is effectual when worn by someone closely related to the individual whom it is desired to influence in this particular way." [1]

In an Australian initiation ceremony described in detail by Mathews, the mothers of the novices are treated in a special way, much resembling that accorded to mourners, and later to those who have been confined—which confirms the idea that initiation comprises an apparent death and a new birth. "At the camp the mothers of the novices belonging to each contingent occupy quarters by themselves a little distance from the camp of their own tribe. Every mother has a fire of her own, and no one else is permitted to use it. . . . Their sisters, or mothers' sisters, or some of the older women provide them with food, and attend to their wants generally. These women are collectively known as *yanniwa*, and none of the other women or the children are permitted to interfere with them. Each mother eats the whole of the food brought to her, as it would bring evil upon her son if she gave any portion of it to the other women present. All the mothers are, however, very abstemious with their food whilst their sons are away." [2] In the province of Victoria, "the mothers of the novices eat practically the same kind of food which is given to their sons in the bush, and must remain silent the same as their sons. They sing the prescribed songs every morning at dawn, and every evening at dusk; and whilst standing singing they lift burning sticks from off the fire and wave them repeatedly towards the direction in which they suppose the camp of the novices to be situated." [3]—Finally, in New South Wales, "during the time a youth is out in the bush with the old men, going through the initiation ceremonies, he must only eat certain kinds of food, and his mother and father are restricted to the same diet as he. And when a novice is released from any taboo regarding food, his mother is freed at the same time." [4]

[1] Spencer and Gillen, *The Northern Tribes of Central Australia*, p. 344.

[2] Mathews, "The Burbong or Initiation Ceremony," *Journal of the Royal Society of New South Wales and Victoria*, pp. 131–51 (1898).

[3] Id., "Aboriginal Tribes of New South Wales and Victoria," *Journal of the Royal Society of New South Wales and Victoria*, pp. 317–18 (1905).

[4] Id., *Thurrawal and Thoorga Tribes*, p. 259

CHAPTER VII

INSTITUTIONS IN WHICH COLLECTIVE REPRE-SENTATIONS GOVERNED BY THE LAW OF PARTICIPATION ARE INVOLVED (II)

INTRODUCTION

THERE are certain practices, the meaning of which, at any rate as far as their object is concerned, does not admit of doubt : such are those which aim at treating the sick, preventing the disease from having a fatal issue, and restoring the sufferers to health. Here again we shall see, when we study the practices almost universally followed by primitive peoples, that they confirm the results yielded by an analysis of their collective representations. Once more we perceive the mystic orientation, the preconceived ideas which allow observation and experience but a very limited area of influence, the connections between entities and phenomena dominated by the law of participation. The facts vary greatly in detail, and yet when they are referred to the mental conditions upon which they depend, they will be found fairly uniform. I shall preferably select those which most clearly demonstrate these mental conditions.

I

A. In the first place, the very notion of illness is a mystic one. That is, illness and disease are always regarded as the product of an invisible, intangible agent, pictured, moreover, in many different ways. Observers are unanimous upon this point. "We must carefully avoid thinking that the Fijian conceives of illness as we do. To his mind, illness is like a wave, an outside influence which weighs down upon the sick

man and seems to possess him. This wave, this influence can
only proceed from the gods or the devils or from living beings ;
but from natural causes, such as cold or heat, hardly ever. . . .
There *is* no natural cause for sickness to the Fijians ; they
seek it *praeter naturum, i.e.* in an invisible world, existing
side by side with this."[1] The expressions which Father
Rougier makes use of are noteworthy. To our minds, indeed,
this invisible world can only be co-existent with, yet outside,
that which we call nature. That which, on the contrary,
characterizes prelogical mentality, as I conceive of it, is that
in its collective representations these two worlds make but
one. Its mystic elements are quite as natural as the others
which participate in them. Junod the missionary helps us
to perceive this participation beneath the distinction he is
endeavouring to establish. " The native regards diseases not
only as physical disorders, but as the result of a kind of natural
malediction of a more or less spiritual nature, and that is
why the patient must not only be treated for such and such a
symptom, but he must have the defilement which he has undergone removed. When he effects this second cure, the healer
has become what is popularly called a medicine-man. Hence
all his efforts to appear a supernatural personage, (his costumes,
paraphernalia, etc.). . . . All these accessories inspire both
fear and confidence in his clients."[2] The illness, however,
does not require the separate, successive intervention of
healer and sorcerer. It is the mystic conception the native
has of it which involves the need of mystic methods of subduing it and escaping from its hold.

This mystic idea may be of almost infinite variety. In
Loango, for instance, the natives affirm that " something
takes the man by surprise, enters into him and ill-treats him.
This something may be powers or malign influences or
poisons—which emanate from natural objects, places, solid or
liquid foods—but also from fetishes, men, wizards. They
may also be souls of any kind, which brush against the sick
man and slip into him, or else definite souls which feed upon
his vital forces, cause him pain, paralyse him, and trouble

---

[1] Em. Rougier, " Maladies et Médicins à Fiji Autrefois et Aujourd'hui,"
Anthropos, ii. pp. 69, 999 (1907).
[2] Junod, *Les Ba-Ronga,* p. 375.

his mind, etc." [1] In Laos, " all illnesses, whatever they
may be, from the smallest to the most serious ailment, proceed either from an angry spirit, or else from a dead person
who is displeased. . . . Thay medicine knows scarcely anything of natural causes." [2]—In Bombay, we are told, that
whatever be the illness which attacks man, woman or child,
or even cattle, the Kolies imagine that it arises from the action
of an evil spirit or an offended deity ; and at the end of a
certain period, after having vainly endeavoured to cure the
malady by remedies known to them, they consult an exorcist
able to expel evil spirits.[3] At Bahr-el-Ghazal, " even where
disease is not directly attributed to the machinations of
enemies, the idea of ' possession ' seems to hold." [4] In short,
without laying further stress upon facts that are well known,
the sick man is a prey to some malign power or influence.

B. The practices relating to diagnosis are the direct outcome of this mystic idea of illness. It is important to discover
what malign power or influence has taken possession of the
sick man ; what witchcraft is being exercised upon him ;
what being, living or dead, grudges him his life ; and so on.
This diagnosis, upon which everything else depends, can only
be made by a man who is qualified to come in contact with
mysterious forces and spirits, and who is powerful enough
to fight them and expel them. The first step, therefore,
is to appeal to the medicine-man, shaman, wizard, doctor,
exorcist, or whatever he may be called ; and if this person
consents to undertake the cure, his first care will be to put
himself into the special state necessary to be able to communicate with forces and spirits, and effectively exercise upon them
his potential influence. This necessitates a whole series of
preliminary operations which may last for several hours,
or even a whole night. There must be fasting, or intoxication ;
a special costume ; magical adornments ; incantations ;
dances to the extent of complete exhaustion and excessive
perspiration ; until at last the " doctor " seems to lose con-

[1] Dr. Pechuël-Loesche, *Die Loango-Expedition*, iii. 2, pp. 443–4.
[2] A. Bourlay, " Les Thay " (Laos), *Anthropos*, ii. p. 620 (1907).
[3] A. Mackintosh, " An Account of the Tribes of Mhadeo-Kolies," *Trans.*
f Bombay Geo. Soc. (1836), i. p. 227 (1864 edit.).
[4] Cummings, " Sub-tribes of the Bahr el Ghazal Dinkas," *J.A.I.*, p. 156
(1904).

sciousness or be " beside himself." Then there takes place
what we should call the " doubling " of his personality.
He has become unconscious of his entire surroundings, but
on the other hand he feels himself transported to the world of
intangible, invisible realities—the world of spirits—or at any
rate he enters into communication with it. It is at this
moment that the diagnosis is accomplished, intuitively, and
consequently without any possibility or error : the patient
and his entourage believe in it blindly. Here is one example
among hundreds. " The most important among the paraphernalia of the shaman " (when about to treat a sick man)
" is a head-dress made of a mat, which is worn in his incantations. . . . Before putting it on they blow on it, and sprinkle
it with water which has been poured over magic herbs. As
soon as the shaman puts on the head-dress, he ' acts as though
he was crazy,' i.e. he puts himself into a trance by singing
the song he had obtained from his guardian spirit at the
time of his initiation. He dances until he perspires freely,
and finally his spirit comes and speaks to him." [1]

Since the diagnosis thus depends upon mystic practices,
both necessary and adequate, very little attention is paid to
physical symptoms. " In West Africa," says Nassau, " this
diagnosis is not made by an examination and comparison of
the physical and mental symptoms, but by drum, dance,
frenzied song, mirror, fumes of drugs, and conversation with
the spirit itself." [2]—With the Cherokees, " the description . . .
is always of the vaguest character, while in general the name
given to the disease by the shaman expresses only his opinion
as to the occult cause of the trouble. Thus they have definite
names for rheumatism, toothache, boils, and a few other
ailments of like positive character, but beyond this their
description of symptoms generally resolves itself into a statement that the patient has bad dreams, looks black around
the eyes, or feels tired, while the disease is assigned such
names as ' when they dream of snakes,' ' when they dream
of fish,' ' when ghosts trouble them,' ' when something is
making something else eat them,' ' when the food is changed,'

[1] F. Boas, " The North-west Tribes of Canada," *Reports of British Association*, pp. 645-6 (1890).
[2] Nassau, *Fetichism in West Africa*, p. 215.

i.e. when a witch causes it to sprout and grow in the body of
the patient or transforms it into a lizard, frog or sharpened
stick." [1]

Moreover, this indifference concerning physical symptoms
also proceeds from the mystic idea of illness. The seat of
the malady is not within the body or the visible organs : it
is the mind or spirit which is attacked. Thus, in West Africa,
" the dogma that rules his (i.e. the doctor's) practice is that
in all cases of disease in which no blood is showing, the patient
is suffering from something wrong in the mind." [2]—According
to the Iroquois, " every illness is a desire of the mind, and
one does not die unless the desire is unfulfilled.—In Acadia,
the sick man is refused nothing he asks, because in such a
state his desires are orders from the guardian spirit,—and
when wizards are called in, it is because they can best learn
from the spirits the cause of the trouble and the suitable
remedy. . . . It is the wizard's duty to discover the sorcery
which has caused the illness. He begins by putting himself
into a perspiration, and when he is tired of shouting, writhing
about, and invoking his guardian spirit, the first extraordinary
thing that occurs to his mind is regarded by him as the cause
of the trouble. Many of them, before beginning to sweat
profusely, take a certain beverage which is calculated to help
them to receive celestial impressions." [3]

C. *The treatment.* We can readily see that, whatever it
may be, it is valuable solely on account of its mystic virtue.
Its efficacy depends entirely upon connections and participations of a spiritual or a magic kind. As a consequence,
the therapeutics of white people are valueless. Their remedies
may possibly do harm (on account of the unknown mystic
proprieties in them) ; it is certain they can do no good,
and they are quite ineffectual in dealing with the maladies
of primitives. " There is a woman here, ill for the last year.
I went to her several times and asked her if she were willing
to take medicine ; her reply was ' the devil has caused this
illness to me, and it cannot be cured by medicine. The
amiluanas (witch-doctors) only can cure me by driving the

[1] J. Mooney, " The Sacred Formulas of the Cherokee," *E. B. Rept.*,
vii. pp. 337, 368.
[2] M. Kingsley, *West African Studies*, p. 169.
[3] Charlevoix, *Journal d'un Voyage dans l'Amérique Septentrionale*, iii. p. 367.

devil out of me.' " [1]   The strong repugnance felt to European remedies, of whatever kind they may be, is very general. From the prelogical point of view, this is inevitable, and we must remember that as a matter of fact the event often justifies it, especially in the case of individuals belonging to the most primitive types.   In Victoria, for instance, " one doctor confessed that as a general rule, every time he had taken any sick native under his especial care, he succeeded only in killing him the sooner. . . . Taken to the bush, they rapidly recover." Why should this be so ?   " In the first place, in the hospital there is the feeling of loneliness ; his spirits droop. Then . . . his hair, perhaps, has been cut, his old clothes taken away from him, and with them probably some valued possession on which his heart is set." (He feels himself at the mercy of strangers who may exercise all sorts of sinister influences upon him without his being aware of it.) " He fears the white man, dreads his medicines, and shrinks from the outward applications which may, for aught he knows, be possessed of secret properties that will cause his destruction." [2]   Certain observers have clearly penetrated the reason for this dislike. Of New Zealand, Elsdon Best writes : " A great distrust of European doctors is manifest in this district. It is probable that this is not due to any disbelief in the medical knowledge of the said profession, but that the natives have an instinctive fear that a doctor will interfere with the state of *tapu*, that the life principle will be endangered by the methods of the Europeans being employed.   A middle-aged woman of this district was taken seriously ill at Rotorua, and it was proposed that she should be sent to the hospital. Her people strongly objected, urging her to adhere to native customs, saying that they would rather see her die than be operated upon by a European.   However, she was taken to hospital by Europeans, was operated upon, and recovered. When she returned here, I heard an old woman asking her : ' In what state are you now ? ' (meaning ' is your *tapu*, your vital principle untouched ? ') The reply was : ' O ! every vessel of the white men has been passed over me.' (Her body had been washed with water heated in a kitchen,

[1] Solomon, " Diaries Kept in Car Nicobar," *J.A.I.*, xxxii. pp. 231–2.
[2] Brough Smyth, *The Aborigines of Victoria*, i. pp. 259–60.

and there is no stain worse than that.)   Her *tapu* has gone,
and she is clinging with great earnestness to European ways
and customs as a means of protecting her vitality.   But
this is a rare case." [1]

On the other hand, the Australian aborigines have infinite
faith in the methods of treatment pursued by their native
doctors, though admitting they could neither cure nor harm
Europeans.   " To prove the imposture practised upon them by
their Baangals, I have offered myself as a subject to be
operated upon by any of them they might select, telling
them that it would not be necessary to complete the process
to prove their case, the mere fact of my being made slightly
ill would be proof to me perfectly conclusive that their Baangals
were all they claimed to be.—To them this offer of mine seemed
so ridiculously absurd, they merely laughed at me, saying :
' Stupid ears you.   Too much you white fellow.   Not that one
Baangal belonging to you.   What for you stupid head ? ' " [2]

Whatever may be the treatment prescribed for the sick
man, the medicines he is to take, the regimen he must follow ;
whether he is to have steam baths, phlebotomy, or, in certain
cases, trepanning—it is the mystic forces alone to which their
efficacy will be due.   All investigators are agreed upon this
point.   Thus, the Dayaks " don't prize any drug, unless it be
covered with mysterious *passes*, with numberless instructions
of how to take it, in what position, and what incantation to
repeat when looking at it.   They can't set a value or trust
on anything, unless it is connected in some measure with
the supernatural." [3]   To the Negritos of the Philippines,
" all disease is caused by spirits, which must be expelled
from the body, before a cure can be effected." [4]—Nassau is
very definite about this.   " To a sick native's thought the
alleviant medicinal herb used by the doctor and its associated
efficiency-giving spirit evoked by the same doctor are inseparable. . . .   It is plain that the component parts of any
fetich are looked upon by them as we look upon the drugs of

---

[1] Elsdon Best, " Maoiri Medical Lore," *Journ. of Polyn. Soc.*, xiii. pp.
223–4 (1904).
[2] Beveridge, " The Aborigines of the Lower Murray," *Journal of the Royal
Society of New South Wales*, p. 70 (1884).
[3] Brooke, *Ten Years in Sarawak*, ii. pp. 228–9.
W. A. Reed, *The Negritos of Zambales*, p. 68 (Manila, 1904).

our *materia medica*. It is plain, also, that these drugs are operative, not, as ours, by certain inherent chemical qualities but by the presence of a spirit to whom they are favourite media. And it is also clear that the spirit is induced to act by the pleasing enchantments of the magic doctor." [1] Miss Kingsley expresses the same idea in a forcible way. " Everything works by spirit on spirit ; therefore the spirit of the medicine works on the spirit of the disease. Certain diseases are combatable by certain spirits in certain herbs. Other diseases are caused by spirits not amenable to herb-dwelling spirits ; they must be tackled by spirits of a more powerful grade." [2]

We must also take into account the fact that prelogical mentality does not deal with concepts as rigidly defined as those of our own thought. There is no clear-cut distinction between the mystic influence which, by means of certain processes, causes or cures a malady, and that which, without being of a medical nature, produces the same kind of effects, by altering the physical or moral disposition of men, animals, or invisible beings. Thus we have here a very general, though not abstract and truly conceptual, idea, similar to the conceptions of *mana, wakan, orenda, mulungu,* and others which we have already studied. Some observers have remarked this particularly. " If the doctor and the magician are usually confused, the confusion is due to the fact that the concept of *mori* (medicine) is an extremely vague one. *Mori* does not stand for the medicinal plant, the healing herb alone ; it means, too, magic methods of all kinds, among them those which change the will-power. The heathen are convinced that if their children become Christians, it is because they have had a medicine, a *mori*, administered to them ; it is *mori* which makes abandoned girls attractive. Everything, even the powder with which the whites clean the rust off their weapons is *mori*." [3]

Very frequently, when the " doctor " has finished his incantations and his magic practices, when he is in communication with the spirits, he applies his lips to the diseased

---

[1] Nassau, *Fetichism in West Africa*, pp. 81, 162.
[2] *West African Studies*, p. 153.
[3] Junod, *Les Ba-Ronga*, p. 468 (note).

part, and after more or less prolonged suction, triumphantly produces, before the patient and his friends, a small piece of bone or stone or coal or some other substance. They all believe that he has extracted it from the patient's body, and that the cure is thereby assured, and even accomplished. We may compare this act to that of a surgeon showing his students a tumour which he has just removed, but the analogy is merely external. The fragment of bone or stone which the " doctor " takes out of his mouth is not the ill that the patient is suffering from ; it is not even the cause ; it is merely the vehicle of it.

" The idea that pains are caused by foreign bodies embedded in the flesh of the sufferer is widely spread among uncivilized people throughout the world, as has long been known ; but, as far as I know, it has not been noted that this foreign substance—at least among the Indians of Guiana —is often, if not always, regarded, not as simply a natural body, but as the materialized form of a hostile spirit." [1]

The true cause of the evil is the malign influence, the sorcery or witch-craft which has introduced into the body, with this fragment of bone or this stone, a principle of decay. Its extraction betokens the superiority of the " doctor's " influence over this noxious principle : it is the visible sign of victory. But this victory is as mystic as the evil itself. It is always, as Miss Kingsley says, the working of spirit upon spirit.

Nothing illustrates this characteristic of prelogical mentality better than the medical practices of the Cherokees, the formulas of which, with their explanation, Mooney received from the lips of the Indians themselves. Let us take, for instance, the formula respecting the treatment of rheumatism. It is composed of two parts : the first consists of invocations addressed in turn to the red, blue, black, and white dogs ; the second gives a detailed prescription, showing how to prepare and to take the medicine.[2] This formula is a " particularly explicit " one. It would, however, be quite unintelligible, at any rate in its first part, without the explanations afforded by the ideas, already noted, which Indians

[1] Im Thurm, *Among the Indians of Guiana*, p. 333.
[2] J. Mooney, " The Sacred Formulas of the Cherokee," *E. B. Rept.*, vii. pp. 346 et seq.

have respecting maladies and the way in which they must be combated.

The Cherokees' most common belief with respect to rheumatism regards it as caused by the spirits of animals which have been slain, generally by those of deer, anxious to avenge themselves on the hunter. The malady itself, called by a figurative name signifying " the one who enters," is regarded as a living being. The verbs used in speaking of it demonstrate that this being is long and narrow, like a snake or a fish. It is brought by the chief of the deer, which makes it enter the hunter's body (particularly his limbs and extremities) and immediately intense pain is felt. The " intruder " cannot be chased away save by some animal-spirit stronger than, and a natural enemy of, the deer : as a rule, by the dog or the wolf. These animal-deities live in a higher clime, above the seventh heaven, and are the great prototypes, of which the animals on earth are but faint reflections. As a rule, they dwell at the four cardinal points, each of which has a mystic name and a colour peculiar to all that pertains to it. (Here we recognize those complex participations which are always expressed in the collective representations of primitive mentality.)[1] Thus the east, north, west, and south are respectively the countries of the sun, the cold, the darkness, and *wă'hă la'* ; and their colours are red, blue, black, and white. The white and red spirits are usually invoked to obtain peace, health, and other benefits of this sort ; red alone, the success of an enterprise ; blue, to unmask and defeat an enemy's plans ; black, to secure his death. The red and white spirits are regarded as the most powerful.

That being so, in the formula for rheumatism the doctor first invokes the Red Dog in the country of sunshine, " as if he were a long way off," begging him to come quickly to the aid of the sufferer ; then supplication gives place to the assertion that the Red Dog is there, and that he has removed part of the evil to the other end of the world. In the paragraphs which follow, the Blue Dog of cold, the Black Dog of darkness, the White Dog of *wahala*, are invoked in the same way, and each carries off part of the trouble. . . .

[1] Vide Chap. V. p. 211.

As a rule, the formulas have four paragraphs. This one
is exceptional, and has five.

Then the physical part of the treatment is set forth. The
remedy consists of a warm decoction made from the roots
of four sorts of ferns, with which the patient is rubbed. This
rubbing is done four times by the doctor, who at the same
time recites the formula of invocation in a subdued voice :
the first at dawn, the last at noon. *Four* is the sacred number
which appears in all the details of these formulas—thus,
four spirits are invoked in four paragraphs ; the doctor
breathes four times on the part attacked ; there are four
herbs in the decoction ; four rubbings ; and often taboos
are imposed which last for four days.[1]

Another Cherokee formula is for the treatment of those
whom " something is causing something else to eat them."
This malady especially attacks children of tender years.
Its symptoms are excessive restlessness and disturbed sleep,
the child waking suddenly and beginning to cry. What
causes this illness ? The birds. A bird has cast its shadow
over the little one, or several birds have " gathered in council "
in its body. (This latter is a favourite expression in these
formulas to indicate the great number of the disease animals.
They have " formed a settlement or established a townhouse "
in the patient's body.) " The disease animal, being a bird or
birds, must be dislodged by something that preys upon birds ;
and accordingly the Blue Sparrow Hawk and the Brown
Rabbit Hawk from above are invoked to drive out the
intruders. . . . The remedy consists of a hot decoction of the
bark and roots of certain plants. The bark is always taken
from the tree on its eastern side, and the roots most frequently, if not always, selected from the same side. The
bark and roots are not pounded, but merely steeped in hot
water for four days. The child is then undressed and washed
all over with this decoction, night and morning, for four
days. . . ."[2]

---

[1] It should be noted that in other places also we find a belief that the
hunter's illness is caused by the vengeance of the game. Thus, among the
Bororo of Brazil, " a hunter falls ill or dies, who has done him this bad turn ?
It is the spirit of an animal he has killed which is taking its revenge." (K
von den Steinen, *Unter den Naturvölkern Zentralbrasiliens*, p. 399.) Cf.
Schoolcraft, *Information*, etc., ii. p. 180.

[2] *The Sacred Formulas of the Cherokee*, pp. 355–6.

D. The *materia medica* used by the "doctors" and the medicine-men of primitive communities suggests similar reflections. Their knowledge of simple remedies varies very much. In some cases their skill amazes explorers ; in others, like the Cherokees, for instance, their actual resources are very scanty. But even supposing that for a certain disease they should prescribe the same medicine as our doctors would do, they would do it in quite another spirit. Nearly always the chief consideration, for them, is to expel the influence or spirit whose presence causes the trouble, or to make the sufferer participate in some known or supposed virtue in the remedy which will enable him to surmount it. In the latter case it is "sympathetic" therapeutics, practised almost everywhere, and which European practitioners were still employing three centuries ago. To take but one example only, in British Columbia, "decoctions of wasps' nests or of flies are drunk by barren women, to make them bear children, as both bring forth many young."[1] Facts of this kind, as we know, are very numerous.

In any case, the healing virtues of the drug are as a rule governed by a good many conditions. If it is composed of plants, they must have been gathered by certain persons, at a given moment, with special incantations and instruments, the moon being in such and such a phase, etc. ; if these conditions are not fulfilled, the remedy will not operate. In Canada, "before the departure of a war-like expedition . . the whole village being assembled, one of these medicine-men declares that he will communicate to the roots and the plants of which he has a large store, the power of curing all sorts of wounds, and even of raising the dead to life. They immediately begin to sing ; other tricksters reply, and it is supposed that during the concert, which is accompanied by many contortions on the part of the actors, the healing virtues are bestowed upon the drugs."[2]—Among the Cherokees, the "doctors" who go in search of the plants and bark and roots must conform with very complicated conditions, which Mooney has not been wholly able to give in detail.

---

[1] F. Boas, "The North-west Tribes of Canada," *Reports of the British Association*, p. 577 (1890).
[2] Charlevoix, *Voyage dans l'Amérique Septentrionale*, iii. pp. 219-20.

The shaman must be provided with a number of white and red beads, (of the kind which play an important part in magical operations, when they begin to move in the shaman's hands, for then the Indians believe that they are alive). He must approach the plant from a certain direction, going round it from right to left one, or four, times, reciting certain prayers all the time. Then he pulls up the plant by the roots, drops one of his beads in the hole, and covers it over with soil. . . . Sometimes the shaman must leave the first three plants he sees, and take the fourth only, after which he may go back to the three others. The bark is always removed from the eastern side . . . because it will have received more healing power by being subjected to the sun's rays.[1]

If the sufferer is cured, all goes well, and the professional healer receives the promised guerdon and an expression of gratitude from the relatives. But if, in spite of his efforts, the issue is unfavourable, it rarely happens—though cases have been known—that he is held responsible. In certain communities where there already is some slight degree of political organization the task of looking after kings and great personages may be fraught with danger. In more primitive societies, failure is as a rule attributed to " the malignant action of a superior magic on the part of some hostile spirit or individual." [2] The medicine-man will not be alarmed, but a fresh question will arise : what is the spirit, and above all who is the enemy whose witchcraft has proved so powerful ? But in a general way, since the idea of illness, its causes and its treatment, remains a mystic one, the failure of the efforts made for the patient are accounted for as easily as their success. It is the more powerful " force " or " influence " or " spirit " which triumphs, establishing or rupturing participations upon which life and death depend. According to the primitive's mentality, nothing is more natural.

Finally, certain observations made prove that the distinction between maladies of mystic origin and those proceeding from causes which *we* should call natural, has begun to be instituted : either the same malady arises from a

[1] J. Mooney, *The Sacred Formalas of the Cherokee*, p. 339.
[2] Spencer and Gillen, *The Native Tribes of Central Australia*, p. 531.

mystic or non-mystic cause, according to circumstances, or else they recognize categories of maladies which are originally different. With the Kafirs, for instance, " when a witch-doctor has diagnosed a case of illness, there are three possible conditions : firstly, the malady may have arisen of itself ; secondly, the spirits of his ancestors have caused it ; thirdly, it is due to witchcraft." [1] Among the Bahima, " sickness is accounted for in four ways : (1) It is thought to be caused by the departed king, who has been offended in some way ; the Mandwa (chief priest to the king) is the only person who can assist in such a case : paralysis is attributed to this source. (2) It is set down to witchcraft (*kuloga*), which is practised by a person with the desire to kill another secretly : (this may be any form of disease). (3) The fever is due to natural causes ; no person is held responsible for it. (4) Illness is attributed to ghosts (*muzimu*), which take possession of people for various causes, and have to be exorcised." [2] These classifications are somewhat confused, apparently ; yet they mark a transition from the wholly mystic idea of illness and the treatment which must be applied to it, to the methods of thought and action in which observation and experience have a little more hold.

II

The mystic idea of illness has a number of corresponding customs which testify to the same prelogical mentality. So, too, the equally mystic idea of death finds its expression in a number of customs relating to the dying and dead, which have been noted by investigators in most primitive peoples, and which would be altogether incomprehensible if we could not interpret them by such a mentality

In the first place, death is never *natural*. This is a belief common to the Australian aborigines and to the but slightly civilized tribes in the two Americas, Africa and Asia. " The native," according to Spencer and Gillen, " is quite unable to realize death from any natural cause." [3]—" To the mind

---

[1] Fr. Aegidius Müller, " Wahrsagerei bei den Kaffern," *Anthropos*, p. 43 (1907).
[2] J. Roscoe, " The Bahima, a Cow Tribe of Enkole," *J.A.I.*, xxxvii. p. 103.
[3] *The Native Tribes of Central Australia*, p. 356.

of the Muganda," says Roscoe, " there is no such thing as death from natural causes. Both disease and death are the direct outcome of the influence of some ghost." [1]—With the Fang, " death is never considered due to natural causes. Disease followed by death is due to *evus* (witches)." [2]—Du Chaillu says the same. " The greatest curse of the whole country is the belief in *aniemba* (sorcery or witchcraft). The African family firmly believes death to be always a *violence*. He cannot imagine that a man who was well two weeks ago should now be lying at death's door with disease, unless some potent wizard had interfered, and by witchcraft broken the thread of life and inflicted sickness." [3]—" In ancient times the Cherokees had no conception of anyone dying a natural death. They universally ascribed the death of those who perished by disease to the intervention or agency of evil spirits and witches and conjurers who had connection with the . . . evil spirits. . . . A person dying by disease, and charging his death to have been procured by means of witch-craft or spirits, by any other person, consigns that person to inevitable death." [4]

When observers tell us that " natives are quite unable to realize death from natural causes," the dictum comprises two statements which it would be well to distinguish.

The first of these means that the cause of death, like that of disease, is always represented as a mystic one ; how could it be otherwise ? If every malady is the deed of a " spiritual influence " or " force " or " spirit " or " ghost," which is acting upon, or in possession of, the patient, why should not the same cause be assigned to the fatal issue of the malady ? That which would *really* be incomprehensible would be for the primitive mind to conceive of a " natural death." It would be a unique idea, quite unlike all the rest. It would mean that this one alone, the most impressive and mysterious of all phenomena, should, through some totally incomprehensible exception, have been released from the mystic sheath which still encloses all the rest.

[1] J. Roscoe, " Manners and Customs of the Baganda," *J.A.I.*, xxxii. p. 40.
[2] Bennett, " Ethnographical Notes on the Fang," *J.A.I.*, xxix. p. 95.
[3] Du Chaillu, *Equatorial Africa*, p. 338.
[4] Haywood (1823), quoted by J. Mooney, " The Sacred Formulas of the Cherokee," *E. B. Rept.*, vii. p. 322.

In this respect, there is nothing more significant than the well-known cases in which death has overtaken a person who is aware that he has violated some taboo, even inadvertently Frazer has quoted a number of these ; [1] and here is another characteristic one. " The lad was strong and healthy, until one day when Mr. MacAlpine found that he was ill. He explained that he had ' stolen some female opossum ' before he was permitted to eat it ; that the old men had found it out, and that he should never grow up to be a man. In fact, he lay down under the belief, so to speak, and never got up again, and he died within three weeks." [2] Here we have a type of " natural death " as the primitive's mentality regards it, if we may venture to lend him the expression. No less " natural " is the death which will assuredly take place if the man has but been lightly scratched by a weapon which has been bewitched. " There is no doubt whatever that a native will die after the infliction of even a most superficial wound if only he believes the weapon which inflicted the wound had been sung over and thus endowed with *arungquiltha*. He simply lies down, refuses food and pines away." Spencer and Gillen have been witnesses of many cases of this kind.[3] The only possible cure for a man wounded by a " charmed " spear is the exercise of strong counter-magic.[4]—Yet more, the mere fact of stimulating the practice of magic suggests to an old man that he himself may have become contaminated, and the travellers seem to have feared that this idea of his might cost him his life. " After the old man had vigorously jerked the pointing stick towards an imaginary enemy, he himself was evidently rather upset, and told us that some of the *arungquiltha* or evil magic had gone up into his head. The natives are people of the most wonderful imagination, and we thought at first it was going to affect him seriously." [5] But this is not a case of even a wonderful imagination being affected. It is the expression of a fear, very natural from the primitive's point of view. The case of the old Australian native might be compared with that of a surgeon who, in giving a demonstration on a

[1] *The Golden Bough* (2nd edit.), i. pp. 321 et seq.
[2] Howitt, " On Australian Medicine-men," *J.A.I.*, xvi. p. 42 (note).
[3] *The Native Tribes of Central Australia*, p. 537.
[4] *The Northern Tribes of Central Australia*, p, 675.   [5] Ibid., p. 462.

corpse, thinks he has pricked himself, and may have become infected.

The second assertion to be distinguished implies that death is never due to natural causes, because it is always violent ; in other words, it is always a crime, an assassination desired, premeditated and accomplished by a certain person by means of magic practices. This leads to those terrible and only too frequent trials for witchcraft, specially common in Africa, of which travellers have given such striking accounts. Nassau even sees in them one of the causes of the depopulation of the Dark Continent. There is no district, however, where this belief applies to every kind of death without exception. Such actions are not instituted when it concerns the death of children of tender age, slaves, or people of no importance, as a rule. Inquiries are only made when dealing with suspicious deaths, and persons about whom it is worth troubling. It is true, however, that among these peoples there are infinitely more suspicious deaths than there are among us. On the one hand, the practice of magic is current there, and everybody makes use of it more or less. No one can do without it, nor has he even any idea of avoiding it : everyone is more or less disposed to suspect his neighbour of practising it upon occasion, and each in his turn becomes the object of a similar suspicion. On the other hand, the very idea, common to all, that illness and death are always due to mysterious influences, leads easily to the conclusion that the death has been a violent one, in the sense that these forces have been set to work by the will of an enemy.

Hence, among primitive peoples, it often happens that the deaths which are the most "natural" in our eyes, being referred to mystic causes, are regarded as violent, to the utter disregard of all that seems to be the evidence. It is a point upon which the difference between our mental habits and those of primitives is most clearly attested. In the Torres Straits, for instance, "death from snake bite is generally supposed to be due to the snake having been influenced by a sorcerer." [1]—" The natives (of Port Lincoln) are not content even when the cause of death is sufficiently clear, but seek

---

[1] Seligman, " The Medicine, Surgery, and Midwifery of the Sinaugolo (Torres Straits)," *J.A.I.*, p. 299 (1902).

to find a hidden cause. . . . A woman, while clearing out
a well, was bitten in the thumb by a black snake. It began
to swell immediately, and in the short space of twenty-four
hours the woman was a corpse. Still it was asserted that
it was not an accident, but that the deceased had pointed out
a certain native as her murderer. Upon this evidence, which
was heightened by the circumstance that no blood flowed
from the wound, the woman's husband and his friends
challenged the accused and his friends to combat. Peace,
however, was made ; and upon the offensive side it was
acknowledged that the woman was in error with regard to
the guilty person. But still not satisfied that the snake
bite should have been the cause of the death, another individual was suddenly discovered and accused." [1] The same
method is followed when an old man dies of senile decay :
his relatives seek to discover whose witchcraft is responsible
for his death, and take vengeance upon the supposed author.
Here is a yet more characteristic case. " The Melbourne
natives lost a man of their tribe, generally supposed from
natural causes. A number of the deceased's friends resorted
to the usual mode of trench-digging,[2] and strictly in accordance
with the straw-pointing, proceeded to Joyce's Creek, and
there at midday attacked a party of natives who were at
the time hunting, and killed a fine young man. . . . The
friends of this young man, although eye-witnesses to his
murder, and in the full knowledge of who the guilty party
were, proceeded in the usual way to tie up the body and dig
the trench. The straw pointing in the direction of the
Goulbura, a strong party, consisting of eighteen men, were
then equipped with spears, etc., and in about a week from
the Joyce's Creek tragedy a similar life was taken by this
party in the locality named." [3]—However incredible such a
fact may appear, Dobrizhoffer quotes similar instances among
the Abipones. " If an Abipone die from being pierced
with many wounds, or from having his bones broken, or his
strength exhausted by extreme old age, his countrymen all
deny that wounds or weakness occasioned his death, and

[1] Wilhelmi, " Manners and Customs of the Australian Natives," etc.,
Roy. Soc., Vict., v. p. 191 (1860).
[2] Vide p. 282.
[3] J. Parker, in Brough Smyth's *The Aborigines of Victoria*, ii. pp. 155-6.

anxiously try to discover by which of the jugglers and for what reason, he was killed." [1]

Such customs as these are best suited to show clearly the extent to which the mentality of primitive peoples is oriented differently from our own. Both the Australian aborigines and the Abipones perceive, as we do, that very serious wounds will inevitably be followed by death. But their thought does not stop there, for their collective representations oblige them, as it were, by some form of preconception or preconnection, to refer the death to a mystic cause. The wound, then, can only be *one* of the ways in which this mystic cause fulfils its end : it might just as well have been a snake bite or a suffocation by drowning. It is no use stopping short at the means employed. The only thing that matters is the true cause, and among certain peoples at any rate, this cause is always mystic in its nature. [2]

The methods employed to discover this cause naturally correspond with the idea formed of it, and are no less characteristic of prelogical, mystic mentality. They have recourse to divination, and the guilty person indicated is executed on the spot. In Africa,—with the Kafirs, for instance—or in the French Congo, and in other parts of the Dark Continent, where trials for witchcraft are extremely common, the following is an abridged summary of the method of procedure. As soon as the death of an important person, or one that appears suspicious, has taken place, all the

---

[1] *An Account of the Abipones*, ii. p. 84.

[2] In peoples slightly in advance of these, we find certain transitional forms. Death, like illness, is still in certain cases attributed to mystic causes ; but in others it is considered natural, in the current meaning of the term. We are told that among the Nez-Percés, for instance, the chiefs say that they and their sons are too great to die of themselves. There is no doubt that they can become ill, grow weaker, and die like others, but it is because some person or some malign spirit incited by him has imperceptibly brought the death about. This is the reason that, when a chief or his son dies, the author of the supposed crime must be executed. (Parker, quoted by Bancroft, *The Native Races of the Pacific States of North America*, iii. p. 157.) So, too, the missionary Brun says : " According to what our colleagues in Equatorial Africa tell us, many negro tribes believe that every man's death is caused by sorcerers or spirits. Among the Malinkas who surround us, this belief is not so absolute, and they do attribute many deaths to their true natural causes, such as illness, old age, starvation, or some kind of accident." (Brun, " Note sur les Croyances des Malinkes. Côte Occidentale Française," *Anthropos*, ii. p. 948.)

relatives, servants, and often the whole population of the
village, collect, and the "medicine-man" begins the magic
practices which are to reveal the identity of the guilty person
Miss Kingsley has furnished us with a striking picture of these
dread assemblies, where the very bravest trembles at the
thought of finding himself pointed at and, in a few seconds,
condemned and done for,—the object of public execration
and hatred, and without the slightest hope of establishing
his innocence. Sometimes, indeed, he is executed on the
spot. Sometimes he has to undergo an ordeal,—he must
swallow a certain amount of poison, for instance—and those
who prepare the dose have decided beforehand what its result
shall be. Europeans who are witnesses of these dramas
cannot but regard them as a horrible travesty of justice.
But the tenacity with which the natives defend such practices
proves that, in their eyes, at any rate, they are strictly bound
up with highly important group ideas regarding illness, life,
death, and social order. Thus, as they put it, they are
"indispensable," from the point of view of prelogical,
mystic mentality, however ridiculous they may appear to
our logical thought.

In the least civilized peoples known to us, it is noteworthy
that divination is frequently resorted to in order to discover
the point of space in which the criminal may be found. There
is a practice, very common in Australia, which consists of
digging a trench in the place where the body has been buried,
and noticing the side towards which an insect turned up by
digging will betake itself. "During the process of digging,"
says Grey, "an insect having been thrown up, its motions
were watched with the most intense interest, and as this little
animal thought proper to crawl off in the direction of Guil-
ford, an additional proof was furnished to the natives of
the guilt of the *boyl-yas* of that place." [1] This is the practice
of trench-digging recently mentioned by Brough Smyth, who
has moreover provided us with a kind of synopsis of the
methods employed. "The Western Port tribe in Victoria,
and the tribes near Perth in Western Australia watch the
movements of a living insect that may accidentally be turned

[1] Grey, *Journal of Two Expeditions of Discovery in North-West and West
Australia*, ii. pp. 325–6.

up in digging the earth; the Melbourne tribe look for the track of a worm or the like; the Yarra black watch the direction which a lizard takes; at Cooper's Creek the corpse is questioned; the tribes at the mouth of the Murray and at Encounter Bay rely on the dreams of a wise man who sleeps with his head on the corpse; and on one part of the Murray they watch the drying of the damp clay that covers the grave, and see in the line of the principal fissure where they are to look for the sorcerer." [1]—We are told that in Central Australia a day or two after the death, there is a ceremonious visit to the exact spot where it took place, and the little mound raised there, as well as the soft earth surrounding it, are both examined very carefully to see whether any trace of the criminal is to be found. ."If, for example, a snake trace were visible, then this would be regarded as a sure sign that a man of the snake totem was the culprit, and then there would remain the task of finding out which particular snake man was guilty." The explorers further relate that if no traces have been seen, the relatives wait until the body begins to decompose, and then the widow's father and brother very carefully examine the liquid that has flowed from the bier upon which the body has been laid, for they believe that the direction taken by the liquid indicates that from which the murderer has come. If the liquid has stopped some way off, the man is still quite near, but if it flows to a yet greater distance, the natives know that the guilty person belongs to a distant tribe.[2]

In New Guinea, too, among other methods of divination, " according to Kunze, some betel ash and a crab are put into the dead man's hand, and a string is attached to his little finger. When the grave has been closed, the string is pulled, and someone walks over the grave calling out ' Arise ! ' The movement of the string makes the crab uneasy, and it moves about. While moving it scatters the ash all around it, and from the direction in which the ash falls, the locality of the criminal can ultimately be found." [3] In Guiana, too, " Schomburgk informs us that even the death of

[1] Brough Smyth, *The Aborigines of Victoria*, p. 28.
[2] Spencer and Gillen, *The Northern Tribes of Central Australia*, pp. 526–9.
[3] Hagen, *Unter den Papua's*, p. 256.

a man who has been attacked by disease is imputed to an unknown *kanaima,* or sorcerer. He has seen the father of a child which had died of dropsy cut off its thumbs and toes and throw them into a vessel full of boiling water, which all the relatives watched most attentively, for it was on the side upon which the boiling water first threw up a finger that the unknown murderer was to be found." [1]

All these practices demonstrate the peculiar importance attaching to spatial relations in the primitive mind. We have already had numerous proofs of this—in particular, of the care taken in most primitive languages to give the express distance, direction, and height, necessary to find the person or thing spoken of. In part, undoubtedly, this care may be explained by the *pictorial* character of languages which are still but slightly conceptual, but it is probably also derived from the attention paid by the primitive to spatial directions. And this very attention arises out of the mystic value of the spatial directions (the cardinal points) and the manifold participations in which these directions are involved. Proofs of this have already been given,[2] such as the " local relationship " of the Australian natives, the mystic symbolism of the Zuñis and the Cherokees, who attribute a colour, an animal, a value of its own, to each point of the compass. The practices we have just described rest upon the belief in a similar participation—so much so, that if the trace of a snake be discovered on soil that has recently been disturbed, it is assuredly a man of the snake totem who has caused the death ; so, too, if an insect thrown up by a digger's spade crawls to the north, it is a sure sign that a man of a northern tribe is the criminal. If we try to regard this as a piece of deductive reasoning, we shall never arrive at any thing but an absurdity ; it is not a deduction or an argument at all, however ; it is a mode of activity peculiar to prelogical mentality, and, for this very reason, almost incomprehensible to us. To such a mentality, there are no accidental circumstances. The insect which took the northerly direction might just as well have crawled to the west or the south, or anywhere

---

[1] Von Martius, *Beiträge zur Ethnographie Süd-Amerika's,* i. p. 651.
[2] Vide Chap. V. pp. 211 et seq.

else. If it selected the north, therefore, there must be some mystic participation between the spatial direction and that which the primitive mind is seeking to ascertain at that particular moment.

That which logicians designate the fallacy of *post hoc, ergo propter hoc*, may help us to form some idea of this participation. An extraordinary vintage occurs in the autumn of a year in which a great comet has been visible during the summer ; a war breaks out after a total eclipse of the sun. Even to the minds of peoples already civilized, such connections are not accidental. The relation of events to each other in time does not consist solely of succession ; a relation, difficult to analyse clearly, connects the abundance of wine with the comet and the war with the eclipse. Here we have an obstinate survival of that which we have called participation. But minds of the most primitive type, which recognize no accidental relations, i.e. minds which assign a mystic signification to all the relations which may figure in their ideas say just as readily *juxta hoc, ergo propter hoc*, as they do *post hoc, ergo propter hoc*. Contiguity in space is just as much of a participation as contiguity in time—even more so, to the extent that such minds pay more attention to the spatial determination than to the temporal one.

Accordingly, in those complex relations of mystic participation which, in the mass, are to prelogical mentality what causality is to logical thought, juxtaposition sometimes plays the part which we should attribute to sequence. We are told by Gatschet, for instance, that it was formerly admitted by universal custom that Indians had the right to attack and slay their neighbours if an owl were heard screeching at night near the hut of the latter.[1] And from a brief tale of the Klamath Indians we learn, too, that a dog having howled outside a certain cabin just as the sun went down, an Indian appeared, to attack, wound, and finally kill its owner.[2] Here is the *juxta hoc* principle at work : it is participation, manifested by contiguity in space, between the Indian at whose door the animal of evil omen is heard, and the misfortune announced—and consequently, in a certain

[1] A. Gatschet, *The Klamath Language*, p. 89.   [2] Ibid., p. 133.

sense, caused by the animal. It is noteworthy that in nearly all the Indo-European languages the prepositions which denote " on account of," " by means of," are words which originally referred to spatial, and not temporal, relations.[1] Possibly the primitive mind at first conceived of relations of time as relations of position, or rather, juxtaposition, and, since it recognizes no relations save those which are of mystic significance, as participation by means of contiguity. It is to contiguity, accordingly, that the primitive mind clings, and whether the one factor of the relation precede the other in point of time, or follows it, is quite a secondary, and possibly indifferent, matter. In Torres Straits, " mishaps or unlucky events are regarded as warnings or omens that something *is going wrong* somewhere, or *will shortly do so.* . . . In 1888, Nomoa, the then chief of Mabuiag, who has perhaps killed more dugong than any other man, one day boasted to me that he was invariably successful. Very shortly after this, he went out to harpoon dugong, and had the misfortune not only to fail in attacking but also to break the dart of his dugong harpoon. I think he made an unsuccessful attempt the following day. Within three or four days, first a baby died in the village, and then two women. Nomoa at once told me that this accounted for his bad luck, and he was quite happy in the belief that it was not his fault that he had missed the dugong." [2] There is then a mystic bond, appreciated by the primitive mind, between the unsuccessful fishing and the misfortunes which occur some days afterwards. But it would be difficult to say which is cause and which effect, if the cause is taken to mean antecedent, since the unsuccessful fishing, on the one hand, is accounted for by the deaths which occur afterwards, and, on the other hand, this unsuccessful fishing is the harbinger, and thus, in a certain sense, the cause of the deaths.

So, too, in North America, " they consider an eclipse as an augury of death or war or sickness : but this augury does not always precede the misfortune it prognosticates ; it sometimes follows it ; for the savages, having seen the lunar eclipse in this year (1642) said that they were no longer

[1] Verbal communication (A. Meillet).
[2] *The Cambridge Expedition to Torres Straits*, v. p. 361.

surprised that the Iroquois had slain so many of their people during the winter ; they saw in it the omen and the sign, but somewhat too late to be able to take precautions." [1]

We find similar beliefs elsewhere. In China, for instance, as De Groot informs us, the spirits of inanimate objects often manifest their baleful presence by predicting misfortunes, and to these simple, illogical minds, this is equivalent to preparing them and bringing them about. Books frequently tell of deaths, conflagrations or other calamities following upon the fact that things have tumbled over without any apparent cause.[2] Here again, it is not the temporal relation of the two occurrences which interests the primitive mind, for that is mainly intent upon the mystic participation which unites them.

The Lolos recognize three bad influences which inflict sicknesses and misfortunes. They are (1) the ghosts of those who have died unclean deaths ; (2) demons ; (3) the *slo-ta*, by which they designate any unusual appearances, phenomena contrary to nature, which not only portend but also cause disaster ; they are monstrous births, hens that crow like cocks, etc.[3]—We find the same beliefs and the same practices in South Africa, where the negroes try to combat these " unusual phenomena " by suppressing them. They call them " *ilolo*," translated by Livingstone as " transgression." Albinos are generally put to death. We are told that a child that cuts its upper teeth before the lower was always dispatched by the Bakaa, and probably by the Bakwains also. In some tribes, only one of twins was allowed to survive (though this may have been for other reasons also). If an ox, while lying in the pasture, beat the ground with its tail, it was treated in the same way, because it was believed that it had invited death to visit the tribe. When Livingstone bearers came through Londa, they brought a specially large breed of poultry with them, but if any of them crowed before midnight, it was guilty of *tlolo*, and killed.[4]

---

[1] *Relations des Jésuites*, xxii. pp. 191–6.
[2] J. J. M. de Groot, *The Religious System of China*, ii. p. 664.
[3] A. Henry, " The Lolos and other Tribes of West China," *J.A.I.*, xxxiii. p. 104.
[4] Livingstone, *Missionary Travels*, p. 577. Cf. Baumann, *Usambara und seine Nachbargebiete*, p. 43.

III

Accordingly, every unusual phenomenon is considered as a sign, and at the same time as a cause of the misfortune which will occur later; but, from another point of view, and just as correctly, this misfortune may be regarded as the cause of the unusual phenomenon. Therefore, if we interpret these collective representations by the law of causality, which implies an invariable and irreversible order in time between the antecedent cause and the consequent effect, we distort them. As a matter of fact, these representations obey the law of participation, a constitutional law of prelogical mentality. It is impossible to reduce to a logical analysis the mystic connection that unites any unusual phenomenon with the misfortune of which it is the sign.

Now the phenomena which play the part, so often difficult to explain, of harbingers, occur but rarely, and the world in which the primitive lives comprises an infinity of mystic connections and participations. Some of these are unvarying and recognized, such as the participation of the individual in his totem, the connections of certain animal or vegetable species with each other, and so forth. But how many others that it is of great, often of vital, interest to know, imperceptibly establish themselves, or disappear. If these connections do not manifest themselves, their appearance must be incited, and this is the origin, or at least one of the main origins of divination. We must remember that to the primitive mind the external world had another orientation than ours; for the primitive's perceptions are mystic, i.e. the elements of perceptions which, to logical thought, are objective and alone real, are enveloped in his mind in an undifferentiated complex of mystic elements. And these mystic elements, as well as their connections, though invisible, intangible, and inaccessible to the senses, are nevertheless the most important of all. It is imperative that he should know all there is to know about them, and it is this end which is served by divination.

To the primitive, divination is an added perception. Just as we employ instruments to enable us to perceive things which are too fine to see with the naked eye, or to supply senses in which we are deficient, the primitive mind makes use of, first and foremost, dreams, then the conjurer's wand, the crystal, the ossicles, mirrors, the flight of birds, ordeals, and an almost infinite variety of other devices, to enable him to apprehend mystic elements and connections which do not otherwise reveal themselves. His desire for knowledge is even more imperative than our own, for our general idea of the world could, if need be, do without the elements which the instruments of modern science have furnished. In its essential features it was constituted before these were discovered, whilst to primitive mentality, from its very construction, divination is absolutely indispensable. The more the mystic elements and connections predominate in their collective representations, the greater the need of mystic processes to enable them to be informed about them.

As a matter of fact, no practices are more widely prevalent than those of divination. I do not believe that there is a single primitive community in which they are altogether wanting. Undoubtedly it is in peoples already somewhat civilized that we find divination as a complex and refined art, with a commonalty and a hierarchy of diviners. But even in the very lowest types we know, divination is already practised, at any rate by means of dreams. It is familiar to the Australian aborigines and to the most primitive social groups of the two Americas. To quote but one example only, we are told of a tribe of Eastern Brazil where a chief made it his business to harangue his followers on the eve of an engagement with the enemy, telling them that they must all recall the dreams they would have that night, and endeavour to have only those of good omen.[1]

To represent the practices of divination as merely designed to reveal the future, is to define them in too limited a sense. It is true that among the mystic connections that these people seek to discover, those which determine that which is to be are of special importance and greater interest. It is these which decide whether one is to act or to refrain from acting, according to the circumstances of the case. But divination, considered in itself, refers to the past as well as to the future,

[1] " The Captivity of Hans Stade in Eastern Brazil, 1547-1555," *Hakluyt Society*, li. p. 98 ; cf. p. 152.

and this is proved by the important part it plays in criminal investigations. In the trials for witchcraft, for instance, the tribe and the individual offender are nearly always pointed out by means of divination. It is the same, too, if they seek to discover who has bewitched a sick man, or what evil spirit possesses him, where a missing article is to be found, whether a man who has not recently been heard of be still alive, etc. " The more one gets to know these tribes intimately," says Junod, " the more surprised one is to see how important a part the ossicles play in their affairs ; they intervene of necessity in all events, however unimportant, both in the career of individuals and in the national life." [1]　De Groot remarks the same about the Chinese, and explorers in general do not fail to state that " savages " are very " superstitious." That means, in our view of the matter, that they act in conformity with their prelogical, mystic mentality. It would be surprising, and even inconceivable, if they were not " superstitious."

With such a mentality, indeed, the consultation of the diviner is an almost indispensable preliminary to every enterprise, frequently even to those which a European would consider the most commonplace, such as resuming the march after a night passed at a stopping-place. It may happen that the native porters manifest the greatest unwillingness, or even, if they dare, refuse to start. The white traveller, (as Miss Kingsley remarks,) unless he knows his men's mentality thoroughly, will perceive in this nothing but laziness, insubordination, failure to keep a promise, incorrigible bad faith, whereas it may possibly be something altogether different. Perhaps when they awoke, one of the negroes perceived a sign which augured ill either for him or for the entire company ; hence their stubbornness. The consultation in this case is offered of itself ; when not offered, it is induced. For if, by virtue of these invincible mysterious relations, that which they are about to undertake should turn out ill, it is as unreasonable to risk it as it would be for us to contravene natural laws, the law of gravity, for instance. And how are they to know this, save by divination ?

Moreover, it will not suffice to resort to it to make sure of

---

[1] Junod, *Les Ba-Ronga*, pp. 455 et seq.

the success of the enterprise as a whole ; the omens must be
consulted and the dreams interpreted at each stage, and almost
at every moment. This is a matter which many explorers
have demonstrated. In war, hunting, in nearly every case
in which individual or collective activity has some end in
view, nothing is done without the favourable opinion of the
diviner, the medicine-man, the witch-doctor. If success is
achieved it is to the strict observance of his injunctions that
it is due. " Yes," said a Dyak chief to Rajah Brooke one
day, " all my people are well off this year for padi, because
we have paid every attention to the omens . . . and appeased
the *Antus* by taking alligators, killing the pigs and examining
their hearts, and we have judiciously interpreted our dreams.
The consequence is a good harvest, but those who have
neglected to do this are still poor, and must pay more attention in the future." [1] When on a campaign, all the movements made by these same Dyaks depend upon omens. They
cannot advance nor retreat, nor attack nor change their
position until the auguries are known. " I have known a
chief who lived in a hut for six weeks, partly waiting for
the twittering of birds to be in a proper direction, and partly
detained by his followers. . . The white man who commands
the forces is supposed to have an express bird and lucky
charm to guide him always ; and to these the Dyaks trust
considerably. ' You are our bird, we follow you.' . . . Besides
the whole way in adventuring, their dreams are religiously
interpreted and adhered to. . . . I well know the names
and can distinguish the songs of their birds . . . the
effect of these signs on myself was often very marked.
. . . A maia's head (the orang-utan) was hanging in my
room, and this was thought to be my director to successful
expeditions." [2]

According to Cushing, many of the Zuñi games were a
kind of divining. For instance, the game of the hidden ball
would be played by two camps, representing east and west,
or north and south, and each camp consisted of members
of the corresponding clans. The indication would be given
by the result of the game. And since the war-dance was
like a preliminary or a souvenir of the battle, represented

[1] *Ten Years in Sarawak*, ii. p. 203.   [2] Ibid., ii. pp. 234-5.

beforehand as a kind of drama, to determine which side
would be victorious—so too this game, celebrating a mythical
decision made by the gods (especially the gods of the wind
and the gods of the water), was a means of interrogating
fate as to which party would prevail. It would show, too,
whether the gods of the wind or of the water would
dominate, whether the season would be dry or rainy, and,
according to the number of points gained by each camp,
would reveal the extent of this drought or humidity. The
players on one side would represent the north and the winter,
the windy, barren season ; those on the other side, the
south and summer, fertilizing showers ; the former stood for
drought and the latter for moisture. Consequently they
could regulate their plans according to the points gained by
the prospective camps, and if the camp representing the
wind won, they would take care to plant their seed deeper,
and in well-watered spots.[1]

This interpretation of Cushing's is valuable in more ways
than one. Not only does it "illustrate" the idea that games
have a prophetic significance, but it shows how divination
serves to obtain exact indications how to proceed, as well as
a revelation of the future. It is certainly important, above all,
that the Zuñis should know whether they may expect rain,
or not. For them it is almost a question of life or death,
and many of their games, among other practices which are
now fairly familiar in their details, have the religious, and at
the same time, magic object of obtaining rain. They need
to know also, however, to what extent, at what time, and
for how long, the rain will fall. This is what divination tells
them, when they interpret, at the same time as the result,
properly so called, the turns of fortune in a game mystically
undertaken between the powers of drought and of rain, the
number of points marked to the credit of each camp, etc.
Thus here, too, divination is an added perception. Strictly
speaking, it is an anticipation of it, to which prelogical
mentality trusts as much as to perception itself. Their
confidence rests on the participations imagined and felt
between the players, their respective clans, the spatial regions

[1] Quoted by Culin in " Games of the North American Indians," *E. B. Rept.,*
xxiv. p. 374.

corresponding with them, their mythical animals, colours, gods, winds, and finally, the rain and drought themselves.

The transition from divination to magic is almost imperceptible. Both are founded upon the same collective representations of mystic relations : divination is primarily concerned to discover these relations, and magic to utilize them. But in actual practice, the differing aims unite once more, since to be able to exercise magic influence it is necessary to know these mystic relations, and, on the other hand, if divination seeks to discover them it is for the purpose of deriving advantage from the knowledge. We may even go further and say that all the practices we have considered hitherto, those relating to hunting, fishing, war, sickness, death, etc., and in a general way, many practices corresponding with the collective representations of primitive peoples are magic in their nature. I have preferred to call them " mystic," because this emphasizes the rigid solidarity with the mentality which I call prelogical and mystic, whereas the word " magic " takes on meanings which vary according to the state of the social type studied. Thus, among Australian natives, or among those of South America, found in Brazil, Terra del Fuego, and other parts, for instance, the majority of the practices which correspond with their most important group-ideas are magical. This is very clearly brought out in Spencer and Gillen's two works. In dealing with peoples who are more differentiated as to type, however, such as most of those in Equatorial and South Africa, the practices which are really magical are different from religious rites, and cannot be designated by the same term. There arises a differentiation of function which is clearly present to the collective consciousness of the group.[1]

Junod tells us, for instance, that there is continual confusion between " diviner, wizard, doctor, exorcist, caster of lots, etc. (among the Ba-Ronga). . . . In my opinion, this is a serious mistake, and African ethnography ought to be very careful to guard against it. Undoubtedly the same person may be both priest, doctor, diviner, etc. But each

[1] Cf. Hubert et Mauss, " Esquisse d'une Théorie Générale de la Magie," *Année Sociologique*, vii. pp. 1–147.

of these functions is a different one, and the native language gives each a special name. . . . The most usual term is that of *mongoma*, which denotes the doctor, especially in his character of *wonder-worker*, as well as the ‘ possessed ’ who have been cured, have undergone initiation and can look after others.

“ *Nganga* is the doctor, but the doctor curing by means of the more or less secret remedies he employs. He is the man of medicine, *wa-mori*. It is his task to prepare, too, the miraculous plants which will confer invulnerability in war. As we see, *nganga* and *mongoma* are very closely related.

“ *Gobela* is the exorcist, who expels the Zulu or Ndjao spirits. There are even two different categories of these, according to whether the north or the south is referred to.

“ *Wa-bula* is the bone-thrower, the diviner *par excellence*, the family counsellor, the interpreter of fate.

“ The *chinusa* is the personage who divines by visions or by ecstasy.

“ As for the word *sorcerer*, that must be reserved for the *baloyi*, those who bewitch, the magicians, if you prefer, those who go by night to place their charms, and kill by their witchcraft. These individuals have no connection with the preceding.

“ Finally, the priest, that is, the *muhahli*, and this, in his own family, is what every father is. He may be only this, but it is also possible that he occasionally has other functions.” [1]

In this stage of development, if we persist in calling all these practices by the name of “ magic,” there would seem to be an official and public magic, as it were, a private and legitimate magic, and an occult and criminal practice of magic. It is evidently better not to include in one and the same term ideas which have become mutually exclusive. Among the Kafirs, for instance, “ if an *isangoma* (diviner) were saluted as a *umtakati* (sorcerer), it would be the most deadly insult that could be offered. It would be just the same as calling a European police agent a thief. To the Kafir mind, the diviner on the contrary is the protector of social order, and his task consists in discovering criminals and sorcerers and

[1] Junod, *Les Ba-Ronga*, pp. 467–8.

putting justice on their track. Whilst the sorcerer exercises his art from motives of personal interest, to attain an end which is prohibited, the diviner must work in a legitimate way for the public good, as a kind of official, and for this reason he enjoys considerable importance among the Kafirs." [1] When a religion, properly so called, has been established, with forms of worship and organized clergy, there is additional reason for the strengthening of the contradistinction between religious ceremonies, either public or private, and magical operations which are more or less secret and malevolent. I do not propose to follow this differentiation further. It is sufficient to have shown that prelogical, mystic representations can but have corresponding methods and traditions which are equally mystic in their nature. The orientation of both is necessarily the same. Their correlation is the more manifest when observation is brought to bear upon the most primitive types, and therefore, to prove my case, I have selected facts drawn from communities of this kind.

Nevertheless, beneath this contradistinction there is a certain relationship. Practices which, from the social point of view, have become very different, none the less imply collective representations of the same nature. That is they relate to a mentality which is prelogical and mystic, still recognizable under the modifications it may have undergone. For instance, the actually religious rites, the prayers and ceremonies by means of which the priests hope to soften the gods who are masters of the rainfall, imply collective representations of the same order as those which form the basis of the *intichiuma* ceremonies. The intermediate stages are to be observed among the Zuñis, for instance. The antagonism between the actually magical practices and the legitimate and religious practices in most aggregates which are already civilized to a certain extent, does not therefore signify that prelogical, mystic mentality is the source of the one and not of the other. On the contrary, we find it more or less unadulterated at the basis of all these practices, and possibly it is this common origin which accounts for the variety and extent of the meaning given to the word " magic." If by " magic "

[1] Fr. Aegidius Müller, " Wahrsagerei bei den Kaffern," *Anthropos*, p. 762 (1906).

we understand every process which supposes that mystic relations and occult forces are at work, there is scarcely any act, even of peoples who are comparatively advanced, which may not be of magic character to some extent at least. In so far as the law of participation more or less governs the mentality, it also more or less determines the modality of its action.

There would seem to be nothing less mystic than for the primitive to satisfy his hunger when food is within his reach. Nevertheless we see him, nearly everywhere, voluntarily abstaining from certain foods which are forbidden. In almost all the aggregates known to us at present, there are a great many taboos with respect to food. In particular, where totemic institutions prevail, on no account—save on certain definite occasions—would a man consent to feed upon his totem. On the other hand, partaking of a being is in a certain sense participating in it, communicating and identifying oneself with it : for this reason, therefore, there are certain foods which should be sought after, and others which should be avoided. This is, as we know, the origin of a certain kind of anthropophagy. The heart, liver, fat, and brain of enemies killed in war are eaten so that their courage and their intelligence may be appropriated ; just as, with us, tuberculous subjects eat raw meat that they may be better nourished. Other foods are rejected for the opposite reason. " They " (the Abipones) " all detest the thought of eating hens, eggs, sheep, fish, and tortoises, imagining that those tender kinds of food engender sloth and languor in their bodies and cowardice in their minds. On the other hand, they eagerly devour the flesh of the tiger, bull, stag, boar . . . having an idea that, from continually feeding on these animals, their strength, boldness and courage are increased." [1]—In the north-eastern provinces of India, " the owl is the type of wisdom, and eating the eyeballs of an owl gives the power of seeing in the dark." [2] In New Zealand, " a good orator was compared to the *korimako*, the sweetest singing bird of New Zealand ; to enable the young chief to become one, he was fed upon that bird, so that he might the better acquire its qualities." [3] The Cherokees had the same idea. " He who

[1] Dobrizhoffer, *An Account of the Abipones*, i. p. 258.
[2] W. Crooke, *Folklore of Northern India*, i. p. 279.
[3] R. Taylor, *Te Ika a Maui*, p. 353.

feeds on venison is swifter and more sagacious than the man
who lives on the flesh of the clumsy bear or helpless dunghill
fowls. . . . Formerly their great chieftains observed a constant rule in their diet. . . . A continuous adherence to the
diet commonly used by a bear will finally give to the eater
the bear nature, if not also the bear form and appearance.
A certain term of white man's food will give the Indian the
white man's nature, so that neither the remedies nor the spells
of the Indian doctor will have any effect upon him." [1] What
is true of men and animals applies also to the gods. " The
idol was very dirty and smeared with blood, but in his right
side was a hole showing the natural white colour of the
material, contrasting strangely with the dusky appearance of
the rest of the figure. This hole owes its existence to the
belief that the power of healing and the knowledge of
mysterious things are acquired by eating a little of the god's
holy body." [2] Facts of this kind are extremely common,
and the reader will find many of them analysed in Robertson
Smith's *Lectures on the Religion of the Semites.*"

It is the same with clothing as with food : the mystic
element plays an important part, and in certain cases pre-
ponderates over utilitarian considerations. Many " savage "
tribes, before coming into contact with white men, wore no
garments of any kind, but there were none among whom
there were no adornments : feathers, beads, tattoo marks,
painting, and the like. Now, as we know, these adornments
are not mainly, nor solely, decorative. They have a mystic
character, and possess magic power. The eagle's feather
assures him who wears it the strength, piercing sight and
wisdom of the bird, and it is the same with other things.
Conversely, if the attention of investigators had been directed
to this point, they would doubtless have noted taboos relating
to clothing as to food : we have already seen the case of the
Malay chief who refused to carry a deerskin in his canoe, lest
the timidity of the deer should be communicated to his young
son. As a general rule, just as one participates in the qualities of that which he eats, so does one secure the qualities of
that which he wears. Here is one example among many.

[1] Adair, quoted by Mooney, " Myths of the Cherokee," *E. B. Rept.*, **xix.**
p. 472.
[2] C. Lumholtz, *Unknown Mexico*, ii. p. 170.

" One morning I shot a hyena in my yard. The chief sent one of his executioners to cut off its nose and the tip of its tail, and to extract a little bit of brain from the skull. The man informed me that those parts are very serviceable to elephant-hunters, as securing for them the cunning, tact, and power to become invisible which the hyena is supposed to possess. I suppose that the brain would represent the cunning, the nose the tact, and the tip of the tail the vanishing quality." [1]

Here we have that " sympathetic magic " so fully described by Tylor, Frazer, and their disciples among the English school of anthropology. May I be allowed to refer readers to their works for facts such as these, to be met with in hundreds ? In them we see how various qualities are communicated by contact and transference, how the whole is attained by means of a part, such as holding a man in one's power when one has his hair, his nail-parings, saliva, water, name, or likeness, and finally how to produce like by means of like (to incite the rain to fall by sprinkling water, etc.). What matters here is to show that these practices of a " sympathetic magic," which are often akin to those which I have analysed, refer equally to the collective representations of the primitive mind and to the law of participation which governs them. In this sphere, too, behaviour is oriented in the same direction as the mental activity. Prelogical, mystic mentality, perceiving everywhere secret relations, actions and reactions which are external and at the same time intimate, between all entities, in short, finding participations everywhere, can only hope to influence nature by establishing, or by rupturing, similar participations. Among the Baganda, for instance, " a sterile wife is generally sent away because she prevents her husband's garden from bearing fruit . . . on the contrary, the garden of a prolific woman bears plentifully.[2] Here the husband of a sterile wife is merely combating a troublesome participation ; in another case, one will try to induce favourable ones. Thus, in Japan, " trees must be grafted only by young men, because of the special need of vital energy in the graft." [3]

---

[1] Arnot, quoted by Nassau, *Fetichism in West Africa*, p. 204.
[2] J. Roscoe, " Manners and Customs of the Baganda," *J.A.I.*, xxxii. pp. 38, 56.
[3] Chamberlain, *Things Japanese*, p. 440.

Contact, also, in certain definite cases, establishes participation. Here is a very clear instance. In Loango, "the *ba nganga* teach that a new fetish sucks in strength, as it were, from contact with other fetishes of proved vigour, next which it is placed—provided only, that it is destined to serve the same end as theirs. For this reason they agree, if the price offered be satisfactory, to put new and untried charms into their collection of effective and well-tested magical objects, and to leave them there for weeks or months. So too, if a fetish has become somewhat doubtful and feeble, its strength is renewed by this process. It is a method of restoring its vigour. If a fetish proves excellent, a duplicate is made, and left for a long time in contact with the first. The duplicate is called the *child* of the original fetish." [1]

Finally, it is participation again, that the well-known practices by whose means "sympathetic magic" seeks to further the principle of "like acting upon like" aim at establishing. If we study them in communities which are already fairly developed, we shall perhaps be inclined to regard as adequate the interpretation which refers them to the association of ideas and the confusion of the objective and the subjective. In China, for example, innumerable practices of this kind may be noted, and sometimes they seem to be like the translating of a punning joke into action. Thus, at a certain period in the funeral ceremonies, " the son of the deceased . . . in concert with most of the attending kinsmen, hastens to swallow a few mouthfuls of cooked vermicelli, wisely inferring that the *long* threads of this food must greatly counteract, nay totally neutralize the *life-shortening* influences which the grave-clothes may have exercised over his person." [2] It seems as if here we have one of those cases of association of ideas which the somewhat abstract subtlety of the Chinese affects : the underlying idea, however, is that of rupturing a dreaded participation. But here is a circumstance reported from South India, the interpretation of which is yet more definite. " Carved wooden figurines, male and female, represented in a state of nudity, are manufactured at Tirupati and sold to Hindus. Those who are childless perform on

[1] Dr. Pechuël-Loesche, op. cit., iii. 2, pp. 366, 380.
[2] De Groot, *The Religious System of China*, i. pp. 68, 208.

them the ear-boring ceremony, in the belief that, as the result thereof, issue will be born to them. If there be grown-up boys and girls in a family who remain unmarried, the parents celebrate the marriage ceremony between a pair of dolls, in the hope that the marriage of their children will speedily follow. They dress up the dolls in clothes and jewellery, and go through the ceremonial of a real marriage. Some there are who have spent as much money on a doll's wedding as on a wedding in real life." [1] This expenditure, sometimes very considerable, attests the faith of the Hindus in the efficacy of the practice.

Is it sufficiently accounted for by an appeal to association by similarity ; is it enough to say that they imagine like will produce like ? It is a " probable " explanation, but it is difficult to maintain when we know that with primitive peoples practices like these proceed, not from an association of ideas in the individual, but from the participations imagined and felt in the group ideas. The Hindu who has a doll's wedding is acting just like the Redskin who dances " to make the buffaloes come," and the rain-maker who sprinkles his neighbours. It is a wholly mystic dramatization, designed to secure for the actors an equally mystic power over the person or the action imitated, creating between them and him a bond which is doubtless unintelligible to logical thought, but quite consistent with the law of participation which governs the collective representations of the prelogical primitive mind. Where prelogical mentality is purest, in aggregates of the most primitive type, the customs reflect it most clearly. We have noted this in the Australian aborigines and in certain groups in North and South America. In the more advanced types modality of action becomes more complicated, and a variety of divergent motives determines it. In nearly every case, however, when we probe this modality to its lowest depths, we discover traces which bear witness to the predominance formerly exercised by the law of participation. We shall find as many proofs of this as we can desire in the great Eastern civilizations, or even nearer home, in the folklore of European nations.

[1] Thurston, *Ethnographic Notes in Southern India*, p. 347.

CHAPTER VIII

INSTITUTIONS IN WHICH COLLECTIVE REPRE-SENTATIONS GOVERNED BY THE LAW OF PARTICIPATION ARE INVOLVED (III)

THERE are certain practices which I have reserved for consideration by themselves, as much on account of the important place they occupy in the life of primitives as of the light they throw upon their mentality. These are the practices relating to the dead, or rather, to the connection between the living and the dead. They are found everywhere : there is hardly any social group, of whatever type it may be, in which observers have not noted customs, taboos, rites which are obligatory at the moment of death, and for a shorter or longer period afterwards.

I

Everybody knows how, from time immemorial, consideration for the dead has imposed a burden on the living, among the Chinese.[1] In Canada, " if a fire should break out in a village where there are any dead bodies, they will be the first to be placed in safety. The people will despoil themselves of their most precious possessions to adorn the dead ; from time to time they open their tombs to change their garments, and they deprive themselves of food that they may carry it to their graves and to the places where they imagine their souls to be wandering. . . . In the grave they are careful to cover their bodies in such a way that no soil will touch them ; the corpse is, as it were, in a little cell lined with skins, much richer and more ornate than a hut." [2]

From the primitives' point of view we can easily under-

---

[1] J. J. M. de Groot, *The Religious System of China*, i. p. 658 et passim.
[2] Charlevoix, *Journal d'un Voyage dans l'Amérique Septentrionale*, iii. pp. 372 et seq.

stand that practices of this kind would be universal. To them, there is no insuperable barrier separating the dead from the living. On the contrary, they are constantly in touch with them. They can do them good or harm, and they can also be well or badly treated by them. To the primitive there is nothing stranger in communicating with the dead than in being connected with " spirits," or with any occult force whose influence he feels, or which he flatters himself he is subduing.

Miss Kingsley relates that she once heard a negro talking aloud, as if conversing with an interlocutor unseen by her. Upon inquiry she found that the negro was talking to his dead mother who, according to him, was present. To the primitive the reality of the objects he perceives does not in the least depend upon his being able to verify this reality by what we call experience ; indeed, as a rule, it is the intangible and invisible that is most real in his eyes. Moreover, the dead do not remain without revealing their presence even to the senses. To say nothing of the dreams in which they appear (and which are, as we know, perceptions which are matter of privilege and solicitation), the dead appear to sight as spectres and ghosts, and to hearing also. Sometimes they afford the living indescribable but very vivid sensations of a contact which has nothing material about it. Occasionally they are heard in the wind. " It cannot be seen ; it is like the wind ; in fact, the gentle rustling of the plantain leaves is said to be caused by the ghosts, and a whirlwind which carries up dust, leaves and straws is said to be the ghosts at play." [1] It is the same in Brazil ; " the Ges thought that the murmuring of the wind betrayed the presence of the dead." [2] In short, without insisting on well-known facts, the primitive lives with his dead as he does with the living who surround him. They are members, and very important members, of a society with manifold participations, a social symbiosis in which the collective representations of his group give him his place.

Hence we derive one of the most distinct differences discernible between the mentality of primitives and logical thinking. Assuming that the latter develops gradually (a

---

[1] J. Roscoe, " Manners and Customs of the Baganda," *J.A.I.*, xxxii. p. 73.
[2] Von Martius, *Beiträge zur Ethnographie Süd-Amerika's*, i. p. 291.

hypothesis which we shall examine later), its ideas relating to the external world have finally become organized in " nature," i.e. in an order which is fixed and immutable, subordinated to laws which the subject may be aware of, but which appear to be wholly independent of him. Ideas with regard to the dead have not provided any such. They have only constituted that nebulous ensemble which we significantly call " the other world." To the primitive mind, on the contrary, the other world and this one make one and the same reality only, a reality both imagined, felt and lived.

Even to such a mind, however, ideas relating to the dead, and the customs connected with them, are distinguished by a more markedly prelogical character. However mystic other collective representations relating to data furnished by the senses may be, however mystic the customs pertaining to them, (such as hunting, fishing, warfare, illness, divination, and so on) it is still necessary, if the desired end is to be attained,—the enemy conquered, the game brought down, etc.—that in some essential points the representations should coincide with objective reality, and the customs, at a given moment, be actually adapted to effect that end. Thus a minimum of order, objectivity and coherence is guaranteed. But in the representations and the customs relating to the dead, this external standard is not in force. The indifference to the law of contradiction which is peculiar to primitive mentality, will accordingly be manifested without let or hindrance. In this domain, therefore, we shall find practices which most strikingly attest the prelogical nature of this mentality.

The law of participation governs in despotic fashion the collective representations upon which these practices depend; and permits of the most flagrant contradictions in these. We are already aware that, to minds like this, there is nothing exactly corresponding with that which we term soul or personality. They regard a soul as both one and multiple, and believe that it can be present in two places at the same time, etc. In their customs, therefore, we must be prepared to find what we, from the logical point of view, regard as inextricable confusion. Our efforts must be directed, not to dispersing this confusion by establishing a logical order in the output of

a mystic mentality which cares nothing about it, but to showing how it is that such confusion is the natural result of the
law of participation which governs the primitive mind.

First of all, then, generally speaking, the primitive finds no
difficulty in imagining the dead as sometimes constituting a
community in the other world quite distinct from living
communities, and again, as intervening on all occasions in the
life of those here. For instance, among the natives of Torres
Straits, "soon after a man dies, his *mari* goes to Kibu, where on
his arrival the *mari* of a previously deceased friend takes the
newcomer and hides him. At the first night of a new moon
the *mari* is introduced by his friend to all the other *markai*,
each of whom takes stone-headed clubs and hits him on the
head and then he is a true *markai*. They then teach the new
markai how they spear fish, and how to do whatever they
themselves do. . . . There was a general agreement that *mari*
or *markai* behaved in every way as do men, and they could
marry mortals." [1]   In China, where the ideas and practices
relating to the dead have been preserved from the very earliest
times, we find the same contradictions. On the one hand,
there is a world of spectres which imitates the world of men.
Its society is organized in the same way, and its clan life
continues. Each one maintains the rank that he had previously held in life, and he continues to practise ancestor-
worship with the same rites as before.[2]   The dead have their
armies and their fights, their burial places and their funeral
ceremonies. Men are as formidable to spectres as spectres
are to men ; the bad influence they exert is reciprocal, and on
both sides this is exorcized by means of sacrifices. De Groot
relates a very significant legend of men penetrating into the
land of spectres, their presence there causing terror. Sacrifices
are offered to them and they are conducted to the frontier with
infinite precautions.[3]

On the other hand, however, according to the same author,
"it is an inveterate conviction of the Chinese people, a doctrine,
an axiom, that spirits exist, keeping up with the living a most
lively intercourse, as intimate almost as that among men.

---

[1] *The Cambridge Expedition to Torres Straits*, v. p. 357.
[2] J. J. M. de Groot, *The Religious System of China*, i. pp. 48, 924.
[3] Ibid., ii. pp. 802-11.

There exists, in fact, a line of separation between the dead and the living, but it is a very faint line, scarcely discernible. In every respect their intercourse bears an active character. It brings blessing, and evil as well, the spirits thus ruling effectually man's fate." [1] These expressions show that the dead are believed to be alive in their graves. " Throughout the whole range of Chinese literature, coffins with a corpse inside are designated ' animated encoffined corpses ' or ' animated coffins.' " [2]   A young girl, widowed as a bride, " when she has acquired the consent of her own parents and those of her deceased bridegroom may renounce conjugal life for ever. She is as a rule allowed to settle for good in the mortuary house, and is then formally united with the dead in marriage." [3] We are told that " in ancient China there existed the curious custom of placing deceased females in the tombs of lads who died before they were married." [4]   Public opinion inclines so favourably to the sacrifice of wives who follow their husbands to the tomb, and the act reflects so much honour on the families that widows often desire it, or at least resign themselves to it, or they may even be constrained to it by their family circle.

The negroes of West Africa hold that when a man dies he only gets rid of his corporeal body and changes his abode, for everything else remains as before. [5]   In North America, among the Sioux, as Dorsey tells us, " the dead in all respects resemble the living. . . . They are not always visible to the living.   They are sometimes heard but not seen, though in the lodge with a mortal.   Occasionally they become materialized, taking living husbands or wives, eating, drinking, and smoking, just as if they were ordinary human beings." [6]—" A young Dakota dies just before marrying a girl whom he loved. The girl mourned his death. . . . The ghost returned and took her for his wife.   Whenever the tribe camped for the night, the ghost's wife pitched her tent at some distance from the others, and when the people removed their camp, the woman and her husband kept some distance behind the main body. The ghost always told the woman what to do ; and he brought

---

[1] J. J. M. de Groot, *The Religious System of China*, ii. p. 464.
[2] Ibid., i. p. 348.   [3] Ibid., i. p. 763.   [4] Ibid., pp. 802 et seq.
[5] A. B. Ellis, *The Ewe-speaking Peoples*, p. 106.
[6] Dorsey, " Siouan Cults," *E. B. Rept.*, xi. p. 485.

her game regularly. . . . The people could neither see nor hear the ghost, but they heard his wife address him. He always sent word to the tribe when there was to be a high wind or heavy rain." [1] An Iroquois legend tells of a dead man who talks to his daughter and gives her advice.[2] Facts of this kind are, as we know, very numerous.

If, therefore, we are to interpret aright the primitives' conceptions and customs with regard to their dead, it will be necessary to rid ourselves, as far as we can, of the ordinary concepts of "life" and "death," just as it is wise not to make use of the concept "soul." It is impossible for us to define these terms save by elements that are physiological, objective, and experimental, whilst the ideas which correspond with them among primitives are mystic in their essence, and to such an extent that they ignore a dilemma which logical thought regards as insurmountable. To us, a human being is either alive or dead : there is no middle course, whereas to the prelogical mind he is alive in a certain way, even though he be dead. While participating in the life of human beings, he at the same time makes one of the company of the dead. To put it more precisely, he is living, or dead, to the extent in which such and such a participation exists or does not exist, for him. The way in which the living conduct themselves with regard to him depends entirely upon whether these participations continue or have been ruptured or are about to be ruptured.

We are thus faced by collective representations and customs which are of extreme complexity. We cannot study their almost infinite detail here, for even in the same country they vary in the different tribes. " No particular description of burial ceremonies can be held applicable to all tribes, or even to any one tribe, if the age, character, or position of the deceased was such as to procure for him more than ordinary respect." [3] Just because the dead continue to live, each one of them is treated according to his rank, sex, and age,— circumstances which observers, when describing these ceremonies, very often neglect to specify. Moreover, the customs

[1] Dorsey, " Siouan Cults," *E. B. Rept.*, xi. p. 490.
[2] Hewitt, " Iroquoian Cosmology," *E. B. Rept.*, xxi. pp. 147 et seq.
[3] Brough Smyth, *The Aborigines of Victoria*, i. p. 114.

relating to death and the dead are possibly the most persistent of all. Consequently, whilst the social *milieu*, institutions, creeds are modified, these customs change but slowly. They remain in use even when their significance has gradually become obscured and been lost. Interpreted in accordance with new ideas and sentiments,—that is, in a contrary sense very frequently—it may happen that they are carried out in such a way as to become self-contradictory in the portion retained. The funeral rites in most social aggregates, if not in all, thus present an irregular stratification in which customs which date back to remote antiquity and relate to a very primitive type of mentality are blended with practices depending upon more recent conceptions, incompatible with such a mentality. Finally, in a great many aggregates the funeral rites and ceremonies vary once more according to the nature and cause of the decease, and whether the individual has departed this life by a " good " or " bad " death.

It is the province of ethnography to give the most detailed and circumstantial description possible of these ceremonies and their very varied nature. It will suffice here to show that it is the mystic and prelogical mentality which inspires them ; that to such a mentality the different degrees of life and death consist in participations or the lack of them ; and finally, that the same man does not pass through two stages of being only, one when he is alive, and the other when he is dead, but goes through a series of states and a cycle of phases in which he participates more or less in what we call life and death. The plan I am about to sketch for you can only be a rough provisional one, and I regard it as applicable (to the extent in which it may be accepted) to communities of the most primitive type only,—communities in which totemistic organization is still recognizable, even if not in its full vigour—such aggregates as the Australian aborigines, for instance. I warn you also that it is impossible to imagine man as an integral whole going through all the phases of this schematic cycle in succession. On the contrary, that which characterizes certain of these phases is that participations have no part in them, and without these, according to our logical thought, there can be no human being. But it is the nature of prelogical mentality to move freely among these participations or these isolations, whilst logical thought feels disconcerted and lost there, for lack of ability to operate upon concepts that are clearly defined and conformable with its own laws.

With such exceptions, our sketch, starting from the state of the adult man who has undergone the initiation ceremonies and has married within his social group, would differentiate the following stages :

(1) Death, and the longer or shorter period which elapses between the last breath and the funeral ceremonies ;

(2) The period which intervenes between the funeral ceremonies and the end of the days of mourning ; i.e. the rite which definitely ruptures the relations between the dead man and those who were closely associated with him in the social group;

(3) The period, indefinite in its duration, but yet finite, in which the dead is awaiting his reincarnation ;

(4) Birth, and the longer or shorter time which elapses between the birth and the giving of the name ;

(5) The period which intervenes between the naming and the initiation ;

(6) The life of an adult initiate man, which ends with death, when the cycle begins once more.

In our language, then, we should say that death, like birth, is accomplished in stages. Death begins with the first period, and is not complete until after the ceremony which ends the second. Birth, too, begins with the actual confinement, and man is not complete until after the initiation ceremonies. Here again our mental habits and our language oblige us to divide into clearly distinct periods that which to prelogical mentality is represented in the form of multiple participations, either beginning or ceasing to be co-existent.

II

According to primitive ideas, death always implies a mystic cause, and nearly always, a notion of violence. It is an abrupt rupture of the ties binding an individual to the social group. New relations, accordingly, are established between this group and himself. Far from being henceforth a negligible quantity, he who has just died is an object of pity, fear, respect, and a number of varied and complex feelings.

The funeral rites reveal group ideas inseparably connected with these feelings.

There are communities in which these rites begin even before the patient has breathed his last, so great is the primitives' haste to remove the dead from the living. Among the Abipones, for instance, " if the respiration of the dying man be not heard at a distance . . . and if his breath stop even for a moment, they proclaim . . . that he has given up the ghost . . . The first business of the bystanders is to pull out the heart and the tongue of the deceased . . . and give them to a dog to devour, that the author of his death may soon die also. The corpse, while yet warm, is clothed according to the fashion of his country, wrapped in a hide . . . and conveyed on ready horses to the grave. . . . I strongly suspect that the heart is sometimes cut out when they are half alive." [1]

Among the Cape Flattery Indians, " I have known several cases where considering the circumstances, there is scarcely any doubt but that people have been buried during a swoon, or when in a comatose state merely. I have often told them how foolish it was to bury these people without having tried to revive them ; but I have never been able to persuade them to wait a single instant after they believe that the last breath has been drawn. . . . A woman had just lost her husband. She was remarkably robust and in good health. I saw her seated beside the brook bemoaning the death of her husband, and I went on to the village a quarter of a mile away, where I had some sick people to see. . . . Suddenly I heard women's lamentations announcing a death. I hastened to return and found that it was the woman I had seen a few moments before. . . . Before I reached her hut she was wrapped in her grave-clothes and squeezed into a box, ready to be buried. Her relatives would not listen to a single word, nor allow me to do anything whatever." [2]

" Frequently," said a Jesuit missionary, speaking of the Canadian Indians, " they were buried according to their own rites before they had actually expired." [3]

Von den Steinen testifies to the same precipitancy among

[1] Dobrizhoffer, *An Account of the Abipones*, ii. pp. 266–8.
[2] Swan, *The Indians of Cape Flattery*, pp. 84–5.
[3] *Relations des Jésuites*, p. 266 (1636).

the Bororos.[1] It is the same thing with the Bakwains of
South Africa. " Scarcely is the breath out of the body," says
Livingstone, " when the unfortunate patient is hurried away
to be buried. An ant-eater's hole is often selected, in order
to save the trouble of digging a grave. On two occasions
while I was there this hasty burial was followed by the return
home of the men, who had been buried alive, to their
affrighted relatives."[2] " In a general way, in the many
communities where they hold that a living man has several
souls, it is enough that one of them should depart (provided
that this departure is a definite one) for him to be considered
dead : it matters little that the soul of his body be there still,
if that which makes his personality has disappeared without
intention of returning. We found this belief prevalent among
the North American Indians. It exists elsewhere also, among
the Dravidian tribes of Bengal. When the sick man is in his
last agony, barely conscious, with the death-rattle in his
throat, they say : ' His body is still moving, but his soul (*roa*)
has already departed.' "[3]

Most frequently, however, the funeral rites and the interment do not take place immediately, precisely because they do
not know whether death is a definite fact, or whether the soul
(I use this term, in default of a better,) will return to the body
as it does after dreams, fainting-fits, etc. They accordingly
wait a while, making use of all the means likely to bring back
the departed. Hence arises that widely spread custom of
calling aloud on the dead, imploring and beseeching him not
to leave those who love him. " The Caribs lament loudly,
their wailings being interspersed with . . . questions to the
dead as to why he preferred to leave this world, having everything to make life comfortable. They place the corpse on a
little seat in a ditch or grave four or five feet deep, and for ten
days they bring food, requesting the corpse to eat. Finally,
being convinced that the dead will neither eat nor return to
life, they . . . fill up the grave."[4] So, too, do the natives of

[1] *Unter den Naturvölkern Zentralbrasiliens*, pp. 350, 397.
[2] Livingstone, *Missionary Travels*, p. 129.
[3] " Sagen, Sitten und Gebräuche der Munda Kolhs in Chota Nagpore,"
Zeitschrift für Ethnologie, p. 371 (1871).
[4] Bruhier, in Yarrow's " Mortuary Customs of the North American
Indians," *E. B. Rept.*, i. p. 166.

the west coast of Africa appeal aloud to the dead, begging him
not to leave them, except in the case of his having been deaf
when alive (for then they believe the ghost or soul to be deaf
also). " Generally speaking, it is only when the corpse begins
to become corrupt, and the relatives thereby become certain
that the soul does not intend to return, that it is buried." [1]
Finally, in China, the custom of "calling back the dead " has
existed from the very earliest times, and is still tenaciously
maintained to-day.[2]

Among the tribes of Eastern Sumatra, " when a man dies,
the corpse remains a day and a night in the house. . . . A
grave is dug ; and the body, with a bottle of water and a
fowl . . . is placed therein and the grave closed. (If the
corpse be that of a woman, her ornaments are included.)
Then bonfires are lighted, and the family live and sleep near
the tomb for a period of three days ; (this is extended to seven
in the case of a chief). This time is necessary, they believe,
for the dead to be really dead, and until that period has
elapsed they must keep him company." [3]

At this moment, then, the dead man's participation in his
social group is suspended rather than actually ruptured.
They believe, or they wish to believe, that nothing is irreparable, and that former conditions may be re-established. If
the soul does not return and the dead awake, however, other
ideas supervene, and with them other feelings are aroused.
Of the Australian aborigines we are told that they believe that
the spirit of a man, especially if he died a violent death,
is extremely miserable and malevolent ; in his anger he is
always ready to become exasperated on the slightest pretext,
and to vent his spite on the living. . . . They seem to think,
too, that the deceased, for a certain number of days after his
death, has not received his spiritual body, which is slow in
forming, and that during this period of transition he is, like a
child, particularly petulant and revengeful.[4] The dead man
finds himself in a state that is painful for himself and
dangerous for others, who henceforward shun contact with

[1] A. B. Ellis, *The Ewe-speaking Peoples*, pp. 106–8.
[2] J. J. M. de Groot, *The Religious System of China*, i. p. 253.
[3] Moskowski, *Stämme von Ost Sumatra*, p. 644.
[4] J. Fraser, " Some Remarks on the Australian Languages," *Journal of
the Royal Society of New South Wales*, pp. 235 (1890).

him. Since he no longer is an integral part of the group like others, he must get away from them.

This feeling is often expressed in the most naïve and vivid fashion. " When a man is dying his friends take food to him, and say : ' Be good; if you leave us, go altogether.' " [1] As for the Igorots of the Philippines, " during the first days the old women and again the old men sang at different times the following song : ' Now you are dead . . . We have given you all things necessary, and have made good preparation for the burial. Do not come to call away any of your relatives or friends.' " [2]—Again, in West Africa, we find from Nassau's account that the feelings of survivors with respect to the dead are " very mixed. The outcry of affection, pleading with the dead to return to life is sincere, the survivor desiring the return to life to be complete ; but almost simultaneous with that cry comes the fear that the dead may indeed return, not as the accustomed, embodied spirit, helpful and companionable, but as a disembodied spirit, invisible, estranged, perhaps inimical." [3] Miss Kingsley has noted the same fear, and it was explained to her that it was due not to malevolence but to loneliness ; the dead did not wish to hurt the members of his own family, particularly the children, but he desired to have their company, and " this desire for companionship is of course immensely greater, and therefore more dangerous, in the spirit that is not definitely settled in the society of spirit-dom." [4] This it is which makes the first few days after death peculiarly critical. Not only is the relation of the dead with his own group only just ruptured, but his connection with the spirit-group is not yet established.

North American natives manifest the same ideas and sentiments. To the Tarahumares, " death means only . . . a change of form. . . . They are afraid of the dead and think that they want to harm the survivors. This fear is caused by the supposition that the dead are lonely and long for the company of their relatives. The dead also make people ill, that they too may die and join the departed. . . . When a person dies his eyes are closed, his hands crossed over his

[1] Basil Thomson, " The Natives of Savage Island," *J.A.I.* xxxi., p. 139.
[2] Jenks, *The Bontoc Igorot*, p. 75 (Manila, 1905).
[3] *Fetichism in West Africa*, p. 223.
[4] *West African Studies*, p. 113.

breast, and . . . the relatives talk to him one by one, and bid him goodbye. The weeping widow tells her husband that, now that he has gone and does not want to stay with her any longer, he must not come back to frighten her or his sons or daughters or anyone else. She implores him not to call any of them off, nor do any mischief, but to leave them all alone. A mother says to her dead infant : ' Now go away ! Don't come back any more, now that you are dead ! ' And the father says to the child : ' Don't come back to ask me to hold your hand, or to do things for you. I shall not know you any more.' " [1]

These fears are so much the more vivid because during the early days one imagines the dead, that is, his soul or spirit, living in the hut or cabin in which he died, in any case not far away from his corpse, or else roaming about the neighbourhood, especially during the night. This belief is almost universal ; even were it not implied in the group ideas a psychic process would arouse it in individuals. Do not we ourselves, when death has robbed us of one of our dear ones, at first expect to see him returning home at his wonted hour and coming out of his room to take his place at table ? With primitives, however, there is something beyond these poignant recollections which amount almost to hallucination : it is the visible presence of the body which, in their collective representations, brings in its train the invisible presence of the soul. " After death, the soul remains for some time in the vicinity of the corpse before beginning its journey to the *bura kure*." [2] Hence it follows that in disposing of the body the fate of the soul can be settled at the same time. The dead man is assigned to the resting-place henceforth to be his, and the living are free from the terror caused by his presence during the intermediate period.

Thus, whatever may be the form of these funeral ceremonies, in whatever fashion the corpse is disposed of—whether by interment, cremation, placing on a platform or in a tree, etc.—the essential characteristic of such practices is mystical, or, if you prefer it, magical, like the rites we have already studied. Just as the essential feature of the chase is con-

[1] C. Lumholtz, *Unknown Mexico*, i. pp. 380–2.
[2] Hagen, *Unter den Papua's*, p. 266.

tained in rites which force the prey to appear, which paralyse
the animal's flight, make him blind, etc. ; just as the essential
part of healing consists of practices designed to reveal the
malevolent cause of the malady and give the medicine-man
power to exorcise it ; so too the essential features of the
funeral rites which take place in the first days after death are
the practices which definitely divide the dead from the company of the living. They prevent him from mingling with
them henceforward, and bring about his admission to the
society of which he will hereafter form a part. Not that all
relations between the living and the dead are broken off ; we
shall shortly discover that such is not the case. Henceforward, however, these relations are to be controlled. In
return for the observance of the regulations made, the dead
man, being pacified, will demand nothing more, and the
survivors on their side have nothing more to fear from him.

On the other hand, it is absolutely necessary that these
ceremonies should take place. We know that the Athenian
and Roman citizens used to think respecting this much as
do the Chinese and most of the peoples actually known at the
present time. On the west coast of Africa, for instance,
" when a person dies abroad, the family try to obtain something that appertained to him, such as pieces of his hair, or
nail-cuttings, over which the funeral ceremonies are then
performed ; for the general belief is that the ghost or soul
lingers near the remains until these ceremonies are performed ;
and either cannot or will not depart to Dead-land before them.
Hence, to declare to a criminal that, after his execution, no
funeral rites will be held over his body, is to him more terrifying than death itself ; for the latter merely transmits him
to another sphere, where he continues his ordinary avocations,
while the former opens to his imagination all kinds of ill-
defined terrors." [1]

Therefore without going into the extraordinarily varied
details of the ritual which takes place from the moment the
sufferer expires until the more or less distant day when the
obsequies, properly so called, are carried out, and above all,
without disputing the fact that by the way in which these are
performed, various distinct ends are often desired ; (such, for

[1] A. B. Ellis, *The Ewe-speaking Peoples*, p. 159.

example, as avoiding contamination from the proximity of the corpse, helping the weakness of the deceased, who is not completely in possession of his human body and has as yet not attained to his ghostly one, safeguarding the survivors from his violence, interrogating the dead to ascertain who killed him, and so on,) we may admit that the general tendency of these customs is to what is mystical, and that they aim at determining, with or without his concurrence, the position of the dead man to his own satisfaction and the safety of the survivors. From a shaman who had been resuscitated, Boas received the following very interesting account relating to the experiences he had undergone in the few days immediately after his death. " When I was dead, I did not feel any pain. I sat by my body, and saw how you prepared it for burial, and how you painted my face with our crest. . . . After four days I felt as though there was no day and no night." (Thus, in the course of these four days, the deceased was by degrees removed from the ordinary conditions of life, which were still his immediately after his death ; during this period, which extends from the moment of death until the celebration of the burial rites, everything that happens is calculated to weaken the connection between the deceased and his living state, and to prepare him for other relations.) " I saw you carrying away my body and felt compelled to accompany it, although I wished to stay in our house. I asked every one of you to give me some food, but you threw it into the fire, and then I felt satisfied. At last I thought, ' I believe I am dead, for nobody hears me, and the burnt food satisfies me,' and I resolved to go into the land of the souls." [1] This shaman, like those to whom he is speaking, has no doubt that the soul wants to dwell among the living, and that it would have remained there, indeed, if the funeral ceremonies had not forced it to follow the corpse.

It may also happen that the soul of the dead does not retire to a distance immediately after the celebration of the obsequies. Among the Zuñis, for instance, although the interment takes place at once, the soul haunts the village for four days after death, and does not start on its long journey

---

[1] F. Boas, " The North-west Tribes of Canada," *Reports of the British Association*, p. 843 (1889).

until the morning of the fifth.[1] Conversely, we often read of
practices designed to expel the spirit of the dead even before
the obsequies. The Baidyas of South India believe that the
ghost of a dead person haunts the house until the fifth day.
" Before retiring to bed on the evening of this day, the inmates
sprinkle the portico with ashes from the spot where the deceased breathed his last, and take great care to abstain from
walking thereon, or approaching the sprinkled spot, lest the
ghost should strike them. Early next morning they examine
the ashes, to see if the marks of the cloven foot of the ghost
are left thereon. If the marks are clear, it is a sign that the
ghost has departed ; otherwise a magician is called in to drive
it out." [2]—" Among the Tyans of Malabar, on the morning of
the third day . . . the nearest relative brings into the room a
steaming pot of savoury funeral rice. It is immediately
removed, and the spirit, after three days' fasting, is understood
to greedily follow the odour of the tempting food. They at
once close the door and shut out the spirit." [3] Lastly, that
we may not multiply facts that are similar, we are told that
among the Iban or Dyaks of Sarawak, when night has come
the *manang* or medicine-man celebrates a ceremony that is
called *Baserara*, i.e. separation. . . . They believe that this
ceremony separates the soul of the dead from those of the
living ; thus they cause him to forget the living, and deprive
him of the power to return and carry away with him the souls
of his relatives and friends.[4] Have we not here as clear a
symbol as possible of the rupture of the relation between the
soul of the dead man and his social group ? Nevertheless
these more or less ingenious artifices, and these infinitely
varied magical practices by means of which the soul of the
dead is expelled or excluded, by depriving him of the desire to
return to the place he occupied when alive, would not be a
sufficient guarantee if the funeral rites, properly so called
i.e. the ceremonious performance of the obsequies, did not
settle the dead in the state henceforth to be his, at least
for a time.

[1] Stevenson, *The Zuñis*, p. 307.
[2] Thurston, *Ethnographic Notes in Southern India*, p. 307.
[3] Ibid., p. 218.
[4] Dunn, " The Religious Rites and Customs of the Iban or Dyaks of
Sarawak," *Anthropos*, i. p. 170 (1906).

III

The period which elapses between the first funeral ceremonies and that which puts an end to the time of mourning varies considerably in length. It may be a few weeks, or a few months, or even longer. It sometimes happens, as Hertz has demonstrated,[1] that the final ceremony tends to be confined to certain rites only, or even to be confounded with the first obsequies. With most primitive peoples, however, there is still a clear distinction. This period differs from the preceding one in that the terror inspired by the dead man has subsided. No longer is he, a dread and unhappy spectre, to be felt prowling around, ready to inflict injuries upon the survivors, and drag them, too, to their death. The mystic force of the funeral ceremonies has severed, to some extent, his participation in the group of living beings. It has secured for him an assured position, and at the same time it has ensured peace to the survivors. Certain relations persist, however : the custom of not neglecting the dead, but of bringing him at regular intervals food and other offerings ; of conciliating him ; above all, of not irritating him ; —(a custom which is general everywhere,) all these prove that even yet the dead man retains some power over the living. On both sides there are duties to fulfil and rights to maintain, and though the dead man is outside the group of the living, he is not yet a complete stranger.

In the Arunta tribe, for instance, " within a very short time of death the body . . . is interred . . . in a round hole in the ground, the earth being piled directly on to the body, so as to make a low mound with a depression on one side. This is always made on the side which faces towards the direction of the dead man or woman's camping ground in the *Alcheringa*, that is, the spot which he or she inhabited whilst in spirit form. The object of this is to allow of easy ingress and egress to the *Ulthana* or spirit which is supposed to spend part of the time until the final ceremony of mourning has been enacted in the grave, part watching over near relatives, and part in company of its Arumburinga, that is, its spiritual double. . . ."[2]

---

[1] " La Représentation Collective de la Mort," *Année Sociologique*, x. p. 120.
[2] Spencer and Gillen, *The Native Tribes of Central Australia*, p. 497.

Even when the obsequies have taken place, the dead man enjoys perfect liberty to come and go, and he pays great attention to the conduct of his relatives with regard to him. In the Northern tribes, " the spirit of the dead person, called *ungwulan,* hovers about the tree (where the body is placed), and at times visits the camp, watching, if it be that of a man, to see that the widows are mourning properly. . . . It is consulted as to the time when the final ceremony shall take place." [1]

It is quite natural that during this period the needs of the dead shall be provided for. In New Guinea, according to Edelfelt's evidence, for some time great care is taken of the grave ; trees are planted there, and feasts given at regular intervals in honour of the dead,[2]—feasts in which he himself naturally takes part. So too, with the Bororos of Brazil. " The first interment takes place on the second or third day. . . . The corpse is buried in the forest near water ; after about two weeks there is no flesh remaining, and the final festival, of which the aim is to decorate and wrap up the skeleton, is then celebrated. In the interval relations are maintained with the dead during the day, and above all during the night, by means of funeral songs. After the second ceremony nobody troubles about the dead again." [3]   In California the Yokaia are accustomed " to feed the spirits of the dead, for the space of one year, by going daily to places which they were accustomed to frequent while living, where they sprinkle food upon the ground. A Yokaia mother who has lost her babe goes every day to some place where her little one played while alive, or to the spot where its body was buried, and milks her breasts into the air. . . . Like the Yokaia and the Konkau, the Senel believe it necessary to nourish the spirits of the departed for the space of a year." [4]

This very rigid obligation is imposed for a limited time only. Whilst the dead man remains in the vicinity, and comes and goes as he will, whilst he exercises surveillance over the group of which he once formed part, he has a right to many things, and he demands that all that is his due shall be

[1] *The Northern Tribes of Central Australia,* p. 530.
[2] Edelfelt, *Customs and Superstitions of New Guinea Natives,* p. 20.
[3] K. von den Steinen, *Unter den Naturvölkern Zentralbrasiliens,* pp. 390–6.
[4] Powers, *Tribes of California,* pp. 166, 167, 171.

rendered him. With the second ceremony all this is at an end. It is permissible to think that the chief, if not the only, object of this ceremony is definitely to break the bond which allows the dead person, despite all, to participate to some extent in the life of the social group. The second or, according to the circumstances, the final ceremony perfects the death and makes it complete. Henceforth the soul of the dead man has no personal influence upon his social group, at any rate for a period of indefinite duration in which it is awaiting reincarnation. Therefore, after a minute description of the final ceremony, in which the most important rite is the breaking of a bone, Spencer and Gillen add : " When once the ceremony of breaking the bone . . . has been performed, and the bone deposited in its last resting-place, the spirit of the dead person, which they describe as being about the size of a grain of sand, goes back to its camping-place in the *Wingara*, and remains there in company with the spirit parts of other members of its totem until such time as it undergoes reincarnation." [1] In Hertz's monograph, *La Représentation Collective de la Mort*, he has cited a great number of cases, principally taken from the peoples of the Malay Archipelago, in which we find that death takes place in two parts, and is only considered to be completed after the second of these. I shall confine myself to relating some similar facts noted among the social groups of American and African primitives. With the Sioux, " when a son dies, the parents with a knife cut off some hair from the top of the head, just above the forehead, placing the hair in a deerskin cover. . . . (They bring it offerings at regular intervals.) . . . At a certain moment the bag is opened, and the hair or ghost is taken out and buried. From this time the parting with his parents is absolute. They think that, until the hair is buried, the deceased is really present with the household, and that when this burial takes place, he dies a second time." [2]—In British Columbia, " a year after the death of a person his relatives collected a large amount of food and clothes, and gave a new feast on the grave. This was the end of the mourning period, and thenceforth they tried to forget the deceased. At this feast his son

[1] *The Northern Tribes of Central Australia*, p. 542.
[2] Dorsey, " Siouan Cults," *E. B. Rept.*, xi. pp. 487–8.

adopted his name." [1] This last is a significant trait, for the name of a person forms a part of his individuality.

In Mexico the Tarahumares celebrate three successive feasts. At the first, which takes place less than a fortnight after the death, all the mourners, headed by the shaman, speak to the dead man, and he is entreated to leave the survivors in peace. . . . The second is held six months later. . . . Three men and three women take food and drink to the tomb ; the relatives remain at home. The third is the final effort to get rid of the deceased, and the proceedings terminate with a race between the young men. " They all come back rejoicing, and show their satisfaction by throwing into the air their blankets, tunics, and hats, because now the dead is at last chased off. . . . According to the names which the Tarahumares apply to the three functions, the main idea of the first is to give food, of the second to replenish the first supply, of the third to give drink. Each generally lasts one day and one night, and begins at the hour at which the dead breathed his last. . . . There are three feasts for a man and four for a woman. She cannot run so fast, and it is harder therefore to chase her off. Not until the last function has been made, will a widower or widow marry again, being more afraid of the dead than are other relatives." [2]

But these same Tarahumares, having once celebrated the final ceremony, know that they have nothing to fear, and act accordingly. " The Tarahumares," says Lumholtz, " had no great scruples about my removing the bodies of their dead, if the latter had died some years before and were supposed to have been properly dispatched from this world. One Tarahumare sold me the skeleton of his mother-in-law for one dollar." [3] " The Huichols are not afraid of dead who passed out of life long enough ago." [4] Knowing that Lumholtz was in search of human skulls they readily brought him some. It is the same thing in Equatorial Africa. The negroes " fear the spirits of the *recently* departed, and besides placing furniture, dress and food at their graves, return from time to time with other supplies of food. During the season appointed for

[1] F. Boas, " The North-west Tribes of Canada, *Reports of the British Association*, p. 643 (1890).
[2] C. Lumholtz, *Unknown Mexico*, i. pp. 384–7.
[3] Ibid., p. 390.   [4] Ibid., ii. p. 285.

mourning, the deceased is remembered and *feared*, but when once his memory grows dim, the negro ceases to believe in the prolonged existence of the departed spirit. . . . Ask a negro about the spirit of his brother who died yesterday, and he is full of terror ; ask him about the spirit of those who died long ago, and he will tell you carelessly : ' It is done,' that is to say, it has no existence." [1]

In Ceylon, " the Weddahs no longer betray any fear of the skeleton of a man who died long ago. We never had the least difficulty in collecting Weddah skeletons. The natives readily showed us the place where, according to the instructions of the English inspector, they had buried them. Whilst we were extracting the skeletons from the ground, they nearly always watched us with interest, betraying not the slightest emotion ; and if it were necessary to search in the dust for the little bones of the hands and feet, they were always ready to help us." [2]

Hertz has clearly shown why the ceremony which closes the mourning period is divided from the early obsequies by an interval which varies in length, but which is, as a rule, fairly long. In order that the final ceremony may be celebrated and the dead be relegated to a sufficient distance to preclude him from any intention to return, as well as to enable him to join other spirits awaiting their reincarnation, he himself must be absolutely discarnate. The flesh must have entirely disappeared from his bones, and the process of decomposition have been accomplished. This stands out clearly in the many cases related by Hertz and also in the detailed description of the funeral ceremonies of the Australian aborigines furnished by Spencer and Gillen. The decomposing corpse is visited from time to time, and the spirit which haunts its vicinity is asked at what moment it considers the bones to be sufficiently bare for the final ceremony to take place.

I find, too, a confirmation of Hertz' theory in a belief which is very common among primitives, and which is still maintained in China. Certain ghosts are particularly dangerous and malevolent ; they are homicidal, and the source of horror and affright when they appear. It is found, moreover, that

[1] Du Chaillu, *Equatorial Africa*, p. 336.
[2] P. and F. Sarasin, *Ergebnisse naturwissenschaftlicher Forschungen auf Ceylan*, iii. p. 494.

when the graves are opened, in order that these terrible
spectres may be " laid," they are seen not to have undergone
decomposition at all. In Loango, " when, on opening the
tomb, the corpse is found intact, his eyes open, . . . it is
destroyed by burning." [1]—In East Africa, " a near relative of
the deceased, wife, husband or sister, dreaming of the departed
night after night, for some weeks after death, wakes up in
terror, goes and looks out of the hut, and finds the ghost of the
deceased sitting near the door of the hut ; or it often happens
that the ghost is seen sitting on the children's playing-ground
close to the village where the deceased was wont to play when
a child. The ghosts are always much bigger than life-size. . . .
Then the grave is opened by one of the near relatives of the
deceased, generally a brother, and the corpse is invariably
found to be quite undecomposed and white. It is then taken up
and burnt, and the ashes carefully re-interred. This procedure
lays the ghost." [2] De Groot tells of many similar cases.[3]

Thus the dead man whose body does not decay is peculiarly
to be dreaded. He is abnormal, because he cannot proceed to
that complete death which will definitely separate him from
the living. He haunts and persecutes them by reason of his
inability to become discarnate, and pass gradually from the
first death to the second. Does not this collective representation, too, make manifest the mystic, prelogical character of
primitive mentality ? The law of participation which governs
this mentality causes the primitive to regard the mystic
relation which binds spirit to flesh and bones as perfectly
simple, incomprehensible as it appears to logical thought. In
one sense, the dead man *is* this flesh and these bones ; in
another sense, he is something quite different, and the two
propositions are not mutually exclusive, because, to the
primitive mind, " to be " means " to participate of." The
decay of the dead man's flesh is what logical thought would
define as the sign, the condition, cause, and the very fact
of the second death. When it has taken place, death, too,
has been accomplished, i.e. the bond between the individual
and his social group is definitely ruptured.

    [1] Dr. Pechuël-Loesche, *Die Loango-Expedition*, iii. 2, p. 318.
    [2] Hobley, " British East Africa : Kavirondo and Nandi," *J.A.I.*, **xxxiii.**
pp. 339–40.
    [3] *The Religious System of China*, i. pp. 106, 127.

IV

Among the customs accompanying either the first or the second funeral ceremony, or even both, I shall refer, by way of example, to a series in which the mystic, prelogical nature of primitive mentality is clearly to be seen. As a general rule it consists of burying with the dead, or else simply destroying, everything that has belonged to him. Such a custom is maintained everywhere among undeveloped peoples, almost without exception. We learn that the Aruntas, in the case of a man's death, cut off his hair, but his neck and arm ornaments and the fur string used for winding round his head are all carefully preserved to be used afterwards. (These are indeed objects possessed of highly magic value which the Australian has himself received either from ancestors or other relatives. He has merely been, as it were, enjoying the usufruct thereof, and they somewhat resemble the *churinga*. . . .) But as soon as the interment has taken place, the camp of the man or woman is immediately burnt, and everything in it destroyed. In the case of women, absolutely nothing is preserved.[1] In South Australia, too, " all that belonged to the dead man, his weapons, fishing-nets, etc., are placed in the grave with his body." [2] In the Victoria district, the medicine-man throws into the grave all the personal effects of the dead man that he has been able to collect . . . he then inquires if there is anything else, and if he hears of anything he has it brought and put with them. Every single thing that has belonged to the living must be placed near his corpse.[3]—In the Bismarck Archipelago, " all the deceased's movable property is placed on the tomb ; and only after the expiration of three weeks is it burnt." [4]—The Bororo suffer considerable loss when a member of the family dies, for everything he has used is burnt or thrown into the river, or buried with him.[5] Dobrizhoffer tells us the same about the Abipones. " All the utensils belonging to the lately deceased are burnt on a bier. Besides

---

[1] Spencer and Gillen, *The Native Tribes of Central Australia*, p. 497.
[2] Beveridge, " The Aborigines of the Lower Murray," *Journal of the Royal Society of New South Wales*, p. 29 (1884).
[3] Brough Smyth, *The Aborigines of Victoria*, i. p. 104.
[4] Parkinson, *Dreissig Jahre in der Südsee*, p. 441.
[5] K. von den Steinen, *Unter den Naturvölkern Zentralbrasiliens*, pp. 384-9.

the horses killed at the tomb, they slay his small cattle if he have any. The house which he inhabited they pull entirely to pieces. His wife, children and the rest of the family remove elsewhere, and having no house of their own, reside for a time in that of some other person, or lodge miserably on mats. To utter the name of a lately deceased person is reckoned a nefarious vice amongst the Abipones." [1] In California the Komacho sacrifice everything belonging to the deceased, even to his horse. With the Nishinam, as soon as life is extinct the body is burned, and with it everything the deceased possessed. The Wintus throw into the grave everything that they possibly can of a man's former belongings, knives, rakes, old whisky bottles, oyster-cans, etc., and everything that cannot be buried is burnt. When an Indian of high rank dies his wigwam is burned down. " The name of the dead is never mentioned more." [2]—" The Hurons either bury or else enclose with the corpse cakes, oil, skins, axes, kettles, and other implements so that the soul of their relative may not dwell in poverty and distress for lack of these things." [3] In Vancouver, everything belonging to the dead is placed near his body ; otherwise he would return to take it away. Sometimes even his house is razed to the ground.[4] The Zuñis, too, destroy or burn nearly everything that has belonged to a dead man.

The same custom is widely prevalent throughout Africa, and even where it no longer obtains, we still find traces of it. On the Slave Coast, for instance, " the children are not the sole inheritors of their parents : the uncles on both sides having also proprietorial rights. For this reason the children take all the valuables from their father's house when they see his end approaching. And his brothers hasten likewise in the last hours to take as much as they can of his movable possessions."[5] The same missionary, however, informs us : " The dead man has been placed in his grave with many coverings, but nothing else is placed inside or upon it. Formerly pots containing fatty substances were broken over it, but this custom is no longer observed." [6]—In the Ba-yaka tribe, " when a man dies all his

[1] Dobrizhoffer, op. cit., ii. pp. 273–4.
[2] Powers, *Tribes of California*, pp. 173, 239, 328.
[3] Fr. Sagard, *Le Grand Voyage au Pays des Hurons*, p. 233 (1632).
[4] F. Boas, op. cit., p. 575.
[5] Spieth, *Die Ewe-stämme*, p. 120.   [6] Ibid., p. 256.

vessels are shattered, and the pieces left on his tomb." [1]   In South Africa, as we learn from Macdonald, when the funeral solemnities have been completed and the party of mourners has dispersed, the house which the deceased was occupying when his death occurred is burnt, together with all its contents, even valuable things, corn, implements, weapons, ornaments, charms, as well as furniture, beds and bedding : everything must be destroyed by fire.[2]

In South India, as soon as a Savara is dead, a gun is fired at his door to help the spirit to escape.   The corpse is washed, taken to the family burying-ground, and burnt.   Everything a man possesses—bows, arrows, hatchets, daggers, necklets, clothes, rice, etc.—is burned with his body.[3]   And lastly, not to prolong the list unduly, we have De Groot's testimony that in China at one time a man's death entailed the complete ruin of his family.   By degrees the custom of burying all his valuables with the deceased fell into disuse, though it has not entirely disappeared.   At the same time, he tells us, the *hiao*, or filial obligations, became more and more imperative. Accordingly children, while avoiding the actual renunciation of their parents' estate, were all the more zealous in preserving the outward aspect of such a renunciation . . . by dressing in the cheapest garments and eating the simplest food possible.[4]

The current interpretation of such practices as these refers them to the following general motives : to provide the dead with all that he requires, so that he may not be unhappy in his new state, and, if it is a case of some important personage, to furnish him with the means of maintaining his rank ; —to rid the living of objects which death has rendered unclean and therefore unusable ; (this would explain, for instance, the almost universal custom of burning or pulling down the house in which the death has occurred) ;—to avoid any risk that the dead man, exercising jealous supervision over the survivors, may be tempted to return and seek his possessions.   That such motives, or at any rate one or other of them, should influence

[1] Torday and Joyce, " Notes on the Ethnography of the Ba-yaka," *J.A.I.*, xxxvi. p. 43.

[2] Macdonald, " Manners and Customs . . of South African Tribes," *J.A.I.*, xix. p. 276.

[3] E. Thurston, *Ethnographic Notes in Southern India*," p. 206.

[4] *The Religious System of China*, i. p. 474.

those who practise these observances, cannot be doubted in a great number of instances. Very often both explorers and missionaries expressly mention them.

Occasionally, however, they ask themselves whether these motives are really sufficient to account for a custom so extraordinary, and apparently so subversive of the evident interests of the survivors. In the Congo, for instance, " the dead man is first adorned with all his ornaments, and everything he possesses that is valuable, for all this must perish with him. Why should this be so ? If it were from motives of avarice, that he should not be separated from his wealth even in the grave, the same sentiment would influence his heir, who would refuse to be thus mulcted. From all that I have been able to gather, they act in this way from blind obedience to the *Kissy* who enjoins it upon them, and they are too ignorant to be able to argue about their religion, to which they implicitly submit." [1]

It is true that it occasionally happens that observers, in relating these facts, confuse them with what seems to them the most natural explanation. We do find, however, that such motives are explicitly attributed to them. " They think and believe that the spirits of these utensils, axes, daggers and all that they dedicate to them (especially at the great Feast of the Dead) proceed to the other world to be of use to the spirits of the dead, whilst the bodies of these skins, utensils, axes, etc., dwell in the bier and in the grave with the bones of the dead. This was their invariable reply when we told them that mice ate the bread and oil, and that moth and rust attacked the skins and the weapons that they buried in the graves of their relatives and friends." [2]

Yet very often these customs are maintained even when their original meaning has been lost. Those who still observe them never fail to interpret them in accordance with their ideas and sentiments at the time, just as myths may be hidden under many layers of additional illustrative matter of a contrary meaning, when the collective representations in which they originated have been modified by the social *milieu*. We may indeed admit that with primitive peoples among whom

[1] Degrandpré, *Voyage à la Côte Occidentale d'Afrique*, i. pp. 147–8 (1801).
[2] Fr. Sagard, *Le Grand Voyage au Pays des Hurons*, pp. 233–4 (1632).

the custom of destroying all that belongs to the dead still
obtains, the motives we have indicated above are those which
natives attribute to themselves, and yet ask ourselves whether,
as a matter of fact, these customs ought not to be referred to
other collective representations which are peculiar to mystic,
prelogical mentality.

According to our view, these customs imply a special
participation both imagined and felt. The things that a man
has used, the clothes he has worn, his weapons, ornaments,
are part of him, *are* his very self, (construing the verb " to be "
as " to participate "), just like his saliva, nail-parings, hair,
excreta, although to a lesser extent. Something has been
communicated to them by him which is, as it were, a con-
tinuance of his individuality, and in a mystic sense these
objects are henceforward inseparable from him. By virtue of
a kind of polarization, they are not weapons and ornaments in
general : they are the weapons and ornaments of So-and-so,
and they cannot be deprived of this distinguishing characteristic, or become the weapons and ornaments of any other.
Now primitive mentality regards the mystic features of things
and their occult properties as by far the most important.
Oriented differently from our logical thinking, this mentality
tends to methods of functioning which are quite unlike our
own, and, from the utilitarian point of view, often irrational.
For instance, the chief may have resolved upon a hunting
expedition early the next day, and instead of going to rest so
that they may be thoroughly refreshed and ready, the Bororo
will spend the night in singing and dancing.[1] Von den
Steinen, who is greatly astonished at such a proceeding, does
not realize that in the opinion of the Bororo the capture of the
game depends far more upon the mystic influence exercised
upon it by the songs and dances, than upon the skill and
agility of the hunters. Again, when we consider the immense
amount of work which the manufacture of their weapons,
canoes, and implements often entails upon the natives, we feel
inclined to ask how they *can* sacrifice the product of so much
effort and patience every time that a death occurs. But to
them the efficacy and utility of weapons and implements is
quite a secondary matter, compared with the mystic bond

[1] *Unter den Naturvölkern Zentralbrasiliens*, p. 367.

which unites them with the individual who has made and used
and possessed them. If this man should die, what is to become of his belongings ? Such a question does not even occur
to the primitive mind.[1] There are not several possible alternatives, for so strong is the participation between him and all
that belongs to him that the idea of utilizing these things
apart from him cannot present itself. These things must of
course go with him. They will be placed near his body, and
since they are usually regarded as animate, they, too, will pass
into the neighbouring region whither death (in its first stage)
has transferred him.

We can readily perceive that the motives just appealed to
do not contradict the mystic origin of such practices. It
would be dangerous to appropriate these things, for instance,
for he who made use of them would run the risk of arousing
the dead man's anger, and might be the object of his vengeance. Or again, the dead man may be grateful for the care
that has been taken in seeing that his belongings accompany
him and, as a recompense, he will refrain from disturbing the
peace of the survivors, etc. These motives are only secondary,
however. They are to be accounted for by the original
mystic bond between the dead man and his possessions, whilst
this bond is not to be accounted for by them, but arises
directly out of collective representations familiar to prelogical
mentality. To it, at this stage, possession, property, use, are
not distinguishable from participation. This mystic bond
cannot be destroyed by death, seeing that the dead man
continues to live, and his relations with the social group are
not ruptured ; far from it. As we should express it, he remains
the proprietor of everything that is his, and the customs we
are studying merely attest that this property is recognized as
his. We must simply understand that, at the moment, this
property constitutes a mystic relation, a participation between
the possessor and the things possessed. It is not even permissible to conceive of the property passing into other hands,
or, if it does pass, that it may be of any use whatever,—to say

[1] " I asked him again why they buried the clothing of the dead with them.
' They belong to them,' answered the Indian, ' why should we take them
away ? ' " (*Relations des Jésuites*, v. p. 130 (1633).—"' We never speak about
the dead again,' he said to me ; ' even the relatives of a dead man never
use the things which he used when alive.' " (Ibid., v. p. 134.)

nothing of the dire consequences which the very violation of this mystic bond would entail.

Although investigators are, as a rule, very far from thinking thus, it often happens that their language more or less clearly confirms the idea. In the first place, they often tell us that the things buried, shattered, or sacrificed are the personal possessions of the deceased, i.e. those things he had himself made, or had exclusively used. The destruction does not usually extend to objects which would be the property (speaking in the mystic sense) of other members of his family. " A widow retains all the baskets and trinkets made by herself." [1] We are told that in New Guinea, some of the bows and arrows belonging to a dead man and most of the things he has used, are broken to pieces on his grave and left there to witness to the fact of his incapability to use them more. A similar practice takes place with regard to cooking utensils, and the materials for women's work ; her skirt is also left on the tomb, with everything she was wearing at the time of her death.[2] Sometimes, too, the observer points out the mystic nature of the bond uniting the dead with the objects he possessed. " The dead man's garments, weapons, utensils are buried with him . . . his canoe of bark is placed upside down on his tomb or else set adrift on the stream. All the objects which have belonged to him and which cannot be concealed with him are sacrificed. They are burned, thrown into the water, or else they are hung in the trees, because they are *etn'áry êtay,* i.e. ' anathema.' This is a new species of taboo, the use of which is often found elsewhere." [3] The comparison is, in my opinion, a very just one ; seeing that this taboo is imposed with regard to those who form part of the same social or religious group, but is not binding on others. So, too, with the Ba-Ronga, when a man is dead, " his clothes and everything else he wore are thrown into his deserted hut. His dishes and drinking-vessels are broken on his grave ; nobody dare touch them again . . ." Junod adds in a note, however : " except the Christians. . . . One of our converts at Rikatla, Lois, told me smilingly that she had been well able

[1] Powers, *Tribes of California,* p. 249 (Shastika).
[2] Edelfelt, "Customs and Superstitions of New Guinea Natives," *Proc. of Roy. Geo. Soc. of Australia,* vii. p. 20 (1891).
[3] Petitot, *Dictionnaire de la Langue Dènè-dindjié,* p. xxvi.

to complete her store of crockery by buying that of a dead man, his heirs having parted with it for almost nothing." [1] This last is a very significant fact. The mystic bond between a dead man and his possessions is doubtless no longer powerful enough in the Ba-Ronga people for it to be necessary to reduce them to the same condition as his present one. They are, however, taboo for the survivors, who destroy them rather than make use of them. But the proof that they do not destroy them so that the dead shall not use them, or for fear he may come to look for them, is seen in the fact that they do not scruple to sell them to natives who have become Christians.

In the same way, among the Hos, the Dravidians of Bengal, on the death of a man all his personal effects are destroyed. This is not with the idea that the dead derives any advantage from it, however. " The Hos have always given a negative answer to this question. They gave me the same explanation as the Chulikata Mishmis of Upper Assam had given : namely, that they are unwilling to derive any immediate benefit from the death of a member of their family, so they commit to the flames all his personal effects, the clothes and vessels he had used, the weapons he carried, and the money he had about him. But new things that have not been used are not treated as things that he appropriated, and they are not destroyed. It often happens that venerable old Hos abstain from wearing new garments which they have become possessed of, to save them from being wasted at the funeral." [2] We could hardly find an instance that more clearly shows that the very essence of property is a mystic bond established between the owner and the objects which participate in it in some way, because they have been used or worn by him, and that if these things are destroyed when their owner dies, it is because death does not break the mystic bond. The participation continues to exist, and on the one hand it is opposed to any use being made of the things, and on the other, it decides the customs which put them, as it were, at the disposal of the dead. It is not even indispensable that the things should be destroyed. A dead man may remain the owner of living wealth. " There are spirits (dead) who become very rich in cattle and slaves,

---

[1] Junod, *Les Ba-Ronga*, p. 58.
[2] Risley, *Tribes and Castes of Bengal*, i. p. 334.

by reason of the continual offerings made to them : these cattle are regarded as sacred, and the parents of the dead man to whose spirit they belong guard them carefully." [1]

Possibly it is in this persistent participation between the dead and that which is mystically united with him as property, that we must seek for the reason of a good many customs relating to mourning, especially to customs which are often so cruel, so complicated, and so prolonged as those imposed on widows among certain primitive peoples. There are many facts which would tend to such a belief. Firstly, as a rule, the widow ceases to observe these practices at the precise moment when the ceremony which ends the mourning has taken place, i.e. the moment when the second time of death is over ; when, death having been perfected, the relations between the deceased and the social group are definitely ruptured. But during the time that elapses between the death and the final ceremony the dead man, even after the first obsequies, pays special attention to the behaviour of his widow. He watches over her, ready to intervene if she does not observe every detail of the mourning. The dead man's near relatives undertake to see that she does not avoid any of them : otherwise, they may chastise her, and sometimes even kill her. Therefore the bond between her and her dead husband must be a very strong one. In the second place, during his lifetime this bond in many respects resembled that which we have termed property, in the mystic sense in which prelogical mentality conceives of it. With many primitive peoples, from the day of her marriage a woman who until then had been allowed the greatest sexual liberty, becomes taboo for the members of any group except her husband's.[2] She only belongs to him because he has acquired her, sometimes at great cost, and adultery is accordingly a kind of theft. Between him and her a participation has been established which no doubt makes her dependent upon him, but at the same time makes her actions reflect upon him. If he is hunting or fighting, for instance,

---

[1] J. Roscoe, " The Bahima, a Cow Tribe of Enkole," *J.A.I.*, xxxvii. p. 109.
[2] With the Maoris of New Zealand, for instance, formerly every woman . . could select as many companions as she liked, without being thought guilty of any impropriety, until given away by her friends to someone as her future master ; she then became tapu to him, and was liable to be put to death if found unfaithful " (R. Taylor, *Te Ika a Maui*, p. 167).

his success and his very life may be endangered by some imprudence or unconsidered act of his wife's. If he repudiates her, the mystic tie is ruptured ; but if he has not repudiated her, and he dies, the participation between her and the dead man still subsists with all the consequences it entails.

Strictly speaking, these should involve the death of the widow. We find innumerable instances of such a custom, even among peoples already somewhat civilized, especially when the dead husband was a person of some importance. At the death of more than one petty African king, his wives, or at least some of them, sacrificed themselves. Formerly, Ellis tells us, the king had hardly breathed his last than the women of the palace would begin to break the furniture, ornaments, vessels, and lastly, kill themselves.[1] We know that in India, in the Far East, above all in China, the suicide of widows upon their husbands' graves is still very common. De Groot speaks of this in very significant terms. " The most numerous class," he says, " is that which comprises the suicides perpetrated by widows wishing to escape the chance of being remarried or of being in some other way deprived of their chastity. Indeed, being the property of her husband after his death, a woman of good principles cannot but consider it an act of the highest injustice towards his manes, nay, of theft, to surrender herself up to another . . . and so rejoin him in the life hereafter in a state less pure than that in which he left her behind. These considerations are obviously very old, being traceable to a certain tribe . . . which was in the habit of casting out many a widowed wife into the wilderness because she was now wife to a spirit, treating her in fact as the Chinese of the present day generally do the inanimate personal effects of the deceased." [2]

But the widow is " the wife of a spirit " for a time only, until the ceremony which perfects death and breaks the last tie between the dead man and his social group can be celebrated. She may therefore be allowed to live, provided that she does so in a way which will not anger the spirit of the dead who is still her master, and cause him to return to vindicate his rights, and thus disturb the peace of the social group

[1] A. B. Ellis, *The Ewe-speaking Peoples*, p. 128.
[2] J. J. M. de Groot, *The Religious System of China*, i. p. 744.

This accounts for most of the practices enjoined upon the widow, even though those who impose them are frequently obeying other impulses, such as avoiding contamination (for a widow is rendered unclean by the death of her husband, and might communicate this impurity to the survivors, etc.). Moreover, in these utilitarian motives there still remains a trace of the mystic bond whence the original meaning of such practices is derived. But these motives are secondary ones, whilst the mystic bond is the main point. Without entering into the very complex details of the mourning customs which it is not my object to explain here, a few examples will suffice to show that until the ceremony which makes death complete, the woman in a mystic sense remains the property of her dead husband, and that special rites are necessary to bring this participation to an end.

In the northern tribes of Central Australia, " the *itia* (younger brother) of the dead man cuts off the widow's hair, and afterwards burns it. . . . We must add that sooner or later the woman will become the property of the *itia*. The woman's hair is thrown into the fire, and she covers her body with ashes from the camp fire and continues to do so during the period of her mourning. If she did not do this, the *atni-rinja* or spirit of the dead, which follows her everywhere, would kill her and strip her bones of their flesh." [1] The mourning over, and the dead man departed for his camp in the *Alcheringa*, the woman is given to one of his younger brothers, but this is not accomplished without much ceremonial. Finally, " one night, the *lubra* comes to the *itia*'s camp, but the two sleep on opposite sides of the fire. On the next day, the *itia* hands her over to men who stand in the relationship of *unkalla*, *okilia*, *itia*, *gammona* and *oknia*, i.e. to men representative of all classes. All of them have access to her and make her presents of *alpita*, red ochre, fur-string, etc., which she carries to the *itia*'s camp, where he decorates her with the string. Previously he has sent by the *lubra*, an offering of spears and shields to each man—a gift which is necessary, or else, later on, they might kill him if he had taken possession of the widow without both offering them the present and allowing them to have access to her. If one *itia* does not

[1] Spencer and Gillen, *The Northern Tribes of Central Australia*, p. 507.

want her, then she is simply passed on to another." [1]   It is
not enough, therefore, that the bond between the woman and
her first husband should be broken by death, for the mystic
relationship to be established between her and her new master.
She must be, as it were, disappropriated, in order to be appropriated anew, and this can only be done by the brother of her
dead husband. We think immediately of the levirate, and
without failing to recognize the utilitarian or legal character
which this custom has assumed among many peoples, we are
inclined to think that it may have originated in collective
representations of the same kind as those which induce the
Australian aborigines to act thus.

Among the Ba-Ronga, the persistence of the tie between
the widow and her dead husband is well shown by the following customs. " In the weeks which follow the death of the
husband two preliminary acts are carried out : (1) that
which is called *the escape into the bush*. The widow leaves the
village of the dead secretly. She goes far away, to a neighbourhood where she is unknown, and there she establishes a
connection with somebody or other, a man of loose character,
to whom she yields herself. In any case he will not make her
a mother. She escapes from him and takes flight once more.
(2) She returns home, assured that ' she has managed to get
rid of her trouble.' She is free from the curse or the stain
which became hers on account of her husband's death. Shortly
afterwards, one of the dead man's relatives, he who is the heir
presumptive of this woman, comes to her, bringing her a
present . . . begging her to take it to her parents and tell
them that So-and-so has ' come for her.' Henceforward this
man will watch over her. He will look after her harvest, will
take her to visit the dead man's village. But she will not
leave her home for a whole year. She will till the land yet
once more *for the dead husband*, and it is only when the last
award of the inheritance is made that she goes to her new
master and becomes his wife. . . .

" But the wife thus obtained by inheritance is not the
property of the heir to the same extent as a wife he would
have purchased. She remains, at heart, the property of the

---

[1] Spencer and Gillen, *The Northern Tribes of Central Australia*, pp.
509–10

eldest son of the dead. She is only a wife *pour le sommeil*.
The children she had by her first husband will not belong to
the second, but to the eldest son of the first. Nor will any of
those which may be born of her new relationship belong to the
heir. He is deemed to be still working for his dead brother
(or his uncle on the mother's side) and the offspring of this
kind of semi-marriage, too, will belong to the real hereditary
heir, the eldest son. *One* of the daughters who may be born
to him will belong to him alone. On the other hand, he has
the advantage of receiving his bowl of cooked food every
evening from this new wife." [1] In this case, the *disappro-*
priation of the widow does not actually become complete and,
since among the Ronga tribe property has already been
moulded into a legal form, the lasting participation between a
woman and her dead husband is interpreted in terms expressive of the conditions governing individuals.

Some at least, therefore, of the customs relating to mourning would seem to refer to that permanent participation
which, in the prelogical mind, corresponds with that which
logical thinking regards as the concept of property. At this
stage, however, it is not a concept : it is still one of the representations which are both general and concrete, many examples
of which we have already studied, which never appear save
enveloped in a complex of mystic ideas and sentiments. The
object possessed participates in the nature of the possessor ;
the objects possessed by a dead man participate in his nature,
at any rate until the closing ceremony of the period of
mourning, and they inspire the same feelings as the deceased.

For similar reasons the property of a living person is no
less inviolable. The objects a man possesses participate in
their owner to such an extent that no other would care to take
them from him. With the Macusis of Guiana, for instance,
" each individual's property, whether it be his hut, his
utensils, or the patch of ground he cultivates, is sacred. Violation of this property, save in case of war, is scarcely possible,
and disputes respecting mine and thine are accordingly
extremely rare." [2] It is therefore sufficient to indicate by
an outward sign that a person possesses a thing for it to be-

[1] Junod, *Les Ba-Ronga*, pp. 67–9.
[2] Richard Schomburgk, *Reisen in British Guiana*, ii. p. 321.

come inviolate. " We are told that the Cumana natives used to surround their plantations by a simple woollen thread or by a creeper two feet above the ground, and that their property was thus absolutely protected ; for it would have been a serious crime to cross this barrier, and all believed that he who tried to do so would shortly die. The same belief still obtains among the Indians of the Amazon." [1] In New Zealand, " a person often leaves his property in exposed places, with merely this simple *tohu* or sign (a piece of drift timber with something tied round it) to show that it is private, and generally it is allowed to remain untouched, however many may pass that way. . . . with a simple bit of flax on the door of a man's house, containing all his valuables, his line, or his food store ; they are thus rendered inviolable and no one would meddle with them." [2] In other words, " if anyone wanted to preserve his crop, his house, his garments or anything else, he made them *tapu* ; a tree which had been selected in the forest for a canoe (which he could not yet use) . . . he rendered *tapu* by tying a band round it with a little grass in it." [3]

Since the property is thus made " sacred " there is no need to defend it by external means, and this is true of that which belongs to groups as of that which is personal. According to Brough Smyth, the area of ground owned by each tribe was definitely known to all its members, and as carefully drawn as if a land-surveyor had defined its limits and reckoned its superficies.[4] It is the same with the aborigines of Central Australia, and Spencer and Gillen tell us that these limits are never disputed and that one tribe would not think of appropriating territory belonging to another. What would it do with it, if it had it ? The idea of such territories is above all a mystic one, and that which dominates it is not the quantity of game or of water to be found there ; it is its division into " local totem centres " in which the spirits which are awaiting their reincarnation in the tribe dwell. How would it avail another tribe to expel the one whose ancestors have lived there and who still inhabit it in mystic fashion ? The participation between the social group and the soil is so close that

[1] Von Martius, *Beiträge zur Ethnographie Süd-Amerika's*, i. p. 86.
[2] R. Taylor, *Te Ika a Maui*, p. 63.   [3] Ibid., p. 58.
[4] Brough Smyth, *The Aborigines of Victoria*, i. p 139.

the idea that the soil may be disappropriated does not even occur to them.   In such conditions the property is, as Schomburgk puts it, "sacred" : it is inviolable and inviolate as long as the collective representations which we have noted maintain their empire over the mind.

In certain cases this mystic sentiment of property may even become an obstacle to exchange.   To give away a thing one possesses is giving something of oneself, and therefore it means giving to another a power over oneself.   Barter is a process which involves mystic elements, and however advantageous or tempting it may be, a primitive often starts by refusing altogether.   Lumholtz tells us " they are chary of selling to strangers.   When a Mexican wants to buy a sheep, or some corn, or a girdle, the Tarahumare will first deny that he has anything to sell. . . . A purchase however establishes a kind of brotherhood between the two negotiants, who afterwards call each other *naragua* and a confidence is established between them almost of the same character as that which exists between *compadres* among the Mexicans." [1]

V

When the period of mourning has been ended by the final ceremony, the death of the individual is complete, in the sense that his relations with the social group of which he was a member when alive are entirely ruptured.   If everything that belonged to him has not been destroyed, it is disposed of, and his widow may become the wife of another.   His very name, which it was forbidden to pronounce, may be heard once more among certain primitives.   Does this imply that all reciprocal influence has disappeared ?   From the logical point of view, not admitting of contradictory standards, this would seem to be the necessary consequence.   It is not so to the prelogical mind, which finds no embarrassment in contradiction, at any rate in its collective representations.   On the one hand, now that the final ceremony has taken place, there is nothing either to be feared or to be hoped from the dead. On the other hand, however, the social group feels that it lives in very close dependence with respect to its dead, in

[1] C. Lumholtz, *Unknown Mexico*, i. p. 244.

general. It exists and subsists only through them. Firstly, it is necessarily recruited from among them. Then there is the respect with which the *churinga* of the Australian aborigines, for instance, is surrounded,—for these *churinga* which represent the ancestors, *are* indeed these ancestors, in the meaning of the word according to the law of participation—the totem ceremonies periodically celebrated by the tribes, upon which their welfare depends, and finally the other institutions testifying to a participation between the living group and its dead, which is most intensely realized. It is not merely a question of the dead who are still near, whose bodies have not yet entirely decayed, but above all of the dead who have started for their camp in the *Alcheringa*, who are no less present in their *churinga*, and also in their *nanja*, in the place in which their mythical ancestor disappeared beneath the soil.

Here we have difficulties which would be insurmountable to logical thinking, which cannot admit the *multipresence* of individuals, and their simultaneous inhabitation of several different localities. We find it hard enough to conceive that in the period previous to the closing ceremony, which marks the definite departure of the dead, a dead man can at one and the same time dwell in his grave with his body, and yet be present, as a kind of tutelary deity, in the house that was his home ; yet to the Chinese, for instance, there is nothing inconceivable in the idea. Still less can we reduce to a thoroughly intelligible schema the collective representations of Australian aborigines with respect to those who are " entirely " dead. We can neither define in one clear concept the personality of these dead, nor form any satisfactory idea of the way in which the living group participates in their existence, and in which it is " participated " by them, according to Malebranche's use of the term. What is actually certain is that this reciprocal participation is real, as we have already seen,[1] that it is not to be confused with that which in other peoples is called ancestor-worship, and that it relates to the characteristics which are peculiar to prelogical mentality.

When a child is born a definite personality reappears, or, to put it more precisely, is formed again. All birth is a reincarnation. "There is a vast ensemble of peoples, negroes,

---

[1] Vide Chap. II. pp. 90. et seq.

Malays, Polynesians, Indians (the Sioux, Algonquin, Iroquois, *Pueblo* groups of the north-west), Esquimaux, Australians, among whom the reincarnation of the dead and the inheritance of the individual name in the family or the clan is the rule. With the peoples of North-western America, the individual is born with his name, his social functions, and his coat-of-arms ready made. . . . The number of individuals, of names, spirits, and rôles in the clan is limited, and its existence is but an ensemble of deaths and rebirths of identical beings. With the Australian aborigines and the Negritos, the same phenomenon obtains, though not so clearly marked . . . as a necessary institution. From its beginning the clan is conceived as attached to a certain spatial district, the ancestral home of the totem-spirits, the rocks in which the ancestors are buried, whence the children which are to be conceived issue, and finally, whence are derived the spirits of the totem animals, the reproduction of which is secured by the clan." [1]

Birth, just like death, then, is merely the transition from one form of life to another. Just as, for the individual, for the first moments at any rate, the latter is but a change of condition and of residence, all the rest being as before, so birth is but the transference, through the medium of its parents, of the child to the light of day. " The child is not the direct result of the intercourse ; it may come without this, which merely, as it were, prepares the mother for the reception, and birth also, of an already-formed spirit-child who inhabits one of the local totem centres." [2] Seeing what the general orientation of prelogical mentality is, and the paramount interest which the mystic factors in every phenomenon claim, would not the physiological aspect of birth disappear from the primitive's field of vision, lost in the infinitely more important idea of the totemic ties subsisting between child and parents ? Birth, like life, death, disease, must inevitably be represented in mystic fashion, and in the form of participation. In the tribes of Northern Australia, " descent both of class and totem are strictly paternal. A spirit-child is not supposed to go into any woman unless she be the wife of a man belonging to the same moiety and totem as the spirit. As a general rule,

---

[1] Mauss, *Année Sociologique*, vol. ix. p. 267.
[2] Spencer and Gillen, *The Northern Tribes of Central Australia*, p. 265.

the spirit is supposed to enter a woman whose children are born into the class to which it, the spirit, itself belongs." These spirits are, as it were, lying in wait for a possible mother, in the various totem centres in which they reside, and each deliberately chooses the mother it desires, without making any mistake. " If the wife of a snake-man were to conceive a spirit at the spot inhabited by bee-spirits, it would simply mean that a snake-spirit had followed the father up from his own place and had gone inside the woman." A woman who does not desire a child carefully avoids passing these local totem centres, and if she finds it inevitable she runs quickly by, begging the spirit-children not to enter her.[1]

The same idea of conception occurs elsewhere. Among the Baganda, for instance, " should a child be still-born, or die in infancy, it is buried at four cross-roads, and thorns are placed upon the grave. Every woman who passes by throws a few blades of grass upon the grave to prevent the ghost from entering into her and the child being reborn."[2]   In the French Congo, children whose mothers have died in childbed are thrown into the bush, but near the road, " in order that their souls may choose a new mother from the women who pass by."[3]

A belief that is widely prevalent among the tribes of different parts of Australia clearly shows that the reincarnation of spirits, or that which we call birth, is conceived of as independent of physiological conditions. White men are thought to be ancestors who have returned to the world. " Miago assured me that this was the current opinion, and my own personal observation subsequently confirmed his statement. At Perth, one of the settlers, from his presumed likeness to a defunct member of the tribe of the Murray river, was visited by his supposed kindred twice every year, though in so doing they passed through sixty miles of what was not infrequently an enemy's country."[4]—" Since they have found out the existence of the race of white people, they have adopted the notion that their souls will hereafter appear in the bodies of such white people. . . . It may be instanced as a proof of how firmly they do believe, or rather, have believed this, that

[1] Spencer and Gillen, *The Northern Tribes of Central Australia*, p. 170.
[2] Roscoe, " Manners and Customs of the Baganda," *J.A.I.*, xxxii. p. 30.
[3] Mary Kingsley, *Travels in West Africa*, p. 478.
[4] Stokes, *Discoveries in Australia*, i. p. 60 (1846).

in the idea they had recognized in some of the settlers natives
long ago departed from life, they actually gave them the names
which these had gone by when alive. This notion is not
confined to the Port Lincoln blacks, but prevails also with
those of Adelaide and Victoria." [1]—" In the south-east
portions of Australia, the old men used to say that the forms
or spirits of the dead went to the westward, towards the
setting sun ; and the natives of West Australia had the same
belief. When therefore they saw white men coming over the
sea from that quarter, they at once took them to be their
deceased relatives reincarnated." [2]—" I found the belief
among the Yantruwunter natives, that white men were once
blacks. I was once asked by some old men how long it was
since I was a blackfellow. . . . I was told that I had once
been one of the Mungalle family." [3]—" Buckley, the white
man who spent so many years with the wild natives of Port
Philip, Victoria, is said to have owed his life to their assuming
that he was one of them who had come to life again. A
similar belief was discovered at Port Lincoln, South Australia,
in 1846, by Mr. Schürmann, who says ' they certainly believe
in the pre-existence of the souls of black men.' " [4]—" On one
occasion, Mr. Bland, in endeavouring to refute their belief,
said : ' Nonsense ! I was never here before ! ' and was
answered, by an intelligent lad, ' Then how did you know the
way here ? ' . . . . This belief, however, began to die out
as they saw that children were born to the white people." [5]
This latter circumstance clearly proves that the natives had
formerly held that the whites were the reincarnation of their
dead relatives, who had not been through the process of actual
birth. This is also the interpretation accorded to it by an
excellent observer, Dr. W. E. Roth. He points out that in
many of the North Queensland dialects the same word is found
to do duty for a European and a deceased aboriginal's spirit,
ghost, etc., and he is satisfied " that instead of a return of the

---

[1] Wilhelmi, " Manners and Customs of Australian Natives," etc., *Trans
Roy Soc., Vict.*, v. p. 189.
[2] Chauncy, cited by Brough Smyth, *The Aborigines of Victoria*, ii. p. 22.
[3] Howitt, *Notes on the Aborigines of Cooper's Creek*, cited by Brough Smyth,
The Aborigines of Victoria, ii. p. 307.
[4] Mathews, " Aboriginal Tribes of New South Wales and Victoria,"
Journal and Proceedings of Royal Society of New South Wales, p. 349 (1905).
[5] Chauncy, cited by Brough Smyth, *The Aborigines of Victoria*, pp. 270, 274.

deceased native's actual body after death in the form of a European, the meaning intended to be conveyed was that the vital principle (spirit, etc.) is reincarnated in the white man." [1] In any case, as a rule, the reincarnation takes place through the medium of pregnancy, and the spirit-child reincarnated already stands in a definite relation to the father and mother who engender it. It virtually formed part of the class or totem of one or other of them. But just as the man who has just expired is scarcely dead, so the child which has just seen the light of day is only partially born. As we should put it, birth, like death, is accomplished in successive stages. As the dead is only " perfectly " dead after the final ceremony ending the mourning period, and by virtue of that ceremony, so the newborn individual will not be perfected until after the final initiation ceremonies, and by virtue of these ceremonies. Perhaps the best way to explain these representations which are so familiar to prelogical mentality is to consider the complex system of participations. To the extent that the individual is engaged in, or apart from, certain of these, he is more completely born or more entirely dead. Most of the customs relating to the dead are intended to rupture their participation in the social group of the living, and to establish their participation in that of deceased members of the same group. So, too, most of the practices relating to the newly-born, to children, and to novices, are designed to effect their increasing participation in the life of the social group to which they belong.

The period immediately following the accouchement is *mutatis mutandis* identical with that which directly follows upon the drawing of the last breath. Like the latter, it is characterized by an extreme sensibility on the part of the subject. Undoubtedly, a newborn child does not inspire the same " mixed " sentiments as a person who has just died : one has no fear of it, nor does one feel a very lively affection for it. But one imagines it as frail and exposed to many dangers, just like the recently deceased. Practices relating to *couvade*, which we have already studied,[2] sufficiently prove the care of

---

[1] *The North Queensland Ethnography Bulletin, No.* 5, p: 16 (1903), cited by *The Cambridge Expedition to Torres Straits*, v. p. 355.
[2] Vide supra, Chap. VI. pp. 256–260

it which is regarded as essential. Its participation in the living social group is still very limited. It has scarcely entered it, just as, at the moment of transition, a man is hardly more dead than alive. Nothing is yet decisive. The friends recall the spirit which has just left the body, they entreat it not to forsake those who love it, they feel it near to them. Similarly, the newborn being uttering its first cry is rather a candidate for life in the social group than a living entity. In this case, too, nothing is yet decisive. If there be any reason, however slight, for not admitting it, they will not hesitate to reject it.

It seems that it is in these collective representations that we must seek the main origin of the infanticide which, in various forms, is so common among many primitive peoples. Sometimes it is the children of the female sex who are sacrificed, sometimes the opposite. Occasionally both twins are put to death, and again it may be only one ; if they are of different sex, it may be in one case, the boy, and in another the girl ; in certain aggregates, moreover, twin births are regarded as a happy event. Westermark has collected a vast amount of data on these practices.[1] They are usually explained in the utilitarian sense : the mother who suckles one child cannot properly feed a second. In the Australian aborigines studied by Spencer and Gillen, infanticide is practised everywhere for this reason. But should the mother have given the breast to the newborn child but once only, it is never killed.[2]

However, this is not the only motive alleged. Among the Abipones, for instance, " the mothers suckle their children for three years, during which time they have no carnal intercourse with their husbands who, tired of this long delay, often marry another wife. The women, therefore, kill their unborn babies for fear of repudiation. . . . I have known some who killed all the children they bore, no one either preventing or avenging these murders. The mothers bewail their children, who die of a disease, with sincere tears ; yet they dash their newborn babes against the ground, or destroy them in some

---

[1] *Origin and Development of Moral Ideas*, i. pp. 394 et seq., 458 et seq
[2] Spencer and Gillen, *The Northern Tribes of Central Australia*, pp. 608–9.

other way, with calm countenances." [1]　In other places it is not the desire to retain the husbands, but economic reasons that make the appeal.　Hawtrey tells us of the Lengua Indians of Paraguay that it is the woman's task to bring the foodstuffs from garden and field, and that she does all the carrying.　The Lenguas are a nomadic race, often covering ten to twenty miles in a day, and the woman carries all the household belongings, pots, water-jars, skins and blankets in a large string bag on her back.　She may have an iron bar, or perhaps some domestic animal or bird to attend to with one hand, and she carries the child upon her shoulders, whilst the man walks ahead, carrying nothing but his bow and arrows. In such case it would be quite impossible for a mother to have more than one child to carry and look after.[2]

The importance of such divers motives is undeniable, and the influence they exert may, in the circumstances described, prove irresistible.　But on the one hand, we do not find infanticide always confined to cases in which the mother was already suckling one child, or indeed to those in which she fears that her husband may take another wife.　On the other hand, these motives would scarcely suffice if the collective representations did not make infanticide—practised at the very moment of birth : this latter point is of capital import- ance—almost a matter of indifference, because the newborn child has but an infinitely small participation in the life of the social group.　Thus the Gallinomero of California " do not seem to have limited themselves to killing twins, or having made any distinction of sex, but cut off boy and girl alike, especially if deformed.　When resorted to, the act was imme- diate. . . . If the child were allowed to live three days its life was thenceforth secure.　They did not call it a ' relation ' until they had decided to spare its life." [3]

Moreover, the newborn who is suppressed does not die like the adult.　The latter, having accomplished the cycle of participations in the world of the living, enters upon the first stage in the life of the dead, and must traverse it entirely before being born again.　But the newborn, who is hardly

[1] Dobrizhoffer, *An Account of the Abipones*, ii. pp. 97–8.
[2] Hawtrey, " The Lengua Indians of the Paraguayan Chaco," *J.A.I.*, xxxi. p. 295.
[3] Powers, *Tribes of California*, p. 177.

alive, in the sense that he only slightly participates in the life of the social group, will remain, if his birth is not completed, at the portals of life, in the terminal period which abuts upon reincarnation. Death to him is scarcely a regression, and he remains an immediate candidate for the next life. Hence there is but slight scruple in disposing of him. He is not suppressed, but delayed : possibly he will enter, even the following year, the very same mother. Spencer and Gillen expressly state this. "It must be remembered that the natives believe that the spirit part of the child returns at once to the *Alcheringa* home" (hence, without undergoing the ordinary stages) "and that it may very soon be born again, entering, very likely, the same woman."[1] This latter belief seems to make the indifference of the mothers in sacrificing their children less strange. The child is only taken from them for a time ; they will find it again, and it will return to them.

The Khonds of India were accustomed to rid themselves of female children at their birth, and the British had considerable trouble in inducing them to abandon this practice. It proceeded from collective representations, the substance of which has been happily preserved for us. "They believe that the reincarnation of a soul in the tribe, when it is first seen to animate a human form is completed only on the performing of the ceremony of naming the infant on the seventh day after its birth ; and they hold the curious doctrine that Boora sets apart a certain quantity of soul to be distributed amongst each generation of men. Thence they believe that if an infant die before it is named, its soul does not enter into the circle of tribal spirits, to be reborn as often as Dinga wills, but rejoins the mass of spirits set apart for the generation to which it belongs." Here we perceive the reasons which make the Khonds act in this way. "Thus by the destruction of a female infant, either the addition of a new female soul to the number of souls attached to a tribe is prevented, and the chance of getting a new male soul in its place is gained, or the return of a female soul by rebirth in that tribe is postponed."[2] But in any case the controlling idea is that the newborn child, since it is but an imperfect being, has not to die as the adult

[1] *The Northern Tribes of Central Australia*, p. 609.
[2] Macpherson, *Memorials of Service in India*, p. 131.

does. For it, there is no question of rupturing participations, since they have not yet been established.

If the child lives, that is, if for some good reason it is not " postponed," its welfare depends (by virtue of a mystic participation) upon the actions of its parents, the food they take, their labour and their repose, etc. ; and we already know how stringent are the regulations to which parents must submit. But above all, in order that the child may be released from the period in which his life is still uncertain, (as the death of the newly-dead is still uncertain) it is necessary for him to receive his name, and this in a ceremony which is more or less complicated. In other words, it must be decided *who he is*. Now it is not a case of choosing a name for him. The child who comes into the world is the reincarnation of a certain ancestor : he therefore has his name already, and this name it is essential to know. Sometimes it may be revealed by an external sign, a mark upon the body. E. M. Gordon tells us that he has found among the Chamars a practice known as *Botlagana*. Before burying any important member of the family they are accustomed to make some sign upon the corpse, either with ghee or oil or soot, and when a child is born into the family they examine its body to see whether the mark reappears. If they find it, they consider the child to be the reincarnation of that particular ancestor.[1]

More frequently, however, they have recourse to divination. The parents send for a witch-doctor or a medicine-man or a shaman—in short, for some person capable of discovering the mystic participations. On the West Coast of Africa, as Ellis tells us, the dead often return to earth and are born again into the family to which they belonged in a previous existence. A mother will send for a *babalowo* to tell her which ancestor dwells in the newborn babe, a fact he never fails to reveal, and when this important matter has been settled, he gives advice as to its bringing-up, so that it may conform in every way with its proper character, since the parents are often taken unawares.[2]—In New Zealand, "when the navel-string came off . . . the child was carried to the

[1] E. M. Gordon, " People of Mungeli Tahsil, Bilaspur District," *Journal of Asiatic Society of Bengal*, iii. pp. 48–9 (1902).

[2] A. B. Ellis, *The Yoruba-speaking Peoples*, pp. 128–9, 152.

priest. . . . The end of the *waka pakoko rakau* (idol) was placed in the child's ear, that the *mana* . . . of the god might be transferred to him, and the following *karakia* was repeated. 'Wait till I pronounce your name. What is your name? ' . . . The priest repeated a long list of names, and when the child sneezed, that which was then being uttered was the one selected." [1]—So, too, with the Khonds. " Khond births are celebrated on the seventh day after the event by a feast given to the priest and to the whole village. To determine the best name for the child, the priest drops grains of rice into a cup of water, naming with each grain a deceased ancestor. From the movement of the seed in the fluid, and other observations made on the person of the infant, he pronounces which of his ancestors has reappeared in him, and the child generally, at least among the Northern tribes, receives the name of that ancestor." [2]

This name is not the only or the most important one which the individual will bear. Among many primitive peoples, at each stage of a man's life he receives a name which is the sign, the mystic medium of a new participation set up for him : at the time of his initiation, his marriage, his first slaying of an enemy, his acquiring a scalp, or securing certain game, his entry into a secret society or receiving a higher rank in it, and so on. The first name given him, as a rule shortly after his birth, is thus merely a kind of mystic registration ; it marks the beginning of definite existence. Henceforth he will have a recognized place in the familial and social group. In it he represents a member who has been in complete participation with it in the past, and he is qualified to participate in it in the same way in the future, when he has undergone the necessary ceremony of initiation.

VI

During the long period which follows, lasting usually from earliest infancy till puberty, or at least until initiation, the growing children are left almost entirely to their mothers. The men do not worry about their daughters, and take no

[1] R. Taylor, *Te Ika a Maui*, p. 74.
[2] Macpherson, op. cit., pp. 72–3.

trouble with respect to their sons except to teach them, by
means of games, that which will later be their actual business :
the fabrication and the handling of weapons and implements.
These children, moreover, much loved and not a little spoilt,
are not yet "perfect" members of the social group. They
are in the period which corresponds with that elapsing between
the first obsequies and the ceremony which terminates the
mourning, when the dead is not yet "perfectly" dead, since
his body, or at least its fleshy part, has not entirely decayed,
and still adheres to his bones. In the same way, whilst the
child's body is growing and developing, he is not definitely
"born." His individuality is not yet complete, and many
characteristic features show that this is clearly understood.
Among the Ba-Yaka, for instance, "even men must observe
certain restrictions with regard to the eating of fowls ; if the
bird be a hen, it may be shared by several, but a cock must be
eaten by one man alone, or illness results. He may, however,
give some to his son if not yet circumcised. This fact is
particularly interesting since it seems to show that a male
child before circumcision is not supposed to possess an individuality apart from the father, although it is regarded as
belonging to the village of the mother." [1]

For the child to reach the state of "perfect" man, it is
not enough to be fully grown, or to have arrived at puberty.
His corporal maturity is a necessary, but not an all-sufficing
condition. It is not even the essential one. That which
matters most, in this as in other cases, governed by the orientation peculiar to prelogical mentality, is the mystic elements,
the mysterious practices, rites and ceremonies which will
enable the young man to participate in the very essence of
tribe or totem. If he have not passed through this initiation,
whatever his age may be, he will always be ranked among the
children. We have many facts in proof of this : here are
some, borrowed from a collection published by Webster.
Fison, speaking of the Fijians, noted that an old Wainimala
man made no difference between the men who had not been
initiated and the children, but spoke of them all as *koirano*

[1] Torday and Joyce, "Notes on the Ethnography of the Ba-Yaka,"
J.A.I., xxxvi. p. 42.
[2] *Primitive Secret Societies*, pp. 25 et seq., pp. 205–6.

(children).[1]—An old native of West Kimberley told another observer that until they had undergone subincision (five years after circumcision), boys were like dogs or any other animals.[2]—Howitt bears witness to a significant fact which occurred during the ceremony known as *kadjawalung*, at which he was present. At that time in the native camp there were two or three men of the Biduelli tribe with their wives and children, and also a Krauatun Kurnai man with his wife and child. When the ceremony began, they all went away, except one, because those tribes had no initiation ceremonies, and therefore the visitors had never been " made men." The only one who remained was the old Biduelli patriarch, " and he was now driven crouching among the women and children. The reason was self-evident he had never been ' made a man,' and therefore was no more than a mere boy." [3]—In Savage Island, " a child not so initiated (through *mata pulega*, a ceremony akin to circumcision) is never regarded as a full-born member of the tribe." [4]

This state of minority, which lasts until initiation has taken place, is accompanied by many disabilities and disadvantages. In Samoa, until tattooed, a boy was in his minority. " He could not think of marriage, and he was constantly exposed to taunts and ridicule, as being poor and of low birth, and as having no right to speak in the society of men." [5] In most Australian tribes, " there are various kinds of meat which he must not eat ; he cannot enter into any argument in camp ; his opinion on any question is never asked, and he never thinks of giving it ; he is not expected to engage in fights, and he is not expected to fall in love with any of the young women. In fact, he is a nonentity ; but when he has gone through the initiatory process of being made a young man, he takes his proper place among the members of the tribe." [6] In South Africa, " at puberty the life of an African may be said to begin." [7] One observer

---

[1] The Nanga, or Sacred stone enclosures of Wainimala, *J.A.I.*, xiv. p. 18.
[2] Froggart, *Proceedings of the Linnean Society of New South Wales*, p. 652 (1888).
[3] *The Native Tribes of South-east Australia*, p. 530.
[4] Thomson, " The Natives of Savage Island," *J.A.I.*, xxxi. p. 140.
[5] Turner, *Samoa*, p. 88.
[6] Brough Smyth, *The Aborigines of Victoria*, i. p. 83.
[7] Macdonald, " Manners, Customs . . . of South African Tribes," *J.A.I.*, xix. p. 268.

has summed all this up in a very striking passage. " Like the dead, the children not arrived at puberty may be compared to seed not yet sown. The child not yet adult finds himself in the same state as this seed, that is, a state of inactivity, of death, but of death with potential life within it." [1]

As long as initiation has not taken place, marriage is forbidden. The man who does not yet participate in the mystic essence of the social group is incapable of begetting children able to participate in it one day. Spencer and Gillen tell us : " Every man without exception throughout the central area, in all tribes in which the rite is practised, is subincised . . . before he is allowed to take a wife, and infringement of this rule would simply mean death to him if found out." [2] In East Africa, " no man can marry unless he had entered the galo, or if he married, his children would be killed." [3] As a matter of fact, these children, even as adults, could never be " full " members of the tribe, their father not having been one at the moment of their birth. With certain peoples, however, where the initiation ceremonies can only be celebrated at very long intervals, this principle has had to be abrogated, and married men, fathers of families, have been seen to undergo the tests at the same time as quite young men. " Bonifaz gave us as an example his uncle, who was already married, but was initiated at the same time as himself, then but eleven years old ; because it was such a long time since the festival had been held." (The case of such individuals is a very special one, and has lasting effects.) " A man married under such conditions has no right to enter the house of the spirits, nor to take part in ceremonies from which women and children are excluded. If he has no children as yet, it will be possible to initiate him when the next public ceremony takes place, but if he already be the father of a family, he will be taken unawares and circumcised, perhaps during a journey. Nevertheless, since he has not been ' made a man ' in a public ceremony, so that the women might know of it, he can never

[1] Passarge, " Okawangosumpfland und seine Bewohner," Zeitschrift für Ethnologie, v. p. 706 (1905).
[2] Spencer and Gillen, The Native Tribes of Central Australia, p. 264.
[3] Dale, " Customs of the Natives Inhabiting the Bondei Country," J.A.I., xxv. pp. 188 et seq.

frequent the house of spirits save by stealth, and without the women and children hearing of it." [1]

The initiation ceremonies, therefore, are designed to "perfect" the individual, to render him capable of all the functions pertaining to a legitimate member of the tribe, to complete him as a living being, as the ceremony ending the mourning period renders him "perfectly" dead. It is thus that Spencer and Gillen, who have given a most minute description of these ceremonies, characterize them. "The Engwura . . . is in reality a long series of ceremonies concerned with the totems, and terminating in what may be best described as ordeals by fire, which form the last of the initiatory ceremonies. After the native has passed through these, he becomes what is called Urliara, that is, a perfectly developed member of the tribe. . . ." [2] I shall not lay stress upon these practices, possibly the best known of all that are habitually met with among primitive peoples : numerous instances of them will be found in Frazer's Golden Bough,[3] or in Webster's Primitive Secret Societies.[4] I shall not enter upon a discussion of the theories which have been proposed as an explanation of them either. I will confine myself to drawing attention to the fact, once again, that the attempt to make such practices "intelligible" is often likely to prove contradictory. If it attains its end it is a failure. In fact, that which is "intelligible" to logical thought is very unlikely to coincide with the idea of the prelogical mind. Without pretending to "explain" these practices, I have merely tried to show precisely how they, as well as so many other customs in use by primitive peoples, are related to the collective representations of such peoples, and the laws governing these collective representations.

Now the general idea of such practices is as follows. An aim which we should consider a positive one, such as the capture of game, the cure of a sick person, is pursued by a variety of means in which those of a mystic character largely predominate. Hunting is not possible unless a mystic participation between hunter and quarry be established, and accordingly a whole system of practices designed to secure this is

---

[1] P. W. Schmidt, "Die geheime Jünglingsweihe der Karesau-Insulaner," Anthropos, ii. pp. 1032, 1037–8 (1907).
[2] The Native Tribes of Central Australia, p. 271.
[3] Vol. iii. pp. 422 et seq. [4] Pp. 21–58.

inaugurated. Illness is due to the action of a spirit and no therapeutic methods will have any likelihood of success until the " doctor " is in communication with this spirit, to subdue and expel it, by force if necessary.

Let us apply this idea to initiation. The novices are separated from the women and children with whom they have lived until this time. As a rule, the separation occurs suddenly, and often takes them unawares. Confided to the superintendence and care of a particular adult, to whom they often are definitely related, the novices must submit passively to everything imposed upon them and bear pain uncomplainingly. The tests they undergo are long and difficult, and often they are actual tortures : deprivation of sleep, of food, being whipped with cords or rods, cudgellings upon the head, pulling out the hair and extracting the teeth, branding, circumcision, subincision, bleeding, the stings of poisonous insects, suffocation by smoke, being suspended by means of hooks fastened in their flesh, ordeal by fire, etc. The secondary motive of these practices may no doubt be to ascertain the novices' courage and powers of endurance, and to test their virility, by seeing whether they are capable of bearing pain and of keeping a secret. But the primal aim sought after is a mystic effect which in no way depends upon their will-power : the important matter is to establish a participation between them and the mystic realities which are the very essence of the social group, the totems, the mythic or human ancestors, and to give them, by means of this participation, a " new soul," as it has been termed. Herein we perceive difficulties which appear insurmountable to our logical thought, since they raise the question of the unity or of the multiplicity of the soul, whilst the pre ogical mind finds no difficulty in imagining that which we call soul as at the same time one and multiple. Just as the North American Indian hunter, by fasting for a week, establishes between himself and the spirit of the bear a mystic bond which will enable him to find and kill bears, so do the tests imposed upon the novices establish between them and the mystic beings in whom they must participate, a relation which is indispensable to the spiritual fusion which is desired. It is not the material aspect of these tests that is of importance ; that, in itself, has as little to do with the case as has the pain of the patient, with respect to the success of a surgical operation. The means employed by primitives to induce in novices the required condition of receptivity are, as a matter of fact, exceedingly painful, but it is not because they are painful that they make use of them, nor would they give them up for that reason, either. Their attention is fixed upon one single point, and it is the only one that matters : this is the condition of special receptivity in which the novices must be placed if the desired participation is to be realized.

This condition of receptivity mainly consists in a kind of loss of personality, and of consciousness, induced by fatigue, pain, feebleness, privations,—in short, in an apparent death followed by a new birth. The women and children, (who are excluded from these ceremonies, on pain of the direst penalties) are made to believe that the novices actually die. The novices themselves are induced to believe it, and perhaps the older men share this belief, to a certain extent. " The colour of death is white, and the novices are painted white." [1] There are numerous features of this kind and, as Frazer has so clearly shown, the testimony respecting it is unanimous. But if we remember what death and birth mean to the pre-logical mind, we shall see that such a mind *must* imagine thus the condition which permits the participation aimed at in the initiation of the young men. Death is in no case the pure and simple suppression of all the forms of activity and existence which constitute life. The primitive has no idea whatever of such annihilation. That which we call death is never, in his eyes, absolute. The dead live and they die, and even after this second death they continue to exist, while awaiting another reincarnation. That which we call death is accomplished in successive stages. The first stage, that which the initiation tests strive to imitate, is nothing but a change of dwelling, a transference of the soul which has momentarily abandoned its body, while remaining in the immediate vicinity. It is the beginning of the rupture of participation. It places the individual in a special state of susceptibility and receptivity, akin to the dream-states, catalepsy, or ecstasy

<hr>

[1] Passarge, op. cit., v. p. 706.

which, in all primitive peoples, are the invariable condition of communication with the invisible world.

Thus by its attachment, in respect to initiation, to practices which produce a kind of death (in the primitive's sense of the word) primitive mentality has followed its usual course. As ever, it has translated into action and reality its collective representations.

VII

In most of the primitive peoples we know, there are personages who undergo an additional initiation. These are the wizards, medicine-men, shamans, doctors, or whatever else they may be called. At the period of puberty, they pass through the tests imposed upon all young men ; and in order to become capable of fulfilling the important functions they will be called upon to exercise, they have also to undergo a further novitiate, which lasts for months or even years, and is carried on under the superintendence of their masters, i.e. witch-doctors or shamans in actual practice. Now the resemblance between the initiation rites of witch-doctors or shamans, and those of the novices of the tribe in general, is a striking one. Still, the general initiation of novices is imposed on all ; it is comparatively public, (except as far as women and children are concerned) ; and it necessarily takes place at fairly regular intervals. The initiation of witch-doctors, shamans, and medicine-men, on the contrary, is reserved for certain individuals who have a " vocation " ; it is surrounded by mystery, and only takes place when these persons meet. As to the details of the tests, and the effect obtained by them, (the apparent death and the new birth), however, analogy occasionally becomes identity. " When they are being made, the candidates are not allowed to have any rest, but are obliged to stand or walk about until they are thoroughly exhausted and scarcely know what is happening to them. They are not allowed to drink a drop of water or taste food of any kind. They become, in fact, dazed and stupefied." [1] When this condition has reached its height, one may say that they are dead. In other words, the spirits (*iruntarinia*) who

---

[1] Spencer and Gillen, *The Northern Tribes of Central Australia*, p. 485.

preside at the initiation, kill them and then cause them to be born again. " At break of day, one of the *iruntarinia* comes to the mouth of the cave, and finding the man asleep, throws at him an invisible lance which pierces the neck from behind, passes through the tongue, making therein a large hole, and then comes out through the mouth. . . . A second lance thrown by the *iruntarinia* pierces the head from ear to ear, and the victim falls dead and is at once carried into the depths of the cave "—(where the spirits dwell).

" Within the cave, the *iruntarinia* removes all the internal organs and provides the man with a completely new set, [1] after which operation has been successfully performed, he presently comes to life again ; but in a condition of insanity.[2] . . . For several days the man remains more or less strange in his appearance and behaviour until one morning it is noticed that he has painted with powdered-charcoal and fat a broad band across the bridge of his nose. All signs of insanity have disappeared, and it is at once recognized that a new medicine-man has graduated." [3]

It is the same in South America. " The *pajé* (witch-doctor) becomes such of his own free will. From his youth up he must prepare himself for his sinister rôle. He must withdraw to some solitary and inaccessible spot, fast, maintain silence, and practise all sorts of deprivations for many years he must dance wild and obscene dances until he falls exhausted, and he must even, like the young men undergoing the initiatory tests, expose himself to the sting of the large poisonous ants." [4]

The same rites, resulting in the same apparent death, are often the indispensable condition of initiation, not to the function of shaman or witch-doctor, but merely to membership of a secret society the candidate desires to enter. For instance, with the Abipones, when a man desires to be raised to the status of *hocheri*, " they make a previous trial of his fortitude . . . to sit down at home for three days, and

---

[1] A ceremony identical with that undergone by the tribal novices during their apparent death.

[2] Again like the novices.

[3] *The Native Tribes of Central Australia*, pp. 524–5 ; *The Northern Tribes of Central Australia*, pp. 480–4.

[4] Von Martius, *Beiträge zur Ethnographie Süd-Amerika's*, i. p. 558.

during that time to abstain from speaking, eating and drinking. . . . On the evening preceding the military function, all the women flock to the threshold of his tent. Pulling off their clothes from the shoulder to the middle, and dishevelling their hair, they stand in a long row (signs of mourning) and lament for the ancestors of him who is, next day, to be adorned with a military dignity. . . . The next day the initiated man directs his course towards all the points of the compass in turn, and then there is a ceremony in which an old woman shaves off his hair, and he receives a new name." [1] He has clearly passed through death and a new birth.—Among the Clallams, a coast tribe on the mainland opposite the south end of Vancouver, " the novice of the order " (a secret society) " must for three days and three nights fast alone in a mysterious lodge prepared for him, round which, during all that time, the brethren already initiated sing and dance. This period elapsed, during which it would seem that the old nature has been killed out of him, he is taken up as one dead, and soused with the nearest cold water, where he is washed till he revives, which thing they call ' washing the dead.' When his senses are sufficiently gathered to him, he is set on his feet ; upon which he runs off into the forest, whence he soon reappears a perfect medicine-man, rattle in hand and decked out with the various trappings of his profession." [2] Lastly, in the Lower Congo territory, we have the *Nkimba*, " an institution which has a wide range among the Lower Congo tribes," (in which) " the initiatory rites are in charge of the *nganga*, or fetish man, who lives with his assistants in an enclosure near each village. The candidate for this order, having previously imbibed a sleeping potion, swoons in some public assembly and is at once surrounded by the *nganga* and his assistants, who take him to the enclosure. It is given out that he is dead, and has gone to the spirit world, whence, by the power of the great *nganga*, he will subsequently be restored to life. The novice remains with the *nganga* for a prolonged period, sometimes for several years, learning a new language, probably an archaic Bantu, and receiving instructions in the mysteries of the order. No woman is allowed to look on the face of one of

[1] Dobrizhoffer, op. cit., ii. pp. 441–5.
[2] Bancroft, *The Native Races of the Pacific Coast of North America*, iii. p. 155.

the *Nkimba*, who daily parade through the woods, or the surrounding country, singing a strange, weird song to warn the uninitiated from their approach. When brought back to the village, and introduced by his new name, he affects to treat everything with surprise as one come to a new life from another world ; to recognize no one, not even his father or mother, while his relatives receive him as raised from the dead ; and for several days the newcomer is permitted to take anything he fancies in the village, and is treated with every kindness until it is supposed that he has become accustomed to his surroundings. . . . He then decides whether he will become a fetish-man or return to his ordinary life." [1]

We might quote many similar instances, but these will doubtless suffice to demonstrate that the initiatory rites for witch-doctors, shamans, medicine-men, fetish-men, etc., or members of some secret society, in their general procedure as, frequently, in their most insignificant details, reproduce the public ceremonies of initiation imposed upon the youths of the tribe when they reach puberty. Now there can be no manner of doubt as to the end sought by the former : they are designed to enable the candidates to participate in mystic realities, to put them in communication, or rather, in communion, with certain spirits. Does not the power of witch-doctor or shaman proceed from the privileges he possesses of entering into relation, when he pleases, by means of which he holds the secret, with occult forces known only to the ordinary man by the effect they produce ? There is therefore no doubt, either, as to the end aimed at by the practices which constitute the usual initiatory rites for the youths of the community. They are magic operations designed to place them in a condition of ecstasy, unconsciousness, " death," indispensable if they are to participate in the essentially mystic reality of their tribe, their totem and their ancestors. Once this participation has been effected, the novices are " full " members of the tribe, for to them its secrets have been revealed. From this moment, these full members, these complete men, are the depositaries of all that the social group holds most sacred, and the sense of their responsibility never leaves them. A man's life is, as it

[1] Glave, *Six Years of Adventure in Congoland*, p. 80, quoted in Webster's *Primitive Secret Societies*, pp. 173–4.

were, " sharply marked out into two parts . . . first, ordinary life, common to all the men and women . . . second, what gradually becomes of greater and greater importance to him, the portion of his life devoted to matters of a secret or sacred nature.   As he grows older he takes an increasing share in these, until finally this side of his life occupies by far the greater part of his thoughts." [1]   At last, death supervenes, and the cycle, of which I have essayed to portray the principal stages, begins once more.

[1] Spencer and Gillen, *The Northern Tribes of Central Australia*, p. 33

PART IV

CHAPTER IX

THE TRANSITION TO THE HIGHER MENTAL TYPES

INTRODUCTION

ANALYSIS of the facts studied in the preceding chapters seems to bear out the essential theses which this books aims at establishing :

(1) The institutions, customs and beliefs of primitives imply a mentality which is prelogical and mystic, oriented differently from our own.

(2) The collective representations and interconnections which constitute such a mentality are governed by the law of participation and in so far they take but little account of the logical law of contradiction.

It is the natural consequence of such a position that I have been endeavouring to demonstrate. It is useless to try and explain the institutions and customs and beliefs of undeveloped peoples by starting from the psychological and intellectual analysis of " the human mind " as *we* know it. No interpretation will be satisfactory unless it has for its starting-point the prelogical and mystic mentality underlying the various forms of activity in primitives.

But it is not only the study of inferior races that comprehension of this prelogical, mystic mentality helps. Subsequent mental types derive from it, and cannot avoid reproducing, in forms more or less apparent, some of its features. To understand these, therefore, it is necessary to refer back to a type which is comparatively " primitive." A vast field for positive research into the mental functioning of aggregates of various kinds, as well as into our own laws of thought, is thus laid open to us. In conclusion, I should like to show, by referring to certain important points, that this research may even now prove fertile of result, if we accept as a working hypothesis the idea of prelogical mentality as defined in this book.

I

In aggregates of the type furthest removed from our own, the collective representations which express the mentality of the group are not always, strictly speaking, representations. What we are accustomed to understand by representation, even direct and intuitive, implies duality in unity. The object is presented to the subject as in a certain sense distinct from himself ; except in states such as ecstasy, that is, border states in which representation, properly so called, disappears, since the fusion between subject and object has become complete. Now in analysing the most characteristic of the primitive's institutions—such as totemic relationship, the *intichiuma* and initiation ceremonies, etc.—we have found that his mind does more than present his object to him : it possesses it and is possessed by it. It communes with it and participates in it, not only in the ideological, but also in the physical and mystic sense of the word. The mind does not imagine it merely ; it lives it. In a great many cases the rites and ceremonies have the effect of giving reality to a veritable symbiosis, that between the totemic group and its totem, for instance. At this stage, therefore, rather than speak of collective representations, it would be wiser to call them collective mental states of extreme emotional intensity, in which representation is as yet undifferentiated from the movements and actions which make the communion towards which it tends a reality to the group. Their participation in it is so effectually *lived* that it is not yet properly imagined.

We shall not be astonished, therefore, that Spencer and Gillen should have discovered in the Australian aborigines they studied " not the slightest trace of anything that might be described as ancestor-worship " . . .[1] very few traditions about the origin of animals ; few myths ; and no objects of worship, properly so called ; no personification of natural

[1] *The Northern Tribes of Central Australia*, p. 494.

forces or of animal or vegetable species.[1] Similar paucity in this respect has been noted by Ehrenreich [2] in the most primitive races of South America—peoples who are unfortunately far less known to us than those of Australia. This fact demonstrates that the prelogical and mystic collective mentality is still actively predominant in the social group. The feeling of symbiosis effected between the individuals of the group, or between a certain human group and one which is animal or vegetable in substance, is *directly* expressed by institutions and ceremonies. At the moment it needs no symbols other than those used in the ceremonies. Such are the *churinga*, the decorations and ornaments with which the actors in the ceremonies adorn themselves, the dances, masks, gestures and traditions relating to the ancestors of the *Alcheringa*, among Australian aborigines ; or again, among the Indians of Brazil (the Bororo, Bakairi, and others), the entire group of customs known as couvade, in which a participation, both mystic and physical, between parents and child is so evidently felt and realized.

This form of mental activity, which differs so notably from the forms which our own aggregates afford us the opportunity of studying, is not yet seeking to understand or explain its object. It is oriented in quite another direction ; it cannot be dissociated from the mystic practices which give effect to its participations. The ubiquity or multipresence of existing beings, the identity of one with many, of the same and of another, of the individual and the species—in short, everything that would scandalize and reduce to despair thought which is subject to the law of contradiction, is implicitly admitted by this prelogical mentality. It is, moreover, impermeable to what we call experience, i.e. to the lessons which may be learnt by observation of the objective relations between phenomena. It has its own experience, one which is wholly mystic, much more complete and exhaustive and decisive than the ofttimes ambiguous experience, the censorship of which thought, properly so called, knows that she must accept. It is entirely satisfied with this.

In this respect there is nothing more significant than the

[1] *The Northern Tribes of Central Australia*, p. 442.
[2] *Die Mythen und Legenden der Süd-Amerikanischen Urvölker*, pp. 12, 15.

primitive classifications I have already cited, to which Durk-heim and Mauss have drawn attention, for in the primitive mentality these, to a certain extent, occupy the position held by the categories in logical thought.[1] The participations felt by the members of the social body and expressed in their divisions and groupings, are extended to all the entities which such a mentality imagines. Animal and vegetable orders, the heavenly bodies, inorganic matter, directions in space, are all fitted into some division or other of the social frame-work. To give but one example only : " In this tribe," says Howitt, " the two main classes and the four sub-classes divide, so to speak, the whole universe into groups. The two main classes are *Mallera* or *Wuthera* ; consequently all other objects are *Mallera* or *Wuthera*. This custom is carried to such an extreme that a medicine-man who is a *Mallera*, for instance, in his magical operations, can only use things which belong to his own class. Moreover, when he dies, the bier on which his body rests must perforce be made of the wood of a tree of the *Mallera* class." [2]

A certain community of being is thus immediately felt, not only between members of the same totemic family, but between all entities of any kind whatsoever which form part of the same class and are linked together in mystic fellowship. And this feeling, which environs a representation still undiffen-tiated, is necessarily accompanied by the feeling (and the undifferentiated representation) of a non-participation with beings and objects belonging to other classes. To a mentality of this kind, the feeling of not being bound by any mystic relation to another being in the vicinity, is not merely a nega-tive sentiment : in certain cases it may be a very definite and positive feeling. We may reconstruct it, to a certain extent, by conjuring up what is now called racial antagonism, and the sentiments which that which is " foreign " may arouse, even among civilized people. From the standpoint of action, therefore, there arises a need to resort to certain individuals or to the members of a certain group, who alone possess the mystic qualifications enabling them to carry out a ceremony or execute a dance or a rite, or merely to be

---

[1] Vide Chap. III. p. 128.
[2] Howitt, " Notes on Australian Message Sticks," *J.A.I.*, xviii. p. 326.

present at it. The result to be obtained depends above all upon the mystic participations between the classes of beings and of objects.

II

In his recent work on *Animism in the Indian Archipelago*, Kruijt believes it necessary to distinguish two successive stages in the evolution of primitive communities : one in which individual spirits are reputed to inform and inspire every being and every object (animals, plants, boulders, stars, weapons, tools, and so forth), and another and earlier one, in which individualization has not as yet taken place, in which there is a diffused principle capable of penetrating everywhere, a kind of universal and widespread force which seems to animate persons and things, to act in them and endow them with life.[1] Here we recognize Marett's "pre-animistic" stage, upon which Durkheim and Mauss have also insisted. Kruijt adds—and this remark of his has a very important bearing upon the subject with which we are concerned—that the differentiation of these two periods corresponds with a difference in the mentality of the social group. At the time when souls and spirits are not yet individualized, the individual consciousness of every member of the group is and remains strictly solidary with the collective consciousness. It does not distinctly break away from it ; it does not even contradict itself in uniting with it ; that which does dominate it is the uninterrupted feeling of participation. Only later, when the human individual becomes clearly conscious of himself as an individual, when he explicitly differentiates himself from the group of which he feels himself a member, do beings and objects outside himself also begin to appear to him as provided with individual minds or spirits during this life and after death.[2]

Thus, when the relations between the social group and the individuals composing it are evolved, the collective representations, the group ideas, are modified at the same time. In its purest form primitive mentality implied a participation which was felt and lived, both by individuals with the social group, and by the social group with the surrounding ones.

---

[1] Kruijt, *Het Animisme in den Indischen Archipel*, pp. 66–7 (1906).
[2] Ibid., pp. 2–5.

Both these participations are solidary, and the modifications of the one reflect accordingly upon the other. In proportion as the individual consciousness of each member of the group tends to declare itself, the feeling of a mystic symbiosis of the social group with surrounding groups of beings and objects becomes less intimate and direct and less constant. Here as there bonds which are more or less explicit tend to take the place of the feeling of direct communion. In a word, participation tends to become ideological. For instance, as soon as individual consciousness begins to grasp itself as such and consequently to distinguish individuals as such in the surrounding groups of beings, these ideas also define, more or less distinctly, that of the groups as such, and as a further consequence, an idea of the mystic relations uniting the individuals of a group, and the different groups in their turn. The communion which is no longer actually lived, the need for which still appears just as pressing, will be obtained by means of intermediaries. The Bororo tribe will no longer declare that they *are* araras. They will say that their ancestors were araras, that they are of the same substance as the araras, that they will become araras after death, that it is forbidden to kill and eat araras, except under conditions which are rigidly defined, such as totemic sacrifice, etc.

Following on the paucity I recently noted in the Aruntas, the Bororo and other aggregates of a very primitive type, we shall find, in those more advanced, such as the Huichols, the Zuñis of New Mexico, the Maoris of New Zealand, an increasing wealth of collective representations properly so called, and of symbols. In the former the feeling of mystic symbiosis is still intense and permanent. To express itself it need but resort to the very organization of the social group and the ceremonies which assure its prosperity and the relations with surrounding groups. In the latter, the need of participation is perhaps no less active. But as this participation is no longer directly felt by every member of the social group, it is obtained by means of an ever-increasing display of religious or magic practices, of sacred and divine beings and objects, by rites performed by priests and members of secret societies, by myths, etc. F. H. Cushing's admirable work on the Zuñis, for instance, shows us how a prelogical and mystic mentality of an already exalted type expands into a magnificent efflorescence of collective representations destined to express, or even to produce, participations which are no longer directly felt.

The " vehicles " of these participations are very diverse in their nature. In many communities we find, concurrent with representations similar to those of the Melanesian *mana*,[1] collective representations of more or less individualized spirits, of souls more or less distinctly conceived, mythical beings with an animal or human or semi-human form, heroes, genii, gods. The observers find names for them easily enough. But the difficulty is not to allow ourselves to be deceived by these names, but to reconstruct under them the mystic and prelogical collective representations which no longer exist for us.

This difficulty never appears so great as when it is a question of defining the " religion " of the most primitive peoples we are acquainted with. For we might say equally well that the mentality which expresses itself in their collective representations is wholly religious, or, in another sense of the word, that it is hardly at all so. In so far as a mystic communion with, and actual participation in, the object of the religious sentiment and ritual practice is of the very essence of religion, primitive mentality must be declared religious because it does realize a communion of such a nature, and indeed to the highest degree it is possible to imagine. But in other respects it does not seem correct to speak of it as " religious," at least to this extent, that by reason of the direct character of this participation it does not recognize as an ideal outside and above itself the beings with whom it feels itself united in mystic and intimate communion. We may recall the definite statements made by Spencer and Gillen on this point.

As a matter of fact, the primitives' " religious " ideas are a constant source of error and confusion to us. Our own way of thinking makes us imagine the objects of their thought in the attitude of divine beings or objects, and that it is by virtue of this divine character of theirs that homage, sacrifice, prayer, adoration and all actual religious belief is directed towards them. But to the primitive mind, on the contrary, these

[1] Cf. Hubert and Mauss, " Mélanges d'Histoire des Religions," *Année Sociologique*, pp. xx et seq.

objects and these beings become divine only when the participation they guarantee has ceased to be direct. The Arunta
who feels that he *is* both himself and the ancestor whose
churinga was entrusted to him at the time of his initiation,
knows nothing of ancestor-worship. The Bororo does not
make the parrots, which *are* Bororo, the objects of a religious
cult. It is only in aggregates of a more advanced type that
we find an ancestor-worship, a cult of heroes, gods, sacred
animals, etc. The ideas which we call really religious are
thus a kind of differentiated product resulting from a prior
form of mental activity. The participation or communion
first realized by mystic symbiosis and by the practices which
affirmed it is obtained later by union with the object of the
worship and belief called religious, with the ancestor, the
god. The personality of these objects comprises, as we know,
an infinite variety of grades, from mystic forces of which we
cannot say whether they are single or manifold, to divinities
clearly defined by physical and moral attributes, such as those
of the Melanesian or the Greek deities. It depends above all on
the degree of development attained by the group studied, i.e.,
upon the type of its institutions as well as its mental type.

III

When we consider myths in their relation to the mentality
of the social groups in which they originate, we are led to
similar conclusions. Where the participation of the individual in the social group is still directly felt, where the participation of the group with surrounding groups is actually
lived—that is, as long as the period of mystic symbiosis lasts—
myths are meagre in number and of poor quality. This is
the case with the Australian aborigines and the Indians of
Northern and Central Brazil, etc. Where the aggregates are
of a more advanced type, as, for instance, the Zuñis, Iroquois,
Melanesians, and others, there is, on the contrary, an in-
creasingly luxuriant outgrowth of mythology. Can myths
then likewise be the products of primitive mentality which
appear when this mentality is endeavouring to realize a participation no longer directly felt—when it has recourse to intermediaries, and vehicles designed to secure a communion which

has ceased to be a living reality ?   Such a hypothesis may seem to be a bold one, but we view myths with other eyes than those of the human beings whose mentality they reflect.   We see in them that which they do not perceive, and that which they imagine there we no longer realize.   For example, when we read a Maori or Zuñi or any other myth, we read it translated into our own language, and this very translation is a betrayal.   To say nothing of the construction of the sentences, which is bound to be affected by our customary habits of thought, if only in the very order of the words, to primitives the words themselves have an atmosphere which is wholly mystic, whilst in our minds they chiefly evoke associations having their origin in experience.   We speak, as we think, by means of concepts.   Words, especially those expressive of group-ideas, portrayed in myths, are to the primitive mystic realities, each of which determines a *champ de force*.   From the emotional point of view, the mere listening to the myth is to them something quite different from what it is to us. What they hear in it awakens a whole gamut of harmonics which do not exist for us.

Moreover, in a myth of which we take note, that which mainly interests us, that which we seek to understand and interpret, is the actual tenor of the recital, the linking-up of facts, the occurrence of episodes, the thread of the story, the adventures of the hero or mythical animal, and so forth. Hence the theories, momentarily regarded as classic, which see in myths a symbolic presentment of certain natural phenomena, or else the result of a " disease of language " ; hence the classifications (like that of Andrew Lang, for instance) which arrange myths in categories according to their content.[1] But this is overlooking the fact that the prelogical, mystic mentality is oriented differently from our own.   It is undoubtedly not indifferent to the doings and adventures and vicissitudes related in myths ; it is even certain that these interest and intrigue the primitive's mind.   But it is not the positive content of the myth that primarily appeals to him. He does not consider it as a thing apart ; he undoubtedly sees it no more than *we* see the bony framework beneath the flesh of a living animal, although we know very well that it is there.

[1] *Encylopædia Britannica.   Mythology* (9th ed.), xvii. pp. 156–7.

24

That which appeals to him, arouses his attention and evokes his emotion, is the mystic element which surrounds the positive content of the story. This element alone gives myth and legend their value and social importance and, I might almost add, their power.

It is not easy to make such a trait felt nowadays, precisely because these mystic elements have disappeared as far as we are concerned, and what we call a myth is but the inanimate corpse which remains after the vital spark has fled. Yet i. the perception of beings and objects in nature is wholly mystic to the mind of the primitive, would not the presentation of these same beings and objects in myths be so likewise? Is not the orientation in both cases necessarily the same? To make use of a comparison, though but an imperfect one, let us hark back to the time when in Europe, some centuries ago the only history taught was sacred history. Whence came the supreme value and importance of that history, both to those who taught and those who learnt? Did it lie in the actual facts, in the knowledge of the sequence of judges, kings or prophets, of the misfortunes of the Israelites during their strife with the neighbouring tribes? Most certainly not. It is not from the historical, but from the sacred, point of view that the Biblical narrative was of incomparable interest. It is because the true God, perpetually intervening in the story makes His presence manifest at all times and, to the Christian idea, causes the coming of His Son to be anticipated. In short it is the mystic atmosphere which surrounds the facts and prevents them from being ordinary battles, massacres or revolutions. Finally it is because Christendom finds in it a witness, itself divine, of its communion with its God.

Myths are, in due proportion, the Biblical narrative of primitive peoples. The preponderance of mystic elements however, in the group ideas of myths, is even greater than in our sacred history. At the same time, since the law of parti cipation still predominates in the primitive mind, the myth is accompanied by a very intense feeling of communion with the mystic reality it interprets. When the adventures exploits, noble deeds, death and resurrection of a beneficent and civilizing hero are recounted in a myth, for instance, i is not the fact of his having given his tribe the idea of making a fire or of cultivating mealies that of itself interests and especially appeals to the listeners. It is here as in the Biblical narrative, the participation of the social group in its own past, it is the feeling that the group is, as it were, actually living in that epoch, that there is a kind of mystic communion with that which has made it what it is. In short, to the mind of the primitive, myths are both an expression of the solidarity of the social group with itself in its own epoch and in the past and with the groups of beings surrounding it, and a means of maintaining and reviving this feeling of solidarity.

Such considerations, it may be urged, might apply to myths in which the human or semi-human ancestors of the social group, its civilizing or its protecting heroes, figure ; but are they valid in the case of myths relating to sun, moon, stars, thunder, the sea, the rivers, winds, cardinal points, etc. ? It is only to an intellect such as ours that the objection appears a serious one. The primitive's mind works along the lines that are peculiar to it. The mystic elements in his ideas matter considerably more to him than the objective features which, in our view, determine and classify beings of all kinds, and as a consequence the classifications which we regard as most clearly evident escape his attention. Others, which to us are inconceivable, however, claim it. Thus the relationship and communion of the social group with a certain animal or vegetable species, with natural phenomena like the wind or the rain, with a constellation, appear quite as simple to him as his communion with an ancestor or a legendary hero. To give but one instance, the aborigines studied by Spencer and Gillen regard the sun as a Panunga woman, belonging to a definite sub-class, and consequently bound by the ties of relationship to all the other clans of the tribe. Let us refer again to the analogy indicated above. In the sacred history of primitives natural history forms a part.

If this view of the chief significance of myths and of their characteristic function in aggregates of a certain mental type be correct, several consequences of some importance will ensue. This view does not render the careful and detailed study of myths superfluous. It provides neither a theory for classifying them in genera and species, nor an exact method of interpreting them, nor does it throw positive light upon their relations with religious observances. But it does enable us to avoid certain definite errors, and at any rate it permits of our stating the problem in terms which do not falsify the solution beforehand. It provides a general method of procedure, and this is to mistrust "explanatory" hypotheses which would account for the genesis of myths by a psychological and intellectual activity similar to our own, even while assuming it to be childish and unreflecting.

The myths which have long been considered the easiest to explain, for instance, those regarded as absolutely lucid, such as the Indian nature-myths, are on the contrary the most intriguing. As long as one could see in them the spontaneous product of a naïve imagination impressed by the great natural phenomena, the interpretation of them was in fact self-evident. But if we have once granted that the mentality which generates myths is differently oriented from ours, and that its collective representations obey their own laws, the chief of which is the law of participation, the very intelligibility of these myths propounds a fresh problem. We are led to believe that, far from being primitive, these myths, in the form in which they have reached us, are something absolutely artificial, that they have been very highly and consciously elaborated, and this to such an extent that their original form is almost entirely lost. On the other hand, the myths which may possibly seem the easiest to explain are those which most directly express the sense of the social group's relationship, whether it be with its legendary members and those no longer living, or with the groups of beings which surround it. For such myths appear to be the most primitive in the sense that they are most readily allied with the peculiar prelogical, mystic mentality of the least civilized aggregates. Such, among others, are the totemic myths.

If, however, the aggregates belong to a type even slightly more advanced, the interpretation of their myths very soon becomes risky and perhaps impossible. In the first place, their increasing complexity diminishes our chances of correctly following up the successive operations of the mentality which produces these myths. This mentality not only refuses to be bound by the law of contradiction—a feature which most myths reveal at first sight, so to speak—but it neither abstracts nor associates, and accordingly it does not symbolize as our thought does. Our most ingenious conjectures, therefore, always risk going astray.

If Cushing had not obtained the interpretation of their myths from the Zuñis themselves, would any modern intellect have ever succeeded in finding a clue to this prehistoric labyrinth? The true exposition of myths which are somewhat complicated involves a reconstruction of the mentality which has produced them. This is a result which our habits of thought would scarcely allow us to hope for, unless, like Cushing, a savant were exceptionally capable of creating a " primitive " mentality for himself, and of faithfully transcribing the confidences of his adopted compatriots.

Moreover, even in the most favourable conditions, the state in which the myths are when we collect them may suffice to render them unintelligible and make any coherent interpretation impossible. Very frequently we have no means of knowing how far back they date. If they are not a recent product, who is our authority for assuming that some fragments at any rate have not disappeared, or, on the other hand, may not myths which were originally quite distinct, have been mingled in one incongruous whole? The mystic elements which were the predominant feature at the time when the myth originated may have lost some of their importance if the mentality of the social group has evolved at the same time as their institutions and their relations with neighbouring groups. May not the myth which has gradually come to be a mystery to this altered mentality have been mutilated, added to, transformed, to bring it into line with the new collective representations which dominate the group? May not this adaptation have been performed in a contrary sense, without regard to the participations which the myth originally expressed? Let us assume—an assumption by no means unreasonable—that it has undergone several successive transformations of this kind: by what analysis can we hope ever to retrace the evolution which has been accomplished, to find once more the elements which have disappeared, to correct the misconceptions grafted upon one another? The same problem occurs with respect to rites and customs which are often perpetuated throughout the ages, even while they are being distorted, completed in a contrary sense, or acquiring a new significance to replace that which is no longer understood.

IV

When the participations which matter most to the social group are secured by means of intermediaries or " vehicles," instead of being felt and realized in more direct fashion, the change reacts upon the mentality of the group itself. If, for instance, a certain family or a certain person, a chief, a medicine-man in any tribe is represented as " presiding " over the sequence of the seasons, the regularity of the rainfall, the conservation of species which are advantageous—in short the periodic recurrence of the phenomena upon which the existence of the tribe depends—the group-idea will be peculiarly mystic, and it will preserve the characteristic features proper to prelogical mentality to a very high degree. Participation, concentrated, as it were, upon the beings who are its media, its chosen vessels, thus itself becomes ideological. By force of contrast, other families, other individuals of the social group, the neighbouring groups not interested in this participation, are represented in a more indifferent and impartial way, a fashion less mystic and therefore more objective. This means that a more and more definite and permanent distinction tends to be established between sacred beings and objects on the one hand, and profane beings and objects on the other. The former, inasmuch as they are the necessary vehicles of participation, are essentially and eternally sacred. The latter only become so intermittently by virtue of their communion with the former, and in the intervening periods they present no more than faint, derivative mystic features.

This leads to two connected consequences. In the first place, since the beings and the objects among which the social group lives are no longer felt to be in direct communion with it, the original classifications by which this communion was expressed tend to become obliterated, and there is a redistribution of less mystic nature, founded upon something other than the ramifications of the social group. Ideas of animal and plant life, the stars, etc., are doubtless still impregnated with mystic elements, but not all of them to the same extent.

Some of them are markedly so, others to a far lesser degree, and this difference brings about fresh classifications. The beings and the objects represented as " containers " of mystic virtue, the vehicles of participation, are inevitably differentiated from those which do not possess this supreme interest for the social group. The latter are beginning to be ranged according to an interest of another order ; their distinguishing features are less mystic, but more objective. In other words, the collective representations of these beings and objects is beginning to tend towards that which we call " concept." It is still remote from this, but the process which is to bring it nearer has already begun.

Moreover, the perception of these entities at the same time loses some of its mystic character. The attributes we term objective, by which we define and classify entities of all kinds, are to the primitive enveloped in a complex of other elements much more important, elements exacting almost exclusive attention, at any rate to the extent allowed by the necessities of life. But if this complex becomes simpler and the mystic elements lose their predominance, the objective attributes *ipso facto* readily attract and retain the attention. The part played by perception proper is increased to the extent in which that of the mystic collective representations diminishes. Such a modification is favourable to the change of classification of which we have spoken, and in its turn this change reacts upon the method of perceiving, as an inducted stream reacts upon the main current.

Thus, as by degrees the participations are less directly felt, the collective representations more nearly approach that which we properly call " idea "—that is, the intellectual, cognitive factor occupies more and more space in it. It tends to free itself from the affective and motor elements in which it was at first enveloped, and thus arrives at differentiating itself. Primitive mentality, as a consequence, is again modified in another respect. In aggregates in which it is least impaired, in which its predominance is at its maximum, we have found it impervious to experience. The potency of the collective representations and their interconnections is such that the most direct evidence of the senses cannot counteract it, whilst the interdependence of the most extraordinary kind between phenomena is a matter of unwavering faith. But when perception becomes less mystic, and the preconnections no longer impose the same sovereign authority, surrounding nature is seen with less prejudiced eyes and the collective representations which are evolving begin to feel the effect of experience. Not all at the same time, nor to the same extent: on the contrary, it is certain that these are unequally modified, in accordance with a good many diverse circumstances, and especially with the degree of interest felt by the social group in the object. It is on the points in which participation has become weakest that the mystic preconnections most quickly yield, and the objective relations first rise to the surface.

At the time when the mentality of primitive peoples grows more accessible to experience, it becomes, too, more alive to the law of contradiction. Formerly this was almost entirely a matter of indifference, and the primitive's mind, oriented according to the law of participation, perceived no difficulty at all in statements which to us are absolutely contradictory. A person is himself and at the same time another being; he is in one place and he is also somewhere else; he is individual as well as collective (as when the individual identifies himself with his group), and so on. The prelogical mind found such statements quite satisfactory, because it did more than perceive and understand them to be true. By virtue of that which I have called a mystic symbiosis, it felt, and lived, the truth of them. When, however, the intensity of this feeling in the collective representations diminishes, the logical difficulty in its turn begins to make its presence felt. Then by degrees the intermediaries, the vehicles of participation, appear. They render it *representable* by the most varied methods—transmission, contact, transference of mystic qualities—they secure that communion of substance and of life which was formerly sensed in a direct way, but which runs the risk of appearing unintelligible as soon as it is no longer lived.

Properly speaking, the absurdities to which the primitive mind remains insensible are of two kinds, undoubtedly closely connected with each other, but yet appearing very different to our way of thinking. Some, like those we have just instanced, arise out of what seems to us an infringement of the logical law of contradiction. These manifest themselves gradually, as the participations formerly felt are "precipitated" in the form of definite statements. Whilst the feeling of participation remains a lively one, language conceals these absurdities, but it betrays them when the feeling loses some of its intensity. Others have their source in the preconnections which the collective representations establish between persons, things, occurrences. But these preconnections are only absurd through their incompatibility with the definitely fixed terms for these persons, things, occurrences—terms which the prelogical mind has not at its command in the beginning. It is only when such a mind has grown more cognizant of the lessons taught by experience, when the attributes we term "objective" get the better of the mystic elements in the collective representations, that an interdependent relation between occurrences or entities can be rejected as impossible or absurd.

In the earlier stage the dictum deduced from Hume's argument, that "anything may produce anything," might have served as a motto for primitive mentality. There is no metamorphosis, no generating cause, no remote influence too strange or inconceivable for such a mentality to accept. A human being may be born of a boulder, stones may speak, fire possess no power to burn, and the dead may be alive. *We* should refuse to believe that a woman may be delivered of a snake or a crocodile, for the idea would be irreconcilable with the laws of nature which govern the birth even of monstrosities. But the primitive mind, which believes in a close connection between a human social group and a snake or crocodile social group would find no more difficulty in this than in conceiving of the identity of the larva with the insect, or the chrysalis with the butterfly. Moreover, it is just as incompatible with "the laws of nature" that a corpse, whose tissues have become chemically incapable of sustaining life, should arise again; nevertheless, there are millions of cultivated persons who believe implicitly in the resurrection of Lazarus. It is enough that their representation of the Son of God involves His having the power to effect miracles. To the primitive mind, however, everything is a miracle, or rather, nothing is; and therefore everything is credible, and there is nothing either impossible or absurd.

As a matter of fact, however—and in this sense the dictum is only partially applicable to the prelogical mind—the pre-connections involved in its collective representations are not as arbitrary as they appear. While indifferent to that which we call the real and objective relations between entities and manifestations, they express others much more important to such a mind, to wit, the mystic participating relations. It is these relations, and no others, which are realized in the preconnections, for these are the only ones about which the primitive mind troubles. Suggest to a primitive that there are other relations, imaginary or actual, between persons, things and occurrences : he will set them aside and reject them as untrue or insignificant or absurd. He will pay no attention to them, because he has his own experience to guide him, a mystic experience against which, as long as it con-tinues to exist, actual experience is powerless. It is not only therefore because, in itself and in the abstract, any relation whatever between entities and occurrences is just as acceptable as any other ; it is above all because the law of participation admits of mystic preconnections that the mind of the primitive seems undeterred by any physical impossibility.

But, granted that in a certain community the mentality evolves at the same rate as the institutions, that these pre-connections grow weaker and cease to obtrude themselves— other relations between persons and things will be perceived, representations will tend to take on the form of general, abstract concepts, and at the same time a feeling, an idea of that which is physically possible or impossible will become more definite. It is the same then with a physical as with a logical absurdity, for the same causes render the prelogical mind insensible to both. Therefore the same changes and the same process of evolution cause it to be alive to the impossi-bility of affirming two contradictory statements at the same time, and the impossibility of believing in relations which are incompatible with experience.

Such a concomitance cannot be merely adventitious. In both cases the impossibility is felt only in a condition common to both : it is necessary, and it is enough, that the collective representations tend towards conceptual form. On the one hand, in fact, participations expressed in such a form can only be preserved, as we have already seen, by transforming themselves in order to avoid contradiction. And, on the other hand, it is when sufficiently definite concepts of beings and objects have been formed that the absurdity of certain mystic preconnections is first felt to obtrude. When the essential features of stone are, as it were, registered and fixed in the concept " stone," which itself forms one among other concepts of natural objects differing from stone by properties no less definite and constant than its own, it becomes inconceivable that stones should speak or boulders move of their own accord or procreate human beings, etc. The more the concepts are determined, fixed and arranged in classes, the more contradictory do the statements which take no account of such relations appear. Thus the logical demand made by the intellect grows with the definition and determination of concepts, and it is an essential condition of such definition and determination that the mystic preconnections of the collective representations become impaired. It grows then simultaneously with the knowledge acquired by experience. The progress of the one helps the other and vice versa, and we cannot say which is cause and which effect.

V

The process which is going on does not necessarily present itself as progressive, however. In the course of their evolution concepts do not submit to a kind of " finalité interne " which directs them for the best. The weakening of the mystic preconnections and elements is not inevitable nor always continuous. The mentality of primitive peoples, even whilst becoming less impervious to the teaching of experience, long remains prelogical, and most of its ideas preserve a mystic imprint. Moreover, there is nothing to prevent abstract and general concepts, once formed, retaining elements which are still recognizable as vestiges of an earlier stage. Preconnections, which experience has been unable to dissolve, still remain ; mystic properties are yet inherent in beings and objects. Even in aggregates of the most advanced type, a concept which is free of all admixture of this kind is exceptional, and it is therefore scarcely to be met with in any others. The concept is a sort of logical " precipitate " of the collective representations which have preceded it, and this precipitate nearly always brings with it more or less of a residuum of mystic elements.

How can it be otherwise ?   Even in social aggregates of a fairly low type abstract concepts are being formed, and while not in all respects comparable with our own, they are nevertheless concepts.   Must they not follow the general direction of the mentality which gives rise to them ?   They too, then, are prelogical and mystic, and it is only by very slow degrees that they cease to be so.   It may even happen that after having been an aid to progress, they constitute an obstacle.   For if the determination of the concept provides the rational activity of the mind with a lever which it did not find in collective representations subject to the law of participation ; if the mind inures itself to reject as impossible statements which are incompatible with the definition of the concepts, it very often pays dearly for the privilege when it grows used to regarding, as adequate to reality, conceptual ideas and relations which are very far removed from it.   If progress is not to find itself arrested, concepts of entities of all kinds must remain plastic and be continually modified, enlarged, confined within fixed limits, transformed, disintegrated and reunited by the teaching of experience.   If these concepts crystallize and become fixed, forming themselves into a system which claims to be self-sufficing, the mental activity applied to them will exert itself indefinitely without any contact with the reality they claim to represent.   They will become the subject of fantastical and frivolous argument, and the starting-point of exaggerated infatuation.

Chinese scientific knowledge affords a striking example of this arrested development.   It has produced immense encyclopædias of astronomy, physics, chemistry, physiology, pathology, therapeutics and the like, and to our minds all this is nothing but balderdash.   How can so much effort and skill have been expended in the long course of ages, and their product be absolutely nil ?   This is due to a variety of causes, no doubt, but above all to the fact that the foundation of each of these so-called sciences rests upon crystallized concepts, concepts which have never really been submitted to the test of experience, and which contain scarcely anything beyond vague and unverifiable notions with mystic preconnections. The abstract, general form in which these concepts are clothed allows of a double process of analysis and synthesis which is apparently logical, and this process, always futile yet ever self-satisfied, is carried on to infinity. Those who are best acquainted with the Chinese mentality—like De Groot, for instance—almost despair of seeing it free itself from its shackles and cease revolving on its own axis. Its habit of thought has become too rigid, and the need it has begotten is too imperious. It would be as difficult to put Europe out of conceit with her savants as to make China give up her physicians and doctors and *Fung-shui* professors.

India has known forms of intellectual activity more akin to our own. She has had her grammarians, mathematicians, logicians and metaphysicians. Why, however, has she produced nothing resembling our natural sciences ? Undoubtedly, among other reasons, because there, too, concepts as a rule have retained a very considerable proportion of the mystic elements of the collective representations whence they are derived, and at the same time they have become crystallized. Thus they have remained unable to take advantage of any later evolution which would gradually have freed them from such elements, as in similar circumstances Greek thought fortunately did. From that time, even in becoming conceptual, their ideas were no less destined to remain chiefly mystic, and only with difficulty pervious to the teaching of experience. If they furnished matter for scientific knowledge, the sciences could only be either of a symbolical and imaginative kind, or else argumentative and purely abstract. In peoples of a less advanced type, even although already fairly civilized, such as in Egypt or Mexico, for instance, even the collective representations which have been " precipitated " as concepts have distinctly retained their prelogical, mystic features.

Finally let us consider the most favourable case, that of peoples among whom logical thought still continues its progress, whose concepts remain plastic and capable of continual modification under the influence of experience. Even in such circumstances logical thought will not entirely supersede prelogical mentality. There are various reasons for the persistence of the latter. Firstly, in a large number of concepts there are indelible traces which still remain. It is far from being *all* the concepts in current use, for instance, which express the objective features and relations of entities and of phenomena solely. Such a characteristic is true of a very small number only, and these are made use of in scientific theorizing. Again, these concepts are, as a rule, highly abstract, and only express certain properties of phenomena and certain of their relations. Others, that is our most familiar concepts, nearly always retain some vestiges of the corresponding collective representations in prelogical mentality. Suppose, for example, that we are analysing the concepts of soul, life, death, society, order, fatherhood, beauty or anything else you like. If the analysis be complete it will undoubtedly comprise some relations dependent upon the law of participation which have not yet entirely disappeared.

Secondly, even supposing that the mystic, prelogical elements *are* finally eliminated from most concepts, the total disappearance of mystic, prelogical mentality does not necessarily follow. As a matter of fact the logical thinking which tends to realize itself through the purely conceptual and the intellectual treatment of pure concepts, is not co-extensive with the mentality which expressed itself in the earlier representations. The latter, as we know, does not consist of one function merely, or of a system of functions which are exclusively intellectual. It undoubtedly does comprise these functions but as still undifferentiated elements of a more complex whole in which cognition is blended with motor and above all emotional elements. If then, in the course of evolution the cognitive function tends to differentiate itself and be separated from the other elements implied in collective representations, it thereby achieves some kind of independence, but it does not provide the equivalent of the functions it excludes. A certain portion of these elements, therefore, will subsist indefinitely outside and side by side with it.

The characteristic features of logical thought are so clearly differentiated from those of prelogical mentality that the progress of the one seems, *ipso facto*, to involve the retrogression of the other. We are tempted to conclude that in the long run, when logical thought imposes its laws on all mental operations, prelogical mentality will have entirely disappeared. This conclusion is both hasty and unwarranted, however. Undoubtedly the stronger and more habitual the claims of reason, the less tolerant it is of the contradictions and absurdities which can be proved as such. In this sense it is quite true to say that the greater the advance made by logical thought, the more seriously does it wage war upon ideas which, formed under the dominance of the law of participation, contain implied contradictions or express preconceptions which are incompatible with experience. Sooner or later such ideas are threatened with extinction, that is, they must be dissolved. But this intolerance is not reciprocal. If logical thought does not permit contradiction, and endeavours to suppress it as soon as it perceives it, prelogical, mystic mentality is on the contrary indifferent to the claims of reason. It does not seek that which is contradictory, nor yet does it avoid it. Even the proximity of a system of concepts strictly in accordance with the laws of logic exerts little or no influence upon it. Consequently logical thought can never be heir to the whole inheritance of prelogical mentality. Collective representations which express a participation intensely felt and lived, of which it would always be impossible to demonstrate either the logical contradiction or the physical impossibility, will ever be maintained. In a great many cases, even, they will be maintained, sometimes for a long time, *in spite of* such a demonstration. The vivid inner sentiment of participation may be equal to, and even exceed, the power of the intellectual claim. Such, in all aggregates known to us, are the collective representations upon which many institutions are founded, especially many of those which involve our beliefs and our moral and religious customs.

The unlimited persistence of these collective representations and of the type of mind of which they are the witness, among peoples in whom logical thought is most advanced, enables us to comprehend why the satisfaction which is derived from the most finished sciences (exclusive of those which are purely abstract) is always incomplete. Compared with ignorance—at least, conscious ignorance—knowledge undoubtedly means a possession of its object ; but compared with the participation which prelogical mentality realizes, this possession is never anything but imperfect, incomplete, and, as it were, external. To know, in general, is to objectify; and to objectify is to project beyond oneself, as something which is foreign to oneself, that which is to be known. How intimate, on the contrary, is the communion between entities participating of each other, which the collective representations of prelogical mentality assures ! It is of the very essence of participation that all idea of duality is effaced, and that in spite of the law of contradiction the subject is at the same time himself and the being in whom he participates. To appreciate the extent to which this intimate possession differs from the objectifying apprehension in which cognition, properly so called, consists, we do not even need to compare the collective representations of primitive peoples with the content of our positive sciences. It will be sufficient to consider one object of thought—God, for instance, sought after by the logical thought of advanced peoples, and at the same time assumed in the collective representations of another order. Any rational attempt to know God seems both to unite the thinking subject with God and at the same time to remove Him to a distance. The necessity of conforming with the claims of logic is opposed to a participation between man and God which is not to be represented without contradiction. Thus knowledge is reduced to a very small matter. But what need is there of this rational knowledge to the believer who feels himself at one with his God ? Does not the consciousness which he possesses of his participation in the Divine essence procure him an assurance of faith, at the price of which logical certainty would always be something colourless and cold and almost a matter of indifference ?

This experience of intimate and entire possession of the object, a more complete possession than any which originates in intellectual activity, may be the source and undoubtedly is the mainspring of the doctrines termed anti-intellectual. Such doctrines reappear periodically, and on each reappearance they find fresh favour. This is because they promise that which neither a purely positive science nor any theory of philosophy can hope to attain : a direct and intimate contact with the essence of being, by intuition, interpenetration, the mutual communion of subject and object, full participation and immanence, in short, that which Plotinus has described as ecstasy. They teach that knowledge subjected to logical formulas is powerless to overcome duality, that it is not a veritable possession, but remains merely superficial. Now the need of participation assuredly remains something more imperious and more intense, even among peoples like ourselves, than the thirst for knowledge and the desire for conformity with the claims of reason. It lies deeper within us and its source is more remote. During the long prehistoric ages, when the claims of reason were scarcely realized or even perceived, it was no doubt all-powerful in all human aggregates. Even to-day the mental activity which, by virtue of an intimate participation, possesses its object, gives it life and lives through it, aspires to nothing more, and finds entire satisfaction in this possession. But actual knowledge in conformity with the claims of reason is always unachieved. It always appeals to a knowledge that protracts it yet further, and yet it seems as if the soul aspires to something deeper than mere knowledge, which shall encompass and perfect it.

Between the theories of the "intellectualists" and their opponents the dialectic strife may be indefinitely prolonged, with alternating victories and defeats. The study of the mystic, prelogical mentality of undeveloped peoples may enable us to see an end to it, by proving that the problems which divide the two parties are problems which are badly couched. For lack of proceeding by a comparative method, philosophers, psychologists and logicians have all granted one common postulate. They have taken as the starting-point of their investigations the human mind always and everywhere homogeneous, that is, a single type of thinker, and one whose mental operations obey psychological and intellectual laws which are everywhere identical. The differences between institutions and beliefs must be explained, therefore, by the more childish and ignorant use which is made of principles common to all aggregates. Accordingly a reflective self-analysis carried out by a single individual ought to suffice to discover the laws of mental activity, since all subjects are assumed to be constituted alike, as far as mind is concerned.

Now such a postulate does not tally with the facts revealed

by a comparative study of the mentality of the various human aggregates. This teaches us that the mentality of primitive peoples is essentially mystic and prelogical in character; that it takes a different direction from our own—that is, that its collective representations are regulated by the law of participation and are consequently indifferent to the law of contradiction, and united, the one to the other, by connections and preconnections which prove disconcerting to our reason.

It throws light, too, upon our own mental activity. It leads us to recognize that the rational unity of the thinking being, which is taken for granted by most philosophers, is a *desideratum*, not a fact. Even among peoples like ourselves, ideas and relations between ideas governed by the law of participation are far from having disappeared. They exist, more or less independently, more or less impaired, but yet ineradicable, side by side with those subject to the laws of reasoning. Understanding, properly so called, tends towards logical unity and proclaims its necessity; but as a matter of fact our mental activity is both rational and irrational. The prelogical and the mystic are co-existent with the logical.

On the one hand, the claims of reason desire to impose themselves on all that is imagined and thought. On the other hand, the collective representations of the social group, even when clearly prelogical and mystic by nature, tend to subsist indefinitely, like the religious and political institutions of which they are the expression, and, in another sense, the bases. Hence arise mental conflicts, as acute, and sometimes as tragic, as the conflict between rival duties. They, too, proceed from a struggle between collective habits, some time-worn and others more recent, differently oriented, which dispute the ascendancy of the mind, as differing moral claims rend the conscience. Undoubtedly it is thus that we should account for the so-called struggle of reason with itself, and for that which is real in its antinomies. And if it be true that our mentality is both logical and prelogical, the history of religious dogmas and systems of philosophy may henceforth be explained in a new light.

INDEX

LIBRARY OF CONGRESS CATALOGING
IN PUBLICATION DATA

Lévy-Bruhl, Lucien, 1857-1939.
  How natives think.

  Translation of: Les Fonctions mentales dans les sociétés inférieures.
  Reprint. Originally published: New York : Knopf, c1926.
  Includes bibliographical references and index.
  1. Ethnopsychology. I. Title.
GN451.L513   1985   155.8'1   85-42662
ISBN 0-691-07298-1
ISBN 0-691-02034-5 (pbk.)